BIKE FOR LIFE

BIKE FOR LIFE

How to Ride to 100

Roy M. Wallack AND
Bill Katovsky

Da Capo
LIFE
LONG

A MEMBER OF THE PERSEUS
BOOKS GROUP

Designed by Pauline Neuwirth, Neuwirth & Associates, Inc.
Set in 11 point Whitman by the Perseus Books Group

Cataloging-in-Publication data for this book is available from the Library of Congress.

ISBN: 978-1-56924-451-7

Published by Da Capo Press
A Member of the Perseus Books Group
www.dacapopress.com

Da Capo Press books are available at special discounts for bulk purchases in the U.S. by corporations, institutions, and other organizations. For more information, please contact the Special Markets Department at the Perseus Books Group, 2300 Chestnut Street, Suite 200, Philadelphia, PA, 19103, or call (800) 810-4145, ext. 5000, or e-mail special.markets@perseusbooks.com.

20 19 18 17 16 15 14 13 12 11

• DEDICATION •

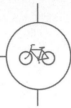

CONTENTS

• INTERVIEWS •

BIKE FOR LIFE

INTRODUCTION

Bike for Life's agenda is simple: wouldn't you like to ride a **century** when you turn a century?

A two-wheel fantasy, you say, pedaling 100 miles at age 100? Hardly. Americans—those who have maintained an active and healthy lifestyle—are living longer. Centenarians now number in the thousands. But science and medicine can only do so much, and studies show that genetics accounts for only 20 to 30 percent of longevity. The rest is due to personal lifestyle choices, mainly exercise and diet, which can radically slow the age-related physical deterioration that naturally starts in your thirties.

Enter *Bike for Life*, a blueprint for longevity, fitness, health, and well-being. Cycling is a sport uniquely suited to the cause of long life, providing the potential for physical and mental challenges, relaxation, achievement, adventure, variety, and social interaction—all at the same time. It works for all abilities, both sexes, and every age and demographic, a great equalizer that unifies generations in fitness and fun. But biking's not perfect. While cardio-healthy cycling can be the linchpin of your longevity program, it suffers gaps in terms of muscular strength, body posture, bone health, and more.

That's why *Bike for Life* has taken a fresh look not only at common cycling topics like training, technique, and sports nutrition, but also at subjects either long overlooked or sensationalized by the cycling community: osteoporosis, relationships, depression, impotence, knee and back preventive care. We don't skip the small stuff, either. In *Bike for Life*, you'll learn how to fight off a mountain lion and a grizzly bear, avoid and manage a car-bike accident, survive a bike-jacking, and deal with a dozen other "it-only-happens-to-someone-else" subjects that can throw your long-life game plan off track.

Proudly, *Bike for Life* breaks new ground on the following subjects:

- **Bone loss:** Want to make sure you don't break a hip when you're 70? See chapter 9—Cycling and Osteoporosis.If you only ride a bike for fitness, and do nothing else, you risk premature bone-thinning. We teach you why you need to hit the weight room and do some jogging and jumping jacks if you want to keep your skeleton as fit as your heart.

- **Back pain:** Read chapter 8—Prehab, long before you visit your chiropractor. The unique posture-saving exercises described there will save you time and money and years of anguish.

- **Age, power, and endurance:** Want to be faster and go farther at 40 than 30, at 60 than 50? Check out "Buttcentric" riding in chapter 7—Bike Fit, which will help you utilize the much-ignored—and highly powerful—gluteal muscles.

- **Yoga for cyclists:** A *Bike for Life* exclusive, the ten-position yoga routine in chapter 1 by renowned yoga and cycling coach Steve Ilg helps counteract many cycling-related imbalances and pain.

- **Reviving your reaction time**: Getting older and afraid to ride because your reactions have slowed so much that you can't avoid road hazards like you used to? Get back up to speed by reading chapter 5—The Anti-aging Game Plan, which describes explosive, rapid-contraction weight lifting, the only thing proven to resuscitate your invaluable **fast-twitch muscle fibers**. A bonus: doing so also restores youthful bulges to age-flattened muscles.

- **The "5 to 1 Relationship Ratio":** Cycling is a demanding lover. Reconciling your significant others and the sport's significant time will be a lot easier with the help of a mathematical plan from some of the world's foremost and fittest relationship psychologists. Find it in chapter 12.

Instinct probably tells you that cycling has a leg up on most other sports when it comes to long-term fitness and health. It's easier on your joints and muscles than running. It's less monotonous than lap swimming. Unless your backyard's a dock, it's a lot more convenient than paddling. With help from a $200 bike training stand, cycling is the rare workout you can do while watching the evening news. And, most telling, it's one of the few sports you can do alone or in a group that does not have an age-specific glass ceiling. For example, ever see a group of 60-year-old men play pickup football or basketball? But go on a century ride, a weekend charity ride, or even **ultra events** such as 24-hour mountain biking or the Furnace Creek 508 [-mile] road race through Death Valley, and you will see plenty of silver-haired men and women pursuing active retirement, often into their 70s. Riding among like-minded enthusiasts is the best social security.

While cycling into your sixth and seventh decades is commendable, why stop there? Why should age be a barrier to health? With a good strategy, it can be a foundation of health. Just take a close look at hard-training cycling legends like John Howard, Gary Fisher, and Ned Overend who are interviewed in *Bike for Life*.

Middle-aged and still riding strong, they have no intention of stopping—ever.

"It's not the older you get, the sicker you get, but the older you get, the healthier you've been," said Dr. Thomas Perls, a geriatrician at Boston University, who was quoted in an August 30, 2004, *Time* cover story titled—get ready for this—"How to Live to Be 100." While *Time*'s news report confirmed our notions about longevity, we think a better tale, told in these pages, is "How to *Ride* to be 100." Using the information compiled in *Bike for Life,* we believe that you can push the age odometer into triple digits.

Because this book was a joint collaborative effort between two stubborn coauthors—think of a **tandem** in which both riders demand to be in front—we decided that the easiest way to get *Bike for Life* rolling is to to summarize our own perspectives on cycling and each other as cyclists.

BILL ON ROY

The first time I rode with Roy was in the summer of 1994 in Santa Monica, California. I had recently become editor-in-chief of *Triathlete* magazine, and Roy was its features editor. The magazine's office occupied several cluttered rooms on the second floor of an office building overlooking the festive outdoor Third Street Promenade. Roy's office was a Category 3 disaster zone of loose papers, clothes, products, and gear sent by manufacturers for testing and review. Parked outside his door was a well-worn Trek 1200 **road bike** festooned with lights and bags. Oddly, two spokes sticking straight up were taped to his handlebars. They were an ideal height to poke out

someone's eye. Roy used the spokes to hold bagels while he rode.

Our initial ride via **mountain bike** that early summer evening took us past the million-dollar mansions in the Pacific Palisades until we arrived at a network of steep fire roads that led into lovely wooded canyons high above Los Angeles. Even though I was deep in **triathlon** training (I had completed the Hawaii Ironman eight months prior and was preparing for the Alcatraz triathlon), he was obviously a stronger rider, so he and his Marin Palisades Trail would invariably be waiting for me and my black Klein at the top of various grades. For a guy who had been the editor of *Bicycle Guide* and *California Bicyclist,* authored a 300-page book about bike touring (*The Traveling Cyclist*), and toured 25,000 miles around the world, including the first-ever bike tour into the Soviet Union, I was surprised to see that this former collegiate wrestler had an awkward, non-fluid, bowlegged riding style. He pedaled in squares rather than circles. But who was I to criticize? I biked the same way—a stocky, muscular guy who mashes the pedals rather than smoothly and efficiently applying force throughout the entire pedal stroke.

We shared another trait besides lousy riding form: we each viewed our bikes as an extension of a freedom-loving spirit for exploration and adventure. This common philosophy shaped our attitude toward bicycling. We often eschewed competition for the intoxication of self-discovery. In 1978, I had biked solo across America; I was 21 years old. That trip marked the beginning of my lifelong addiction to cycling. In subsequent years, I bike-toured—on- or **off-road**—three times up the California Coast, throughout the

Canadian and Colorado Rockies, the Sierras, Utah, Arizona, Baja, Death Valley, New Zealand, and the Dominican Republic.

In 1982, the year I was training for my first Hawaii Ironman, Roy and his brother Marc rode 6,000 miles from Pacific to Atlantic to the Gulf of Mexico. That led to his first published article in *Bicycling* ("How to Take the Tour of Your Life") and a series of cycling trips through 15 countries and 34 states that included the length of the Mississippi River, Alaska to San Diego, London to Moscow, and Budapest to Lisbon.

When our career paths finally intersected at *Triathlete,* we had plenty of stories and experiences to swap, especially during the half-dozen times we rode together after work; we would find the steepest hills and challenge each other up them. I could beat him trail running, but had no chance on a bike.

Our first big two-wheel adventure together occurred in Costa Rica at the La Ruta de los Conquistadores, maybe the toughest mountain bike race on the planet. It's a three-day stage race of extremes— beauty, distance, weather, and difficulty. La Ruta follows the historic path of Spanish conquistadors who crossed Costa Rica in futile searches for gold. Racers travel 250 miles from the Pacific Ocean to the Caribbean Sea, crossing several distinct ecosystems and climatic zones. Through humid, mud-soaked rain forests, towering mountain passes, and lowland banana and coffee plantations, the race clobbers participants with heat, cold, and a cumulative elevation gain of 22,000 feet. Each year, 50 percent of all racers don't finish all three days.

I had first learned about La Ruta in 1997 at the annual **Interbike** industry trade show in Las Vegas when the event promoter, a cheerful adventure athlete and wilderness guide named Roman Urbina introduced himself at the *Triathlete* booth. He was having difficulty convincing American bike journalists to come to his country to experience the race. On a whim, I playfully said I'd go, despite being undertrained for an event that was scheduled to take place in a month. I asked Roy to join me. Every Don Quixote needs his Sancho. When we showed up in Costa Rica, there were only a dozen other U.S. riders joining a field of 150 locals.

In a later magazine article, Roy described the riding conditions: "Costa Rican roads don't traverse mountains as much as go straight up. The climbs involve endless **granny-gear** chugging and hiking. Your quads, calves, and hip flexors cry with pain. La Ruta doesn't wait; with blistering heat and rain and humidity and hills and endless mud, it tries to break you from the get-go. Day One is a shock to your system. Most people—even the well-trained—have never experienced anything like it in their lives."

Roy and I rode together for the first 10 miles on Day One, which began at the Pacific Coast and went 90 miles to San Jose. We were already at the very back of the pack. As we passed several small farm villages, I would hear the stray *"Andale"* (keep going) from a curious farmer or student walking to school. I wanted company, a slowpoke sidekick. I even felt like bribing Roy to hang back with me, but I could tell that he silently nursed more ambitious plans. He almost seemed apologetic when he gradually peeled away from me during one brutal, 12 percent uphill grade. Watching his back disappear behind the next switchback, I had resigned myself to spending a very lonely day in the Central American tropics.

Just before the halfway mark, in a desolate region of raw, pristine jungle beauty of mountains and steep ravines, I began suffering severe stomach spasms caused by drinking a local sugary lemony sports drink called Squenchy. I was walking the hills by then anyway, but now I was doubled up in pain and forced to use my bike as a walker. When the Jeep Safari race **sag wagon** checked on me, I accepted a ride, without pause, to the finish zone—a nauseating, three-hour journey over boulder-strewn dirt farm roads.

At the finish area, racers—over half the field had dropped out—were being fed a catered dinner. Dusk was approaching and the course would soon close. Roy was still out there riding. He arrived at the finish just before nightfall—with four minutes to spare.

The next morning, feeling a spring in my step and a bounce in my quads, I was ready for Day Two—the ride up a volcano. At least I thought I was. As for what happened that memorable day and the next, well, that's a story best told by Roy.

ROY ON BILL

I felt bad about leaving Bill on the morning of Day One. I was here in the sweltering rain forest, one of the first Americans to participate in La Ruta, because of him. Bill's always on top of the trends. He raced in the Ironman Triathlon back when you didn't have to qualify for it, then started a magazine, *Tri-Athlete,* about the fledgling sport. He put on one of the first mountain bike races in Berkeley in 1984, and participated in 24-hour mountain bike races and adventure races when both were in their infancy. He heard about La Ruta before almost anyone. Before I knew it, I was on a

plane and atop a new Cannondale F-1000 mountain bike, a deal Bill had arranged with a local bike shop. Thanks to Bill, I was a pioneer in an unknown epic that would soon become famous in the mountain bike world, a "must do" for those who savor daunting physical and mental tests.

But on Day One of La Ruta, as Bill and I fell farther behind, losing complete touch with the pack and shadowed by two bored policemen on Kawasaki motorcycles ready to ferry us to civilization, I couldn't babysit him any longer. It was agonizing to take this event lightly, to pretend I was a hapless desk-jockey rather than what I see myself as: a participant, an athlete, a cyclist. Not a stellar one, maybe, but one whose work ethic and lust for adventure helped me survive events normal folk often consider crazy, like the 1991 **Paris-Brest-Paris** (750 miles in 90 hours or less), a 1994 honeymoon tour from Nice to Rome on a tandem (600 miles with a complaining wife), and the 1995 Eco-Challenge (300 miles of hiking, paddling, mountain biking, and climbing in a week); La Ruta would be a worthy addition to my endurance resumé. But time was running out. Glancing at my watch again and again, I guiltily bid my benefactor adieu and finally headed into the rain forest alone.

Redlining all the way through dozens of river crossings and lakes of foot-deep mud, it took me two hours to finally catch the next rider. "*No más.* You cannot finish," said the Tico (what Costa Ricans call themselves), who had called it quits at the checkpoint. *Screw you, amigo,* I said to myself, more determined than ever. Over the next ten hours I picked off a dozen more dehydrated, **bonked** riders who hadn't learned what I had from years of touring and double-centuries: eating and drinking a lot is as important as training when riding 79 off-road miles in 90-degree heat and near 100-percent humidity. That's fortunate, because having found out about La Ruta from Bill just two weeks earlier, I was severely undertrained.

And I paid for it. Entering San Jose after 11 hours and 51 minutes—five hours after the leaders and 92nd of 97 finishers—virtually every muscle on my legs from calf to butt was lurching into violent spasms. I could only make it by continually shifting the position of my feet on the pedals to find fresh muscle fibers. The inner thigh of my right leg was a bloody, stinging mess, as the chamois of my cycling shorts had sandpapered a grapefruit-sized welt into my skin; any sweat dripping on it felt like acid. My triceps were seizing up whenever I stood on the climbs. When it was over, I couldn't walk—make that shuffle—without whimpering like a wounded dog.

But even worse was a bigger problem: there were two more days to go.

There is a famous saying in La Ruta, *"Quien gana el primer día, gana la carrera"*—"Whoever finishes the first day finishes the race." But it wouldn't apply to me. I felt like my body was booby-trapped. I was so intimidated I could barely sleep thinking about Day Two, a relentless 8,000-foot climb from the capital of San Jose up the chilly, fog-shrouded Volcan Irazu, piercing the clouds at 11,600 feet. I was almost relieved when my quads seized up as I rolled out of bed that morning. Gasping and stumbling around the hotel room, I thought, *Thank God. I'll have to do it by Jeep.*

If someone was going to carry the ball for journalism up the volcano, known for its radical changes in weather and temperature, it would have to be Bill.

At least Bill was fairly well rested, having ridden only 50 miles on Day One. He'd thus preserved his strength for the Day Two climb up Irazu—and he'd need every bit of it. The steep, muddy, eroded farm roads that snaked up the volcano, coursing through fields of onion, potato, coffee, olive, and other crops that thrive in volcanic soil and cool weather, were often unrideable. Riders had to carry their bikes 50 yards on their shoulders dozens of times; when you could ride, it was 5 mph, max. It got miserably cold as the elevation rose so high that one could easily see 30 miles south to Cartago, the former capital destroyed by an earthquake a century before. The view soon disappeared in a foggy drizzle that blanketed the mountain, subjecting the slower riders to a splattery coating of the infamous "Costa Rican cocktail"—a thick stew of mud and cow excrement.

After five hours, the leaders—nearly all mountain-bred Ticos, save an occasional Colombian or Venezuelan—crested the top and began a two-hour descent on a rutted, lava-rock-strewn farm road. Many riders donned plastic trash bags to keep their torsos warm in the soupy fog for the daunting, finger-numbing plunge, which disintegrated the rubber on many brake pads.

I ascended Irazu in a sputtering 1972 Toyota Land Cruiser, shooting photos for my magazine story and learning important Spanish phrases from my driver such as, *"Este tiempo está gueiso"*—"This weather sucks"—and *"Mis piernas me duelen"*—"My legs are broken"—my pitiful explanation of why I wasn't riding that day. I also learned, but didn't say, the phrase, *"Yo tengo dolor en mi cabeza"* ("I have pain in my head")—a profound sadness over having chosen not to ride when I should have at least **blown up** trying. I decided then and there that I would never make this mistake again.

After a while, people began to ask me, "*Dónde está su amigo?*" Where was Bill? Nearly everyone had passed, and there was no sign of him. Someone suggested that he had quit riding and had taken a siesta.

That's why, gunning it downhill toward the next checkpoint in the Land Cruiser, we were surprised to see a man *jogging* up.

It was Bill!

Finding that he could run faster than he could ride uphill, the wily Ironman veteran had a sag wagon trailer ferry his bike up to the top, where the turnoff to the 5,000-foot descent began. His multisport plan worked so well that it even affected another competitor. A 39-year-old Costa Rican car mechanic named Rafael Pacheco, who had decided to quit La Ruta and was rolling back downhill to San Jose, told me he was so shamed to see someone running up the volcano that he turned around and finished the big climb.

Two hours later, as we waited inside the Toyota in torrential rain on the lower slopes of the neighboring Volcan Turrialba, American ex-pat and cattle rancher Nat Grew emerged after the 25-mile downhill. "You heard of whitewater rafting? This was brownwater rafting!" shouted the 63-year-old five-time La Ruta participant. The boulder-strewn farm road was now a raging, hip-high river.

And Bill? "That crazy bastard?" said Grew, trying to get feeling back into his frozen hands and feet before the final descent toward town and the hotel. "He stopped to take pictures!"

I felt a torturous mixture of envy and joy by the time Bill finally emerged from the torrent 40 minutes later, hardly able to speak, but looking as if he had seen the face of God. One policeman escorting him had broken his arm and his motorcycle in a terrible wipeout, but Bill had survived the descent with nary a scratch, eventually arriving to awe and applause two hours after the cutoff time.

Normally, you can't shut Bill up, but now he was stunned into speechlessness, except for one word: "Epic." He was euphoric at what he'd accomplished and seen.

Unfortunately, there was no happy ending on Day Three, the final 90-mile ride up the 5,000-foot Turrialba volcano and down through the steamy banana plantations of Limón Province. Feeling strong enough to show off while riding mid-pack past coffee farms and dairy pastures, I did a 20-mph **bunny hop** for some villagers as they hosed us off. Unfortunately, I landed slightly sideways, slammed chest-first into the rocky cobble road, blew my tire, put my rim out of true, and smeared a lot of blood all over the place. Then, after slipping halfway through a dilapidated train trestle and nearly becoming an hors d'oeuvres in an alligator-infested river, I caught a water bar longways and crashed at 30 mph, separating my left shoulder. Determined to finish, I stupidly rode until my chain broke. With the mechanic's truck long gone, I wearily flagged down the last vehicle on the course, literally a broken man.

Bill finally found me back at the hotel in San Jose that night. Much to the relief of the two motorcycle cops who were still trailing him as the last rider, he'd been forced off the course by officials who were tired of him going so slowly. When the Jeep that had picked him up broke a wheel, Bill, who doesn't speak a lick of Spanish, had to sit, alone, in front of a farmhouse in the sweltering heat without food or drink for five hours. He had nibbled on green coffee beans for sustenance.

Bottom line? Between the two of us, we *did not finish* La Ruta.

They have a saying about La Ruta de los Conquistadores: *"Competiendo contra la tierra"*—"You are racing against the country." Against endless, roller-coaster mountains. Against wicked changes in temperature. Torrential rains. Stultifying humidity. In 1997, the country won. But the next year, I was back, finishing the race except for a 20-mile hitchhike due to a broken **derailleur**. I finally conquered Costa Rica without incident in 2000.

By then, I'd added to my catalog of cycling adventures: a self-declared **Masters** title at the World Solo 24 Hours of Adrenalin Championship in Canada (there was no official Masters category yet; I beat a portly 53-year-old wearing a Santa Claus outfit), and completion of the 400-mile, eight-day TransAlp Challenge mountain bike stage race across the Alps. These races were helped immeasurably by lessons I learned about training and surviving that incredibly difficult trio of days riding across Central America from Pacific to Atlantic. La Ruta is indelibly stamped on my cycling soul, with me every time I take on a new challenge.

As recently as October 2004, I tapped La Ruta while climbing 4,000 feet out of Death Valley at 2 AM in the four-man team division of the Furnace Creek 508, one of the world's toughest road endurance rides. The 508-mile 2004 race was the hardest in the race's 20-year history, with 40- to 50-mph headwinds for the last 250 miles. Feeling wasted and dis-illusioned on the ascent of 3,630-foot Salsberry Pass, I suddenly remembered Bill running up the volcano in Costa Rica and chuckled. This was a piece of cake compared to La Ruta! I stood up as

if I were running on the bike and didn't sit down for an hour, passing a half-dozen competitors. Four hours later, the best rider on our team, 508 Hall of Famer Ron Jones, stood up for 30 minutes as he powered us into first place. "I got inspired when I saw you standing so long," he said to me and our other teammates, Steve Ilg and Keith Kostman, as we celebrated our victory at the finish line. Thanks, Bill.

Oddly enough, extreme events like La Ruta and the 508 are rife with examples of people who embody the principles we espouse here in *Bike for Life*. Nat Grew, the cattle rancher who ran into Bill on the Irazu volcano, is now in his 70s—and still getting into crazy adventures. At the 508 finish line, I came across retired Berkeley scientist Gerd Rosenblatt, 71, who does a dozen double-centuries per year and competed on a two-man team with his friend Ron Way, 69. Half the starters at La Ruta are over 35, and three-quarters at the 508. Each one of the four guys on my team, all in their 40s, said they were stronger now than when we'd last teamed up eight years earlier, in our 30s.

That's the message we hope to make clear here in the pages of *Bike for Life*: with planning and enthusiasm, cycling is a unique lifelong sport that can not only help you live a very long, healthy life, but even improve as you age. Most importantly, perhaps, is what it can do for you mentally. When 23-year-old soloist Ian Tuttle was asked if he was "an old man in a young man's body," given that he was half the age of many of his 508 competitors, he shook his head. "It may be that all these old men are young men at heart."

Leave it to cycling and lifelong events like La Ruta and the Furnace Creek 508 to prove that feats of athletic wonder are not limited to youth, and that wisdom is not limited to the old.

WE'VE WRITTEN THIS book for selfish reasons: we both see life as a bike tour, and we don't want it to end. Whether it's a 20-mile cruise on the beach bike path, an extreme challenge like La Ruta, a 12,000-mile trek from Nome to Tierra del Fuego (topping Roy's wish list), or another Hawaii Ironman (Bill's 50th birthday wish to himself), we want to be able to hop on our bikes and do what comes naturally whenever the urge strikes, today or decades from now. So read the training and anti-aging strategies outlined in the book. Stay as young as you can. And join us for the ride.

Roy M. Wallack and Bill Katovsky

Have suggestions or a good cycling-longevity story to tell? Let us know at bikeforlifebook.com.

TRAINING

*Building a bigger engine with goal-setting,
Periodization, weight lifting, and
cycling-specific yoga*

"L ARRY! *LARRY!!* Wake up! *WAKE UP! YOU ARE GOING TO DIE!*"
I wasn't exaggerating. At 1 AM, deep in California's High Sierra after 27 straight hours of riding, my friend Larry Lawson and I and 60 others were rolling down a 10,000-foot mountain at 45 mph, and he was nodding off. So I kept us both awake by screaming at him all the way down to the little town of Susanville, where we'd finally get some sleep before riding back to our car, 310 miles west and south in Davis, near Sacramento. It was June 1991, and this was the final qualifier for the mother of all bike rides, the Paris-Brest-Paris Randonee, to be held the next month in France. Inches from a 1,000-foot drop-off, every fiber of my being consumed by the most monumental challenge of my athletic life, it didn't dawn on me at the time that I was simply about halfway done with a training ride. A 620-mile training ride.

That was a pretty extreme distance for a guy who, four months earlier, had rarely ridden over a century in any one day and never formally "trained" a day in his life on a bicycle.

During the '80s, I ran for fitness and biked for adventure, only yanking my trusty Univega touring bike out of the garage the day before a two-week or two-month bike tour. I gave no thought to doing any organized death march, much less training for it. I paid the price occasionally—one time bailing out of a five-day ride from San Francisco to L.A. on Day Three at the San Luis Obispo Greyhound Bus depot because I hurt so bad I could no longer walk—but on most slower-paced trips I'd just pedal into shape. Train? What for? Then Larry, who'd toured the length of the Mississippi River with me in 1989, suggested we do Paris-Brest-Paris.

Say what you will about the French, but they have a strikingly beautiful country that is heaven for bike touring, a deep love for cycling, and an uncompromising knowledge of training. If you wanted to do their beloved, quadrennial 1,200-kilometer (750-mile) ride from the capital to the

Atlantic Coast town of Brest and back, a tradition that began in 1891, you were required to survive a butt-numbing training series of progressively longer, time-limited qualifiers called **brevets**: a 200k, 300k, 400k, and 600k. For me, each brevet, spaced about three weeks apart, was a new landmark of distance and agony . . . and revelation.

As I pushed myself further and harder than ever before, then collapsed back home in an orgy of relief, rest, and healing, I was amazed again and again to find my body emerging remarkably stronger and more powerful at the next brevet. Before my very eyes, I was transforming, every 21 days mutating like the Incredible Hulk, ramping up to a new **PR (personal record)**, a new level of cycling insanity—186 miles, 248 miles, 372 miles. When we survived the final, 1,000k brevet from Davis to Susanville and back—a special requirement the French imposed solely on U.S. riders in response to our exceedingly high drop-out rate at the '87 P-B-P—I crossed the line wasted, moaning with every pedal stroke, barely able to walk, hating the very sight of that vile pain machine. In fact, I wouldn't touch my bike again for a week. But I wasn't worried a bit.

I knew by then that this amazing, stair-step training effect of "kill-yourself-and-rest"—an extreme example of the "Periodization" program outlined in this chapter—would morph me into a cycling cyborg by the next month in France. Despite numerous mechanical problems and major time off the bike, I finished P-B-P in 88 hours, 55 minutes, an hour under the 90-hour cutoff; Americans as a whole that year had the highest finishing percentage of all nationalities among the 5,000 participants.

This experience changed me; now, I crave the hard challenges and the training they demand. Yes, I still love the freedom of touring, of randomly exploring, of going out with no goal other than to be as free as a bird to see what I can see. The bike allows that like nothing else in this world. But discovering that you are in possession of a strange, wonderful, self-improving machine—your own body—that in a few months can be molded and transformed through training into a high-performance being that can survive P-B-P or La Ruta or the Furnace Creek 508 or a **double-century** or that 10-mile hill climb in your local mountains, is a different, empowering kind of freedom that can be even more satisfying. —RMW

Situation: A friend who you haven't seen in five years since he moved to Singapore calls up one day and says, "Hey, I'm flying into town tomorrow for a business meeting. How about on Tuesday we get together and do our old four-hour mountain bike loop up Silverado Canyon?"

You freeze. You haven't done anything athletic in weeks—months if dog walking doesn't count. If you say yes, you know what to expect: lung-wheezing, leg-burning, back-aching pain, followed by a week of limping with sore knees and frayed tendons. Maybe a doctor visit, too. "Yeahhh,

uhhh, okay," you stammer, too embarrassed to say no, all the while wondering how you managed to get so out of shape.

The answer might be that you're lazy or too busy. But more likely, we'd bet that you simply don't have a training plan.

Fact: People tend to respond to plans—and slack off in the absence of them. On the job, you follow a business plan—one-year, five-year, ten-year. You plan for your retirement with 401(k)s, IRAs, and income property. By the same token, if you want to ride like you did at 30 when you're 50, or do the Furnace Creek 508 race at 71 like

Berkeley's Gerd Rosenblatt, or generally be confident enough to take on an unexpected ride at any age, you can't just wing it. You need a plan. Cycling, with its huge menu of highly motivating events and exhilarating biomechanical efficiency that encourages long, fun hours of exercise, is the ideal sport to build an athletic training plan around.

"Training" may seem scary to some because it sounds like—and is—hard work. But if you understand that training should not be a daily hammerfest but a structured process that encompasses a logical series of easy and hard, long and short, on- and off-the-bike workouts, the hard work won't seem so daunting. In fact, given training's benefits—a regular endorphin rush, almost-instant feedback in the form of identifiable, enhanced fitness, a more youthful appearance, and the Superman-like pleasure of knowing you can perform feats younger people can't—you may come to look forward to, even love, the hard work of training. Yet in the same way that you can't truly love a person unless you understand her/him, you can't love training unless you understand its logic.

This chapter tells you how to train for an event and, by extension, how to train for longevity. It addresses bike training in the context of the traditional "three-legged stool" of fitness—aerobics, strength, and flexibility.

Since there is no longer any doubt that weight lifting is a key to keeping all people strong into old age, we had Los Angeles cycling coach/personal trainer Chris Drozd put together a strength program geared to cycling's specific strengths and weaknesses. In the flexibility section, *Bike for Life* introduces a groundbreaking "Yoga for Cyclists" plan from renowned yoga instructor,

author, and cycling coach Steve Ilg. For building the all-important aerobic system, we go to Tudor Bompa, the originator of Periodization, the foundation of all modern training. Based on an endless series of varying challenges and recoveries that strengthen your body and keep your mind fresh, Periodization is a virtually foolproof training regimen.

Before any of this, however, you need a focus that gives you the motivation to train in the first place. That's why Step One of any training is setting goals.

• GOALS •
Make Your Life a Nonstop Event

Rich McInnes, 45, wanted to be a top-level competitor, just like he was back in college. Dan Crain, 60, wanted to set an untouchable record. Wendy Skean, also 60, demanded the opportunity to become a world champion. These three people, profiled at the end of this chapter, are each getting stronger and younger every day, because they each made a decision to give themselves an extremely important gift: a goal.

Goals give you a reason to get on the bike. They give your training purpose, urgency, and excitement. Big ones, small ones—you need a whole series of them to reinforce one another—lifelong goals (i.e., ride a century at age 100), decade-by-decade goals (i.e., climb Maui's 10,000-foot Mt. Haleakala faster at age 50 than you did at age 40), annual goals (i.e., earn a California Triple Crown T-shirt by doing three double-centuries), and monthly goals (i.e., do at least one four-hour bike ride with your friends; gravitate to younger friends if the oldies pass). Mix the goals up, changing the annual goals every year to keep you fresh. Write down all your long- and short-term goals in your appointment book as your would business deadlines.

It's easy to get motivated to train for a challenging event a couple of months down the road. That's near enough to keep you focused for a while. But training to maintain a fitness lifestyle that keeps you strong enough to hammer at 40 or 60 or 80 requires at least one major challenge per season to focus the year on, plus several smaller "booster shots" to keep you on track. Cycling offers a vast variety of activities to keep your interest high: multiday cross-state rides, charity benefit rides, hill-climb challenges, and epic one-day events (see chapter 14 for many of these). To keep the training fever hot, also take advantage of the age-group format of Masters racing and triathlons; thousands actually look forward to "aging up" to, say, the 55–59 age group, where they'll be the young stud for a couple of years.

Beyond keeping you focused, goals provide definable memory markers that are often missing in adult life, when one year of fighting traffic and paying bills can seamlessly blend into another. Kids instantly identify years with grades, teachers, proms, and soccer championships. But after college, life can fade into a fuzzy morass of adult responsibilities. Yet it's easy to prevent the decades from slipping by unannounced: mark the years with memorable fitness benchmarks.

"2010? What a year!" you'll tell your great-grandchildren 50 years from now. "That's the year I turned fifty and did the TransAlp Challenge." They'll look at themselves and wonder, *How did the old codger do something that crazy at 50? And how does he remember all that stuff a half century later?*

Answer: it was something worth remembering—and training—for it kept you in shape and excited for the next year's goal. Heck, even if your memory frays, you'll have the photo albums and finisher's medals to jog it.

However you do it, the ultimate objective of setting goals is to turn your life into a nonstop event—which, by definition, requires nonstop training. When that happens, training may become an end in itself, the chicken *and* the egg, a necessary and enjoyable part of life that you look forward to much like eating, sleeping, and brushing your teeth.

• PERIODIZATION •
Planned Variation— the Basis of All Training

The Einstein of athletic training is Tudor O. Bompa, who outlined the framework on which most modern training today is based. In 1963, the Romanian developed his own "Unified Theory" of fitness: "Periodization," a relatively simple series of stair-step training schedules that were first used successfully by athletes in communist countries. Bompa originally developed Periodization for weight lifters, but it is now applied to nearly everything athletic—from cycling to running to swimming—and virtually ensures success when followed. Lance Armstrong, like all pro riders, follows a program based on Periodization. It develops remarkably high fitness by making every workout count.

Periodization, in a nutshell, is a series of methodical, progressive physical challenges, peppered with variety and punctuated with rest. It starts with a goal and plans a workout schedule around it, breaking the training year up into four "periods," or training phases, that vary the volume, timing, and intensity of workouts. Many call it "planned variation."

Why the need for variation? Researchers predating Bompa found that doing the same thing over and over eventually causes the body to stop improving, a process known as the "General Adaptation Syndrome." Turns out that the body is a very efficient adaptive learning machine; it improves in response to incrementally increasing stress for a while, but at a certain point will adapt and plateau. Over time, your body actually "learns" how to ride your favorite 20-mile loop (or bench press that same 150 pounds at the gym) more efficiently—but after a while your muscles don't get stronger. What they get is more efficient—building the neural pathways that let you do that same work with less muscle. So, ironically, you can actually *lose* some of the strength that you don't need to accomplish that particular task.

Solution? Stress your body, rest it, then stress it again even more. That's Periodization. By altering your workouts (add more hills to your bike route, add ten pounds to your bench press, or use a different hand position), you force your muscles to grow in new ways, recruiting new fibers in a different order and adding to overall strength.

In Periodization, deliberate rest and recovery is planned, too. That's because your body actually consolidates the gains of your workouts during downtime. Hard workouts in particular must be followed by rest and easy "recovery" workouts. Technically, the body doesn't get stronger during a workout; it gets broken down. It is during rest when it repairs and rebuilds itself stronger.

What exactly gets stronger? Periodization simultaneously develops two types of fitness: aerobic and structural. Aerobic, or metabolic, fitness builds your cardiovascular system (heart, veins, and capillaries), the pulmonary system (the lungs), the endocrine systems (hormones), the nervous system, and the energy production in the muscles themselves. Structural fitness includes strengthening muscles, tendons, ligaments, and bone.

Summary: If you ride the same miles at the same speed all the time, you'll plateau. Your body responds to Periodization's escalating variety of challenges and subsequent rest by getting fitter and better able to handle hard work, safely and gradually making gains in strength, speed, power, and endurance. The changing variation also alters motor coordination and gives muscles balanced shape and size. On the other hand, "variation" doesn't mean chaos. While random workouts will aid overall fitness, they won't help you reach a sport-specific goal as effectively as Periodization.

FOUR PERIODIZATION PHASES:
Base, Strength, Peak/Taper, and Transition

Periodization uses four periods, or phases, to prepare you for your goal. Each phase has a specific conditioning purpose and can last anywhere from four weeks to several months, depending on your objective, whether it be riding a century on June 1 in seven hours; riding a mountain bike across Costa Rica in November; or keeping up with your eleven-year-old grandson on the bike path by Christmas. In Periodization, every workout in a months-long agenda is performed with this objective in mind.

Sample goal: Let's say it's February, you've spent most of the snowy winter swimming or cross-country skiing, and you want to do a moderate hilly century ride in June. Here's your plan:

Phase 1: Base Training
Type: Long, slow rides
Duration: 3 months
Intensity: 55% to 75% of maximum heart rate
(Maximum heart rate = 220 minus your age)

A three-month Base Phase would contain three four-week sub-phases—Base One, Base Two, and Base Three—in which training volume (duration and frequency) slowly increases in stair-step fashion. When you begin a new sub-phase, you start at a higher level than the old one ended at.

A key to success: go slow. Start slowly, and ramp up the miles and pace slowly, no more than a 10-percent increase per week. Be patient. Hold back. Fight the urge to pick up the pace, to sharply increase intensity. Triathlete Mark Allen successfully demonstrated the benefit of this in the early '90s with Low Heart Rate Training, a then-unique training method in which he deliberately kept his **heart rate** below 150 at all times, slowly building his base on his way to the last of his six Hawaii Ironman championships. Base training is all about low-intensity workouts at maximum volume—long, slow, distance rides, or LSD for short. (Note: Some people, like two-time Race Across America rider Chris Kostman, think the "S" in LSD means "steady." "Forget 'slow,'" he says. "The only thing accomplished on a physiological level by riding slowly is learning how to ride slowly." He likes "steady"—keeping it challenging without pushing it over the limit.)

The purpose of these gradual, stepwise increases in training time or mileage is to prepare your body and gain confidence for the harder work to follow. Physiologically, you are building up the components of your aerobic foundation: stronger heart and leg muscles, thicker tendons and bones, and miles of capillaries. The latter, the tiniest pipes in the vascular system, serve to distribute and remove fuel and waste products from all parts of your muscles. They are much slower to respond to stimuli than muscles and lungs—all the more reason to throttle up very slowly.

Another purpose in ramping up very slowly during Base Training is to teach the body how to burn your body's most abundant fuel: fat. You do this by slowly increasing the density of the muscle cells' mitochondria, the tiny aerobic energy production factories that use fats and oxygen to make energy. Before you are trained, intense exercise will outrun your ability to process enough oxygen to burn fat, and you go "anaerobic" (without oxygen): your body, trying to keep going, then reaches for a quicker-burning fuel—your precious, limited stores of carbohydrates. More mitochondria help you meet the muscles' demand for more oxygen and allow you to stay longer in fat burning mode.

Rest is key: each four-week sub-phase ends with a rest-and-recovery period. Three weeks on, one week off. The fourth week is the all-important recovery week— a vastly reduced workload that refreshes your mind and body, letting all your systems consolidate the stresses of training and come back even stronger. Warning: Don't train hard through your recovery week. You'll exhaust your body, stall your progress, and maybe get injured.

But recovery is not limited to this one week. A recovery day should follow any hard workout, no matter the week or the phase.

Recovery doesn't necessarily mean sitting on the couch, although a day of that won't hurt. You can go out for shorter, lower-intensity rides. Here, cross-training comes in handy: swim, do the elliptical machine, play tennis. Stay aerobically active, but lower the burners. A recovery workout doesn't produce additional stress; its low intensity is rejuvenating—like a massage. Recovery permits body (and mind) to test the limits of athletic potential without falling over the edge into overtraining/under-recovery.

By the end of the three-month Base Training period, a prospective century rider should have built his body up to the point where it can survive a 75- to 85-mile ride. Now, it's time to add the strength and speed that will allow you to survive 100 miles with a fair amount of hills.

Phase 2: Build/Preparation

Type: Shorter, faster rides with more hill climbing
Duration: One month
Intensity: 75%, with progressive intervals ranging from 85% to 92% of maximum heart rate

Now that you've built your metabolic and structural foundation, you enter the Build Phase, where you maintain volume and further increase aerobic capacity and build speed and power. One objective of this period is to raise your body's ability to tolerate the kind of hard work your goal requires—to, say, climb several miles without significantly slowing down. Your tools: hill climbing, sustained hard efforts, and shorter, higher-intensity training sessions than the previous phase.

Technically, in the Build Phase you are trying to raise your "lactate threshold" (or LT), the point at which a metabolic waste product called lactic acid starts flooding your body and cramping your muscles. The only way to get true LT readings is to ride a stationary bike in a lab and have the technicians prick your fingertips and do a blood analysis. Fortunately, you can approximate LT by looking at your heart rate. Roughly, it's when your breathing's heavy and your working muscles are close to feeling a burn. This means that you are going anaerobic—so hard that you are outstripping your body's ability to bring in enough oxygen for its needs. That's often somewhere in a range around 85 percent to 92 percent of approaching maximum heart rate, which you can sustain only for a short period, or "interval" of time. Therefore, your Build Phase training sessions might be mainly at 75 percent of maximum heart rate, with occasional interval sessions at 85 percent, 88 percent, and 92 percent. Try to push the intervals a bit higher each time.

Since what isn't trained gets de-trained, long efforts are still part of the Build Phase. Every second week ride a distance close to your longest day of Base, and follow it with recovery time, to prevent overtraining.

Phase 3: Peak and Taper

Type: Continued fast rides, but for less time
Duration: One to three weeks
Intensity: 75%, with intervals to 85% to 92% of maximum heart rate

Relax—but only a little. With the Build Phase over, you're at peak fitness, but not well rested. For that, you must "taper"— back off on the volume. You'll work out just enough to stay sharp but gain a deep recovery that will leave you fresh. Work out too much and you'll be fatigued on game day. It's a fine line that plenty of elite

The Evil Fifth Stage: Overtraining

IS Periodization fail-safe? In theory, applying stressor forces to the body in a progressive manner, broken up by rest and variation, will always compel muscles to adapt by getting stronger. But what happens when you apply too severe a stressor for too long? After all, cycling is a sport that tends to encourage hard daily training. And an average load for you one year may be too much the next, when personal circumstances have changed.

Answer: When the body lacks the energy source and/or recovery time to continue adapting, it gets overwhelmed and simply capitulates. This is the dreaded exhaustion stage, most commonly known as "overtraining." For lab rats, overtraining often means death. For humans, it could manifest as tendonitis, frequent colds, unexplained edginess, or worse, poor race performance. It behooves you to be aware of its signs, so that you can make adjustments before a crisis occurs.

In the book *Andy Pruitt's Medical Guide for Cyclists,* co-written by Pruitt, director of the Boulder Center for Sports Medicine, and Roadbikerider.com cofounder Fred Matheny, Pruitt identifies four causes and seven symptoms of overtraining:

Causes of Overtraining
1. **Nonstop hammering:** Too much training and racing without adequate rest and recovery.
2. **Runny-nose riding:** Exercising through sickness and injury.
3. **Too much, too soon:** Intense training without a sufficient mileage base.
4. **Empty gas tank:** Poor nutrition, particularly a failure to eat enough carbohydrates and protein soon after a ride to replenish glycogen stores.

Signs of Overtraining
Each of the signs described next are warnings that you need to back off.

1. **Steadily deteriorating performance:** You're getting worse despite—and eventually due to—hard training.
2. **Depression:** "I've never seen an overtrained athlete who wasn't clinically depressed," said Dr. William Morgan, who in the 1970s was one of the first to establish a link between overtraining and depression.
3. **Persistent soreness in muscles and joints:** Since cycling doesn't pound your joints, muscles shouldn't get excessively sore even after hard rides, says Pruitt.
4. **Abrupt weight loss:** A 5 percent loss of body weight over several days can mean two things, says Pruitt: Chronic dehydration, or a lack of glycogen during hard training, in which case the body may begin to devour muscle tissue for fuel.
5. **Diarrhea and constipation:** Chronic fatigue can disrupt digestive system function.
6. **Rise in resting heart rate:** A 7-to-10-beat rise in your normal morning heart rate means your body is tired and your heart is trying to deliver more oxygen and nutrients.
7. **Increased incidence of illness and rise in white blood cell count:** A weak body can't fight off viruses and infections well. Pruitt advises serious cyclists to get a complete blood count four times a year to establish your normal blood count levels.

athletes have botched from time to time. You can walk the line successfully if you follow two rules:

Rule #1: Avoid the urge to go for one last long ride. You cannot develop any more fitness, but you can tire yourself out and sabotage the event for which you've been training for months. The stress levied on your body must now be unloaded for your top-level fitness to show up with you at the start line.

Rule #2: Maintain intensity, but cut training volume by 30 percent. Then the next week reduce it another 30 percent. Shave duration from longer efforts. Maintain frequency, if possible. You may be able to hold a peak for a month, but not much longer, so when targeting several events keep them close together on the calendar.

Phase 4: Transition
Type: Easy riding and cross-training
Duration: At least a week, depending on your next event
Intensity: 55 to 75% of maximum heart rate

After the event is over, especially if it's something as tough as a hilly century, spend the next week recovering. Swim or row for aerobic fitness; give your legs a break. Spin a bit on Wednesday and Thursday if another event is planned in a week. If you have an event planned for a month away, recover for a week, build for a week, and recover for two.

The four-stage Periodization plan is a proven formula that works for all athletes of all abilities for every sport. It also works for the activity for which it was originally designed, weight lifting, which, not coincidentally, is the next subject of this chapter.

• WEIGHT TRAINING •
No Debate—Cyclists Must Pump Iron

Cyclists love the outdoors and often hate going indoors, unless if it's for a **spin class**. But every cyclist needs to get familiar with the weight room, and not just because lifting weights is a must for longevity and quality of life (see chapter 5) and protecting against early bone-thinning (see chapter 9). Weight training will actually help you become a better cyclist.

"Many cyclists believe that weight training is unnecessary for them, given the fitness they derive from riding," says Christopher Drozd, C.S.C.S., a Los Angeles–based personal trainer, cycling coach, and Ironman triathlete who has developed a weight training program specifically for cyclists. "Wrong! Strength training may be *more* important for cyclists than for other athletes. That's because cycling itself is such an incomplete activity." Example: You need glutes to cycle effectively and fast, but cycling itself doesn't develop glutes well. You can only build glutes by some form of weight training.

Weight training provides two important functions for cyclists, says Drozd, one on the bike and the other off the bike. It can reinforce and strengthen cycling movements, helping to make your riding more powerful and stable. And it can correct imbalances caused by cycling, making your off-the-bike life safer, easier, and healthier. Here are the details.

WEIGHT TRAINING'S ON-THE-BIKE BENEFITS

1. ***Strengthens the core.*** Ironically, while the core muscles—the abs, hips, and lower back are largely ignored by

cycling, you need a strong core to ride effectively, says Drozd. "A strong midsection helps you in standing out of the **saddle**, negotiating obstacles, turning, generally controlling the bike, avoiding falls, even creating a foundation for the legs to push against," he says. "If you're a noodle, you're shifting all over the place, losing energy and power." Use weights to build your core, and you're automatically better on the bike and off the bike in all real-life movements.

2. *Improves your power.* Weight lifting is an easy way to quickly and thoroughly strengthen cycling-specific muscles, including the quads, hams, glutes, and calves. Pulling exercises, like rows, give your upper body more power when pulling up on the handlebars while rocking the bike out of the saddle.

3. *Maintains reaction time and balance.* Lifting with fast contractions and heavy weights resuscitates the **fast-twitch fibers** that can rapidly diminish and lose power and speed over time.

WEIGHT TRAINING'S OFF-THE-BIKE BENEFITS

1. *Corrects imbalances caused by cycling.* Muscles are stressed through a limited range in cycling, often to the exclusion of others. The quads get worked more than the hamstrings; the *vastus lateralis*, the outside muscle of the quad, get worked and built up more than the *vastus medialis*, the inside of the quad, which is fully flexed only when the leg is completely straightened (which never happens during pedaling). Good balance

dictates that agonist and corresponding antagonist muscles (i.e., quads/hamstrings, abs/low back, biceps/triceps) be of complementary strength. With weight lifting, you can spot-strengthen the underworked muscles, restoring balance.

2. *Adds stability to all movements.* Cycling stresses leg muscles in one direction, a one-dimensional fitness that is not as resistant to traumas from other directions. Weight lifting can provide more omni-directional stress that provides stability during standing, walking, and lateral movement sports like tennis and basketball.

3. *Strengthens unstressed muscles.* The cycling position is very static. Many muscle groups—nearly all those in the upper body and back—do not see much use during riding.

4. *Generally keeps you younger.* Need more motivation to hit the iron? Consider that weight lifting also provides great benefits for general longevity. Described in detail in chapter 5, regular strength training can help you slow the body's natural rate of decline of muscle mass (normally 1 percent per year after age 35), fast-twitch fibers, oxygen-processing capacity, power, reaction time, testosterone, and human growth hormone (HGH) production.

A successful strength training strategy includes lifting with the same muscles no more than once every 48 hours to allow muscle recovery; a warm-up set with light weights; rapid contractions with heavy weight to build muscle and maintain power; heavy circuit training with no rest between sets to spike HGH; a recovery workout following a hard workout; and periodizing (changing) your routine to keep muscles fresh.

THE EXERCISES

The strength exercise routines described below, put together by Chris Drozd, are separated into three categories: (1) those that develop cycling-specific muscles; (2) those that develop the muscles ignored by cycling; (3) those that undo the damage cycling does. The exercises can be done with dumbbells, a weight bench, a Swiss inflatable ball, as well as weight machines, making it possible to do most of them at home.

"You're a cyclist, not a bodybuilder, so you don't want to be in the gym much," says Drozd. That's why he favors a "less is more" philosophy with regard to weight lifting: train movements rather than muscles. Focusing on big, complex movements not only provides the best bang for the buck, but gets you out of the gym (or your garage) quicker—squats, dead lifts, pull-ups, sit-ups. Keep in mind that we all function with multijoint movements; hip, knee, and ankle joints all work together as you run and jump.

How many reps?

For all exercises below, for general strength do three sets of 10 reps to failure (the point at which you can no longer maintain form). For stamina, do 20, 25, or even more reps; for power do 1 to 4 reps, all out. Be careful with ALL of these, especially if you're new to weight lifting. Hire a trainer—a good one—to get you started. To warm up, use lighter weight for the first set. Always warm up well, for about ten minutes, at least. Do this riding, too.

A word about timing

There is debate as to the best time of year to lift weights. Through the early 1990s, the common belief was that weight lifting was strictly an off-season endeavor for cyclists. Late-season weakness, however, led innovative triathletes like six-time Hawaii Ironman winner Mark Allen to maintain strength training throughout the season, and performances increased as a result. *Bike for Life* recommends that all cyclists—except possibly top-level racers concerned with having too much muscle mass—follow Allen's lead. One caveat: don't do any heavy lifting, especially with your legs, within a week of an event you've been training for. Six-time Ironman champ Dave Scott blames his poor bike ride in the 1996 race on lack of recovery time from a heavy lifting session three days before the event.

Cycling-specific strength exercises

These exercises will give you more power on the bike by strengthening the muscles used.

1. ***Barbell Dead Lift***

   Benefit: "There is no better cycling-specific movement," says Drozd. The dead lift develops the calves, quads, hamstrings, glutes, low back, mid back, forearms, and midsection stability.

   Description: Standing with feet at "pedal" width, holding barbell at thigh height, hands about shoulder width, fold over at the hip joint—*not the waist*—kind of like that party favor from the '60s, the plastic bird that looked a bit like the road runner, that would pivot from the top of its legs, dip into the martini glass and return, only to dip again and again.

There are variations in the dead lift with regard to knee bend. If there's too much knee bend, you're doing a squat. Bend the knees no more than about 25° to 35° and maintain that bend throughout. If you do these straight-legged, fine, but you probably won't handle the same amount of weight and it'll be more load on your back. You only need to lower the bar to a little below your knees, but if flexibility allows, you can go further. Keep your back neutrally aligned, not rounded during this movement.

A dead lift can also be performed with dumbbells and with a bench and the low row station of a cable weight machine. Standing on the bench with the handles in your hands, rise from a squatting to standing position. To emphasize balance even more, some even perform dead lifts one leg at a time.

2. **Decline Sit-up**

Benefit: Conditions the hip flexors and abdominals, which together are integral to a good pedal stroke. Also useful in building a "six pack."

Description: On a slant board with your hips beneath your bent knees, sit up and lean back with a smooth, controlled motion, keeping the midsection stable. Fight the tendency to over-arch the back. Keep it "neutrally aligned"—flat, with a natural standing-posture arch. The total range of motion is about 30° to 60°, depending on your strength. Maintain stability by drawing your navel in toward your spine throughout. Maintain overall abdominal tension at top.

Reps: To failure.

3. **Push-ups**

Benefit: Conditions the midsection as well as strengthening the "pushing" muscles of the upper body, including triceps and chest. You do use all arm muscles when you climb, and holding a line while mountain biking requires good stability on an unstable surface. Staying stable while pushing up from the ball is more challenging than a simple ground push-up and a machine or free-weight bench press. To increase the ground push-up challenge, do them with hand positions altered (one forward, the other back), different-sized balls under each hand, and with feet elevated on an exercise ball.

Description: Keep back neutrally aligned and move the whole body as a unit. Tilt your pelvis back, draw your navel into your spine, keep your butt low, and switch hand positions to increase instability factor. Note: For added benefit, perform on an inflatable exercise ball; put your feet on top of the ball and walk out on your hands to normal push-up position.

Reps: To failure.

4. **Single-Arm or Single-Leg Dumbbell/ Cable Rows**

Benefit: Works the back and midsection in a cycling-specific position under conditions that require balance and build stability and alignment. Balance is important on a bike, especially as you age.

Description: Warm up with conventional double-arm rows with both feet on the ground. (This works the back well but requires little stability, especially if performed on a row weight machine.) Then release the left dumbbell/cable handle, hold on with the right, stand on the left foot, and pull the right-hand weight toward your body as your right elbow moves straight back.

5. Leg Curls

Benefit: Strengthens the hamstrings and calves. The gastroc part of the calf crosses the knee. This is not a multijoint exercise, but the leg curl is similar to the cycling upstroke and develops hamstring strength, which is necessary to balance a cyclist's often-overemphasized quads. This exercise will help you avoid pulled or torn muscles.

Description: Lay belly-down on a leg-curl weight-stack machine. With your heels beneath the pads and knees aligned with the hinge, bend your knees, "curling" the weight toward your butt. As you do this, press your hips into the bench if you feel them start to rise from the bench. Lower slowly. There are other "leg curl" machines, and they're all useful.

6. Single-Leg Leg Presses or Step-ups

Benefit: Allows for concentrated effort on one leg at a time, providing better strength symmetry. The leg press position is quite cycling-specific, and the ability to load weight onto the legs in such a position, without the need for stability, is of great use in building high local strength and stamina. Conversely, step-ups require great balance, and large loads cannot be easily used; this makes for far better three-dimensional conditioning, improving stability and alignment under load. Further, the height of the step can be used to target specific strength-range deficiencies, if needed.

Description: Sit in a leg-press machine and only push with one leg. Concentrate on staying aligned. Keep your knee, hip, and toe all on the same plane. Avoid twisting to the side, and avoid allowing your knee to collapse to the inside.

Step-ups (standing on a step and pushing up, as if walking up the stairs) accomplish the same thing but ramp up the difficulty by adding imbalance. It conditions stability from ankles to ears. Do them with or without weights in hand. Do not let your right foot swing behind the left.

7. Calf Raises

Benefit: Isolates calf in a near-cycling position. Also, the stronger you make the connection between the foot and leg, the better for power transfer.

Description: Standing on the edge of a step on the ball of your foot, with the heel down as far as it can go, push up on your toes and raise your heels as high as you can. This conditions the full range of motion. It also gives you strength at the end of the range, and will help prevent injuries. Avoid bouncing. Make sure knees are bent about 25° to 35° and keep that bend throughout the movement. There are plenty of calf machines in the gym, and all are valid.

8. Modified Plank with Leg Raise

Benefit: This exercise works your body in a position similar to cycling's **aerobar** position and develops the *serratus anterior*, but more importantly it develops midsection stability and stamina, especially when, as an advanced exerciser, you raise one leg, supporting yourself and remaining aligned with only a single leg.

Description: Get in flat-back push-up position, but on elbows instead of hands. Then raise one leg at a time as high as it can go. Hold it as long as possible, up to a couple of minutes.

9. **Squats**

Benefit: Increases hip, knee, and ankle muscles' strength in a fairly cycling-specific manner. Relies on the body's ability to stabilize and align itself, rather than neglecting that three-dimensional aspect, as leg machines and Smith squats do. Because of its difficulty and whole-body involvement, this is a great exercise to encourage overall strength and stamina and work the core and low back.

Description: Standing erect with a barbell over your shoulders, bend the knees, lean forward slightly, and lower yourself. Don't go beyond the point where your butt is lower than your knees. This exercise can also be done on a squat machine.

Muscles that don't get worked in cycling . . .

. . . but that you need in order to be a balanced person.

1. **Glutes**

Benefit: While not completely neglected in cycling, the glutes, in a phenomenon known as "reciprocal inhibition," release in response to hip flexor tightening. As the latter reflexively shorten, their opposing muscles, the glutes, have to stretch to accommodate and can become saggy, flaccid, soft, and weak. This exercise tightens the glutes and restores their power. Ideally, it is done in conjunction with the hip flexor stretch, below.

Description: Using a leg-press machine, press through with your heels (not your forefoot, which uses more of your quads than glutes).

2. **Upright Rows**

Benefit: The shoulders are largely ignored in cycling. Pulling up a barbell, dumbbells, or bar from a low pulley also somewhat replicates the pulling you do on a handlebar, especially while climbing.

Description. Standing straight up, hold a barbell at thigh level with hands at shoulder width. Pull the bar up until your elbows reach about shoulder level. Avoid shrugging.

3. **Pectoral Flys**

Benefit: Builds the pecs, ignored in cycling. Turns your cyclist's upper body (roughly that of a ten-year-old boy) into a he-man's (or Amazon woman). "May even put hair on the chest (of men)," jokes Drozd.

Description: Lie face face-up on a Swiss ball, with dumbbells directly over the chest at about nipple line. Palms facing each other, slowly lower weights out to the side, still directly in line with the chest. Pause briefly at the bottom, elbows just below rib cage, and without shifting or twisting, raise the weights back to starting position. There should be a slight to moderate bend in elbows throughout. In the gym, use the pec-fly machine.

4. **Triceps**

Benefit: These rear upper-arm muscles are little used in cycling, except for balancing the upper body when leaning on the handlebars, and, more actively, during climbing. They can become sore during long rides.

Description: In a standing position with dumbbells straight overhead, palms facing each other, lower your hands to ear level, then arc the dumbbells back to their original position.

5. **Pull-ups or Lat Pulls, Palms Supinated**

Benefit: Helps in strengthening the connection between rider and bike, allowing for greater power transfer to the road. Uses arms and back muscles.

Description: Grab a pull-up bar with palms facing back, hang and then begin raising your chest toward the overhead bar. Return slowly, under control. If pull-ups are too hard, use a high pulley and a lat bar, and while seated at the machine draw the bar down toward the bottom of your rib cage. Keep the chest high and shoulders back.

6. **Deltoids**

Benefit: Delts are used little in cycling, except during standing climbs.

Description: In a crouched "action position"—with knees bent, waist bent more than 90°, head forward—hold dumbbells hanging straight down from arms one foot from the ground. Then lift the bells out to the side like the wings of a bird. Keep shoulders from elevating, or shrugging. Keep hands and elbows aligned with each other and on the same plane throughout. The movement is about 90° from side to shoulder level.

Exercises that undo the damage cycling does

1. **Back Extension**

Benefit: This exercise contracts the spiny erector muscles, which become stretched out and weak from the riding position. Restores back posture to concave, from convex.

Description: Lying face-down, rounded over a Swiss ball, uncurl yourself by arching your head and back up one vertebrae at a time from your head, neck, back, and then hips. Your arms can be included in this stretch, too. From the slumped position, you'll lightly grasp crossed arms by the elbows, and as you rise, bring each arm out to the side, up and back, rotating as in the chest stretch, below. Also, do this exercise on a machine at the gym or on a flat floor.

Reps: To failure.

2. **Hip Flexor Lunge Stretch**

Benefit: Lengthens the hip flexors, which are shortened by cycling and daily sitting at a desk, in a car, etc.

Description: Kneel on one knee and place the other foot directly in front of its hip. Make sure that knee is vertically aligned with the ankle of that foot. Knee will be at 90° to shin, shin will be at 90° to floor. Place both hands on top of the forward knee and keeping upper body upright and vertical, slide the rear knee backward until a stretch is felt in or about the top front of that leg, near the hip and "lower" ab region. The stretch will feel "deep." Sink further into the stretch with each deep exhale. Back off a bit if stretch is "burning."

3. **Swimming (Crawl and Backstroke)**

Benefit: Elongates the posture with arms reaching overhead and waist straight; it is the antithesis of the protracted, hunched cycling position. Also, this stroke's exaggerated twisting at the hips works the midsection, which is largely ignored in cycling. Also a terrific means of unloading cycling muscles while still conditioning heart and lungs; great for adding condition to the upper body, which is typically ignored by cyclists; develops a proprioceptive and kinesthetic sense that, though not specific to cycling, can have some neural carryover improving positional and spatial awareness.

Reps: Ideally, a couple of times a week for 15–30 minutes.

4. **Chest Stretch**

Benefit: Restores lung capacity and expands and lengthens the chest muscles, which shorten over time because of cycling's flexed and protracted shoulder positions, especially in the aerobar position.

Description: Standing erect, straighten arms, hold them to the sides parallel to the ground, then pull them behind you by pinching the shoulder blades together; focus on holding an imaginary pencil between the blades. Perform this stretch frequently—at the gym, in the elevator, when you get out of bed or your car.

5. **Scorpion Tail Raises**

Benefit: Restores strength to spiny erectors, curvature to lumbar spine, and de-humps upper back.

Description: Lying face-down on a Swiss ball, raise both legs and arch back as high as possible in the air, balancing on your hands and abdomen.

Reps: To failure.

• QUICK PRE-RIDE • WARM-UP EXERCISES

Don't hop on your bike cold. For the four functional, non–weight training exercises below, which offer simultaneous strength and stretching benefits for cyclists, *Bike for Life* talked to Dr. Michael Yessis, a former consultant to several Olympic and pro Los Angeles sports teams. He is a proponent of active-isolated stretching (AIS), a highly effective method that moves the muscle through a range of motion that includes contraction (strength) and elongation (stretching). Yessis selected the following exercises based on what would be most beneficial to cyclists.

1. **Calf Raises:** Very effective at warming up the calf and Achilles tendon and providing ankle flexibility, this stretch is conducted while standing on the edge of a step or curb on the ball of your foot. Raise the heel as high as possible, then lower back down below the plane of the step. Can be done with and without weights. Initially do with both legs, then switch to single-leg.

2. **Good Mornings:** This movement strengthens a cyclist's weak back muscles while stretching/strengthening the glutes and hamstrings. While standing, arch your back and bend forward at the hips. Don't lose the arch. Think of it as a flat-back, arms-outstretched bow. Do with or without a dumbbell resting on your shoulders.

3. **Squats:** Long considered the king of exercises, the squat strengthens the quads, hamstrings, and glutes. Feet shoulder-width apart, bend your

knees, lean forward at the waist, keep your back arched, and head looking forward. Keep heels on the floor to align knees over your feet. Do with or without a dumbbell on the shoulder.

4. *Back Raise:* Cyclists have weak backs, and this exercise is the only way to work the *erector spinae* muscles through their full range of motion. Lay belly-down on the back hyperextension bench with feet locked in place, legs straight, and torso draped downward. Raise your head and the thoracic portion of your spine first, then raise your trunk until it is slightly arched and higher than your legs.

If you do the same exercise while holding a broom handle over your shoulders, you can twist while at full extension, which will stretch and strengthen back muscles used during out-of-the-saddle climbing.

• HIGH PERFORMANCE YOGA® •
FOR CYCLISTS

Ten yoga poses from fitness guru Steve Ilg will strengthen your cycling—and help you repair the damage it does

Steve Ilg knows a cyclist when he sees one. "Three out of four who first come in to my classes are not flexible—and that hurts them big-time," says the USCF coach and inventor of High Performance Yoga. A high-level road cyclist, cross-country skier, snowshoer, and rock climber, Ilg was once dubbed "the world's fittest human" by *UltraCycling* magazine and was pictured on a 1992 cover of *Outside* magazine next to the headline "This man can break you—

and build you up again." A dozen years later, at age 44, Ilg remains as chiseled as a bodybuilder, as flexible as a yogi, and, as *Bike for Life*'s Roy Wallack saw while teaming with him at the Furnace Creek 508 relay race in October 2004, in possession of an aerobic engine worthy of a champion half his age.

"Flexibility is huge for cyclists for two reasons: proper bike fit and quality of life," says Ilg. "Yoga can open up your power and get your flexibility back fast."

The problem with cycling, he says, is that it is "strange on the body; it can suffocate it.

"The sport mandates long hours of intense exercise in an imbalanced position with a constricted range of motion, a closed kinesthetic loop that does not fully extend legs or arms and shortens connective tissues," he says. "So when cyclists come in to my yoga classes, I immediately see a number of muscular weaknesses and biomechanical inefficiencies: weak midsections and undeveloped 'internal flotation,' humped backs and slumped shoulders, and stiff and weak hip flexors, top of the feet, ankles, and knees."

INTERNAL FLOTATION

If you were stopped by the yogic term "internal flotation," as we were, Ilg describes it as "a natural, fluid state of inner mobility and support based upon appropriate breathing." It's a key concept for cyclists to understand and use, given that the sport unwittingly has a tendency to work against it.

"When we are internally supported," says Ilg, "we breathe and move from a mobile core—our abdominals, hips, an lower back. When we are internally supported, our breath becomes a turbine; it creates a fusion of powerful breath and physiology that creates and radiates action from the inner toward the outer. All animals move this way; think of a starfish and you've got the idea."

The trouble is that cyclists often don't move this way. "Most cyclists are overly concerned with their leg strength and speed and remain untrained in yogic breathing," says Ilg. As a result, we are grossly unbalanced throughout our core. We have super-strong hip flexors and virtually nonexistent hip extensors. Just have a cyclist perform a standing backbend with his arms extended overhead and see how far he gets. This imbalance weakens our riding—and our postures. We tend to skeletally brace ourselves on our bike with locked-out arms, shoulders pinned close to our ears, our spines unable to maintain a flat, low, aerodynamic position. Without internal flotation, cyclists collapse inward and restrict their most powerful forces from within. When we internally float our postures with turbine-like breath, we are in "attack" mode more often instead of "survival" mode.

The yoga poses that Ilg prescribes below, taken from his recent book, *Total Body Transformation*, are designed to erase those cycling-specific restrictions on a cyclist's body. He says they'll maximize power transfer, elongate the vertebral chain, and stabilize pelvic alignment for enhanced biomechanics and riding technique.

THE MENTAL SPOTLIGHT

The poses are also designed to take you beyond purely "physical" fitness. "These positions will enhance 'ekagrata' . . . the ability of 'one-pointed' mental

concentration," says Ilg, referring to another yogic concept that has important applications to cyclists.

"In the mental training sciences," he says, "mental energy can be directed in two primary ways: One Pointed Concentration (OPC) and High Perspective Mental Energy (HPME). The latter can be likened to a traffic helicopter; the vision is all-encompassing as it looks down onto the ground to see which freeways are congested and which are clear. To cyclists, HPME is required while riding in a large **peloton**. The cyclist must process a lot of incoming data while sensing surges and attacks from all around them. OPC, on the other hand, is like a narrow-beamed spotlight at night from that same helicopter; the spotlight deletes everything save for that narrowed beam of vision. A cyclist needs OPC while high-speed descending in the rain or when opening up his final sprint to come around an opponent(s). If HPME is a floodlight, then OPC ("ekagrata" in yoga) is like a surgeon's laser scalpel. HPME is peripheral awareness, OPC is focused awareness."

Now that you know more about yoga than you probably wanted to know (go to www.wholisticfitness.com for his Wholistic Fitness Online Training), it's time to, as Ilg says, "feel the *chi*"—the life-force. Here's his yoga workout designed specifically for cyclists.

The 30-Minute Cycling Yoga Workout

The following 30-minute "asana" workout (defined as "conscious breathing while sustaining postures") consists of moving deliberately, with little rest, between ten traditional, challenging yoga poses. Ilg says the workout can be used on in-season recovery days and more regularly throughout the off-season. It starts with a general warm-up routine, adds important core poses, and moves on to cycling-specific poses.

Important rules:

- Perform all yoga poses barefooted in a draft-free, clean, warm space where you are not to be interrupted.
- Hydrate before and after, but not during, a session.
- Allow at least three days of recovery between sessions.
- Hold each pose for a minimum of 45 seconds to a maximum of 90 seconds unless otherwise prescribed.
- Consciously engage in deep nasal breathing (technically known as Ujjayi Pranayam in the yoga world) throughout the entire program. "Do not move without the presence of conscious breathing," says Ilg. "Breath dictates movement. When your mind wanders, draw it gently back with deep breathing."

Step I
Warm-Up Exercises

This dynamic sequence, which flows unbroken from one pose to another, generates internal heat to promote elasticity of connective tissue, helps remove cellular toxins, and focuses the mind within the body, according to Ilg. Cycling-wise, it builds postural strength on the bike.

1. *Downward-Facing Dog*
   This classic yoga position looks like an upside-down V. Standing with feet flat on the ground, bend down, put fully extended hands flat on the floor, and walk back three feet. Lift butt high in the air. Let the spine lengthen

by keeping the thighs firm, as if you are trying to lift the kneecaps up to the thighs. Lift your toes to lower your heels.

This pose loosens restricted shoulders, lengthens the spine, and stretches the Achilles tendon, hamstrings, and arm muscles. It also bathes the brain stem with oxygen and nutrients.

Hold the Dog for three breaths, inhale, and move on to . . .

2. *Plank Pose*
   This simply is the "up" position of a push-up, with arms vertical, hands flat, on toes, with back and legs in a straight line. From the Dog, simply lower your butt, rock your head and shoulders forward, and walk your feet back.

   The Plank builds midsection and shoulder strength.

   Hold it, exhale, and lower halfway down to . . .

3. *Chaturanga*
   This is the "down" position of a push-up. It works your midsection and arms. Keep your elbows pinned to the sides of the ribs.

   Hold it, inhale, and move to . . .

4. *Upward-Facing Dog*
   Rock forward, lower your legs and tops of the feet to the ground, and push your head and torso straight up by fully extending the arms.

   Hold it, exhale, push back to . . .

5. *Chaturanga*
   Hold it, inhale, press to Plank; hold it, exhale, move to Downward-Facing Dog.

   Repeat the entire five-exercise sequence five times, recover for 30 seconds, and then move on to the Core Sequence.

Step II
Core Sequence

6. *Navasana/Ardha Navasana Superset*
(repeat two to three times)

The following two poses condition a cyclist's upper and lower abdominal muscles, gastrointestinal tract, core strength and balance, mental focus, and build strength and power by developing the "internal flotation" described above.

"These are killer ab exercises—they make ab machines at the gym seem easy," warns Ilg. "Just do your best until the strength comes on line, which happens remarkably quickly."

▶ *Ardha Navasana (Half-Boat Pose)*

From a sitting position with legs stretched out in from of you, raise both hands so arms are parallel to the ground with palms forward and fingers outstretched, grow your spine tall. Then exhale as you lean the upper torso away from your feet while you raise both legs off the floor until both feet are at eye level. Spread the toes and draw them and the inner arches of the feet toward you, pressing the balls of the feet into the air. Balance on your sacrum (tailbone) and experience the burn of the abdominals.

Breathe for a few moments before moving into . . .

▶ *Paripurna Navasana (Full-Boat Pose)*

Inhale and draw both legs higher while simultaneously raising your heart center toward the knees, taking the shape of a V while still balancing on the sacrum. Keep raising the feet until they are above or even with the top of your head. Make your back as concave as possible and move your navel toward the upper thighs, but without rounding the back.

Exhale into Ardha Navasana and repeat back and forth between the two for 30–90 seconds. This equals one Superset.

Step III
Cycling-Specific Sequence

Sustain each of the following postures for 60–90 seconds of deep, nasal breathing before moving on to the next one. This sequence targets cycling's power-chain musculature, releasing the tightness and strengthening the weaknesses created by its imbalances.

7. *Utkatasana (Fierce Warrior Pose)*

"The worst biomechanics that I see in cyclists of all categories—rounded spine, weak torso stability, scrunched-up shoulders, knees and feet out of alignment—can all be solved by this one yoga pose!" says Ilg.

Assume a pedal-width stance. Bend both knees deeply until the top of your thighs are parallel to the earth. Do NOT allow your heels to come off the ground. Point your toes forward, in alignment with your knees. Raise both arms overhead by feeling a backbend in the back of your heart area. Do NOT allow your elbows to bend. "Your arms are your Warrior Swords!" says Ilg. "Make sure your swords are strong and long!" Press your head back and keep soft eyes looking forward. Nasal breathing only. Hold for 60–90 seconds.

Note: If your heels refuse to touch the earth, it is because cycling has shortened the connective tissues in your calves and hamstrings. If so, widen your stance until the heels do touch. Over time, you will close the gap.

8. **Virasana (Hero Pose)**

"When cyclists come into my yoga classes, they are notoriously stiff and weak in their hip flexors, top of the feet, ankles, and knees," says Ilg. "Weakness is not something I want my athletes to carry into their cycling. This one pose, Hero Pose, excels at removing stiff, brittle, and weak trigger areas of a cyclist and replaces them with strength, suppleness, and life energy. I call it a 'gateway pose' because it opens the gate to making other postures more available to you."

Sit on the ground in a kneeling position. Press your knees together and splay your feet apart so they rest beside the hips and you are sitting between your heels. Turn the soles of your feet directly behind you, and point your toes backward as well. (If this is too much for you, options include sitting on the heels, sitting on the inside edges of the feet, or crisscrossing the feet under your buttocks.) Bring your spine beautiful—tall and erect.

Rest your palms on top of your knees, puff out your heart center slightly, and gaze softly in front of you. Breathe and dance your edge here for the prescribed time. After doing one, you may repeat the pose, or move on to the next pose.

9. **Eka Pada Sarvangasana (One-Legged All-Parts Pose)**

This pose counteracts the limited range of motion in cycling that causes waste-product build-up and shortening of connective tissue. "It trains the body to become more 'lymphatically fit'—to better process exercise-induced cell toxins while providing a beautiful full range of motion for the entire spine and lower body," says Ilg. "It also benefits heart rate, reduces tension, and improves thyroid and parathyroid functioning—meaning more strength endurance for cyclists."

Lying on your back with arms at your sides, bend your knees and draw both heels into your buttocks, press fingertips against the ground, and raise your torso and legs simultaneously as you roll back into a shoulder stand (head and shoulders do not move). With knees still bent, quickly bring your palms into your lower back and use your elbows as small support pillars. Walk your hands down closer to your armpits. With thumbs placed on the side ribs, press the back ribs toward the spine with the fingers. Now, you should be looking straight up into your mid-thighs.

Exhale and push your legs and torso straight up to the sky. Press hands deeper into your back as you move your sternum toward the chin. Relax your face and work on steadying your entire body. ("As your 'internal flotation' strength develops, you can try removing your hands from your lower back to an overhead position," says Ilg. "By doing this, you will quickly discover why it is called All-Parts Pose. It requires great strength to do this movement purely!")

After 60 to 90 seconds in this pose, exhale and arc your right leg down until all five toes touch earth. Keep both legs fully extended. Reach the left heel away from the right to ensure maximum height and length of the left leg. Exhale, raise the right leg back, and repeat with the left.

After working both legs, slowly bend both knees toward the forehead, and then straighten the legs until your toes touch the ground. Exhale. Then remove your hands from the lower back and clasp fingers from each hand around your two big toes. Slowly, keeping your legs straight, roll your upper spine, the middle spine, then lower spine, down onto the ground, all while keeping your legs close to your torso. Exhale and squeeze both knees into your chest with your hands. Breathe, then relax and extend your legs to your original supine position.

Step IV
The Grande Finale

10. *Savasana (Corpse Pose)*

"Learning how to relax into the body is, without a doubt, the pivotal quality of champion athletes," says Ilg. "Learning how to mentally 'let go' is precisely what is needed when high-end suffering is trying to convince your ego to quit. This pose, your final relaxation posture, is tantamount for relaxing your mind and body, the only way we gain better health, healing, and self-knowledge."

Lie supine, facing upward, with both legs stretched out in front of you to complete extension, hip and shoulder-width apart. Heels in, feet fall out to the sides like an open book. Stretch both arms, fingers outstretched and palms facing upward, at a 45° angle from your torso.

Inhale and raise your chin to your chest. "Take one loving last look at the body that has served you so well in the last few minutes," says Ilg. "Thank it, close your eyes, gently lay your skull down, and calm the inner war. *Namasté*."

(Oh, in case you were wondering about that last word, it's what they say in India instead of hello or good-bye, according to Ilg. "*Namasté* means that the Sacred Space that lies within me recognizes and honors that same Sacred Space that lies within you," he says. "When you and I communicate from that space, we are one.")

Three Case Studies: The Glory of Goals

There is no incentive to train without a dream. Here are the stories of three middle-aged dreamers who set lofty cycling goals and are achieving them in impressive fashion.

The Carmichael Plan . . .
. . . turned a 45-year-old into The Man

CHRIS Carmichael is known for being the coach of Lance Armstrong, but just as good an advertisement for his training methods is Rich McInnes, a 45-year-old father of three from Louisville, Kentucky. In fact, *Bike for Life* called McInnes for an interview when we saw his picture in a Carmichael Training Systems (CTS) magazine ad. As expected, he was a worthy poster boy. In less than a year, the traveling operations-efficiency expert had lost over 30 pounds, went from non-racer to Cat 3, and from watching Masters races to winning them.

Carmichael's system won't be a surprise to anyone who's followed the sport and read this chapter. It combines standard Periodization base- and strength-building with the fast cadence that Armstrong made famous. "Carmichael works on the cardiovascular system first—strengthens your heart and gets you processing oxygen well," says McInnes. "The fast cadence is difficult at first, but it takes the stress off the legs. Then he slowly builds your power and has you practice active recovery. It plays real well for an aging athlete."

The Carmichael program starts out as all should: finding where you are now and setting future goals. McInnes was a high school and college runner who got heavy after he "fragged" his knee in a church softball game. A cyclist friend dragged him into the sport and he fell in love; after three and a half years, he owned a $5,000 road bike, did tandem trips with his wife, and could ride a century in five and a half hours. Then, when he saw a buddy race at the 2003 Masters Nationals, he said to himself, "I can do that. I just need a coach."

In August 2003, the 206-pound McInnes went into the CTS offices. First, he listed his goals: drop 20 pounds, ride a sub-5 century, climb L'Alpe d'Huez (he flies to Europe a lot for work), and do a tour from Louisville to the Upper Peninsula of Michigan. Then, he got to work. First, to measure his wattage output, he did a field test—2- to 3-mile intervals with a ten-minute rest in-between, an ordeal he says "left me with my tongue on the ground." Also measured: lactate threshold, maximum heart rate (174), and body-fat percentage. A bike fit revealed that McInnes was sitting too far back; as advised, he got a longer stem to put his weight more over the front wheel.

After that, he was given a diet plan from a nutritionist and a training plan from a coach, Colorado Springs–based Kate Gracheck. He signed up for Expert level—four hours per month, $150 per month. For that "dirt cheap amount," says McInnes, Gracheck gives him a monthly schedule in advance, and modifies it based on his situation, such as his trip to Abu Dhabi in April. Likewise, if he wants to run and swim, weight train, do yoga, or Pilates, she will build that in.

"Initially, my bike handling was much improved from the bike fit; I could instantly corner better," says McInnes. "But the training plan they set me up with was too easy, which was frustrating. Kate had set me up at 90-minute rides—half of what I'd normally do on my own—at no higher than 135 to 142 heart rate. I rode at a cadence of 95; normally, I ride at 85.

"I'd download my files and send them to her—and she'd verbally—or e-mail—spank me. 'You're not racing now—you're training,' she'd say.

"I started to get it after a couple months when I noticed I dropped ten pounds and felt stronger. It was amazing! But then, instead of letting me go faster, Kate told me to rest, shorten my rides even more, slow down, and pedal faster. Like a girl.

"A while later, I did a field test; it was crappy. I was mad, but Kate just laughed. 'What'd you expect? We haven't done anything to strengthen you yet.'"

Over winter, strengthening commenced. Two months later, McInnes's tests showed a quantum leap. In February, he tried his first Cat 5 race. In March, he won two of them.

Entering Masters races, he began learning that the strongest often doesn't win—team tactics are key. By July, a year after he began the CTS program, McInnes was doing his sprints in the hills instead of the flats and training nine to twelve hours per week. He then rode a hilly, 25-mile **time trial** in over 26 mph with a maximum wattage of 1,200—double that of a year before.

"I'm 172 pounds now, headed for 168, the lightest I've been since college," he says. "Watching my body literally morph has motivated my wife, who now does aerobics three to four times a week and is getting ready to do her first triathlon. The training has kept me out of bars at night and out of trouble. When I'm at an account, they all know that I won't eat late. I get up early now. I've got shaved legs now—went through the whole thing—Nair, razor blades.

"It's been a rebirth," he says. "I was once a top-level athlete, and I'd always wondered if I could get back to that level. Well, now I'm a Cat 3, placing high in multiday races in the 1 and 2 levels, and I've rediscovered the old Rich.

"At the '04 Nationals in Park City, I saw 70- to 80-year-olds racing. Well, I'll be riding into the sunset for sure."

Going from 0 to 3,100 miles a month . . .
. . . and, at 60, getting younger every day

IN March 2004, Dan Crain got up at 4 AM every day and rode a century before work. "I was fatigued all the time, all month long. But it paid off," said the corporate insurance manager from Irvine, California, whose 3,100 miles won him the March Madness competition of the Davis Bike Club, of which he is a remote member. "After a few week's rest, I was surprised to feel like I was supercharged. I came back stronger than I've ever been—at age 59!"

Crain laughs, amused by the unlikelihood of a near-60-year-old being at his peak, especially with his history. For the first half-century of his life, he did no aerobic activity at all. He surfed in college and skied regularly in his 30s, period. At 50, worried his legs were getting weak, he began cycling. He gradually moved up to double-centuries and participated on a 4-man team and two 2-man teams at the famed Furnace Creek 508. Over time, to maintain leg strength, he added kickboxing and twice-a-week lower-body strength training—low reps/heavy weight one day and high reps/light weight the other. He did tons of squats and dead lifts—but no upper body exercises. That oversight would hurt him when he put his neck on the line—literally—at his first solo 508 in October 2004.

Three-quarters of the way through the race, after 380 miles—the longest ride of his life—Crain was in fourth place in a field of 61 solo riders and feeling invincible. Not only had he traversed an immense, forbidding swath of Southern California against 40 mph winds, but he'd traveled light-years from 1995, when he was a nonathlete. Now he was an entirely different person—and about to join the endurance gods: The 500-mile club.

He didn't plan, however, on "Shermer Neck."

"With less than 100 miles to go in the 508, I could no longer hold my neck up," he said. "It was falling forward like a rag doll. I literally couldn't see." It was a classic case of the condition first suffered by **RAAM (Race Across America)** pioneer Mike Shermer, in which riding in an aerobar tuck causes the muscles of the hyperextended neck to collapse.

Crain's crew tried in vain to keep him riding. First they cut a four-inch strip of sleeping pad and fashioned it into a neck brace, but "I couldn't breathe and it compressed my aorta–it was stopping blood from getting to my head." Next, they hooked bungee cords from the back of his helmet, down to a strap under his arms, around his chest and back again. "But it didn't feel safe to me. I could feel the vertebrae in my neck being pinched–felt like I was going to damage myself." After 420 miles, with his legs feeling great, Crain had to drop out of the 508.

But there's a silver lining. "I DNF'ed [did not finish] but had the ride of my life!" he shouted. "So I'm very optimistic for next year. I'll add neck exercises to my training, do wrestler's bridges, raise my handlebars an inch or two, and be back even stronger."

Crain plans to stick his neck out twice in '05. In June, he'll ride from San Diego to Atlantic City on a 2-man RAAM team. In October, he'll attempt to set a new 60-plus record of 33 hours at the Furnace Creek 508.

"Is it possible to continue improving as you get older? Yes–I'm proof of that," says Crain. "My body is far younger than it was two decades ago."

The Grande Dame of Dirt
In 24 hours, Wendy Skean realized a 50-year-old dream

"DON'T be intimidated by your own age." The advice tumbles from 60-year-old Wendy Skean's lips with an assurance that is undoubtable, undeniable, irrefutable. After all, the kindly, polite, kindergarten teacher from Idyllwild with the grandmotherly shock of white hair looks like a poster girl for the AARP–and just happens to be a two-time world champion mountain biker.

You see, nothing intimidates Skean–not taking up bike racing for the first time in her mid-40s, not riding for 24 hours straight, not even riding through a near-tornado. In September 2002 at British Columbia's Silver Star Resort, she won the 45-plus age group at the 24 Hours of Adrenalin Solo World Championship, because she rode 165 miles, climbed 11,000 feet, and kept going when everyone else, including male **NORBA** [National Off-Road Bicycle Association] riders three decades younger, was just too scared.

It had been a miserable night of rain and cold in the Canadian Rockies, and at dawn it got worse. A surprise Arctic storm blasted gale-force winds out of the north, dumped sleet at the course's 7,000-foot summit, knocked the already-frigid temperatures down by 20 degrees, and tore through the 24 Hours of Adrenalin tent city like a buffalo stampede. Half of the 84 soloists' tents and 800 team riders' tents were laid waste. Frightened and hypothermic, the course emptied as hundreds of panicked riders scattered for cars, hotel rooms, and any nearby building, bundled in blankets with heaters turned on full-blast. Race leader and two-time defending champion Chris Eatough fled the course. So did the man on his heels, off-road superstar Tinker Juarez, who thawed out in a hot bath, went to sleep, and didn't wake up in time to finish the race. No one went back out into the maelstrom. Except for the oldest.

Clad in over-the-knee knicker bike shorts and five layers of wool and polyester under a windbreaker, Wendy Skean paused ten minutes for a cup of hot chocolate and plunged back into the fray. Ultimately, that's why she finished 24 minutes up on Debi Sheets, a 51-year-old from Pennsylvania who had led to that point.

"I wanted that world-championship jersey in the worst way!" she explains. "I figured I'd ride until I blew up—or was blown away."

It was a very logical way to think for someone who had been nurturing a dream for 50 years.

From an Ending, a Beginning

"I had a goal as a child: I wanted to go to the Olympics as a swimmer," said Skean. But growing up in America in the 1940s and '50s wasn't a good time for such fantasies. Wendy grew up in South Pasadena, California, in an era when women didn't do sports, when the girls in her P.E. class actually weren't allowed to run past the half-court line in a basketball game. There was no girls' swim team at the Alhambra City Pool, and no pool at all at South Pas High. As a teen, Skean taught swimming to neighborhood kids. She swam endless circles in the above-ground pool in her backyard—figuring 99 laps to a mile—and dreamed of what might have been.

It took a divorce decades later for Skean to rekindle her old athletic flame. A career schoolteacher who'd done a lot of backpacking and hiking with her husband, she started running in 1986 to deal with the frustration of her broken marriage—and immediately began medaling in races. At the same time, she felt compelled to take up mountain biking.

"I had two teenage boys, and I needed to figure out something that we could all do together," she says. "My ex and I had bought mountain bikes a few years before, but we didn't ride much. Now, I figured, why not use them?"

To say that decision had an effect on the family is an understatement. As Wendy and the boys spent summer after summer taking three-week mountain bike camping trips all over Colorado and Utah, the trio bonded. "In the '80s, no one was doing what we did," she says. "My parents thought we were crazy. But it made us a cohesive family unit and changed our lives." Soon, they were entering off-road races from the Grand Tetons to Crested Butte to Big Bear and buying road bikes to do triathlons. One son became a serious bike racer. Both eventually ended up running bike shops for a living.

Queen of the Hill

By 1996, Skean had progressed to the Leadville 100 race in Colorado, and two years later became the oldest-ever woman to officially finish the legendarily difficult 100-mile mountain bike race under the 12-hour deadline. Soon, she discovered 24-hour racing and began organizing groups of her middle-aged friends to do team events.

In 1998, the first 24 Hours of Adrenalin race came to Hurkey Creek State Park, just a couple of miles from Skean's hometown of Idyllwild. "There were three women in the race, and I figured that it was my big chance," she said. She finished second to a 40-year-old and beat a teenager, "who was real upset that she'd been beaten by an old lady."

Skean won the '99 Idyllwild race over a woman in her 20s, and took fifth in 2000 in a field of ten in which she was the oldest by a decade. She missed the 2001 race due to broken ribs and blunt-force trauma to the pancreas she suffered in a crash while training for Colorado's fabled Montezuma's Revenge race. "But there was a silver lining to those injuries," she says. "Like Lance Armstrong, I lost fifteen pounds, so I got a lot faster." So much faster that it reminded her of her childhood quest for a world title.

Realizing that goal took persuasion as well as fitness. In 2002, Skean cornered Stuart Dorland, the owner of the 24 Hours of Adrenalin series, and told him she had no reason to travel to the Silver Star race unless she had a chance to compete for a championship. With professional men and women now racing for big money and championship jerseys as 24-hour racing took off, that meant setting up age-group categories for the first time. Dorland always planned on instituting age groups when the fields grew large enough, and the result was the solo field's sudden doubling in size, from 43 riders in '01, to 83 in '02. By the 2004 Solo Worlds in Whistler, B.C., the field had doubled again to 186. Soloists poured in from around the globe—including Austria, Australia, New Zealand, and England—and Idyllwild. Skean was back again, and the results were predictable: first place in the 60-plus division. The second Solo world title for the Little Old Kick-Ass Lady from South Pasadena.

Wendy's Tips: How to Ride Like an Old Woman

"I'm not an exercise maniac," says Wendy Skean. "But I certainly don't sit around." Here's the champ's training and racing tips for pulling off a world-class age-group performance at a 24-hour race.

Long training rides. Skean typically does a five-hour, 32-mile route with 6,000 feet of elevation gain up a peak in her neighborhood, Thomas Mountain. "It gets boring—I've done it 50-plus times, but it's all quality mileage with no junk that makes the most of my time."

Don't overtrain. "If my legs are tired walking up the stairs, I'm grumpy, or don't wake up easily, it's a sign to take it easy the next day," she says. In general, Skean rides only three or four days a week and takes a day or two off to hike or swim between rides for recovery.

Lift weights. "My upper body and arms got tired and beat up on the rocky sections until I started lifting," says Skean.

Don't pig out. "Weight slows you down and kills your DNA as you age," says Skean. "Oldies have to cut their calorie consumption. I'm faster since I started eating oatmeal for breakfast, just a little red meat, and two salads a day."

Newbies: Try a "women's-only" race. "Lots of gals get scared off from racing by rude hotshot guys who push you and yell at you when they pass," says Skean. She has introduced friends to the 24-hour scene at women's-only clinics at the annual Big Bear 12-hour relay at the beginning of June. For information, go to www.teambigbear.com.

Gary Fisher

THE JOY OF BEING
MR. MOUNTAIN BIKE

There may be no one who embodies the sport and culture of mountain biking as completely as Gary Fisher. He is a bike maker, athlete, promoter, and most importantly, a pioneer. He was there at the creation and, along with early partner Charlie Kelly, gave the world the first exclusive mountain bike business and the name "mountain bike"—earning both of them lifetime "Founding Father" status. With a knack for innovation and marketing savvy, Fisher pioneered the use of the unicrown fork, oversized **headsets**, **suspension forks** *on production bikes, long-top-tube/short-stem cockpits, and oversized wheels with 29-inch tires. As an athlete, he's been a top* **road racer**, *cyclocrosser, and age-group mountain biker. He's raced the Coors Classic road race, set the record at the fabled "Repack" race on Mt. Tamalpais, and, as he's aged, pushed the envelope by winning Masters off-road championships, tandem off-road races, and monumentally difficult events like the 400-mile, eight-day TransAlp Challenge stage race across the Alps. In 1988, he was among the first inductees into the inaugural Mountain Bike Hall of Fame. Outside magazine named him one of the 50 most influential outdoorsmen of the 1980s. He saw hard times—a failing business—turned into a dream lifestyle when bike industry behemoth Trek bought his trademark in 1993 and turned "Gary Fisher" into a mainstream brand. For over a decade, Fisher's had what many think is the best job in the bike business. He travels to cycling events around the world, exerts influence as a board*

member of social programs like Trips for Kids, which takes poor urban kids mountain biking, and spends his days riding and thinking of new ideas for the bikes that bear his name. All the while, he remains superfit, endlessly creative, and, as he told Roy Wallack in his Bike for Life interview on March 10, 2004, feeling decades younger than his chronological age. That'll come in handy; Fisher became a father again in 2004 at age 53.

LOTS OF PEOPLE say that they don't have a chance to ride, but I think people allow themselves to be worked into a place where they can't ride.

There's more to cycling than exercise and the fitness benefits. Just lately my girlfriend [now wife], Amanda, and I have had a lot of fun riding "town" bikes [low-tech, relaxed-geometry **cruisers**] around. We take them shopping. And along the way, we do this thing where we try to find the most arcane way to get from Point A to Point B.

Take the trip from Fairfax to San Anselmo [in Marin County, California]. Normally you come down Center Boulevard. Well, we go off and try to find another route on one side of the valley and find a different route back on the other side. Sometimes we find ourselves walking the bikes up some staircases and down others, just because they connect a couple of streets together. Every time, we end up going to all these places we've never been before—just to get to the grocery store about a mile and a half away. It's the serpentine route, and no one else is on it.

The sense of discovery is one of the things that makes me happy, and there is no better way to find a new place than on a bike. They're the get-off point. Besides not having to find a parking place, I love the instant gratification. The being in the now—taking the back routes, spending more time together, having fun. A lot of it is like, do you like what you are doing, here and now?

I STARTED ROAD racing when I was twelve, in 1962, and **cyclocross** a couple years later. I was attracted to it because there were older guys doing it, 15-, 17-year-olds who were working at the San Mateo Bike Shop in San Mateo. I couldn't quite hang with them. I was small for my age, one of the smallest kids in school. I wasn't even 98 pounds; I was 89 pounds when I was in eighth grade. As a freshman at Burlingame High School, there was one kid smaller than me. But from the first ride those older guys couldn't get rid of me. I kept following them. Then they said, "Well, OK. We'll let you come."

You've got to realize that it was so different then. There were a thousand registered race riders in the whole USA. And there were 50 or so in Northern California. Every time you saw somebody on a bike who wasn't a kid on the sidewalk or was obviously someone convicted of a DUI [and therefore had no license to drive a car], you went up to 'em and asked who they were, where they were from, and if you could ride with them. There were that few riders.

So we all stuck together—and we stood out. When I was in seventh grade, some girls from school saw me and said, "You farmer!"

That was a big put-down back then. The first six months, all I heard was, "Look at this farmer. With his little girl socks, little black wool shorts, and funny-looking jersey."

I thought about the total injustice of it.

All these things that I was wearing had a reason. So I didn't care that much. Because I had my own pace, my own world. The style was accepted by my peers.

It's ironic now that kids that age accept it, even like it, to some degree. My son has even come around. He's 16 now. But for years, he'd say: "Lose the Lycra, Dad."

A Mountain Bike and an Image Change

I DIDN'T KNOW mountain biking was going to be big at first. In the beginning, I thought, *This is for athletes. This is really tough. This is really cool. But there's only a few people that are into something this hard-core.* Then I remember this guy, Bob Burrows— a local fireman, not in particularly good cardiovascular shape, older, in his 40s. In about 1975, I made him a clunker—you know, the old cruiser frame, precursor to the mountain bike, cobbled together with all old, found objects for parts. And I thought to myself, *Here is another bike that will wind up in a garage or just ridden around the neighborhood.*

Well, I was so wrong.

We took Burrows out on a ride. He took forever to make the climb. But at the end of the ride, his eyes were so big and he was just so . . . new. It just changed him. Right there. It really surprised me, how much he liked it. And that was it.

Then I knew—This was going to be really big. This was going to go somewhere, by hook or by crook. Because people would do it. The percentage of 'em that said, "This is incredible. I'm gonna do this all the time and then follow through with it," was amazing. Amazingly high.

They loved the thrill so much, they were willing to get the fitness. So Burrows's bike didn't stay in the garage. He kept it out. And he rode it a lot.

BIKE FOR LIFE

WHAT IF YOUR doctor prescribed cycling and your insurance company co-paid it?

Why not? Hell, they do it with all these other stupid things. And who says it helps you or not? But I KNOW cycling helps. There's nobody that rides a bike that doesn't get better.

I worked some for Rodale Press in the late '70s, writing bike reviews for *Bicycling* magazine. In 1979, I went back to Emmaus, Pennsylvania, and there were people in the office who would give me hard-ass because I rode my bike the six blocks from where *Bicycling* was to the main headquarters. They'd ask me, "Can't you rent a car?"

Can you believe that? That's insane. But if you think about it, it was typical for the times. Back in the '70s and '60s, people were in the mind-set of "the bicycle is a primitive device."

So, in 20 years, everything's changed. We were at the bike messenger championships a few years ago in San Francisco. It was the coolest thing you could go to. Here I am, riding through Broadway Tunnel in a **Critical Mass** with all these people on a Friday night. There were 3,000 riders. And I was thinking, *Cycling has gone from being totally uncool to being totally cool.*

Aging Ungracefully

I'M 53, BUT I feel like I'm in my 20s.

That's because I can get on my bike and do what I do. It's still the same. I'm not as strong or as fast as I used to be. But that's just the sheer speed. All the same actions are there; standing up out of the saddle, powering through this, climbing in certain gears. The act of being able to do this is really important. I've been in places where I wasn't able to do that, like when I broke my wrist last summer [2003] and I had to spend three straight months at home.

The incident happened a couple of miles from home. I was riding with insolence. I was just too full of myself.

I was alone. I'd ridden to the top of Mt. Tam on July 5. I found out that morning that the UCI [Union Cycliste Internationale, cycling's governing body] was going to change the 29 rule. [In 2001, Fisher had introduced a mountain bike with fast, huge 700c wheels and 29-inch tires and had been lobbying to get it legalized for racing.] I'd been to see the UCI on June 13 at their headquarters just outside of Geneva, Switzerland, and sat in on a mountain bike commission meeting and presented my case. It went very well. I was really surprised at how cordial and logical they seemed in their approach.

I had gone there six months earlier. I knew the rules: make a face visit. That's what I did the first time and said, "When can we talk about this?" That's all I said. I didn't bug 'em. I know how to do these things. That's the nice thing about getting older. You've been through every scenario. And I've made most mistakes maybe once. Maybe twice. I've learned a lot over the years. That's how you do it with people like that—a face visit.

I didn't know what was going to happen. People all around were telling me, "Oh, you can't deal with those guys. They won't do what ya wanna do. They'll just ignore you." And it didn't turn out that way. I found out, by e-mail on July 5 in the morning, that they okayed it. They had changed the rules.

So I was full of myself. I rode by myself to the top of Mt. Tamalpais. It felt great. And I'd just been to Crested Butte the entire week before, for the Mountain Bike Hall of Fame. There was a big party and a big reopening of their museum. I went riding all the time. You know? Nine thousand-, 10,000-, 11,000-feet elevation with a bunch of hard-cores and just going crazy. Perfect. Didn't fall. Didn't hurt myself. Didn't even get a flat. And then I come home and I ride up to the top of Tam. On the descent I was looser and faster, and faster and looser. Just ripping through everything. Because I know every square inch. This one section near the bottom I felt, *I'm just going to wind it out in the biggest gear.* I think I was going about 35 and my front wheel was going through a rut. Nice sculptured little rut, and I let the front wheel get outa grip. The bars flipped around and I'm stepping off the bike at about 35 and saying: THIS . . . IS . . . STUPID!

And I just rolled around. I looked up at my right hand and said, "Oh my beautiful wrist!" It was in a Z-shape.

But it turned out to be a beautiful experience. I just laid back; suddenly there was another cyclist there, another Mt. Tam regular. She went down and got Matt, the ranger in the mountain district and an avid mountain biker. He came up and said, "Gary, what are we gonna do?" "Little ice, please," I said, "And get an ambulance down to the parking lot." And they did that. And the ambulance driver was Helena Drum, who's a road racer that I used to ride with.

That's what getting old does—you know everybody in your neighborhood. She says, "Gary, are you allergic to morphine?" When I get to the hospital they say, "Don't worry. We know who you are. We have all your medical insurance stuff online. Don't worry."

And it was fine. I stayed home for three months. It was the first time I stayed home in like 20 years. That went through the summer.

It's the worst injury I've had mountain biking, but it won't stop me. A big part of staying young is staying at-risk—despite being cautious to some degree. People will say, "You're really fast." But that's not all. I'm also really cautious. It's like both times I rode the TransAlp Challenge; I finished it, but didn't crash once.

I'll ride within myself and ride fast. But I'll ride within what I know I have confidence I can do.

Part of it is that, you know, as you get older, healing and recovery slow down. In lieu of a cast, they put a couple of long screws into the biggest bone on my hand and the big bone on my forehand, then held them together with a *RoboCop*-like device that goes from one to the other. Now if I was a young punk, they'd have taken that off in five and a half, six weeks. But it took eight to grow back.

I see all the signs of growing old. I can't recover like I used to. I'll stay tired longer. My muscle growth won't be as fast. Overall I don't have that total energy output. Take my heart rate: I can get it up to about 177. In the old days I could take it to about 200. When I was a kid, I had that much more burst power. And recovery has changed for me. I could ride harder more often back then. No doubt. For a competition over 100 miles, what used to take two days off to recover now takes five.

But there are fitness advantages at this age. When I'm well-rested, I can go really steady, really hard. In fact, I think the way I'm fit now allows me to perform better than what I could do in my 20s. That's because I've been able to really prepare myself correctly and feed myself during the ride. I'm a better coach to myself than I ever was.

I can still bolt from the get-go, but I gotta get a good warm-up beforehand. When you

BIKE FOR LIFE

rode the TransAlp, you didn't have time for a huge warm-up. You'd start and it'd be cold for a while. There'd be a lot of bumping around at the front. It was crazy.

In one sense, though, riding when you get older is easier. For me, easier to win.

I was a good rider when I was young. I rode Category One for ten years, and would be in the top 10 in Northern California, and maybe the top 100 in the nation. But my age started to become an advantage when I got into my 40s, because there are fewer guys that do it, that ride hard, and have avoided injuries.

Taking on New Challenges

MOUNTAIN BIKING IS tough. Guys stay away from it because they are worried about hurting themselves. Yes, the risk of injury is there. But that's back to what I said about youth, about continuing to push it.

It is really helpful to give yourself a challenge and a chance to ride with people who are just a little bit better than you; sometimes, radically better than you. Just to see how people are doing it, to keep up the urge to master something. Some things, like mountain biking, you've got to master to a certain extent to enjoy. You master the bike—the same brand tire, your position, get it all dialed. If you're changing equipment all the time, it's a little more difficult to master it. And you master riding technique. You've got to work on it a lot so you can have it embedded into your memory and you can do things automatically. There's a real simple pattern to improving: You look for a weakness. Identify it. And then start to do something that works on that weakness.

It's like when I swim, which I started to do during the time I had the wrist injury. It was the hardest thing I've ever done. Amaz-

ingly, I'm not really efficient with my legs. So I gotta make sure I do a lot of paddleboards. It's like if I'm having a lot of trouble with a trail drop-off or something, I'll go back and do the same one over and over and over again. In a little tiny lap pool. I'll just go and do it again and again and again. Very soon you get very familiar and you do it. Not to overpush it, not to be obsessive about it, but to the point where you give yourself a chance. Finally you get it and you step on. I will always do that. I do it with surfing, which I got hooked on in Australia at the Olympics four years ago. It's hard to do something brand-new, that I'm a beginner at. It's the process of learning and relearning and doing it over.

I didn't really plan on having all this— the success, the notoriety. A lot was luck—like Trek reviving the brand name when my company was dead (in 1993). I never tended to look off too far into the future, to make myself promises, because I think that's a big source of disappointment. However, I could never imagine not being able to use my body. My philosophy has always been "Use it or lose it." That's why you have to continue to do things, and then go back and redo them again. It's like swimming again. Even though I had taken lessons when I was four and five years old, my body had grown, changed, and forgotten how to do it. Your body adapts to whatever lifestyle you go to. If you neglect a part of it—i.e., don't use it— you'll lose it. I'd lost my ability to breathe properly above water, to move properly and coordinate all these things together. That's where I bought it back.

It's important to try different things and push new challenges. For years, I'd only ridden a bike and done a little yoga. It's good for me to get off into some different

BIKE FOR LIFE

things. The bike, though, is the cornerstone. I don't know of any tool that elicits such amazing physical things out of a person. And it has such tonic qualities. Some people might think of it as a torture rack, and it can be at times. But it does something to the body that helps you recover and perform better. It's a really special thing that way.

I've gotten a lot more active in advocacy in the last ten years. I'm lucky I'm able to do something as simple as just show up someplace and help somebody. That's unbelievable to me. I'm on the board of Trips for Kids, which takes inner-city kids on rides. I'll be at about four events a year in the Bay Area, and I'm going to start doing some more chapters. The kids don't know me, but they have seen the name on the bikes. They knew nothing about cycling heroes, and nothing about Olympic athletes or anything like that. But they know what they like. Once, when I brought along [two-time gold-medal mountain biker and longtime Fisher endorsee] Paola Pezzo, all dressed in gold, with a totally gold-plated bike, they just went ape! They didn't know who she was, but they just knew she was important. It was hilarious. A world-class photo op. [Amanda] was more of a commuter in the city and bike activist. That's how I met her. She's got it going naturally. We got a couple of commuter bikes—a Breezer for her and a Dutch bike for me . It's a real Dutch bike. Single speed. Fifty pounds. Old school. Brand-new. And it's so much fun.

You should see her; my god, she's a good rider. But she can't hoist her bike and walk up stairs too easily right now. She's six months pregnant. We're going to have a new kid. A boy. I'll be a new father at age 53. [Gary's son Miles was born on May 14,

2004.] Now I gotta keep it going like that 90-year-old guy [see interview of John Sinibaldi at end of chapter 4].

Advice: Ride Often, Eat Better, Think Young

WHEN I WAS young, I read the *CONI Blue Book*, a cycling manual originally published in Italy. It was like the bike racer's bible and it still rings true to me. It had a section in there about having joy and youthfulness in your riding. It said things like that you gotta have that flair—like bike racers should have a fast car, not a slow car, just because of the feeling of it. And a racing cyclist should feel youth in their training. It was a way of saying don't overtrain. And don't lose that youthful feeling. As you get older, keep a balance. Ride every day, ride hard once in a while, but keep it fun.

I'm lucky. I have an unusual job situation. At the end of the day, my sponsor won't fire me, no matter how I do in the race. For me it's ride, smile, and finish. I don't have to win. But when I want to, I have the time to train almost full-time—20 to 25 hours a week plus time to recover. For fitness, though, just riding every day, even if it's only like half an hour, makes a huge difference. After I broke my wrist and couldn't ride for three months, I rode in a celebrity chase race in San Francisco. Whoa! It hit me so hard. Not having stressed my body on a fairly regular basis, I was hurting bad. I think, as a rule, you need to do whatever it takes to do a good and hard ride at last once a week—maybe three times a week if you want to get better. Then make the time to recover between. On just a small amount of riding, I can maintain an amazing amount of my strength.

I am much more careful than I used to be. In my late 20s, I had a pretty good quality diet, but I could eat as much as I wanted. As I got older, I stayed away from dairy, which shrunk my gut, and ate the things I could digest thoroughly and relatively easily. I'll eat a huge salad or something that doesn't have much dressing—just olive oil and some lemon or something. And a ton of organic vegetables and a little of some kind of protein. You know, now I almost do the Atkins Diet. But then when I'm actually on the bike, I'll have three-quarters carbohydrate and one-quarter protein. And then try to stay away from the carbs after the recovery. I always try to get drinks and foods where you get a little bit of protein in there.

To keep a balance as you get older, I think of three areas: building yourself up in one aspect—requiring some intense workouts and a fair amount of time; maintaining—daily riding and once-a-week stress; then there are new skills—the one that is a lot of fun. I'm learning to swim. I'm learning to surf. I wanna go back and ride a fixed-gear bike at the **Velodrome**. There are things within the sport that you used to do and you need to pick up again. Then there are brand-new things. I want to go up to Whistler and do the freeride park more.

If you don't mountain bike, try it. Those new physical experiences will keep you a kid at heart.

2

TECHNIQUE

Skills to get you there faster, safer, and in style

"**J**AM THE OUTSIDE *foot down. Don't just let it hang there.* **Jam it down!**" *Those words reverberated in my brain as I tore down twisty, treacherous Northern California mountain roads one day in June 1994 at speeds that would have scared me out of my gourd two months earlier, before I took a weekend course at John Howard's Cycling School of Champions in San Diego. I had no choice but to use what I'd learned from the Cycling Hall of Famer. Due to misreading the map, I arrived 90 minutes late in Santa Rosa for the start of the Terrible Two, one of the world's hardest, most beautiful double-centuries, including 16,500 feet of climbing through Napa and Sonoma counties. I spent another hour taking wrong turns. My only hope of catching up to the pack and winning my fourth consecutive "California Triple Crown" T-shirt (representing the completion of three double-centuries in a year) was to throw caution to the wind.*

Yet as I let loose and heeded Howard's instructions—"Lift the inside foot, lean into the turn, and drive the outside foot straight down with most of your body weight"—I surprisingly felt safer, not riskier. Just as John promised, "sticking" the outside foot gave me remarkable control at high speeds, virtually gluing my wheel to the road like a slot car in a track. For the first time in my life, I wasn't nervous on the steeps and was making up huge amounts of time on them. After four hours of being told repeatedly by organizers I should quit, I began catching some of the laggards.

By 10 PM, after 14 hours of one of the best rides of my life, maybe the first time I actually felt like a competent cyclist, I had conquered all four major climbs, some up to 11 percent grade, and was homing in on the finish when I was spotted in the darkness and pulled from the course for safety reasons. Damn—I had done the work: 201 miles. But that year was the last time the Terrible Two measured out at 211 miles; it was shortened to exactly 200 thereafter.

So I drove 600 miles up from L.A., did all this work, and didn't get my Triple Crown T-shirt. But at least I learned a couple of valuable lessons about efficient cycling that day, Number one, I better figure out how to read a map. And number two, technique works. —RMW

The last chapter gave you a blueprint for building a high-performance machine. This chapter gives you the technical skills to drive that machine. The brief clinics outlined below will help transform you from dilettante to connoisseur—from mere "bike rider" to a true "cyclist." At any level, whether you do charity rides or centuries, ride a $200 Costco cruiser or a $7,000 custom carbon fiber–titanium dream machine, it comes in handy to know the basics of riding a bike—how to stop, climb, corner, descend, and draft. Ultimately, it's not just about the extra mph they confer; it's about the safety of being in control of your new-found power, the pride of mastering real skills, and flat-out fun, pure and simple.

·1·
HOW TO STOP

"Sooner or later," says John Howard, "you are going to come face-to-doorhandle with a distracted soccer mom who is talking on her cell phone and screaming at her kids. What you need is a Hot Stop."

A Hot Stop is an emergency technique that can save skin, bones, and, possibly, funeral-home paperwork. It is the nearest thing to stop-on-a-dime braking. Done right, you won't skid out and will live to ride another day.

1. *Shift your weight rearward.* At the first sign of trouble, slide your glutes very far back and low, behind the seat. This lowers your center of gravity,

improving rear-wheel traction and preventing an end-over.
2. *Level your pedals.* This keeps you from pulling to one side or clipping a pedal if you do lean.
3. *Grab the front brake hard, the rear easier.* Apply far more pressure to the front brake than you otherwise think would be safe. The correct percentage of braking bias is two-thirds front and one-third rear; in the rain, use equal braking pressure. It will probably take several tire-sliding sessions before you can get the hang of it. If you don't lock up the wheel and catapult into a truck, you'll stop amazingly fast and under control.
4. *Get ready to bail.* Find an escape route or stopping point and focus on it, rather than what you want to miss. The bike will naturally follow your eyes.

·2·
HOW TO TURN

Good cornering skills not only make you faster—allowing you to make up time without working any harder—but they also make you safer, less likely to crash. Here are the basics, according to Howard.

1. *Push your butt back.* Your hips should be slightly to the rear of the saddle, and your back as flat and parallel to the **top tube** as possible.
2. *Raise the inside foot.* If you are making a right turn, put the right pedal/foot

up, in the 12 o'clock position on the crank, and shove the left leg straight down on the pedal in the 6 o'clock position. The right knee should fall out toward the turn as you lean, providing a lower center of gravity and more stability. To handle higher speeds, drop your shoulder, or even the head, slightly.

3. ***Have one finger over the brakes at all times.*** Be ready to use a light, featherly brake. Don't grab the brakes hard and risk a skid.

4. ***Enter the turn wide and cut in.*** Be at your preferred speed 10 feet before the turn. Drift to the outside of the straightaway before entering the turn, then cut an arc toward the apex. (Enter the curve on the inside, and you may have a date with the hay bales on the outside curb.) The flow is: outside, inside, outside. The idea is not to steer the turn, but to set up for it, then adjust your body weight so that your knee comes out in the direction of the turn.

5. ***Weight the outside pedal.*** The more weight you shift to the outside pedal, the more traction you have. Drive your body weight into that pedal. "Jam it!" Howard says. You'll stick like glue to pavement.

· 3 ·
HOW TO CLIMB

Don't dread the hills—relish them. With proper hill-climbing technique and strategy, climbing can actually be relaxing (see John Sinibaldi interview at the end of chapter 4). In fact, climbing can be a time-efficient staple of training, providing superb conditioning in an hour or less. It can even help you make a name for yourself, as it did for Tom Resh, one

of the best-ever American climbers. At one time, Resh, now retired, held hill-climbing records at three of the toughest hill-climb competitions in North America: Mt. Baldy in Southern California (4,700 feet of elevation gain in 12.7 miles; Resh's time: 56:15); Mt. Charleston, Nevada (5,700 feet in 17 miles; time: 1:16:05); and the world's longest known climb event with the greatest elevation gain, Maui's Mt. Haleakala (10,000 feet in 38 miles, 2:45:32.). Here's how Resh rushed 'em.

1. ***Big gear, fast spin.*** Generally, be in the biggest possible gear that will allow you to keep the pedals spinning above 85 percent of your flatland rate. That would be above 76 rpm in the hills if you pedal 90 rpm on the flats. Any slower than 60 to 70 rpm and your heart rate, energy use, and perceived exertion jack up.

2. ***Beware Armstrong-style spinning.*** A super-fast spin rate isn't the answer if you're not trained for it. High rpm may save your legs, but leads to a high heart rate and heavy breathing. "The key to climbing is to achieve a cadence which balances the pain in your chest with the pain in your legs," says Resh. Let experience—and the 85 percent rule—be your guide.

3. ***Bigger isn't necessarily better.*** For short climbs under a half-mile long, it's okay to use an extra-large gear. But for longer distances, smaller gears will be faster, more efficient, and less tiring. If you struggle in a big gear for too long, your legs will wear out before the hill ends.

4. ***Match body position to steepness.***
   a. ***Shallow grade: Sit.*** Stay in normal or aero position. After all, you don't

want to fight the wind as well as the hill.

b. *Moderate grade: Push butt back.* The back-of-the-saddle position provides extra power by increasing the extension of your leg, utilizing the glutes, and boosting the effectiveness of the calf muscle. A good blueprint to follow: Drop your heel at the top of the pedal stroke, then push through the ball of the foot. Scoot your butt back and forth to alternate the focus on the glutes and the quads, respectively. Flex elbows. Don't hunch shoulders or round your back; try to fold forward at the hips.

c. *Steep grade: Stand up.* As the hill steepens and your cadence slows, the sitting position may not deliver enough power. You'll need to stand. Standing also can provide relief during long climbs or that extra burst of power you need to drop an opponent.

5. *Standing technique.* Grip the **hoods** of your brake levers while still seated, and stand up by putting your weight on the pedal that is traveling downward. At this point, rock the bike side to side for leverage, using your body weight and arms to push the pedals down.

If standing gives you more power, many wonder why not stand for the entire climb? Simply, you use more energy standing. You have to support your weight as well as push the pedals. Again, it's a trade-off between speed and efficiency.

6. *Don't weave.* Studies show that a 3° change in your steering angle makes you work up to 30 percent harder. It also increases the distance traveled.

7. *Hill-training intervals.* Heading for the hills is a fast way to develop power. Find a hill two to three miles long. It doesn't have to be really steep, because you can always make it steeper by using bigger gears. "Two or three times up the hill are enough as long as you make a hard effort the entire way," says Resh. "Just pretend your archrival is up the road." Use the ride downhill as your recovery. Constantly monitor your body while climbing. Go as hard as you can go without blowing up.

8. *Join an expert climber. Try this virtual ascent with Tom Resh:*

To show you how it's done, *Bike for Life* asked Resh to create a simulated climb. Clip into your virtual pedals, imagine a tall, thin rider next to you, and heed his words:

"Get ready, rookie. Up ahead of us looms a one-mile-long hill. But notice as we approach that I don't shift gears. I wait until the hill slows me before I shift.

"Now we are starting to go up. I move my hands to the top of the handlebars and slide back on my saddle to give me a little more leverage.

"Now my pedal cadence is beginning to slow, so I stand up to get a little more power and keep my speed up.

"Even with the extra power, however, my pedal cadence is still slowing down. So I sit back and finally shift to an easier gear. My goal is to keep my rpm's within 15 percent of what they are on the flats.

"Now, just as I am starting to adjust to the increase in effort, I look ahead to see a short, steep section. Rather than shift down to an easier gear, I stand up and power over this section.

"After the steep part, I sit back down. Immediately, I monitor myself: How do

TECHNIQUE

BIKE FOR LIFE

my legs feel? How is my breathing? Can I go faster and drop you, or should I be nice since this is our first ride together?

"Whew! This is getting to be a long one. So I'll stand up once in a while to stretch the legs.

"Thank god, the last 100 meters. I stand again. Standing up uses more energy, but there is always a rest on the downhill. See you at the bottom!"

MOUNTAIN BIKE CLIMBING TECHNIQUE

Off-road climbs are far different than asphalt ascents. That's because the main concern is traction on the loose ground, or rather the lack of it. That all but eliminates standing while climbing, as the seat must be weighted to keep pressure on the rear wheel. Do this:

Steep climbs.
- Scoot butt rearward for back-wheel traction, but bend at the hips and elbows, and drop chest toward handlebar to maintain front-wheel control.

  For more rear traction, raise chest away from bar; to keep front wheel grounded, lower chest. Don't move your butt.

Super-steep grades.
- Perch your butt on the tip of the saddle.
- Lean waaaaay over the bar to keep the front wheel from popping up.
- Accompany each downward pedal stroke with a forceful pull down and back on both ends of handlebar. Perfect timing adheres the back wheel to the trail, while your weight keeps the front wheel down.
- Do upper-body training at the gym. Otherwise, you won't last long. Shoulders and arms will fatigue—it's tiring.

· 4 ·
HOW TO DESCEND

Tearing down twisty mountain roads involves the same skills described above in the "cornering" section. But mountain biking is a whole different animal.

1. **Get back.** Push your butt back and drop your chest to lower your center of gravity. The steeper the descent, the farther back and lower, to the point where your rear is floating behind the seat altogether. Make the mistake of straightening up, and you'll eventually be launched over the bars.
2. **Momentum is your friend.** Inertia will carry you over most minor obstacles without a problem, but those same rocks and roots can knock your front wheel sideways if you slow to a crawl and ride over them timidly. So learn to lay off the brakes, build some speed, pick a line, and go for it.
3. **One-digit braking.** Put just one finger on each lever. The best mix of steering and braking control comes when your index fingers loop over the levers and the rest of your fingers hold the bar.
4. **Front-brake-centric.** Use the front brake for 70 percent of your braking power; use the rear on more technical sections to avoid skidding the front wheel.

· 5 ·
HOW TO RIDE IN A PACE LINE

Riding behind others, front wheel to rear wheel—known as a **pace line**—helps you cheat the wind. This "drafting" is part of the sport, even in casual riding and touring. Some say it can save up to 40 percent of your energy, especially if you are riding into headwinds. Here's how to do it.

1. **Hook up with a group.** Hey, break out of your shell. You can't draft by yourself, unless you've got a thing for 18-wheelers.
2. **Pick a wheel.** Stealthily latch on to a rider who's steady and smooth. See how long you can go without him or her noticing you.
3. **Stay close.** Start about 3 feet away; work up to within 1 inch of the wheel.
   Modulate speed with brakes; instead use soft pedaling or sit up in the wind.
4. **Keep a steady pace.** Aim for 20 mph, a good speed for first-time drafters. Don't go any faster at first; you'll get tired and lose concentration.
5. **Factor in the wind.** In a headwind, stay directly behind your **mule**. In a crosswind, position yourself between it and your benefactor.

Still a Slow Climber?

The heck with technique; just lose weight. Here's how:

LANCE Armstrong was a one-day World Champion who lagged in mountainous stage races; then he lost 20 pounds to chemotherapy in 1997 and won six straight Tours de France. Miguel Indurain was an awesome time-trialist who fell off in the hills; then he dieted off 12 pounds before the 1991 season and won five straight Tours. See a pattern here? If you want to ride faster—especially climb better—just lose weight.

For several decades, coaches have known that there is a proven demarcation line that separates champions and also-rans: a power-to-weight ratio of 6 watts per kilo of body weight for a sustained 45 minutes. Below it, says former Motorola team doctor Max Testa, now director of sports performance at UC Davis, a pro can't keep up in both the flats and the hills; but above it, he's a potential mutitime Tour winner. Thanks to James C. Martin, PhD, assistant professor of exercise and sports science at the University of Utah and a 1988 national Masters track champion, we even know how much faster you'll climb. His study, "Validation of a mathematical model for road-cycling power," published in the 1998 *Journal of Applied Biomechanics,* estimates that every five pounds of weight loss will help you ride 30 seconds faster over a 3.1-mile, 7 percent hill climb.

Of course, a proven way to melt the fat is to increase your mileage and reduce your caloric intake, but this may be difficult for those with limited time, and can also risk weakening muscles, according to David Costill, PhD retired director of the human performance lab at Ball State University. "Don't start hard training before you have your body weight where you want it," he says. "You lose weight only by burning more calories each day than you eat, and if you do that while training hard, you will not only be burning fat, but causing a sizeable breakdown of muscle protein." Case in point: Armstrong's rival, Jan Ullrich, who routinely puts on 10 kilos (22 pounds) over the winter. "He has to diet and train harder during the season to get ready for the Tour," says Testa. "Sometimes, he weakens himself."

BIKE FOR LIFE

Although this issue may be less acute for noncompetitive and heavier athletes, experts like Dr. Arny Ferrando, director of the performance lab at the University of Texas Medical Center at Galveston, say the safest weight loss is gradual, not rapid. "You won't jeopardize muscle mass if you drop the pounds gradually—no more than a pound or two a week," he says.

Below are ten ways to help you lose weight gradually and painlessly—off the bike. These dietary and lifestyle changes are so easy to incorporate into your daily routine that you may forget you're doing them—until the day you realize that you arrived two minutes ahead of your riding buddies on Hell Hill, rather than two minutes behind.

1. **Do a light workout the moment you wake up.** "It is a fact that you burn more fat before eating breakfast," says Asker E. Jeukendrup, director of the Human Performance Laboratory at the University of Birmingham (England) School of Sport and Exercise Sciences. "Although there is no scientific evidence yet, we assume weight loss." With a minimum of easy-to-access fuels like muscle glycogen or bloodstream sugar in the system (your body utilizes a good deal of glycogen during the night), the body reaches for "intermuscle" fat, the plentiful but hard-to-access fat within the muscle, according to Dr. Gabrielle Rosa, coach of many top Kenyan marathoners, known for their early runs.

   Intensity is not important. "There's no need to work out hard," says Max Testa. "A 20- to 30-minute light jog, spin, or even brisk dog-walking increases your metabolism and primes you for a better workout later in the day." Jeukendrup recommends no more than 70 to 75 percent of maximum heart rate.

   That jibes with studies indicating you should exercise hard later in the day, not earlier. Building on previous findings of increased afternoon body temperature and metabolism, Dr. Boris Medarov at the Jewish Medical Center in New Hyde Park, New York, found that resistance in air passages decreases as nightfall approaches, increasing air-gathering capacity in the lungs by 15 to 20 percent.

2. **Walk after dinner.** "A 20-minute 'Dine and dash' immediately after dinner burns up to 100 calories and helps you burn more later," says Carl Foster, PhD, of the department of Exercise and Sports Science at the University of Wisconsin–La Crosse. "That's because, while slow enough not to interfere with digestion, briskly walking one or two miles raises your metabolism." It also cleans your pipes and clears your head, he adds, reducing by 20 percent the glucose and insulin that flooded into the bloodstream with the meal.

3. **Eat more dairy.** Studies led by Michael Zemel, PhD, author of *The Calcium Key,* show that diets high in calcium appear to set off a chain reaction that prompts the body to metabolize fat more efficiently. Calcium supplements aren't nearly as effective, he adds. Dr. Robert P. Heaney, professor of medicine at Creighton University in Omaha says three or four servings of low-fat yogurt or milk a day could help Americans lose an average of 15 pounds a year. Another factor: many say dairy makes you feel full, so you eat less.

   For those who are lactose intolerant, eat dark leafy greens (kale, collards, etc.), which have high levels of calcium.

4. **Don't starve.** It leads to bingeing and kicks the body into survival mode, which encourages fat storage.

5. **Graze.** Eat more small meals throughout the day. Long stretches without eating—i.e., a noon lunch to a 7 PM dinner—kick the body into survival mode, which encourages fat storage. Eating and digesting numerous smaller meals "prevents blood sugar spikes and costs lots more energy," says Dr. Arny Ferrando of the University of Texas. To avoid junk food, keep fresh fruit like apples, grapes, pears, and bananas around. They're low in calories and portable, says Suzanne Havala Hobbs, RD, and faculty member at the School of Public Health at the University of North Carolina at Chapel Hill.

6. **Avoid liquid calories.** A Coke won't make you feel as full as an orange will. Studies show that your body doesn't register a feeling of fullness from liquid calories, which helps you gain weight by leading to overdrinking and overeating later. So, instead of a soft drink, slurp zero-calorie, noncarbonated water. (Beware carbonation; it leeches calcium from bones. See chapter 9.)

7. **Eat "mindfully."** "It's hard to overeat if you follow a wholistic approach and eat slowly and elegantly," says Los Angeles performance yoga and fitness trainer Steve Ilg, the author of *Total Body Transformation.* That means sit with an elegant posture, back erect, cross-legged in a chair or on the ground, put the fork down between every bite, consciously breathe between every third bite, and chew the first bite of food 30 times. "Doing this, an astounding insight arises: Digestive secretions give the body a deeper feeling of satisfaction," says Ilg.

8. **Don't eat much after 8 PM.** A large meal before you go to bed, especially one high in carbs, stimulates insulin, changing your sleep time to fat storage instead of fat-burning and inhibiting the body's production of muscle-maintaining growth hormone. If you must snack late at night, go for a piece of turkey breast, not an orange. "It seems odd at first, but it's better to eat lean meat than fruit before bed," says nutritionist Betty Kamen, PhD, the author of *1001 Health Secrets.* "Fat-free meat is all protein."

9. **Cut fat, not carbs.** "Reducing fat intake is the most important step for weight loss," says Jeukendrup. "For exercisers, it is not a good idea to cut carbs; that simply reduces the fuel for your workouts and increases the risk of overreaching/overtraining." Example: Eat a salad with your burger, instead of fries.

10. **Change—don't cut—your carbs.** Switch the majority of your daily carbs to low-glycemic-index carbohydrates like yogurt, fruit, nuts, and bananas, which are broken down slowly by the body. They provide you with an appetite-curbing feeling of fullness that you don't get from high-GI foods like bagels, cereals, and rice cakes that are burned quickly as sugar.

11. **Cut down on alcohol.** Booze is a double whammy: a dead calorie with no nutritive value that has a negative domino effect. The liver has to pay attention to it first in the metabolic sequence, because it's toxic. While being stored as fat, it crowds out good calories and gets them stored as fat, too.

12. **Read before you eat.** Look at a $.99 bag of corn chips. One serving is 150 calories. Then read further: there are five servings in a bag. That's 750 calories—one-third of an adult's daily requirement.

John Howard

THE MAN WHO CAN DO ANYTHING

Many people have called John Howard "Greg LeMond before there was a Greg LeMond," but that characterization is far too limiting. A monster talent who blew out of the backwoods of Missouri at a time when few Americans raced a bike and none had yet tried their luck in Europe, Howard has pushed the envelope in every imaginable sphere of cycling. He won a national championship (in 1968) before he could vote, added three more in the 1970s, and so stunned the U.S. Olympic Committee with his 200k win at the 1971 Pan Am Games that it restored financing to a sport it had planned to let expire. The three-time Olympian saw Black Power fists raised in Mexico City in 1968, heard terrorist bullets in Munich in 1972, and competed in Montreal in 1976. He was still America's top road cyclist in 1979, when he was unceremoniously booted off the U.S. Pan Am team for, as he remembers it, not being a "team player."

Seeking new challenges outside mainstream cycling, Howard won the Hawaii Ironman Triathlon in 1981, finished the first Race Across America in 1982, and risked his life in 1985 in setting an astounding bicycle speed record of 152.2 mph behind a custom-built land rocket. Since then, he's built and sold pedal-powered water bikes, accumulated scores of Masters road and mountain bike championships, broken dozens of bones, authored hundreds of articles about form, training, and bike fit, acquired a taste for antique cars, and, of course, been inducted into the U.S. Cycling Hall of Fame (in 1989).

Infinitely curious and open-minded about unorthodox technologies and fitness regimens (don't get him started about lung trainers and belly breathing), Howard lives in a house in North San Diego County that includes a self-designed spinning studio and a cycling museum. He runs one of cycling's best-regarded coaching clinics, the John Howard School of Champions and the John Howard Performance Sports FiTTE™ Clinics. And, by the way, as he told Bike for Life's Roy Wallack during their interview on March 4, 2004, he claims to have ridden 800,000 miles. That's about 31 times around the circumference of the Earth.

A COMIC BOOK changed my life. When I was 16, I saw *Schwinn Bike Thrills* at the local Schwinn shop in my hometown of Springfield, Missouri. I was fascinated. It told the story of Alfred LeTourner's world record—108.92 mph on a Schwinn Paramount drafting a race car in 1941. LeTourner, known as "the Red Devil," was the most famous six-day bicycle racer in French history and one of the most famous in the world. I thought, *God! I've got to do this.*

I went to the library and found a book called *The Big Loop*, a story about the Tour de France. I thought, *God! What a wonderful sport.* So I went back to the bike shop and bought the first ten-speed in Springfield, Missouri—a Schwinn Continental, a high-end race bike.

Trouble was, nobody in Springfield knew anything about bike racing. The closest I could find was the AYH—American Youth Hostels. They're into touring—the kind with **panniers**. I wanted some organization, to ride with a group, to find a connection. But after I rode with them, I realized quickly that they were way below my level. Some were serious, but not many. I was just this young stud. . .

I was a good intramural athlete in baseball, football, and basketball, but the only varsity thing I did was running. I did the mile and would call myself mediocre, even though I won the Ozark Conference mile-championship race. But from the beginning, cycling was my forte. I always seemed to be able to outdistance the rest of the kids in the neighborhood. And I was always into the lightweight equipment; got a three-speed at 12 or 13, a big step up from the cruiser bikes. Then came the move up to the Continental with its derailleur gears—pretty hot stuff back in 1963. My brother and I prided ourselves on being on the cutting edge. He's about a year younger than me—my competitor and best friend.

I always rode more than he did. I loved the blue sky and fresh air. Even on my three-speed, I was traversing hills in the Ozark Mountains—some of the toughest little climbs anywhere to be found in the country. As soon as I got the Continental, I would take that thing down to the Lake Country, a 70-, 80-, 90-mile ride, alone. There was nobody else who would do it. Why'd I do it? [*long pause*] Because it was there. Because I saw the potential. Everyone wants to be good at something. In my case it was covering ground.

I had good cardiovascular, but cycling was different. With a bike I could make progress more rapidly, because the sport itself was on such an infantile level back then. The true competition in the United States in the '60s was in the Velodrome. And right away, I found that it didn't take much to get to the top of the sport. By the time I was 19, I was there.

I would literally ride away from the field and cover 50 miles on hilly courses under two hours, which was unheard of. So I knew this is what I am good at. This is what I can do. At 19, I won the 1968 national championships. The top guys—Parsons, Hiltner, Butler, Van Boven. I beat all of them.

Religion, RAAM, and 152 MPH

PEOPLE DON'T LET me forget that I once called my bike my "Iron Mistress." Metaphorically, it means it was a tool. I won't say that I hadn't discovered girls, but the girlfriends I had were short-term. I can't believe I was ever this way. But back then, I was more focused on the bike. It gave me much more than another person could—particularly a spirituality.

I found myself practicing a very profound, personal form of worship when I turned those pedals. On a bike, passively covering ground for two or three hours, I would experience a wonderful sense of self-discovery, of being a part of a universe that was much more powerful than myself. I say *passive* for a reason. I can remember covering 20 to 30 miles and having no recollection of being anything but in a complete form of perfect bliss.

Growing up, I was religious—did go to church quite a bit. Being of the Bible Belt, my parents were fairly religious Presbyterians. It was what I did, who I was. But the bike replaced that. It brought me into a whole different landscape. The spirituality of the bicycle was a self-discovery that went much deeper than the four walls of a church. The feeling of being in control of my own destiny, as opposed to having it scripted through the organization of religious doctrine.

To go there by myself, with no training partners, these journeys into the spiritual world, into a separate universe, were powerful motivators. The spiritual focus changed as the world became more complex and competition came into the mix. But it came back as I got older.

Today, I practice kind of a mix of optimism, Taoism. I believe we are what we practice. I really put more emphasis on the positive nature of things. I feel like that's really the essence of it—coming back to just feeling good about yourself and practicing exactly that. I meditate on this; meditation has been a profound step. I learned to do this during the Race Across America.

For me, the Taoist view of life was extremely profound during RAAM. In 1982, John Marino, Lon Haldeman, Mike Shermer, and I did the first RAAM, the true cycling ultra event: L.A. at the Santa Monica Pier all the way to the Empire State Building in New York City. It took me ten days, ten hours. Tough ride. Headwinds all the way from Kansas through Illinois clear into West Virginia. It was a tough, tough ride.

The sleep deprivation had an impact on me. Going into a trance state, some of my visualizations were extremely powerful. I really didn't associate them at the time with what reality was or should be, but over time I could see that it was an experience that shaped me as an individual. I really understood a lot more about my limitations. My inflexibilities. My temper. All the things I didn't like about myself, I had to come to grips with. In a real powerful way, I realized what I needed to discard and what I needed to work on and where I needed to go with my life. I would never do RAAM again for anything—it was so grueling. Yet it was a unique time for me—a self-analysis that lasted ten days; I saw myself at my best and I saw myself at my worst. Where do you have an opportunity to do that?

Since RAAM, I've been better able to control my anger and channel that into more positive progressive experiences. I've been able to use those experiences to understand what I need to do to advance in business, to make a living—what works, what doesn't, what to discard, what to keep. I realize that a lot of the anger that was directed at my crew was really a reflection of my own insecurity problems. I'm still working on it, but I think I've come a long way since 1982.

I clearly see one of my [RAAM] visualizations even today. I was standing by the motor home, waiting for the fog to clear so we could get back on the bikes. Freezing cold. It was in West Virginia, probably less than two days out of New York. Three in the morning and no traffic. Appalachian Mountains. It was so foggy on the descent, it was actually dangerous. I so badly needed sleep. I didn't want to take a risk. While somebody was gathering up something—I don't remember if it was food or what—I was leaning against the motor home. Then this black Lab came up from out of the ditch and started nuzzling me. I remember the cold snout of his nose against my warm palms. And I thought that was great. I played with that dog for a while. Then it was like my eyes were like shutters on a camera. I clicked and the dog was lying down at my feet. Here I am, so tired. I looked around. And when I looked back down a second later, the dog was a pile of bones. Road kill.

I could feel that warm snout. I can feel it—even today. But that experience, God, I get cold chills every time I think about it.

I'm not sure I can apply any meaning to it. Maybe I just chose not to. But there were four or five experiences like that that happened en route at various times during the ride. Through sleep deprivation and lack of good, consistent diet, I just put myself over the edge. But I look back and like I said, I'd never change anything. But I'd never want 'em repeated.

Although I didn't win, RAAM was the hardest thing I'd ever done, much harder than winning the Hawaii Ironman Triathlon the year before. Then I had to face something even harder: the third act in my four-year post-bike-racer plan, the new bicycle world speed record.

By 1985, I wasn't at my peak anymore—nearly 40 years old, I had been spiraling down since 35. So I had to develop something else: mental fortitude. I was heavily into meditation then, and that was my key to getting over the incredible pressure of the speed record, a confluence of stress I'd never experienced. There was training stress, the monetary stress, the stress of organizing everything—building the supercar, building the superbike, hiring all the people, getting the *Sports Illustrated* article, the sponsorship deal with Pepsi and Wendy's and Specialized, the training, the worrying about the weather conditions on the Bonneville Salt Flats, the fear of death—a very real fear at the speed I'd be going. I didn't want to push the safety envelope, but I had to push it to get the ink we needed to pay off the sponsors, to sell the show to *That's Incredible*. Total pressure—far more than anything I'd ever done. More than winning the Tour of Baja (the first win ever of a big international stage race by an American), scoring high in the Milk Race (the Tour of Britain), and taking third in the Tour of Ireland (then the best-ever placing by an American in Europe), winning the Ironman, and doing RAAM.

This speed record was half terror, half exhilaration. I badly needed an edge. It would either bring me to a new realm of self-discovery—or a nightmare that could leave me permanently broken. So as I meditated, I came to my method of dealing with the pressure: visualization. It's the deepest I've ever gone. The image replays like a video camera in my brain. I visualized it—streaking above the vast, endless ribbon of salt flats, a mirage on top of a mirage, the image above me flashing in giant red numbers in the sky: 152. I saw it before it took place. And that day, it was 105°F. I'm covered in my leather suit. Three years of putting this all together—for five minutes of action. No mistakes possible. No do-overs. And when it was over. I looked at the number: 152.2 mph. Didn't just beat the old record (140 mph), but did what we said I'd do: Shatter it.

Fitness, Aging, and Wives' Tales

IN THE EARLY '70s, I had a **VO$_2$ Max** of 82 milliliters per kilogram, up there with all the best pros today. Now, thirty years later, I'm 18 percent lower. I've done my best to counter it, and think I have done quite well.

There is a popular belief that decline is bullshit and we don't deteriorate. But it is very much a genetic issue and it can happen to the best of athletes any time. We all reach a point where we diminish in terms of vital capacity. You can accept it or just deny it.

I've tried to fight it. One way is that I've vastly improved my range of motion, using specific stretches to gain maximum utilization of my lung capacity. Some of it is Pilates-based. Some of it is yoga. I've used a number of sources to create a program which is the nucleus of our training school. Because I feel like my career has been a guiding point for us and I've used that to help other athletes. I'm very proud of the fact that we've had over 130 national championships won by people I've worked with.

Much of coaching in cycling is steeped in tradition. Old-school stuff. And some of it's good, most of it isn't good. We really believe in following technology as much as possible. Without naming names, let me say that the old way of bike fitting that the French taught us 25 years ago is backwards. It doesn't take into consideration the biomechanics, much less the aerodynamics. Christ, I back-test everything I do using the most sophisticated programs available anywhere in the world. We have access to the Allied Aerospace wind tunnel, the most sophisticated low-speed wind tunnel in the world. What the hell. I love [name withheld by request] like a brother. But the bottom line is he's not a coach and all he knows is what the French told him 25 years ago.

It's frustrating to be so clear on the way to improve performance and yet this kind of bogus crap is being pitched out there in [cycling publications]. Old wives' tales. That is exactly what it is. There is very little scientific documentation. On the other hand, my coaches have done a thousand fits a year, and we have an understanding of the way it should be done. We have the electronics to back up what we do. To see it done so wrong is kinda frustrating.

Example: The age-old formulas for saddle height don't take into consideration a lot of important factors. Overall, the traditional bike-fit seems to have absolutely no scientific basis whatsoever.

Everybody should be different with regard to saddle height. It's based on trochanteric leg length. It's based on hamstring flexibility. It's based on the tilt of the saddle. It's based on amount of hip rotation you have. It's based on how the IT [iliotibial band, the tough muscle sheath on the outside of the thigh running from hip to knee] is lined up. It's based on bone configuration. All of which can be systematically tested. Our work we do is like dyno-testing a race car. We can show minute changes in performance in terms of torque and wattage. The average guy just can't do it on his own. But we can use our principles to show the simple way to do it—to make somebody comfortable and fast.

People typically have their saddles too low and too far back. You can change the pivot point of the **cleat** and change torque and watt output for optimal performance. In many cases, the cleat is jammed all the way forward—or too far back. You should be on the ball of your foot, absolutely, for optimal power.

There's an optimal way to do everything—even falling. I've gotten hurt way more mountain biking than road biking. But you can minimize breakage by developing a strategy for going over the bars— essentially a tuck and roll. Very difficult to do, but effective. It needs to be second nature, which means you need to practice it. Throw your shoulders back and try to stay off the collarbone. Stay off the shoulder. Or let the bike absorb the crash. Don't put your hands straight out to break the fall—that breaks the collarbone. I dunno one in a hundred people who'll practice that sort of thing. But if you have the presence of mind to tuck and roll, you're always going to come out of it better. You may lose a lot of skin on your back and shoulders. But believe me, that grows back a lot faster than a collarbone.

My diet hasn't changed appreciably over the years. I eat a lot of vegetables. A lot of good solid protein. Basic food groups. The essence of it is to try to get the macro levels to supply as much of the nutrients as possible. Failing that, or to supplement that at harder levels, you need some micro nutrients. Generally, as you age, think about prevention issues. In males, think prevent prostate cancer. Eat roughage. Leafy vegetables.

On the bike, I still try to put in the miles and do the training—100 to 160 miles per week. But it's smart training. It's what I can do to stay at the top of my game without being competitive. My emphasis has changed. After a life of competition, I no longer compete. Riding for me now is therapeutic. It's beautiful. I go out and experience the bicycle the way it should be. I don't see that [feeling] with retired European pros—they sit back, get fat. Not all of them, of course. But generally, they don't see the bike as I see it: A life tool.

More than a Wheelman

YET A BIKE's not the only tool. Even though people may raise their eyebrows at this, I resent being labeled a "cyclist." I think in the human body there are generative vital spirit energies; while cycling brings those out, the ultimate manifestation of energy is not to be tied down to one medium or one source—that is risky. For example, cyclists tend as they get older to be stoop-shouldered, because they are not balanced.

The last thing I would want for somebody to say is, "Oh, there's a cyclist." I don't want to be labeled that way. I want to have balance. To me, that balance is more than physical. It's mental as well. And I look now at the Masters cyclists who are really the ultimate manifestation of what I do, and I think, *You know, I don't*

need that racing anymore. Racing doesn't do it anymore. I don't need to prove that. I've been there. Done that. I have all the titles I'll ever need. And I don't want the degenerative break in what is important physically, you know? I want to have good muscle control. I don't want my low back to be compromised by sitting in the saddle for hours and hours. I came to a conclusion which sort of relates to one of the most important things I learned from the RAAM—that all of us are geared for X-number of miles at effort. When you use that up, it's probably going to be gone and you're going to have to find something else to do.

I really believe in it. I've tempered my whole life with the idea that I don't want to use this energy up. Now I understand that there's a yin and a yang. But I choose on my own now not to race; to me, that's wasteful dissipation of the energy. I'm not saying I'll never race again. But I see it better spent in using it to prolong my feel for life and just enjoying the body shell until it eventually wears out and dies and it will be gone. I've reached a point where I know that there is no immortality. What's important for me is to prolong, elongate the process of life and to experience it on a positive, blissful level. Play with it. Use the pattern that is set up in a positive way. Move out of this belief that we have to express it in a competitive realm. Because to win something, to win a race, means to make other people lose; in and of itself, that is a hypocritical way of looking at things. I really feel I have evolved beyond the point where I have to compete anymore. It's not the same. It's not international competition. Where are we getting? We don't get on TV anymore. Why do we need to express it that way? I just feel like there is so much more I can impart in terms of coaching, from all of the millions of things I've learned. That to me is the real importance of what I do and where I'm going. I want to be the best coach in the world. I want my other coaches to experience what I know so that we collectively can be the best at what we do.

One of my campers said something that really clicked. He'd been to the Carmichael program, and said it pampers you. It lets you experience just what it's like to be a pro cyclist. "But you guys," he said, "you show us *how to be* a pro cyclist." To me, that was the ultimate compliment. It told me that after all these years, I've learned how to do my job right.

3

THE GREAT INDOORS

*How to use indoor spin classes
to be a better outdoor rider*

IT'S A COOL *and casual 1994 fall night in West Los Angeles, but inside The Garage it's a different world. The lights are off. The music is alternately zen-like, disco, mystical, throbbing. The air is heavy with perspiration and breathing and incense and a familiar mechanical hum. It's the sound of pedaling—hard pedaling, slow and labored pedaling, standing and sitting pedaling, pedaling so much faster than you've ever gone before that you feel like you're a passenger in flight, sitting atop a spinning, whirling, perpetual motion machine, your legs a blur, independent of your body. You sweat like you've never sweat, dripping like a prizefighter in the eighth round, grossly, embarrassingly, frantically blotting, hoping to dam the rivers for a few seconds. Faintly before you, in silhouette, is a circle of ten people on unadorned, industrial-looking stationary bikes. From one of them, the muscular rider with the mane of wavy hair, comes an accented voice, bold and soothing, pushing, motivating, pulling you with the power of pure conviction. "Turn the resistance up," he commands, and you twist the numberless dial in front of you to the right—too far probably, because you're so swept up in it. "Become one with the mountain, one with the bike, one with your dreams," the faintly British voice implores. "Dare . . . dream . . . hunger . . . to believe . . . to achieve . . . to find . . . to feel . . . the champion within!"*

As we file outside into the backyard when it's over, the theatrical setting and relentless intensity having left me drained but exhilarated, I'm surprised. It's a strange mix toweling off on the driveway: hard-core athlete types and housewives. Everyone is aglow, basking in victory, but for different reasons. The bike racers got an awesome workout, kept their training up. The affluent Westside matrons are more emotional. They tell of how they never enjoyed exercise before spinning, how they lost 40 pounds, how they got a deal on clipless pedals and shoes at Helen's, how they just bought their first bike to ride in the mountains, and how they've become something that was never part of their self-image: athletes. They glance over at the charismatic Voice, the leader of the journey, his Superman physique and leading-man cheekbones glistening with the aura of a cult leader. Eyes light up as they clasp his hands. Thank you, Johnny, they say, it was incredible. See you next Tuesday.

A year later, the workout and the bike that Johnny G honed in his garage exploded into the health-club world. Spinning changed fitness as we know it, drawing millions of dyed-in-the-wool cyclists and average Joes and Jills into the same aerobics class for the first time. Serious riders like it because it's a time-saver, packing two hours of intensity into 45 minutes. And everyone likes it because it helps them find "The Champion Within." —RMW

Cycling begat Spinning. And Spinning begat cycling fitness, confidence, and a sense of achievement. But it doesn't have to stop there. By following the skill-building drills outlined in this chapter, spinning can help all cyclists develop and reinforce the real-world skills that can take years of outdoor riding to learn—whether they are grizzled veterans who remember steel frames with lyrical Italian names or newly minted, health-club-honed rookies who are pedaling outdoors for the first time.

The fitness, of course, is undeniable: many think Johnny G's claim that a standard 45-minute Spinning class is the fitness equivalent of 90 minutes of riding on the road is too modest; one class is worth two or three hours on the road, most say. Coming from a cyclist's perspective—Johnny raced the Race Across America twice in the late 1980s—he designed his Spinner to be the first stationary bike with the fit and feel of a real bike: normal handlebar positions, a performance bike saddle, and a standard **bottom bracket** (the assembly that houses the pedal spindle) and crankset, allowing for use of clip-in pedal systems. Then he went further, adding a 44-pound **flywheel** that did not allow coasting. The result, when combined with the music-charged group energy of a Spinning class, was revolutionary: 45 concen-

trated minutes of legs scrambling at a furious, faster-than-normal rate, never coasting downhill or resting at a stoplight. The Johnny G Spinner did more than replicate cycling. It supercharged it.

Word of Spinning's high bang-for-the-buck fitness spread like wildfire to regular folk and hard-core athletes alike. Health clubbers weaned on Lifecycles became addicted to the relentless Spinning pace. Serious cyclists and triathletes, people you couldn't pay to take a step aerobics class, poured into spin classes. Superstars could even be found teaching. Six-time Hawaii Ironman champ Dave Scott was a regular spin instructor in Boulder, Colorado. Former pro mountain biker Tammy Jacques taught once a week in the winter and spun in-season whenever bad weather hit. Emilio DeSoto, former pro triathlete and president of De Soto Sports triathlon clothing, packed them in to his classes in La Jolla, California. World champion downhiller Missy Giove is now the master trainer for the Trixter **X-Bike**, a novel "mountain" spin bike that simulates off-roading via its **freewheel** and rocking handlebar (see Missy's interview at the end of chapter 9).

Quickly, Spinning and its many knock-offs—Cycle Reebok, SpeedCenter, Road Racers, and others (now, virtually every fitness equipment manufacturer makes a spin bike)—mutated to satisfy those seeking bigger challenges. Johnny G led once-a-month two- and three-hour "Super-Spins" that took advanced students on virtual century rides. Once a month in the summer, New York's Reebok Sports Club moved bikes out to the sundeck for a two-hour workout. A small club in New Jersey offered a four-hour "Mt. Everest Spin." In Denver's Rocky Mountain Aerobic Network club, Reebok master trainer Marsha Macro led a "Mountain Bike Spin" that featured "Explosions" that simulated powering over trail-blocking logs and vertical-rise "Lifts" to simulate bunny hops. Several clubs tried to combine indoor cycling with calisthenics, dancing, and aerobics. At the Workout Warehouse in West Hollywood, California, spinners lowered their seats, stood for an entire hour, and did one-arm twisting crunches, lat pulls, and handlebar push-ups. Voight by the Sea in Santa Monica added dance-troupe-like choreography.

Individuals used the club setting to make up their own challenges. Part-time spin instructor Ruben Barajas, 39, the director of the Scott Newman drug prevention charity in Los Angeles, says Spinning helped him to qualify for the Hawaii Ironman several years ago. Slipping on cycling shoes right after a swim, he'd teach a couple of Spin classes in a row, then put on running shoes and hit a treadmill. "I called it 'my own private Ironman,'" he said.

While it took hard-core athletes inside, Spinning began pushing former non-cyclists outside. "It's a natural progression," explains Johnny G. "Spinning changes you. It gives a nonathlete the *mind of an athlete*—taking on a challenge, toughing it out to the end. When you get out of Spinning class, that impossibly steep hill in the distance that used to seem daunting now

suddenly begs you to conquer it." That explains Linzi Glass, an L.A. novelist who never rode a bike before she began Spinning in 1997; within a year, she was leading group rides into the Hollywood Hills. After he started Spinning, famed New York hairdresser Louis Licari upped his outdoor mileage from ten miles a year on an old, beat-up clunker to 200 miles a weekend in charity events on a new $3,000 racer. One of the most extreme Spinning-to-cycling converts may be Phyllis Cohen of Santa Monica, California, who became a twice-a-day Spinning addict under Johnny G's tutelage in the mid-1990s and went on to organize the first team of 50-plus women to complete the Race Across America. Ironically, there was one downside to her cross-country experience. "When I was training for RAAM," says the granny-gear granny, whose curly gray locks tumble halfway down her back, "I rode so much in a slower cadence that I got out of spinning shape."

Nathan Micheli, a tile-setter-to-the-stars from Redondo Beach, California who hadn't exercised in years, became a three-times-a-week spinning addict in 2004. "I'm a workaholic who couldn't have imagined cutting short a business meeting to catch a normal aerobics class," he said. "But Spinning class leaves me feeling so fit, so fresh, so relaxed and filled with energy, so like I was just born. I plan my day around it. I can't wait to buy a bike—my first since I was ten years old—and do the Rosarito-Ensenada Ride."

If Micheli ever does the 50-miler down the Mexican coast, usually attended by up to 10,000 Southern Californians, he'll join millions of former non-cyclists who now crowd into organized bike tours and benefit rides. In fact, in the week before the popular Boston to New York and San Francisco to L.A. AIDS rides, instructors report that Spinning rooms often empty out by half as their students practice on the road.

"As people—especially women—get into it," said Reebok instructor Glen Philipson, "they remember how much fun it is to ride a bike." He guessed that 80 percent of women—compared to only half of the men—come into studio cycling with no real cycling experience, and that up to a quarter of those will eventually buy bikes.

People who spin three or four days a week have the potential to ride "as good or better" than regular cyclists, says Chris Kostman, who worked closely with Johnny in the early days, founded the RoadRacers indoor cycling program at the L.A.–based Bodies in Motion fitness chain, and now organizes numerous endurance events in the western U.S., including the Death Valley–crossing Furnace Creek 508. "You come out of Spinning with exceptional cycling-specific fitness," he says. "The intensity, the **leg speed** (pedal turnover), quick heart rate recovery and lactic-acid flushing after sprints and hill climbs, and the focus on good form is similar to high-level cycling. But once you get out on the road, there's more to learn than switching gears and learning how to reach over and eat an energy bar at 18 miles per hour. It can take some people, especially those who have never ridden before, six months to get truly comfortable on a bike. That's because Spinning is specially designed as an indoor workout—and most of the instructors don't know a thing about cycling."

In fact, most spin class teachers are indeed aerobics teachers in clipless pedals. Many have never even ridden a bike on the road. They know how to select good music and exhort their followers through a killer 45-minute workout. But few can help

make you a better cyclist. "Cycling skills are not what people get out of my classes," says Emilio de Soto. "Fitness is."

"That's why you're going to have to develop those skills yourself—in class," says Kostman, a two-time Race Across America racer. "Spinning classes are an ideal place to work on classic, old-time technique—a traffic-free laboratory environment that can go a long way toward replacing the on-the-road instruction once handed down by veteran riders. By the same token, it's a great place for the vets to refresh their technique—as long as they remember *not* to ride an indoor bike the same way they do their 'outdoor' bikes."

Here's what he means.

· 1 ·
GENERAL CLIMBING
Spread the load

If you've ever seen a pro rider climb a hill, you've seen a thing of beauty. Forget words like "plodding" or "inching" or "agonizing." The pros, using all the muscles of their body in a synchronized dance, look like they are gliding. Spinning can help you achieve some of this efficiency.

"There is no greater confidence builder—and time-saver—than good climbing," says Kostman. "And good climbers stay fresh by using as many muscles as possible throughout their entire body to get up the mountain—not just pushing and pulling from the quads, hamstrings, and glutes. Spreading the load saves your legs over the long haul, and the emphasis on other muscle groups can provide a welcome psychological diversion, especially on lengthy climbs. There's no better place to focus on this than indoors."

An Orthodox Spin

Audrey Adler never spun in Johnny's garage. But she makes a difference in hers.

"ALTHOUGH I'd always been fit and athletic, I never considered myself a real athlete until spinning. Aerobics keeps you fit, but doesn't give you skills you can use, like this does. The minute I started spinning, I felt like I was preparing for something, as if I was training to be an astronaut." Or a cyclist. Or a changer of lives.

Audrey Adler, a Los Angeles mother of four, bought her first bike at age 36 after six months of spinning in 1995. She went on her first serious road ride six months later, her first mountain bike ride in the Santa Monica Mountains a month later, and her first all-day ride a few weeks later. She'd never swum before, but by 1997 did a half-Ironman triathlon. She began changing lives later that year.

The new "Road Racers" spin program at the Century City Bodies in Motion needed instructors, and Adler, who kickboxed at the club, was first in line. "It was the first time I'd ever spoken into a microphone," she says, "but I took immediate command." Soon, she was teaching six classes a week, all of them jammed. Her energy was infectious.

"A guy came up to me once after class and said, 'You kicked my butt.' I said, 'No, you kicked your own butt.'" That fellow was a board member at the Santa Monica public school system. And Adler was soon hired to organize the district's first indoor cycling program for school kids.

"You see, in spinning, you control the [resistance] dial, so you work as hard as you make yourself work," she says. "The feeling of accomplishment is immediate. Even people who aren't athletic feel athletic. And there's a camaraderie involved. Whether you're an adult or kid, you get swept up in it. You feel like you can do anything."

In 2000, when Adler's brother was struck down in a motorcycle accident, she used indoor cycling to work through it. "In my grief, I decided to set up a three-hour charity spin to raise money to buy Adaptive Sit Skis for disabled skiers," she said. Her brother was a family physician and an expert skier. She drew in thirty riders, raised $5,000, and presented it and a memorial plaque in the name of Dr. Aaron Pretsky to the National Center for the Disabled in Winter Park, Colorado. The following year, she did it again, raised another $5,000, and bought two adaptive mountain bikes.

A new challenge presented itself in 2001. "People were approaching me more and more about personal spin training—busy people who didn't have time for a gym. I thought about opening my own storefront, but the costs were out of sight—and would have taken me away from my family too much. As I pulled the car into the garage one day, it dawned on me: This is a perfect studio!"

She discussed it with her husband. "What are you—nuts?" he said.

Thirty thousand dollars and twelve spin bikes later, "Homebodies Workout" opened for business. Opening day was January 1, 2001. It was oversold.

"I had to throw people out," says Adler. "I had unwittingly uncovered an untapped market just dying for something like this: Orthodox Jewish women. There's a huge population of them in this area. They don't know a thing about fitness and won't work out in a co-ed environment [their religion prohibits it]. Spinning is a very liberating thing for them.

"I lecture them a lot. 'You'd never blow off taking your kid to a play-date. Well, why blow off a play-date for yourself? You're not getting any 'me' time. Just read the papers. You gotta stay healthy."

Adler, who has shelved her decade-old, part-time interior-design consultancy and still teaches a few classes at Sports Club L.A. and the Spectrum Club in Santa Monica, has 30 steady clients ranging in age from mid-20s to mid-50s; dozens more show up at Homebodies on an occasional basis. The fee is $15 per class or $120 for ten classes; the latter "encourages them to make a commitment," she says. All advertising is word-of-mouth. Spinners reserve a spot in class via e-mail.

"I'm not getting rich off this," she says. "But to hear someone tell me, 'You've changed my life,' is priceless."

Adler told of her most recent success story—a young, overweight mother of two named Darline, who worked a production job at HBO. "She was cute, in her 30s, but getting fatter and more depressed," she said.

"She came over three days a week. It took her a couple of months to get through a whole class without slowing down. And by the time she did, she'd lost three dress sizes. 'You look so hot!' I told her, and she was so flattered. I felt so worthwhile later, when she told me I'd changed her life.

"There is absolutely no reason why a woman in her 30s shouldn't feel fabulous."

Once her clients are fit enough, Adler repeats a deeply imprinted pattern: She takes them out on mountain bike rides.

"It's a thrill for them, as it was for me, to see the fitness and skills learned indoors translate to a real sport," she says. "And very quickly, they learn what I learned: cycling is a life-changing experience.

"I always get my best ideas when I'm riding, and meet pivotal people. Just the other day, I was riding on PCH [Pacific Coast Highway] in Malibu, cookin' along at 17 to 20 miles per hour, when I slowed down to ask an old struggling 70-year-old guy on a Colnago if he was okay. Turns out he was a retiring psychiatrist who worked in the same building as my [surviving] brother. I ended up getting my brother a bunch of new clients."

Last year, Adler retired from triathlons and mountain bike racing. "It's not about me proving myself as an athlete anymore," she says. "It's about everyone else."

"The combination of spinning and my brother dying had a huge affect on me. I realize that people have a lot of living to do, and being able to help them do it is a gift. Making a difference anywhere on this planet is a very good thing.

"You know that old cliché, 'Random Acts of Kindness'? That's nice, but it's not good enough. Why not plan them?"

When Kostman teaches, he stresses two techniques that can aid climbing. In the first, the spinner hinges forward at the waist, keeping the spine flat and parallel to the ground, then she slides a few inches off the back of the saddle and uses arm and shoulder muscles to pull on the bars to exert more leverage on the pedal. In the second, she slides forward a bit and cultivates the lower abdominals to push the butt into and back on the saddle to increase leverage on the pedals.

"When you add that all up," he says, "you are using the majority of the body to push and pull yourself uphill."

Another indoor method that Kostman advocates for developing outdoor climbing skills is a low-rpm cadence. "It's popular these days for everyone to emulate Lance Armstrong's climbing prowess, which involves keeping a cadence of 90 or 100 [rpm] even on the climbs, which saves his legs. But the fact is that the average person can't do this well without daily training—the high rpm on the hill will wear him out. On a shorter climb, the average guy is actually better off standing up and pushing a low cadence—something a spin bike is perfectly set up to do."

Spin bikes, after all, only have one gear. In fact, to climb, you don't downshift, as you would do on a road bike, but you turn the tension up and slow your leg speed down. Kostman recommends that spinners fight the urge to ease off on the tension. "In fact, the longer you can hold a high tension at a slow speed, the better," he says. "It'll pay off when you go outside."

SEATED CLIMBING: Butt back, heel down

On long climbs, seated climbing is generally more economical than standing climbing, because it unweights your legs and keeps your heart rate lower. Technically, the bike seat—not your legs—supports your body weight when you're seated, and your legs have the luxury of focusing on pushing the pedals. To further lighten the load on the quads, cyclists should pull up on the pedals on the upstroke. "But they rarely do it for long outdoors," says Kostman. "Either they shift to an easier gear, and therefore stop pulling up, or just lose focus on their pedaling technique altogether."

He says one relatively simple spin class technique can help you keep that focus: lower your heels.

"Suck in your lower abs to help push your butt to the back of the seat, then drive the pedals down with your heels lower than the toes," he says. "Keep the heels low when you pull up, too; as soon as you lift the heel above the ball of the foot, you turn off the calf muscle." Kostman believes most cyclists sit too high and too far forward on their bike, often because they don't hinge their torsos forward enough or push their butts far enough back. By keeping their heels up, they are only pulling up with their shins and quads, rather than their shins, quads, calves, hams, glutes, and lower back. [Note: The dropped heel Kostman advocates jibes with many top bike fitters. Paul Levine of the Serotta Fit School says the dropped heel helps you utilize the glutes for more power. See "Butt-centric" riding in chapter 7.)

STANDING CLIMBING

Because a stationary bike does not angle upward while "climbing," as does an outdoor bike, Kostman says that the indoor cyclist must make a posture adjustment to cultivate the hamstrings, glutes, and back muscles in the same way that they'd normally be used outdoors.

His advice: to replicate the outdoor position, hinge at the hips, keep your back straight and parallel to the ground, push your nose down to within a few inches of your handlebar, and shove your butt so far back that it barely brushes against the saddle. Look down, not forward, to keep your spine in a neutral, comfortable position; in fact, literally lengthen the spine by inching your tailbone back and the crown of your head forward.

"Many indoor cyclists are misinformed about movement of the upper body in outdoor cycling," says Kostman. "Many indoor cycling instructors tell their students not to move their upper body, period. But this is wrong and counterproductive.

"Outdoors, the bike moves side to side beneath the rider," he says. "Since a stationary bike cannot be rocked beneath you, simulate the effect by moving your upper torso side to side." On a slow-cadence "all-body climb," rock your chest from one side of the handlebars to the other with each pedal stroke. The movement is strictly side-to-side, not up-and-down, and the hips/lower torso remain fixed in proper alignment with the feet and knees.

· 2 ·
SPEED WORK

STANDING POSITION—Run for your life

Standing tall on the pedals and doing what Johnny G called "running" looks strange to outdoor cyclists. "But forget about that," says Kostman. "Cyclists used to think lifting weights and yoga was weird, too. Running on a spin bike can make you a better cyclist, forcing you to go anaerobic, building explosive power, raising your lactate threshold and turnover, and increasing your ability to make hard efforts. Most people working in a gym have had their HR [heart rate] in the anaerobic zone for a couple of minutes at a time or more, far longer than the brief efforts most people do during intervals."

Here's how to "run" while you spin: stand tall on the pedals by putting the entire weight of the body on the quads with ears, hips, and bottom bracket in a straight line. With the upper body stabilized by tensed abs, and virtually no hand pressure on the bars (using only fingertips for balance), use the momentum of the weighted flywheel to blast your cadence up to 200 rpm—far above the 150 rpm most top cyclists can manage outdoors.

"This particular technique skyrockets the heart rate like nothing else," says Kostman, who claims to have recorded a max of 212 with this technique. In fact, he warns, newbies in the spin room should beware of getting in over their head. "Just do this for 10 to 15 seconds, max. Don't push it." Either sit back down—or read on to the next technique.

STANDING IN "HINGED" POSITION—Still standing

Whereas standing tall and running (the aforementioned technique) can be tolerated only for a short burst of time, hinging forward and standing can be held for an entire song (3 to 6 minutes) at a cadence of 110–150 rpm. To do this, says Kostman, assume a climbing posture, but don't push as far back over the saddle as you would do while climbing with a slow cadence. In this position, you're still lengthening your spine when hinged forward, but resistance is light, and leg speed is high.

"As compared to standing tall, this off-the-saddle position won't 'burn' as much," he says. "Therefore you can hold a high leg speed for a longer period of time—raising your endurance, leg speed, and lactate threshold."

SITTING POSITION

Kostman likes sprinting during each chorus in a song, rather than sprinting for arbitrary periods of, say, 30 seconds. Ideal for building rapid turnover, the sitting technique is easy: use very little resistance, sit forward on the saddle, suck in abs to stabilize hips and upper body, and go like hell. Again, shoot for 200 rpm.

• 3 •
GRADUAL WARM-UP IS BEST

The one "problem" that irritates Kostman about many noncyclist spin class instructors is a tendency to force their classes to "redline" from start to finish. "That shoots your heart rate up—and once it's up, it'll never come down the rest of the session," he says. "Consequently, you never train for recovery—allowing your heart rate to drop—a key to cycling endurance."

Recovery means that a truly fit person will see his or her heart rate drop by as much as 50 beats on a 30-second down-

hill. That is important because it allows the body to rest. "The problem with charging out of the gate and freezing your heart rate at a high level is that you never train your heart to rest," says Kostman. "You'll burn out."

His advice: regardless of what your class is doing (unless you've done your own spin warm-up before class began), ride the first two songs seated with light resistance, followed by a seated and standing climb for one song each. Be sure to warm your muscles in conjunction with a gradually rising heart rate. Never do speed work until 12 to 15 minutes into the class. Then, go for it.

And when you get outdoors . . .
1. ***Know your pedals.*** Before you go out for a ride, repeatedly practice clicking in and out of your clipless pedals comfortably. Otherwise, your first stop at a red light will be terrifying—especially if you land on your hip.
2. ***Look up.*** Never look down, as you might when concentrating in a studio. Always keep your head up, hyperaware of traffic and road conditions.
3. ***Butt back.*** Keep the same form taught in class—butt slid to the back of the saddle, straight back, sucked-in abs, relaxed shoulders, with as much weight as possible off hands.

Gear: Taking a Spin at Home

HOME spinning takes the final excuse not to work out away from you, especially given six distinct categories of indoor trainers to choose from today—some of them so cheap that they surely are among the best deals in the fitness world. Relatively inexpensive compared to quality treadmills, steppers, and other serious aerobic machines, and sometimes downright cheap, indoor cycle machines are offered in a variety of categories. The Johnny G Spinner and a host of copycat group-cycling spin bikes, including models from LeMond, Kettler, Schwinn, Monarch, and many more, typically run a grand or less. The newest development is the Trixter X-Bike ($1,299), its articulating handlebars and coastable freewheel attempt to replicate the feel of mountain biking. Although trust-funders can drop $35,000 on a state-of-the-art cycling treadmill, a mere $100 can buy average folk a bike-world staple—the simple, reliable, and safe bike-training stand, which places the rear wheel of your own bike atop a small flywheel. Rollers, the original, turn-of-the-century (1900, that is) bike trainer favored by hard-core riders, haven't gone away, either. And if you like that old-fashioned (pre-spinning) health club feeling, the venerable Lifecycle and its ilk, in upright and **recumbent** configurations, are still going strong. Here's a quick overview of what's out there, with features, advantages, and disadvantages noted.

Hardware: Group-cycling spin bikes

Category Thumbnail: Stationary bike featuring heavy, momentum-driven flywheel that can result in leg speed approaching 200 rpm.

Example 1: Star Trac Spinner® (several models)

Price: $1,025.00 (Pro model), $1,225.00 (Elite), $1,625.00 (NXT)

Where to buy: www.StarTrac.com

Details: Latest version of the original Johnny built. Includes 43-lb. flywheel, twist-turn resistance, adjustable seat and handlebars, and room for two water bottles. New Spinner Elite model adds backward-pedal Smart Release braking. Simpler, basic, Johnny Spinner ($499) available at Madd Dogg Athletics (800-847-7746).

Upside: Momentum of huge flywheel develops leg speed impossible to attain on a street bike. Unlike Lifecycles, Spinners have fit, adjustability, and positioning of a street bike and allow use of performance bike pedal systems.

Downside: You may pine for the music-saturated group environment of a spin class at the club. Solution: Johnny G–hosted video from Madd Dog Athletics.

Competing models: LeMond RevMaster (www.LeMondFitness.com); Schwinn Indoor Cycling Pro (www.SchwinnFitness.com); Ironcompany ICS-1 Indoor Cycle Sport Bike (888-758-7527, www.ironcompany.com); For all brands, go to www.exercise-bikes-direct.com/catalog/buy/Indoor_Group_Cycling_Bike/

Example 2: The Trixter X-Bike

Price: $1,195.00

Where to buy: www.Trixter.net

Details: Tries to simulate mountain biking via a unique design that constitutes the first major change of the classic spin bike: articulating handlebars and freewheel.

Upside: Workout incorporates a dynamic upper and lower body workout. Rocking the bar back and forth adds a fun and challenging new element to indoor cycling.

Downside: None

Competing models: None

Example 3: Electronic wizard: CycleOps Pro 300PT

Price: $1,699.00

Where to buy: 800-783-7257; www.cycleops.com

Details: Sleek, aerodynamic spin bike with a large handlebar monitor jammed with performance feedback, including mph, odometer, calories burned, power output in watts, downloadable to a PC.

Upside: Highly motivating. All the info makes you work out longer.

Downside: None

Competing models: None

Hardware: Standard "triangle" bike training stands

Category Thumbnail: Simple, no-frills stand that uses your own bike. The rear **hub** clamps in place, holding the rear wheel (slick tires only) against a small flywheel that employs one of several resistance mechanisms: magnetic, fan-blade air-friction, sealed fan-blades pushing through viscous fluid, and centrifugal force.

Example: Performance Travel Trac Century Fluid trainer

Price: $169.00

Where to buy: 800-888-2854, www.performancebikes.com

Description: Resistance provided by small fan encased in a sealed oil-water chamber; to up resistance, speed up.

Upside: Dirt cheap, compact. Real cycling workout (sans handling) on your own bike. One-minute set-up. Fluid is the smoothest and most quiet of the resistance mechanisms. To add resistance, simply pedal faster or switch gears. Simple design; nothing to break, no wires. Can be used with mountain bikes, recumbents, and beach cruisers with slick rear tires. Transportable; folds up instantly, fits in a car trunk. Travel Bloc front wheel holder ($11) provides level riding position. Reliable; cyclists have used them for years.

Downside: None

Competing models: Blackburn (800-456-2355, www.blackburndesign.com); Graber CycleOps (608-274-6550, www.cycle-ops.com/); Minoura (800-601-9592, www.minoura.co.jp)

Hardware: *Electronic Cycling Simulators*

Category Thumbnail: Bike, video game, and test lab combined. Computer software translates rider's effort into visual feedback on a video screen in real time and stores for analysis.

Example: Racermate Velotron

Price: $5,175.00

Where to buy: 800-522-3610 x 338; www.velotron.com

Description: Displays on-screen every imaginable variable—speed, power output in watts, pedal cadence, heart rate, left-right pedal-stroke analysis, and more—with lab-quality accuracy in striking 3-D graphics. Includes 100 built-in courses, including the Hawaii Ironman and Lance Armstrong's Appalachian climbs. You can download your own courses.

Upside: Highly motivating; race against a computer-generated opponent—or yourself—by saving your workouts and recalling them. Simulates hills, headwinds, drafting.

Downside: Big $

Competing models: Racermate's Computrainer ($1,399) offers similar features with less accuracy (www.racermateinc.com); CycleOps electronic-control ($800, www.cycleops .com/); Performance Power Train ($500, www.performancebikes.com).

Hardware: *Bicycle Treadmill*

Category Thumbnail: A huge, fast treadmill that a bike could ride at speeds up to 25 mph.

Example: Inside Ride Super Trainer

Price: $35,000.00

Where to buy: 503-647-5883; www.insideride.com

Description: The ultimate indoor trainer. Ride your own bike all-out, at grades up to 16 percent. Requires 5 by 12 feet of floor space. Has a sensing tether for computer-controlled speed and resistance, programmable slope and course profiles, and interval training.

Upside/Downside: Natural feel of real cycling. Cyclist must balance and steer. Ideal for long rides. As safe or safer than outdoor riding; light-beam perimeter switches will stop the belt if any part of the bike or rider breaks the beam. Safety rails with cable-activated shutoffs are also easily tripped by the rider during either controlled or panic stops. Full-speed stops or power outages will bring the belt to rest in as little as three feet.

Downside: Takes up a garage, costs you a BMW.

Competing models: None

Hardware: Conventional Exerbike

Category Thumbnail: Home versions of a health club bike.

Example: Life Fitness Lifecycle c9i and r9i

Price: $2,200.00

Where to buy: www.lifefitness.com

Description: Packed with gym-style features, including 20 levels of resistance; four preprogrammed workouts; detailed message center; built-in cordless heart rate monitor. The r9i is the recumbent model of the same bike. They are powered by pedaling, so you don't have to plug them in.

Upside: Plenty of feedback to keep you amused. Tried-and-true gym-bike workout.

Downside: Lacks true cycling fit, position, and feel of a real bike or a spin bike.

Competing brands: Diamondback (253-395-1100/800-222-5527, www.diamondback fitness.com); Horizon (888-993-3199; www.horizonfitness.com)

Hardware: Rollers

Category Thumbnail: Used and refined for a century, rollers consist of three narrow, yard-long drums, arrayed on two rails, that allow you to ride your bike in place. Has a superb, road-like feel.

Example: Kreitler Dyno-Myte Rollers

Price: $379.99

Where to buy: www.competitivecyclist.com; www.tristore.com

Description: High-performance rollers with narrow, 2.5-inch diameter drums, which provide greater resistance than any other Kreitler unit.

Upside: Best road-like feel of all indoor trainers (other than the treadmill). Great for learning balance and pedaling fluidity, since the bike can list and veer side to side as it does on the road. The small drums are ideal for superfit riders. The unit is compatible with the Killer Headwind Fan ($159.99), which makes the workout harder by mimicking what you get on the road: wind drag, not magnetic or fluid resistance. The adjustable unit simulates a range from a 2-mph tailwind to a 10-mph headwind.

Downside: Lose attention for a split second, and you can crash. For those concerned about safety, note that larger size, 3-inch drums found on Kreitler's Dyno-Lyte ($409) or Poly-Lyte make it nearly impossible to spin out during a tough workout. Use of a **forkstand** (in which you remove the front wheel and attach your fork to the stand; $79.99) eliminates the need to focus on balance.

Competing brands: Tacx, Cycleops (for both check www.cbike.com, fax 773-445-7008).

Johnny G

HE TOOK CYCLING DEEP INSIDE

Bodybuilders don't ride bikes. And cyclists don't bodybuild. But a South African immigrant named Johnny Goldberg did both with such passion and charisma and vision that he singlehandedly changed the health-and-fitness industry and improved the fitness and outlook of millions around the globe. In the early 1980s, Johnny got into the Los Angeles personal-training phenomenon at the ground floor, then took himself to the limits in the 3,000-mile Race Across America. Frustration over the un-bike feel of standard exercycles led to his hand-welded invention, the innovative Spinner stationary bike, which uses a heavy flywheel and standard cycling bottom bracket and pedals. That morphed into Spinning, the cycle-to-the-music group workout sensation now used by 6 million Americans a year and even more in bike-crazy Europe, where massive outdoor spinfests have attracted over 500 Spinners at a time in Holland and 1,000 in Italy. Perhaps millions have used spinning as a springboard to outdoor cycling. Spinning fundamentally altered our view of group aerobic exercise class from organized dancing and jumping to a quest, a challenge, a journey into heart and soul that could be appreciated by men and athletes, not just housewives. But as the man now known simply as Johnny G told Bike for Life's Roy Wallack in their interview on March 11, 2004, he couldn't have come up with it until he'd been on his own amazing journey first.

I WAS FOUR years old when I got my first bike and fell in love with cycling. A bike was more than a workout tool. It was a place to sink my sorrows, to dream. It was a place to break through boundaries, to get myself out of this box or cage. It was a place for me to liberate myself, to find peace and harmony. To take that trip on to the coattails of God. To find the sense of freedom that lots of people find using the bike. It has always been a staple in my life. The martial arts and the swimming and the squash and the music—they were all cool. But none of them made me feel the way the bike did.

We were very primitive in South Africa. My dad was a pharmacist and we had very little money. I used to work on my bikes for hours. When I was twelve years old I put on ape-hanger handlebars. When I was sixteen, I actually rode across South Africa for an organization called TEACH—Teach Every African Child.

At twelve or thirteen, I met Arnold [Schwarzenegger] when he came to see Reg Park, who won the Mr. Universe a couple of times in the 1960s. I was best friends with Reg's son. He and I watched *Pumping Iron* together. We went through all the magazines—*Ironman, Muscular Development*. I met Frank Zane and some of the all-time greats, and started getting into bodybuilding. I was very much excited about the prospects of health and fitness, as it was just starting to unfold in South Africa.

About 1978, when I got out of the army, I was running a gym for Reg. I was like a sponge to him. Over the years, I'd practically spent more time with Reg than his own kid. He and I used to talk bodybuilding at length. Exercises. Philosophy. Diet. His fears. Reg was extraordinary. He hit the gym every morning from six to eight. He wasn't just a bodybuilder; being in the fitness business, he'd say he was a " physical culturist." That was the beginning of

BIKE FOR LIFE

my search for self-development and under-standing. The first building block.

I wanted to come over to the States. My big dream was to go over to California to go to Venice Beach, to Muscle Beach, and to train at the Gold's Gym.

In June 1979, at age 23, I came to the U.S. on a 30-day tourist visa. Went right to Gold's, worked out, then got held up. Welcome to America.

I hadn't really found out what I was looking for, but I wasn't going to leave. Soon, I met a guy in Venice Beach who was selling Ginsu knives—possibly stolen merchandise. He would drive the car with product and I'd walk in and visit the shops. He paid me a dollar per sale.

One day I walked into a health club on Motor Avenue in West L.A. called World for Men and World for Women. It had separate wings, which was a big deal—they could work out at the same time. Back then, most clubs had separate hours for the sexes, so the owner had his own niche in the market. I told the head guy that I had experience running a health club and that I could raise their business by 10 percent—and they hired me. I worked for a month, and when it came to pay day, there was no pay.

So I've got no money. I'm eating sugar cubes to stay alive. Sleeping on a couch. I've got my fair share of challenges.

But I stay working there, making my $3.25 an hour, and finally get paid. We run a successful "two memberships for the price of one" ad campaign—my idea: one man, one woman—in 1980 and get a lot of traffic.

At Ground Zero of the Fitness Revolution
My BIG BREAK came in 1981, when I answered a phone call from a huge Hollywood agent named Sandy Gellen, who handled the biggest names in the industry—Cher, Dolly Parton, Barbra Streisand. He was looking for a private trainer to come to his house. At the time, personal training was almost unheard of. There were no fitness organizations, no exercise physiology classes. You just had a background in bodybuilding or sports or something. I went up to Sandy's house in Beverly Hills, gave him a workout, and sometimes ended up training him seven days a week.

I was making a hundred bucks for two hours—pretty good money. With my $3.25 per hour at World for Men, plus commission on sales, I was bringing home about nineteen hundred bucks a month.

Soon, I started picking up all the celebrities and started working the Hollywood scene. It was amazing. Victoria Principal, Andy Gibb, Jack Scalia. Soon, I was making $8,000 a month.

Training exploded. Jake Steinfeld—"Body by Jake"—did the first big show, *Entertainment Tonight.* He was training Spielberg. Dan Issacson was doing Linda Evans and Christopher Reeve. The movie *Perfect*, with John Travolta and Jamie Lee Curtis, came out.

My style was always different, real world. My clients were always ultra-skinny and ultra-fit. I'd run them on trails in the Santa Monica Mountains, up the stairs at UCLA, and combine it with weights.

I started getting a reputation—that I was really tough. If someone really wanted to go to another level, almost a sportsman with philosophy, I was the guy.

All this time, I'd never stopped riding my bike. I got into triathlon and bike racing in 1984. My marriage started to fall apart in about 1985, and I needed out. I needed space. Cycling gave me space.

BIKE FOR LIFE

Everything in cycling was pedigreed—Cat 3, Cat 4, certain distances. I hadn't made Category 2 yet, and I was having a lot of conflicts between traveling and my clients and the races and sponsorships. It was tough. And family and kids and responsibility was really difficult. I dealt with it by putting in more miles.

Then I went to Texas and did the Spenco 500. Five hundred miles from Waco to Comfort and back. A thousand cyclists from all over the world. Pro teams. KLN. Schwinn. Icy Hot. Thomas Prehn. Ultra-distance cyclists—Pete Penseyres. Mike Shermer. *Randonneurs*. I had no idea about long-distance riding, no support, no proper gear. Specialized gave me a pair of **slick tires**. I tried a liquid diet. Carried my stuff.

I took a 17th in that race. There was prize money to 20th and I won $280, maybe $320, which was pretty cool. Took me a week to recover and get back to L.A.

I'd never gone over, I think, 105 miles before. But here I went 500 miles at that pace! With packs and motorcycles and copters! I mean this was the real thing. The real deal—my first ultra. It gave me such a sense of awe. It was incredible. There was something about the distance. It was about facing my weaknesses, about being totally exposed and limited. My brain started to fly.

The Concept: A Stationary Bike Workout

In 1985, I opened the first "Johnny G Cross-Training and Nutrition Center" at Matrix 1 on Westwood Boulevard. I started [leading] 30 minutes of high-intensity drills on a stationary bike—which was very different. The stationary bike had always been used as a warm-up, not for workouts. I added combinations of squats with pullovers, extreme super sets, giant sets with no rest, and ended it by doing their body work. It was sort of an all-in-one workout.

I was inspired by my teenage memories of the Donavet stationary bike, a German-made machine with a built-in heart rate monitor. At Matrix, we used Windracers, a competitor of Lifecycle. The bike gave the clients a real good sweat. It gave them a feeling of conquering terrain—and fears. I could talk to them like an athlete. And, of course, it gave me my own niche. No one had a bike workout.

Combining the bike workout with the South African accent and my appeal and the whole thing, and it was cool. I got in all the magazines. I was in *Variety*, the opening show of *Geraldo*, *Hour Magazine*, *Gary Collins*. I trained Melissa Gilbert for a movie. And my results were very dramatic.

The next year, I opened my own Johnny G Cross-Training and Nutrition Center in Beverly Hills. Arnold was there at the grand opening. I hired a lot of guys, including Rob Parr [Madonna's longtime coach]. I set up four road bikes on turbo-trainers, not the old Lifecycle-style bikes.

That was an important step. I was getting really aggravated, annoyed, and frustrated with the old bikes. The pedals were wrong. I wanted to get people into real bike shoes. I wanted them to have this experience of what it felt like to get out of the saddle. To sprint, to do intervals. To sit back and close their eyes. To create a really cool environment that could help me get people into a really athletic state. If people weren't going to go outside and actually ride the bicycle, I had to take them there indoors. I had clients I was taking out on bikes on the weekends, triathletes and other guys who already had ten-speeds, but from a commercial point of view, this wasn't where the business was. The business was in being able to take people on this journey where I could get into their heads and talk to them. They would look into the shadows of themselves in the mirror, and I started to give them visualizations. With the music—and I was using Pink Floyd and the coolest music, not just typical aerobic tempo—it was incredible! It was a very exciting time.

It was really the start of Spinning. The name and the specially designed spinning bike and 40-minute training session wasn't there yet, but the concept was.

Aerobics had limited a lot of people. It never gave them an opportunity to be self-expressed. Aerobics was becoming very dance, very choreographed. So guys and people who weren't very coordinated started to find a different sense of power on the bike. And this was a great thing, because I could tap into them using the bike as a tool, as an analogy. I wasn't sophisticated, I never understood what I was doing, I never had the wisdom or the experience or the foresight to know what would happen later. But at the time my instincts were sharp and I was coming from a very intuitive place. This place was spot-on for where people needed to go. I was definitely on the right track.

Spinning worked for super athletes and it worked for average people. In 1985 I had met pro triathlete Brad Kearns while out on a training ride. I asked if he wanted to ride with me, and eight hours later we were near Santa Barbara before we turned around and went back home. Brad was in third place in the Desert Princess duathlon series. Then I brought him into my cross-training center and helped him visualize, and I made him believe in himself. He saw the winning time, which was

eight minutes faster than his best time. And he beat that time I think by 1.6 seconds. And he became the world champion in 1987. When I met [actor] Jack Scalia, he had just gone through recovery. And he could dream about doing a triathlon. Back then, there weren't a lot of guys who were taking just ordinary people and getting them into sports.

The RAAM Revelation

I HAD NO idea what the Race Across America was in 1985, but in 1986 I was trying to qualify for it. I did the John Marino Open [the 500-mile western states' RAAM qualifier] from Tucson to Flagstaff and back. I was still trying to do a few private clients. I was trying to get a divorce. I was dealing with not being the dad on weekends. I started doing these long miles and the riding started taking over more of my life.

Having absolutely no idea what I'd bitten off and what I'd gotten myself into, I entered the 1987 RAAM with very little sponsorship, very little support. Got a couple of buddies together. I was a raw-food vegetarian and I suffered for eight days in the rain. I quit 400 miles from the finish.

The problem was I never knew at the time that I was bipolar manic-depressive. Sleep was very important. If you start losing sleep and you're not medicated, you start getting really delusional. I started having huge spiritual conflicts and psychological conflicts. Five hundred miles was great distance for me. Everybody has their distance; you just have to know what yours is. You just have to find it. Well, I outreached my space. I outreached my parameters. I broke my boundaries.

I never had any boundaries before. I was invincible. My mind had no sense of boundaries. I never laid any down. It was

BIKE FOR LIFE

just possible. Training would make it possible. No doubt. It's OK to have a very positive state of mind, yet, it also can work against you. For me in this event, it worked against me. It was too much, too hard. I had too many conflicts. Too many emotional things going on, too much chaos going on within myself. These also became huge principles which I used later. Chaos and emotional traumas and how the mind would work in ways that could be far more effective, if the right pieces were put in place. What happened was this RAAM was an extremely fruitful and productive learning experience. Yet athletically it was disastrous. I lost about 26 or 27 pounds. It took a long time for me to recover.

When it was over, I decided I was finished with the ego. I was finished with being the best. I got in my vehicle and drove to a friend's house who said I could recover at his house. And.I drove back to California and began a three-month recovery. I lost my clientele base. I couldn't go back into the gym. I didn't want to go back into the gyms.

.

To SURVIVE, I had to sell everything. There were a lot of nutrition companies sending me a lot of high-tech stuff they were working on—carbohydrate diets, meal replacement. I was sort of selling the stuff to a couple of guys that I knew and cashed out all the money I had, maybe a thousand bucks, maybe twelve hundred bucks. And I borrowed some money to buy a bike and I started training again, because I wanted to go back and get my RAAM ring.

Because I didn't finish RAAM, I knew I'd have to requalify in 1988, put a crew together and get back to the Race Across America in 1989. So I was facing a two-year ordeal to finish what I'd started.

Finishing RAAM was gonna take a lot of work. A lot of planning, getting the crews together, and a lot of guts and courage. Because I wanted to finish it. Ego-wise I couldn't let this thing go. It was the first time I'd really been outmatched. Yah, it was the first time I'd felt worthless. Or acknowledged not being capable of matching up to the mind of the great Johnny G. And it was a really interesting time.

I was doing incredibly long miles. But I was training on a 24-hour cycle, not a normal 12-hour day. Because of my bipolar, I wasn't sleeping a lot—three or four hours every other day. That is why I couldn't talk in sentences. I was just like I was on speed all the time. You get into the manic states, you get abundant energy. You start to fly. You get very scattered. You just become delusional. Graham Obree [the record-setting Scottish 24-hour rider] just wrote a book on his bipolar disorder and how it helped him achieve what he did. If you can channel and focus it, you can harness unbelievable energy. Boundaries and limitations start to disappear. And so I would dream. I would have ideas, a thousand ideas a second. I was always creating something new. And this was my four-day training cycle. What I started to find was Tuesday I would start at 6 AM and finish at 6 PM—go 200 miles. But I would switch it up. Tuesday I would go into the deserts. Thursdays I would go into the mountains. But Friday night, I would start at 6 PM and then I could come back at 6 PM Saturday night. Brad Kearns would usually meet me at 6 AM on Saturday morning and spend a 12-hour day with me. I'd do my 24-hour ride on the weekend.

In four days I would clock anywhere

between 760 and 830 miles. . . . The rest of the time, I had just met a wonderful girl and had fallen in love head over heels. For the first time in my life, true love. And we found a little bungalow in one of my clients' backyard. He let us use it. We had a little futon. An old-fashioned bathtub. A little refrigerator. And that was our life. She would sell sweaters and make jewelry and I would go out and train.

I had given up everything—a complete lifestyle change from big-time trainer to cycling monk. But I had a two-year task. See, this is where life is beautiful. And this is one of the most special parts of the journey. Really about this process, about as an adult being able to say, okay, this is what I need to do.

So I went and did the qualifier—the John Merino Open, otherwise known as RAAM Open West. And I won by four and a half hours in 29:36.

I averaged 18.1 miles an hour, climbing 36,000 feet and with temperature changes from 106°F in the day to 11°F and 12°F at night. It was such a severe event, so challenging. And my time was so fast that it was the only time in history, I believe, that there was only one qualifier for RAAM besides the winner. Second place came in just within the 15 percent cutoff—the rule that qualifiers for the RAAMs have to qualify within 15 percent of the winner's time. No one else made the cutoff. This is a pretty cool thing.

So I went into the RAAM knowing I would have a good shot of finishing it. And I rode really fast for the first four days. I was in great shape. I thought I could break eight days—my goal. And halfway through I just realized it wasn't going to happen. I dropped to riding 16 hours a day, not the 22 I'd planned for. I finished in ten days. But I

got my RAAM ring!

And I was happy. In my first RAAM, I thought my athletic god would set me free, get me recognition, love, fame, be the key to a life of accomplishment, to the road to nobility. I didn't know until I finished the second that it was just a race.

I'd first used the term "spinning" in 1985 or 1986 when I had bikes on a trainer in my garage, "Come on over and catch a spin," I'd say. Harvey Diamond, the author of *Fit for Life*, was talking to me about my training once and latched onto the term "spinning."

RAAM was a profound and interesting lesson. The bicycle became a universal metaphor. Talking about headwinds, intensity, the struggle in a way that everybody [in a class] could relate to. In cycling, an individual must be able to participate in the group without being restricted to the group. In 40 minutes of spinning, people get stuff from the great masters.

The Spinner Is Born
DURING MY RAAM training, I'd put a specialty bike together—the early version of what is now known as the Spinner. Jody was pregnant. I'd ride at night when the air is clean. So that became my race strategy: rock and roll at night, sleep in the day, 2 PM to 4 PM In the end, I couldn't maintain that plan during the race. But I came away from the training with the basics of Spinning, the rhythm and combinations and movements, the three hand postures, the heart rate training zones. The principles that would end up in the manual.

After I finished RAAM, Jordan was born. Now I have to make a living. I took two of my Spinners to the Mezzaplex and told the owner I don't want to go back to private training. I gotta get back to the gym

BIKE FOR LIFE

business. I issued a challenge: if anyone can stay with me on a Spinner workout, they get $10. The mirror, the music, it's like Russian roulette. I'm hammering them to death. Nobody can last ten minutes. It creates a big buzz.

I needed more bikes. I went to Helen's Bike Shop to buy a Schwinn DX 900 stationary bike, but it couldn't handle the standing and the jumping. Or take regular pedals.

At the end of 1989, I built a fleet of my own bikes and opened the first Johnny G Spinning Center, in Santa Monica. I never thought about training people. It was my thing. Training session with my mates. I'd take them on a journey. I built fifteen more hand-welded bikes, then moved the class to Karen Voight Fitness in 1992, thinking Hollywood was better exposure. It worked. It was amazing.

When people began trying to rip off the program, I started working on the trademarks and took it back to my garage for a couple of years. I sold bikes and trained people at Crunch. I met John Baudhuin, now my partner. We got a call from Schwinn, made a deal, and launched it at the 1995 IHRSA [health-club] trade show. It was profound. In three months, Spinning was in 400 gyms, in 1,000 within a year, and in 1,500 by the end of 1996. We formed Madd Dogg Athletics, traveled to three countries every ten days, and logged a million miles in the first year training instructors.

It was unique—the first time equipment, training, and philosophy was sold together. We've trained 65,000 instructors over the years from Brazil to Moscow. By 1999, I was overworked, dead tired. And Schwinn was trying to rip us off. Luckily, we sued just before they went bankrupt. In 2003, we made a big deal with [equipment manufacturer] StarTrac, and I went traveling again. Went to lots of six-hour and eight-hour events for charity in Italy and Brazil.

I took up surfing and paddleboarding when we moved up to Santa Barbara. Training for a 200-mile ocean paddle right now. Been training for Orlando Kani, a Brazilian martial art, to go along with my black belt in Shodo Kan and study of Chi Gung, a stick-based martial art. Actually haven't been on a real bike in two months.

Will Spinning be here in twenty years? Spinning is a style so effective, so functional, so new for so many people, so easy to learn, and the bicycle's been here forever. The rhythm, the lack of impact, the inertia of a weighted flywheel, the sense of empowerment it gives to people is so powerful. People may decide that cardiovascular training is not the way to go in the future, who knows? We're just starting out on a journey of human development and growth.

4

MEALS ON WHEELS

The strategy and science of high-octane food and drink

WHEN I PULLED up to the starting line of the 1997 La Ruta de los Conquistadores on the morning of Day Two, someone asked me what happened to John Rodham, a friendly, chatty guy I'd briefly met a couple of nights before. The 35-year-old New York school-teacher was the top-finishing American on Day One, an impressive feat given the 79-mile mountainbike ride through jungle, mud, and humidity. But now, he was nowhere to be seen. By the end of the day, we got the grisly news: Rodham had gone to bed and hadn't awakened. A hotel maid opened the door at noon and found him in a coma. He fluttered near death for four days until he finally woke up.

Of course, we all figured it had to be severe dehydration. Even in the era of the hydration back-pack, when office workers carry around water bottles and six-year-old soccer kids can define the word "hydrate," you easily could underdrink in a race with this heat, this distance, this inten-sity. Heck, you can even get dehydrated swimming. Back when I first did the Hawaii Ironman in '82, we were warned before the 2.4-mile swim that we'd be in a minor state of dehydration by the time we touched land. "Drink the moment you start to pedal the bike toward the lava fields," veterans counseled—sage advice I obeyed that year and in the 1993 event. Each year, 20 per-cent of Ironman competitors require medical tent IVs for fluid and mineral replacement. Not me. I guzzled in Kona and at La Ruta.

That's why it was a shock to discover, months later, that John Rodham hadn't gotten dehy-drated at all. He'd slurped plenty of water—too much, in fact. He'd developed hyper-hydration, medically known as **hyponatremia**, or "water intoxication," which means drinking too much water without replenishing lost electrolytes—salts and minerals easily replaced by Gatorade and *salty snacks. Its symptoms can include nausea, dizziness, and cramps, but the real life-threatening danger is swelling of the brain.*

We've all heard about people drinking themselves to death. In cycling, a sport you can do for hours—or days—without stopping, this behavior takes on new meaning. You can drink like a camel, but you'll need more than water in your Camelbak. —BK

Napoleon once famously remarked that an army marches on its stomach. Cyclists, however, ride on their bellies. Tour de France racers consume between 6,000 and 7,000 calories per day. If you prefer empty-caloric analogies, this amount is roughly equivalent to six pints of Ben & Jerry's Chunky Monkey ice cream, 34 Krispy Kreme glazed doughnuts, or 43 bottles of Sam Adams Boston Ale. Lean-as-toothpick Tour riders learn to gorge like Sumo wrestlers throughout the day—breakfast, pre-race meals, dinner, and constant snacking and drinking fluids while in the saddle. Most of these calories while riding come from carbohydrates since they are the primary fuel source for energy. Since there is a finite amount of carbs you can store in muscles and liver—between 1,600 and 1,800 calories—after three hours of riding, you will be sputtering and clanking on empty unless you fill your tank with more carbs.[1]

"Lance Armstrong aims to get 70 percent of his calories from carbohydrates, 15 percent from protein, and 15 percent from fat," writes his longtime coach Chris Carmichael on his Web site www.Train Right.com. During their regular meals, continues Carmichael, "Lance and his teammates get their carbohydrates from potatoes, rice, pasta, cereal, whole grain breads, and fruits and vegetables. Protein comes from eggs, meat, chicken, and yogurt." As for fat, that comes courtesy of how their personal team chef Willy Bal-mat, who during the off-season runs the kitchen at the St. Moritz Hotel in Switzerland, prepares meals with monounsaturated oils such as olive oil. "On the bike, riders eat a mixture of real food, energy bars, and gels. The *soigneurs* prepare musette bags with small sandwiches, often ham or turkey and cheese with butter on a roll, and the bags almost always contain baked potatoes. The riders eat the potatoes like you would normally eat an apple. Lance also consumes about two to three Powerbars during each stage as well. Riders aim to ingest 300 to 400-plus calories per hour while racing, and take small bits of food every ten to fifteen minutes."

While the body can extract energy from its fat stores, the primary fuel for extended aerobic performance is carbohydrates. **Bonking** often happens when the brain is running low on glucose, or sugar, from the blood. It can even happen to Lance, like at the 2000 Tour's 16th stage on the infamously steep Col de Joux Plane with its five climbs averaging 8.5 percent. The final climb witnessed a very weary Texan. As he later told reporters, "Today was the hardest day of my life on a bike. I didn't have enough to eat on the final climb and suffered a 'bonk.' I didn't have enough energy. I was in trouble, but I stayed regular and rode conservative."

A bonk can manifest itself in varying degrees of intensity. "The confusion, nausea, and disorientation that go along with bonking are more due to the brain running low on glucose than a problem with energy-starved muscles," notes Carmichael. "When push comes to shove, the brain acts defensively to make sure it gets enough fuel." A critical source of carbs and electrolytes come from sports drinks. In hot weather, Tour riders can drink between two and three bottles per hour on the bike. "Immediately following the stage," he continues, "riders are handed another musette bag containing more food and bottles. The big difference is that these post-stage bottles usually contain a recovery-oriented drink with a 4 to 1 ratio of carbohydrate to protein. The body is most efficient at replenishing carbohydrate stores in the first 60 minutes after exercise, and the protein in the drink helps muscles absorb carbohydrates from the bloodstream."[2]

Those first 60 minutes have come to commonly be known as the "**carbohydrate window**," and represent the optimum time for your body to replenish its lost energy stores. For a brief peek into this window, let's turn to Dr. John Ivy, chairperson of the Department of Kinesiology and Health Education in the College of Education at the University of Texas at Austin, who has spent several decades investigating when to eat and drink after hard aerobic exercise.

When you exercise, "the muscles become very sensitive to certain hormones and nutrients, and you can initiate many highly desirable training adaptations if you make sure the correct nutrients are present quickly," he told *Outside* magazine (May 2001). "This increased sensitivity of the muscles only lasts for a limited length of time, so the element of time becomes absolutely crucial."

Ivy also was surprised to discover that ingesting a small amount of protein assists glycogen recovery. While the rate of glycogen storage could not be increased by eating more carbs, the addition of a limited amount of protein—the aforementioned 4 to 1 ratio—sparked a chain reaction that boosted the insulin concentration in the blood. Another end result is a higher rate of glycogen recovery and speedier muscle recovery.

Cyclists who have come of age in the post–Greg LeMond era will be mistaken to think that Tour riders have always carefully considered what they munched, nibbled, swallowed, chewed, digested, guzzled, or swigged. Before sports drinks, energy bars, and gels became a multibillion-dollar industry, riders made do with much less. "We used to race with a bottle of water and a bottle of Coca-Cola," says Jim Ochowicz, who raced in Europe in the 1970s. "That was it. Maybe a sandwich. Or a cookie. You could get cookies then that were wrapped individually."

• NUTRITION • FOR THE LONG HAUL

Monitoring your energy and hydration needs is critical to success on the bike—whether it's for a three-week stage race or a Sunday group ride. The more consecutive hours you spend riding, the more attention you must pay to proper food and fluids.

Let's consider one end of the extreme gastronomic scale: endurance mountain bike riders, including Iditarod Trail record holder Mike Curiak and 2002 La Ruta de los Conquistadores women's winner Hillary Harrison. In a *VeloNews* interview, Curiak admitted that "at a supported event I eat as many Clif or Luna bars as I can get my hands on. When I set the record on the Iditarod Trail, I averaged 16 [bars] per day for 15 days—240 total. I typically revert to Twizzlers licorice, gummy worms and ice cream bars, especially the chocolate chip-cookie sandwich kind."

Harrison says she likes "foods you don't really need teeth to eat. That is why waffles are so enticing. You make them yourself with a waffle iron and then just stick them in a Ziploc." She also likes pretzels with peanut butter, plain boiled red potatoes with salt, peanut butter and jelly on whole wheat bread or crackers, sliced apples with peanut butter, grapes, Rice Krispies Treats, and gummy bears. At La Ruta, a three-day stage race in Costa Rica that is billed as the toughest mountain bike race on the planet, with 250 miles and 20,000 feet of climbing, Harrison says, "The big challenge is putting calories in without upsetting your stomach in the heat. The first year I raced it I just used [an energy powder] in my water bottles and electrolytes in pill form. My stomach started getting upset towards the midway point of the first day, and I ate boiled potatoes. It seems to me that my stomach shuts down the hotter it gets. At first I can use Gatorade watered down and I count that for my calories, but the hotter it gets I just need plain water."

Both Harrison and Curiak are extreme athletes. They have extreme appetites. (Not to be confused with the sport of extreme eating.) For those on moderately paced weekend rides, certain energy and hydration requirements ensure maximum performance and muscle recovery.

"We're really just big bags of fluid—our blood contains about 50 percent water," observes Fred Matheny, an experienced competitive cyclist who is the cofounder of the popular online site www.roadbikerider.com. "Because water helps keep us cool, a loss of only 11 percent of our body-weight as sweat means a significant loss of speed and endurance. I know you've heard it before—drink, drink, drink! But it's amazing how few cyclists heed this advice." There is also only enough muscle fuel (glycogen) for a couple of hours of hard cycling. For everything from century rides to multiday tours, Matheny suggests these useful, time-tested tips:

- *Enjoy the last supper.* Eat aggressively the night before a long ride to cram your muscles with glycogen by morning. Emphasize carbs—pasta, vegetables, bread, whole grains, and fruit.
- *Don't skip breakfast.* Cycling's smooth pedaling motion means you can eat just before a long ride without risking stomach upset. Fill the tank. Cycling consumes about 40 calories per mile, or 4,000 calories in a century ride.
- *Pre-ride meal.* Three hours before the start, eat about 60 grams of carbohydrate if you're an average-sized woman, 80 to 100 if you're a man. (Cereal, skim milk, a banana, and a bagel with jam equals about 90 grams of carbs.) Many riders find that adding some protein and fat, like scrambled eggs or an omelet, keeps their stomach satisfied longer.
- *Pedal, chew, repeat.* Eat 20 grams of carbs every 30 minutes while riding, the equivalent of half an energy bar, several fig bars, or half a banana. Most organized rides have aid stations every 20 miles or so, but always carry food, fluid, and cash for a 7-Eleven stop. A hydration backpack jammed with Powerbars is a must on unsupported rides.

- **Prehydrate.** Fluids are as important as food. Drink at least eight big glasses of water the day before the ride. If you don't, your performance and comfort may plummet by mile 50. Most people are chronically dehydrated becuse they simply don't drink enough water. Keep a bottle on your desk and sip all day. Also, prehydrate the day of the ride. During the hour before the start, sip 16 ounces of a sports drink.

- **Drink before you're thirsty.** Your body's sensation of thirst lags behind your need for liquid, so grab your bottle every 15 minutes and take a couple of big swallows (about four ounces). Most riders generally need one big bottle (16 to 20 ounces) per hour, depending on conditions—temperature, intensity of the ride, and body size.

- **Hydrate after the ride.** No matter how much fluid you drink while riding, in hot weather you'll finish the ride depleted. Your stomach doesn't empty fast enough to keep up with the demand.

- **Weigh yourself before and after the ride.** Compare the figures. If you've lost weight, drink 20 ounces of fluid for each pound of body weight you're down. Keep drinking until your weight has returned to normal and your urine is pale and plentiful. Rehydrating is especially vital during multiday rides. If you get a little behind each day, by the end of the week you'll be severely dehydrated, feeling lousy, and riding poorly.

- **Restore sodium levels.** Those white stains on your clothing and helmet straps after a hot ride come from the salt that you sweat out. It needs to be replaced. Low sodium levels are associated with increased incidence of cramps. Heavy sodium losses lead to **hyponatremia**, the potentially life-threatening condition that affected John Rodham in La Ruta. Your sports drink should contain at least 100 mg of sodium per 8 ounces (check the label). It may also help to salt your food when you're riding frequently in hot weather.

- **Eat for tomorrow.** Muscles replace glycogen better if you consume carbohydrate immediately after riding. So within 15 minutes of getting off the bike, eat or drink 60 grams of carbohydrate if you're an average-sized woman or 80 to 100 grams if you're an average male. **Remember the carbohydrate window and the 4 to 1 ratio.**

• A BRIEF LOOK AT • OUR NATIONAL TASTE BUDS

Let's step back in time to see why we eat the kind of foods we now do. Long before the discovery of the wheel, humans were searching to improve a diet that paralleled shifts with changing living and climatic conditions. Our diet witnessed a radical change when our ancestors migrated from the African savanna—and a meal plan that depended on hunting and gathering for sustenance. The move to other regions eventually developed into farm-based grain economies. In fact, there is a modern dietary trend—the Caveman Diet—that attempts to mimic the pre–grain eating habits of the Fred Flintstones.

BIKE FOR LIFE

Hydration vs. Hyper-Hydration: Water Ain't Everything

JOHN Rodham's near-death experience at the 1997 La Ruta race (see the anecdote at the beginning of this chapter) occurred not from being severely dehydrated, as you might think from the race's tropical locale, but just the opposite—he was *hyper-hydrated.* He had developed a once-rare but increasingly common condition among extreme endurance athletes called hyponatremia, or "water intoxication."

Like most of us, Rodham replaced lost fluids by religiously slurping water from a hydration backpack, but neglected to replace another crucial substance lost through sweat: salt. Salt is made of sodium and chloride, the electrolytes in sports replenisher drinks that help the body distribute water essential for the effective functioning of muscles and organs. Skip your electrolytes in an hour ride, and it's no big deal; but do it in challenging, all-day endurance events—which can drain one to three quarts of sweat an hour—and you risk dizziness, nausea, cramping, headache, confusion, and disorientation. If electrolyte depletion is severe enough, there's brain swelling, which can lead to a coma.

Counterintuitively, hyponatremia has been exacerbated by the ubiquitous hydration pack. If you occasionally fill it with Gatorade and nibble on salty snacks like pretzels or potato chips, especially on long rides, hyper-hydration won't be an issue. Even adding one teaspoon of salt to a quart of water may

"Following a prehistoric, or Neolithic, diet is simple. If a food is perfectly edible as it grows in the wild, it's okay," says Ray Audette, author of *NeaderThin.* "But the diet forbids foods that require man's intervention to grow or make edible. So, you can hunt, gather, or buy fruits, vegetables, meats, fish, roots, berries, eggs, legumes, and nuts. But throw away your alcoholic drinks, refined sugar and such mainstays of the modern diet as potatoes, wheat, corn, rice, beans, soy, peanuts, milk, and cheese."

The contemporary nutritional message is to eat like your physically active ancestors, according to the online nutritional site www.welljournal.com. "What's so new and improved about a high-fat, high-protein diet—up to 30 percent protein and a whopping 40 percent fat each day? Not much, and that's the appeal. Paleolithic proponents contend that agriculture, domestication, and industrialization have introduced foods that man isn't created to handle."

"Our over-reliance on grain-based nutrition is especially problematic," says exercise physiologist Loren Cordain, PhD, author of *The Paleo Diet.* "The best path for avoiding diabetes, heart disease, and other diseases of civilization," he says, "is to follow the hunter-gatherer diet that mankind spent two million years adapting to." Other beneficial prehistoric habits include eating leafy vegetables, low-sugar fruits, and constant grazing instead of bingeing.

Before modern scientific measurements were available to athletes and coaches, diets were pursued through instinct, myth, and faith. In ancient Greece, for example, Olympic athletes ate the meat of oxen for strength in the belief they could gain those qualities if they ate them. It was only about a century ago that chemists were able to break down food into major components of

carbohydrates, protein, and fat, while measuring caloric energy input and output accurately; the modern era of diet and nutrition was born. During the last two decades sports nutrition has come out of the (kitchen) closet, with supermarket aisles jammed with bars, drinks, powders, gels, and supplements, and diet books like *The South Beach Diet, SugarBuster,* and Barry Sears's *The Zone* series on the *New York Times* best-sellers list.

The intensive athletic quest for the golden meal ticket has spawned a mini-industry of claims and counterclaims. New studies debunk old ones. Sports nutritionists debate conflicting dietary regimens and theories with the fierce partisan flavor and fervor formerly reserved for politics and religion. The two overriding questions involve quantity and quality: (1) What is the ideal dietary breakdown of carbs, protein, and fats? (2) Just what kind of carbs, protein, and fats should they be?

How we, as athletes, think about nutrition often mirrors popular social and cultural trends. While most athletes watch what they eat (we hope), the nation's waistline continues to expand—61 percent of Americans are overweight. Sales of diet products and weight loss programs total $33 billion a year. Talk about a growth industry! Fifty million Americans are currently trying to lose weight. Our nation has a long history when it comes to the weight loss merry-go-round. Who's to blame? Some say the government is partially at fault. Take for example the U.S. Department of Agriculture food pyramid, rolled out in 1992, which showed fats, oils, and sweets at its tip, broadening to grains and cereals at the base. Its dietary guidelines advised daily consumption of six to eleven servings of bread, cereal, rice, and

also stave off hyponatremia and help you with gastric emptying. So how much should you drink?

For athletes, water is often the most common nutritional deficiency. Sweating leads to dehydration, and the result is poorly functioning muscles, blood, and organs. Even a deficiency of less than 1 percent can bring on signs and symptoms of dysfunction. At 5 percent dehydration—between six and eight pounds of fluid—your body begins to deteriorate. As your blood thickens, the heart works harder since your natural cooling mechanisms of sweating and evaporation are impaired.

A young male athlete's body is typically 60 percent water and may contain 42 kg (more than 92 pounds) of water. A female athlete's body is slightly less aqueous at 50 percent of total weight. Approximately two-thirds of this water is in the intracellular areas—predominantly the muscles, with most of the remaining one-third in extra-cellular compartments in the blood.

Don't wait for your sense of thirst to signal that it's time to drink. Thirst is sensed only after dehydration has started. More importantly, once you are dehydrated, it may take as much as 48 hours to properly rehydrate. This is why so many athletes, unknowingly, are in a constant state of dehydration. Just make sure you top off your electrolytes as well.

pasta; two to three servings of meat, poultry, fish, dry beans, eggs, and nuts; and sparing consumption of fats, oils, and sweets. An outspoken critic of this eating plan, Harvard scientist Dr. Walter Willett, a leading U.S. nutrition researcher and author of *Eat, Drink, and Be Healthy,* believed that the pyramid placed too much emphasis on red meat and grouped too many types of carbohydrates together, while not placing enough emphasis on nuts, beans, and healthy oils like canola, olive, and soy, which have positive health effects. He recommends eating more vegetables, fish, poultry, and eggs. Still, politics play a big role in how the government built its pyramid, with the meat, dairy, and sugar industries influencing what the pyramid ends up looking like on our cereal box. And perhaps in a concessionary measure to our obesity epidemic, the USDA announced in July 2004 that the food pyramid is being overhauled.

"Ours is a culture where a meal is measured by how fast it's served or how many grams of fat it may contain. We ignore, to our detriment, the wonderful social aspects of a long leisurely lunch that one experiences in other parts of the world. We have become, in the midst of our astounding abundance, the world's most anxious eaters," wrote Michael Pollan in a *New York Times* essay aptly titled "The National Eating Disorder." "*How* we eat, and even how we feel about eating, may in the end be just as important as *what* we eat. So we've learned to choose our foods by the numbers (calories, carbs, fats, RDAs, price, whatever), relying more heavily on our reading and computational skills than upon our senses. Indeed, we've lost all confidence in our senses of taste and smell, which can't detect the invisible macro- and

micronutrients science has taught us to worry about, and which food processors have become adept at deceiving anyway."

The idea of just how and what we eat also affects the dining habits of athletes. In fact, there is a dietary correlation betwen world-class athletics and illness. As part of its Athens Olympics coverage, the *New York Times* reported that while athletes normally cart around very little body fat, sickness was "foremost in the athletes' minds," according to Professor Peter Fricker, the medical director of the Australian Olympic team in Athens. "The Australians, long at the forefront in sports science with their Institute of Sport in Canberra, have done extensive research on athletes' immune systems. 'There's no doubt that athletes are playing hard enough to suppress immune defenses,' Fricker said. 'The normal population in Australia expects to get between three and four upper respiratory infections each year. But if you look at groups of elite athletes, about 15 percent of those athletes can have six or seven or more, up to even eleven or twelve. They seem to get more vulnerable as they train harder.'"

A common misperception is that forced reduction of body fat is a good thing. "The truth is that body fat, as a percentage of a person's weight, is influenced more by the body's water content than by any other single factor," writes Philip Maffetone in *Eating for Endurance.* "Studies show that restricting calories as a means of losing body weight can result in diminished athletic performance. In addition, athletes who restrict energy intake to promote weight loss can also decrease bone density."

Still, excess weight works against you if you are a cyclist, especially if you enjoy being the fastest hill-climber on your weekend group ride. Everyone knows what happened after Lance Armstrong dropped amost 20 pounds after his cancer comeback, thereby significantly reducing his upper-body muscle mass; he gained Superman-like hill-climbing ability.

The point here is this: to be fit is one thing, but to be so obsessively fit that a rigidly followed diet can be your undoing is something you should avoid. Listen to your body. Are you often getting sick? Are your training injuries increasing? Do you feel listless or unmotivated? In the give-and-take between between gym-honed aesthetics and healthy athleticism—just how many cut, carved, and chiseled bodybuilders do you ever see running or biking?—there are certain nutritional responsibilities associated with a lifetime of biking, which means striking a balance between proper eating and society's cult of thinness. You want to be fit and you want to be healthy; they are not neccessarily synonymous.

The Ten Commandments of Cooking

"WITH proper nutrition and training your endurance could—and should—actually improve well into your 40s," says Philip Maffetone in *Eating for Endurance.* "Eating habits directly affect your fitness."

Maffetone says that how you prepare food affects digestion, absorption of nutrients, hormone balance, and energy production. An ideal diet would include lots of raw and uncooked foods (loaded with nutrients), no hydrogenated oils (they create problems for the body), and no ground meat (laden with bacteria). That and more can be found in what he calls his Ten Commmandments of Cooking, below. There's no downside to healthy eating, he says; it's not only better for your body, but tastes better, too.

1. **Avoid hydrogenated and trans fats:** Hydrogenated or partially hydrogenated fats such as margarine or shortening, and highly processed vegetable oils aren't good for your body, according to Maffetone. "They interfere with normal metabolism and cholesterol balance, and promote inflammation," he says. "Stick with high-quality, unsalted 'sweet' butter." Not surprisingly, food companies are now making much-publicized moves to eliminate transfats and hydrogenated fats from a wide range of products, even potato chips.
2. **Don't cook in vegetable oil:** "Heating the oil causes unhealthy chemical changes in vegetable oil, including converting it to archidonic acid (found in saturated fat) and increasing the amount of **free radicals**," says Maffetone. Instead of sauteeing your food in oil, steam your vegetables, bake or broil meats and fish, or pan-fry using the fat naturally found in the food. Also use butter and olive oil, stable monosaturated fats that don't break down when heated.
3. **Steam with a teeny bit of water:** "Many vitamins and minerals are lost in the water in which foods are cooked," says Maffetone. "Steam rather than boil, and drink the water—as tea or soup to reclaim the minerals."
4. **Don't overcook:** "Many nutrients are unstable in heat," says Maffetone. "Take glutamine, the amino acid; if you cook a steak medium, you lose half the glutamine. If you cook it well-

BIKE FOR LIFE

done, almost all the glutamine is destroyed. When fish is cooked, valuable EPA fatty acid is destroyed." The rule: the rarer, the rawer, the better. No worries about hygiene, either, considering that bacteria, found only on the surface in solid (non-ground) meat, is killed quickly by heat. Part of our diet should be raw. EPA, a fatty acid in fish, gets destroyed when cooked. Raw fish is ideal.

5. **Use whole foods, not processed:** Raw foods are jammed with disease-fighting bio- and phyto-nutrients such as bioflavenoids and vitamin E that are often destroyed in cooking and processing

6. **Avoid ground meat:** Bacteria, initially only on the surface of solid meat, becomes intermixed throughout with grounding, says Maffetone. To kill all the bacteria in a hamburger, order it well-done. Outbreaks usually are traced to ground beef.

7. **Use fresh foods first, then frozen, and canned as a last resort:** "Same story," says Maffetone. "The more the processing, the more the nutrients lost. Lots of nutrients are lost sitting around. Eat all food quickly. An old, sour orange means the natural chemicals inside are breaking down."

8. **Have raw food at each meal:** Avocado, soft-cooked egg yolk, tomato, greens, radishes, and carrots come packed with the stuff nature gave them.

9. **Use coarse sea salt:** "Traditional sodium chloride has other ingredients in it—even sugar sometimes," says Maffetone. "Sea salt has a better balance of minerals—and the best chefs use it because it tastes better. And since we evolved from the sea, you can argue that it is more compatible with the body."

10. **The presentation of a meal is important:** "Making the environment lovely and dishes healthy, tasty, and attractive to the eye prepares the brain and the rest of the nervous system to digest," says Maffetone. "It's like foreplay in sex—preparing the body for what's to come. Good music, known to add to the enjoyment of a meal, actually helps you digest better and get more nutrients out of it."

•1•
CARBOHYDRATES
Don't Cut them

In the last several years, carbs have taken a beating, a result of the commercial popularity associated with the Atkins diet, a yummy regimen rich in protein and tasty fats. But two recent studies published in the *Annals of Internal Medicine* found that the Atkins low-carbohydrate diet outperforms traditional low-fat diets in the short term but offers no weight loss advantage after one year. Furthermore, an over-reliance on a low-carb diet can overtax the kidneys and contribute to minor health problems like constipation, muscle cramps, diarrhea, general weakness, and headaches due to a lack of fruit, vegetables, and whole grains. And because all that protein produces ketosis, which triggers bad breath, it's probably a good reason not to hang out with Atkins dieters anyway.

Dr. Arne Astrup, a Danish obesity expert interviewed by the *New York Times*, says normal body function requires 150 grams

of carbs per day—five times what some Atkins dieters get. When you add vigorous exercise, like cycling, the issue becomes carb addition, not carb restriction. Cyclists need to figure out how to get more carbs, not less. But not all carbs are created equal; there are good carbs and bad carbs. There are simple carbs that cause a sudden yo-yoing spike in your blood sugar for instant energy. Those candy bars, fruit juices, and soft drinks in the company lunchroom are bad carbs. And there are good, complex carbs (for example, grapefruit, peanuts, lentils, peaches, barley) that have a less errratic and more sustained energy effect with a less dramatic rise in insulin levels. "Individuals need to understand that healthy carbs such as vegetables, fruits, beans, and whole grains (eaten in proper amounts) are essential components of a well-balanced diet," says Dr. Cedric Bryant, chief exercise physiologist for the American Council on Exercise. "The consumption of these healthy carbs has been linked to a reduced risk of heart disease, certain types of cancer, and a number of other chronic ailments."

To CLOSELY EXAMINE the precise role that carbs play in the lives of cyclists, *Bike for Life* asked world-champion adventure racer Ian Adamson to share his bike- and trail-tested insights. Few people combine academic and real-world knowledge of sports nutrition like Adamson, who has competed at the highest levels in endurance events ranging from a couple of hours to a month in duration. A world-record holder in marathon kayaking and named by RailRiders Adventure Clothing as "the toughest man on the planet," Adamson lives in Boulder, Colorado, and has a master's degree in sports science.

Q: How does the body turn carbs into blood sugar into energy?

Ian Adamson: Carbohydrates are processed in the digestive tract and converted through various biochemical processes into blood sugar (glucose). If the blood sugar is not used to fuel the brain and/or working muscles, then it is stored in the muscles and liver as glycogen. Protein and fat are also converted to blood sugar but much more slowly and at a higher energy cost through more complex processes.

Q: What's the difference between simple and complex carbs?

IA: Simple carbohydrates have a simple molecular structure. The most basic carbohydrate is glucose, followed by fructose (fruit sugar), lactose (milk sugar), etc. At the other end of the spectrum are the complex carbohydrates that make up the starches of rice, grains, beans, and other foods. Simple carbohydrates are easier for the body to metabolize; they have a high calorie yield (to the working muscles) and generally have a higher glycemic index. Complex carbohydrates are generally slower to metabolize and (generally) have a lower glycemic index, and are digested to blood glucose at a slower release rate. Energy food formulators try to balance simple and complex carbohydrates to acheive a graduated release of carbohydrate into the body's system. One challenge here is that some complex (and some simple) carbohydrates can cause gastric distress in some people.

Q: Do men and women have different carb requirements?

IA: Women generally require less volume in carbohydrate than men, but this is due mainly to differences in muscle mass. Both men and women require the same percentage of carbohydrate in their diets depending on physical output or training load.

Q: How important is body fat, and eating fatty foods, in relationship to carbs in providing energy?

IA: Interestingly, stored body fat (adipose tissue) is an important source of energy for humans at low heart rates. At rest, it is the primary souce of energy, but this decreases as energy output (and commensurately heart rate) increases until it is essentially nil beyond the **anaerobic threshold**. It is important here to distinguish between stored fat and dietary fat. Dietary fat has a very low yield as an energy source for exercise and becomes a problem as exercise intensity increases. The complexity of the metabolic pathways to convert dietary fat to glucose means that it is slow and difficult to digest. Consequently, high-fat intake while exercising can cause gastric distress. The function of fat in the diet is to provide a vehicle for absorbing fat-soluble vitamins, for example vitamin E, and to add palatability to foods. Fat also has a high energy density, so it is useful for providing calories in very cold environments or when caloric output is extremely high. Human physiology is remarkably adaptable and can cope with a dramatic change in diet; however, it can't overcome basic biological constraints. Blood sugar is the *only* fuel that can be readily utilized by the working muscles, no matter what it is derived from.

Q: For someone's first century ride, what would be a sensible eating plan, before, during, and after?

IA: A century ride is a substantial endurance challenge for most people, and will entail anything upward of five hours or more to complete. Being in the saddle for this length of time will require a full tank of glycogen and frequent ingestion of carbohydrate during the ride. The first thing is to ensure a good taper, or reduced training volume, for the week prior to the event, while maintaining a high carbohydrate diet. This will ensure your glycogen supplies are topped up, providing a significant fuel reserve. Each glycogen molecule is stored in the body along with two water molecules, so it is common to add several pounds of body weight in this period. During the ride a combination of endurance sports drink, like GU2O (formulated for long endurance), and high carbohydrate snacks should be consumed. Sports drinks help maintain adequate hydration, which is of primary importance in long endurance, and the carbohydrate provides readily available fuel. Drinks should be on the diluted side to aid in palatability and absorption, especially in hot environments, and should be taken at regular intervals. In mild conditions this might be four to six ounces every 15 minutes. Small portions of carbohydrate-rich food should be consumed as well, with as much as can be comfortably eaten every half hour or so. This will generally be about half an energy bar (up to 100 grams of carbohydrate). Diet is very important post-event to aid in recovery— refueling, tissue maintenance, and repair. It is best to consume a high carbohydrate drink within 20 minutes after the finish of the ride, and also some complete protein in a well-balanced meal to provide vitamin and mineral replacement.

Q: What are the best types of food to eat during aerobic exercise?

IA: Certain foods cause gastric distress while exercising, and this is due primarily to the ability of the digestive tract in absorbing (or not) its contents. As exercise

MEALS ON WHEELS

load increases, progressively more blood is shunted between the working muscles, heart, and lungs and away from the gut. This lowers the ability of the body to process food and fluid and inhibits gastric emptying. The more complex the metabolic processes in digesting a food, the more gastric distress it will cause. Fat is the worst, followed by protein and various high-fiber complex foods.

Some people have a sensitivity to fructose and lactose even though these are relatively simple sugars. On the other end of the spectrum, a solution of about 5 percent sodium chloride (table salt) and 5 percent glucose has been shown to be most effectively absorbed during highly aerobic exercise.

Q: What about the glycemic index of certain foods? How does this affect the metabolic process?

IA: The glycemic index measures the speed at which a food is converted to blood sugar. High glycemic foods are fast (sugar, fruit, candy bars, sodas), low glycemic foods are slow (bananas, rice, grains). You may choose high glycemic foods if your blood sugar is very low or you are in a bonk, and low-glycemic index foods if you want more sustained energy and you can handle the additional gastric demand (in general, low glycemic foods are harder to digest.)

Attention Vegetarians: How to Avoid That "Deficit"

WITH rising health fears associated with mad cow disease, E. coli, salmonella, and listeria contamination of meat and poultry products, coupled with increased revulsion at how cattle—a "food delivery system"—are penned, fed, drugged, and slaughtered, vegetarianism is gaining adherents—and not just in green meccas like Berkeley, Cambridge, Madison, and Boulder. Fourteen million Americans call themselves vegetarians. But vegetarian athletes are especially at risk due to certain deficits in their diets.

Does a vegetarian diet leave some important nutrients out? Do vegetarians need a booster shot of meat once in a while—or at least a booster shot of supplements? Most agree that protein and minerals like zinc and iron, all found in important quantities in meat, are necessary for a healthy diet. Below, we examine whether these non-meat-linked nutritional deficits can be filled, as total vegetarians maintain, with beans, pasta, and rice, or require more extreme measures.

Deficit: Protein

Besides eliminating fat and cholesterol, a meatless diet reduces protein, which is loaded with essential amino acids the body uses to repair its tissues. That is critical for cyclists and endurance athletes, who are constantly stressing their muscles. There are many ways to make up the protein gap, depending on your brand of vegetarianism:

▶ *Chicken, fish, and dairy (milk and eggs):* These non-beef animal products pack as much protein as red meat, supplying all the essential amino acids you need to make new proteins for the body. But strict vegetarians technically won't touch a drumstick, and vegans (who ban any animal derivative) won't do dairy.

► *Combining grains and legumes (for example, the peanut butter sandwich):* Vegetable sources of protein lack some of the amino acids the body needs for renewal, unless you eat grains (whole-grain wheat, barley, rice, quinoa, amaranth, kasha, spelt, oats, rye, corn, millet, kamut, etc.) with legumes (chickpeas, black beans, lima beans, pinto beans, lentils, black–eyed peas, split peas, etc.) every day. Find them in vegetables and whole grains–whole-wheat bread and whole-grain rice. Eat both together or at least on the same day.

And eat a lot: For a 160-pound sedentary man to get his daily requirement of 8 grams of protein per kilogram (3.66 grams per pound) of body weight, about 60 grams, he must consume 4.5 cups of pasta, three cups of broccoli, and 1.5 cups of tomato sauce. Athletes, who burn protein as a form of energy during exercise, need nearly double that–about 1.2 to 1.6 grams per kilogram of body weight, which adds up to about 80 to 110 protein grams for a 150-pound person. It's easy for them to get there with meat; a lean, broiled 4-ounce sirloin steak has 31.3 grams of protein. A non-meat diet requires a lot of eating unless you include . . .

► *Soybeans:* This super-legume is the only veggie that can go head-to-head with milk and meat, offering comparable protein quality and amino acids. It doesn't need to be combined with anything. In addition, soybeans contain antioxidant phytochemicals that help protect against cancer and heart disease–ailments, not surprisingly, that are not nearly as prevalent in Asian countries with soybean-rich diets that include tofu, tempeh, and soy milk.

Deficit: Iron

Red meat is a great source for iron, which is essential for preventing anemia, particularly in women, who lose iron through menstruation. The RDA of iron is 10–15 mg a day. A lean, 3.5-ounce steak has 3.5 mg. A similar portion of dark turkey or chicken has 3.1 mg.

While vegetarian fare isn't hurting for iron–firm tofu (10 mg per 3.5 ounce) and fortified breakfast cereal (12–28 mg), plus lentils, kale, collard greens, and dried fruit lead the pack–plant-based iron isn't as well-absorbed as the "heme" iron of animal foods. One sure-fire way to increase iron absorption is to drink orange juice and eat lots of fruit; their vitamin C aids iron absorption.

Deficit: Zinc

Zinc, needed for protein synthesis, wound healing, and proper immunity, is also harder for the body to absorb when it comes from plant sources rather than from meat. The RDA for zinc is 12 mg a day. Four ounces of beef has 4 mg, fowl 2 mg. Corn and wheat germ, fortified cereals, beans, nuts, tofu, and other soy products have it in decent quantities, but to be safe, you need a booster shot. Dairy foods and a 10 mg zinc supplement will do the trick.

Deficit: Calcium

Women need at least 1,200 mg a day of calcium, which builds strong bones and prevents osteoporosis. If you consume dairy products, don't worry—a couple of cups of milk or yogurt will suffice. If dairy is out, try calcium-fortified soy milk and dark green, leafy vegetables like broccoli, collard greens, and kale. Easiest route: calcium supplements.

Deficit: Vitamin B_{12}

Long-term deficiencies of vitamin B_{12}, found only in red meat, poultry, shellfish, and dairy products, can cause anemia and nerve damage. This essential vitamin keeps blood cells healthy and maintains the covering around nerve fibers. You need at least two micrograms of this nutrient every day, an amount available from 8 ounces of skim milk. Athletes may need double this, since they consume more calories.

Unlike calcium and others, a B_{12} deficiency can't always be made up with dairy. Milk and eggs contain B_{12}, but vegetarians who eat them often still have low levels of the vitamin. If you've cut dairy, it's no easier getting adequate B_{12}, even though they are many good non-meat sources: fortified cereals, fortified soy, rice, nut milks, and nutritional yeast. Fermented vegetable products, such as miso and tempeh, contain some B_{12} because of the fermenting bacteria.

Best bet if you've cut all dairy products from your diet: a daily 2-microgram supplement of vitamin B_{12}, especially since it can be more easily absorbed than B_{12} in food.

Q: What are your favorite carbs in competition and why?

IA: For short races (under 12 hours) I drink GU2O and eat Balance Bars and GUs. For longer races I start to include more whole foods like sandwiches, breakfast bars, plain water, and salty snacks (chips, nuts).

Q: What is the correct proportion of carbs in a diet for a cyclist? For someone who rides 50, 100 miles a week? How about 300?

IA: Active endurance athletes need a high proportion of carbohydrate in their diet, primarily to provide fuel for their increased energy expenditure. For moderate endurance, 50 miles a week of cycling, at least 60 percent by calories of carbohydrate needs to be consumed, 65 percent at 100 miles per week, and 70 to 80 percent at 300 miles. Adequate dietary carbohydrate is critial to raise muscle glycogen to high levels in preparation for the next day's endurance competition or hard training session. During the 24 hours prior to hard exercise, athletes should consume 7–12 grams of carbohydrate per kilogram of body weight [1 kilogram equals about 2.2 pounds, so 15.4–26.4 grams of carbohydrate per pound of body weight]. During the 24 hours prior to a moderate or easy day of exercise, 5–7 grams of carbohydrate per kilogram of body weight should be consumed[3] [11–15.4 grams per pound]. Consequently, the percentage of carbohydrate in the diet should be increased as length and intensity of exercise are increased.

Q: Are there any inherent risks with a high-protein, high-fat diet for an endurance athlete?

IA: High-fat and/or high-protein diets are extremely detrimental to endurance performance and are well known in the scientific and medical communities to cause long-term health damage. Kidney damage, elevated cholesterol levels, loss of calcium, and atherosclerosis (clogged arteries) are some of the known risks. See www.atkins dietalert.org for more information. The American Heart Association, American Dietetic Association, and the American Kidney Fund have all published statements warning about the various dangers associated with low-carbohydrate, high-protein diets. For endurance athletes like cyclists, the immediate effects are lack of fuel for the muscles—effectively a chronic bonk.

Q: Do carbs have a significant role in post-workout muscle recovery? What about protein? Or should I stick to complex carbs?

IA: Post-workout muscle recovery is aided firstly by fluids (rehydration), then carbohydrate replacement (to replace blood sugar and glycogen stores), protein (for tissue repair), and vitamins and minerals (repair and maintenance). Complex carbohydrates are more slowly metabolized than simple carbs in general (related to glycemic index, more below), which helps attenuate blood sugar spikes. At rest, complex, high-fiber carbs are more healthful than simple ones. Complete protein should be consumed, since all nine amino acids need to be together for their bio-availability for metabolism. This is particularly relevant for vegetarians, who don't eat any animal protein. Complete protein can come from various sources including all meats (beef, chicken, fish, eggs, dairy, etc.) or botanical sources like whey and soy. Most protein powders contain a mixture of soy, whey, milk, and egg protein isolates combined with various vitamins and minerals. No protein source is better than

another if it is complete—that is, it contains all nine essential amino acids. Consuming adequate protein is a huge challenge for vegans, since they don't eat most natural and readily available sources of complete protein. Combinations of various vegetable sources of protein can yield all amino acids, but it is a lot of work and volume-eating. Rice and beans eaten together in large quantities can provide a complete protein meal. The short answer to the efficacy of absorption of protein is that unprocessed sources are preferable, since our digestive systems have evolved to readily digest them—meat, that is. I recommend eating a piece of meat, chicken, fish, or eggs. Formulated protein powders are good, but they also tend to expand dramatically when mixed and can cause gastric discomfort; try mixing half a cup of protein powder like MET-Rx with a cup of water in a blender and watch what happens.

Q: How can one weigh the competing claims and benefits of all those energy bars, gels, and powders that promise the latest and greatest in carb energy?

IA: The solution to figuring out which energy food to use lies with the user's palate and a few essential ingredients. Your choice should include fluids, readily metabolizable carbohydrate (simple sugars), and some electrolytes (salt) for training and competition, and fluids, complex carbohydrate, protein, vitamins, and minerals for recovery. As distances get longer, your nutrition choices should include more solid and everyday foods, like sandwiches and meals. As distance increases, palatability becomes an issue. It is virtually impossible to consume high-carbohydrate foods exclusively (especially simple sugars like sports drinks) for more than a few hours. Sugar coats your gums and teeth and over a few days leads to dental problems like sore gums and mouth ulcers, making eating difficult and painful. Meals generally provide a balanced diet, replacing electrolytes, carbohydrates, protein, vitamins, and fat.

·2·
FAT
Don't Fear It

Let's now turn our chat to fat—an integral, if often overlooked, part of the athlete's diet. Fat has a critical function here—physiologically, hormonally, and nutritionally. But first, here are some broad facts regarding fat.

▶ *Fat's goal is survival:* The body's largest endocrine organ is fat tissue. The fat cell's main job is to store enough excess calories as fat to keep a normal size person alive without eating for 90 days.

▶ *A "fat" fat cell is dangerous:* The fat cell of an obese person can swell to three times its normal size, and a swollen fat cell retards the body's production of insulin, which is the hormone that instructs the muscles to burn energy and fat cells to store the excess amount. The pancreas must work harder to produce more insulin, which in turn can lead to insulin resistance, artery damage, and inflammation, because the fat cells are leaking fat and proteins into the blood system.

▶ *Beware trans fats:* The U.S. Food and Drug Administration in 2004 ordered food manufacturers to list trans fats alongside saturated fats on product labels (chief culprits are margarine, chips, cookies, and fries) starting January 1, 2006. Some trans

fats occur naturally in beef, lamb, and dairy products. But most are created when hydrogen is added to liquid vegetable oil to create solid margarine or shortening. Both trans fat and saturated fats, which are prevalent in meat, raise blood levels of bad cholesterol. But trans fats also reduce levels of good cholesterol, increasing the risk of heart disease even more. They also increase blood levels of triglycerides, the chemical form in which most fat exists in food as well as in the body.

Trans fats accounted for about 0.5 to 2 percent of daily calories for Europeans. That compares with an estimated 2.6 percent for Americans, according to the U.S. Food and Drug Administration. Mediterranean countries were at the lowest end of the scale, reflecting their use of olive and other vegetable oils rather than spreads.

▶ *Some fat is very good:* Until recently, fat had a Rodney Dangerfield reputation among athletes. It got no respect. But that should only apply to "bad" fats like saturated fat and trans fatty acids. "Good" fats (oils and spreads of almonds, avocado, nuts, and olives, or cold-water fish like salmon) can help promote your immune system, ward off common infections, and stem inflammation. They also aid in the manufacture of hormones, such as testosterone and estrogen. Morever, fat is the body's best source of energy. "Theoretically, even the skinniest athlete has enough fat stored to last for forty hours or more at a low intensity without refueling," writes Joe Friel in *The Cyclist Bible*, "but only enough carbohydrates for about three hours at most."

Friel further makes this claim: "After three decades of believing that very high-carbohydrate eating is best for performance, there is now compelling evidence, albeit in early stages, that increasing fat intake while decreasing and properly timing carbohydrate may be good for endurance athletes, especially in events lasting four hours or longer. Several studies reveal that eating a diet high in fat causes the body to preferentially use fat for fuel, and that eating a high-carbohydrate diet results in the body relying more heavily on limited stores of muscle glycogen for fuel."

By the mid-1980s, endurance athletes, particularly triathletes, recognized the value of fat. Six-time Hawaii Ironman winner Mark Allen substantially increased his fat intake. His diet took on a ratio of 30 percent fat, 30 percent protein, and 40 percent

Eat the Clock
Mark Allen on When and What to Ingest

THESE days, long retired from triathlon competition, Mark Allen, continues to spread his nutrition message via his online triathlon-training program at www.markallenonline.com. In the August 2004 issue of *Triathlete*, he outlined fueling basics and key differences in athletes' caloric needs based on exercise time.

Sub-90-minute rides: Short sessions will be affected very little by the calories you take in during the event, according to Allen. "The calories you have stored up as glycogen plus your pre-race meal should get you through with flying colors," he says, adding that "the biggest issue on short rides is water."

Long rides: By two hours, a hammering 160-pound male ripping through 700 calories in an hour will have exhausted his carbohydrate stores and must replace them to keep the engine going. The problem, says Allen, is that "research shows that a person cannot absorb more than 500 calories per hour—and that, over an extended time, the stomach has increasing difficulty breaking down carbohydrates to their simplest form for absorption."

Solutions: (1) *Good aerobic fitness,* which trains your body to take a lot of its calorie needs from stored fats. (2) Ingest *short-chain carbohydrates.*

"The shorter, the better," says Allen, "with glucose being the absolute champagne for the working muscle because it does not need to be broken down to be absorbed. On long rides, that energy bar, rich in complex carbs, might give you cramps and a bloated feeling." In day-long events like the Ironman, Allen recommends sucking on salt tablets, since the "sodium helps activate the secretion of stomach acid which will help absorption going again." First-time century riders should heed this advice.

Above all, Allen believes in one word: experiment. Try different sports drinks and gels on your rides. See which one agrees with your taste buds, digestive system, and how they replenish your energy reserves. Those sweet-tasting bars or drinks with high-fructose content might give you a quick energy boost, but that power surge will quickly taper off and leave you listless again; seek out products with low-glycemic ingredients that might give you a less rapid but more long-lasting, sustained energy effect.

carbohydrates—radically different from conventional wisdom of the day where 70 percent of the diet was prescribed for carbs, 20 percent for protein, and 10 percent or less for fat. Combining weight training with careful training at low aerobic heart rates, which maximized fat burning for energy, Allen nobly embodied the marvels of his dietary approach. In 1996, after he retired, he was hailed by *Outside* magazine as "The Fittest Man in the World."

· 3 ·
PROTEIN
The Muscle Builder

While carbs and fat are necessary for endurance and energy, you need adequate amounts of protein in your diet. Though protein provides only a small amount of energy—up to 15 percent—it serves these vital roles: muscle and tissue repair, growth and maintenance. Protein is a major component of cell structure and vital for enzymes, such as those necessary for the production of anti-inflammatory hormones.

But how much protein should cyclists eat? Daily protein requirements for adults, established by the World Health Organization, are pegged at 0.75 grams per kilogram (2.2 pounds) of body weight for Western diets, but this number tends to be higher for Americans (0.8 grams). (Excess protein is converted to fat and stored. An overabundance of protein may produce metabolic stress on liver and kidney function.)

Because endurance training depletes carb reserves, protein may also become a necessary fuel source for longer workouts. How is this possible? When glycogen supply runs low, the body's amino acids, which are stored in the muscles can be converted to glucose.

When glycogen stores are sufficient, that number can decrease to 5 percent.

"What is most important is that your elevated protein requirements are easily met by a well-planned sports diet," writes Monique Ryan in *Sports Nutrition for Endurance Athletes*. "For endurance athletes consuming enough calories to meet their energy needs, this often translates into increased protein intake. When calories go up, the percentage from protein often remains constant, and the total grams of protein you consume increase. Average protein intake for most endurance athletes range from 70 to 200 grams daily depending on calorie intake."

Beware of protein and amino acid supplements, Ryan warns. Manufacturers' claims "that these products are more reasily digestible and absorbed than protein found in foods is simply false," she says. Your body is well-equipped to handle protein from whole foods by secreting a number of enzymes that renders amimo acid absorption at 90 percent effectiveness."

· SUMMARY ·
A Moveable Feast

Your life on and off the bike should be a moveable feast. Active cyclists will burn enough calories to eat whatever they like—as long as they steer clear of caloric potholes like refined sugar and artery-clogging foods made with trans fatty acids. Assuming a sensible eating plan, diet is an individual matter. Go with your gut, but aim for fruits, vegetables, grains, and healthy snacking throughout the day to avoid irregular sugar mood swings. Don't depend on good ole joe to keep your alert. The caffeine in coffee and Coke may give you an energy boost, but it's a diuretic—it can cause dehydration. Your

Better Med Than Dead: Do or Diet

A study published in the September 22, 2004, issue of the *Journal of the American Medical Association (JAMA)* detailed sufficient evidence that the Mediterranean diet, combined with regular exercise (30 minutes daily), is the key to longevity. For ten years, the study followed 2,300 active elderly Europeans, aged 70 to 90, whose diets emphasized whole grains, fruits, vegetables, legumes, nuts, and olive oil and were low in saturated animal fats, trans fats, and highly processed grains. They died at a rate that was more than 50 percent lower than those who didn't excercise and ate poorly.

The same issue of *JAMA* also cited a study that looked at the Mediterranean diet's cardio-protective benefit, suggesting that it may inhibit inflammation in blood vessels, which is believed to be a major player in heart disease and type 2 diabetes. According to a WebMd (www.my.webmd.com) news report, "Patients at high risk for these diseases who followed the Mediterranean diet for two years showed more improvements in weight loss, blood pressure, cholesterol, and insulin resistance—conditions that promote heart disease—than a similar group placed on a conventional diet. Adherence to the Mediterranean diet was effective in reducing inflammatory blood markers, which have been linked to a high risk of heart disease."

goal is to find a balanced eating plan, that if followed, will improve your health and fitness—and give you the energy you need to ride successfully.

If you are concerned about whether your own diet is providing you with the right nutritional building blocks, consult a health professional, dietician, or pay for a computerized analysis of your diet, available from many online companies, such as NutriAnalysis, which will provide you with a 14-page record. When seeking a personal assessment, pay particular attention to these categories: total calories; percent carbohydrate, protein, and fat; vitamin and mineral levels; amino acid levels; essential fatty acid levels; Omega 3 and Omega 6 fat ratio; percentages of monosaturated, polysaturated, and saturated fat; and amount of fiber.

Although this chapter commmunicates basic dietary rules, we know that nutritional and energy needs differ among individuals. What might work for your riding partner may not work for you. Metabolism and energy needs differ; bodies respond differently to the same food, rendering across-the-board generalizations that spell out exact proportions of carbs, protein, and fat dicey. For example, consider the diets of five accomplished endurance cyclists who *Bike for Life* queried in a survey sent to the membership list of a popular endurance cycling Web site, www.adventurecorps.com. You'd expect similar eating habits amidst this rarefied circle of ultra-marathon riders, all of them male, ranging in age from early thirties to fifties. Each have competed in superlong events like RAAM, the Furnace Creek 508, and double-centuries, but that is where the similarity ends.

Todd Teachout: "I'm pretty bad with nutrition. Dry cereal in the morning, fast food (chicken and beef burgers, salad, fries, onion rings, burritos, pizza sometimes [for lunch], a mix of low-fat, high fiber). Dinner is prepared by wife and stepdaughter with low metabolism so we eat a Weight Watchers–friendly meal. I supplement dinner with cookies and wine or beer. I can no longer digest milk in quart quantities like I used to. On long rides the only thing that worked, somewhat, is a mix of Hammer Nutrition products, with a little Cytomax and a little sea salt. My gut works as long as it stays below 85°F. Above that glands/organs regulating things are very inconsistent. I often experience digestive distress, nausea on events longer than 175 miles. Throwing up about 30 percent of time. Major water loss on 60 percent of long events despite effort to drink. Rarely feel thirsty on rides of any distance."

John Axtell: "I usually eat cereal for breakfast, peanut butter sandwich for lunch, chips, cookies, four pieces of fruit, chicken or fish for dinner. On 100 mile or more rides I use sustained energy. I have a close friend who I usually ride with on Fridays, he eats mostly candy bars and Dr Pepper. I ride about 8,000 miles a year, while he rides over 12,000. We are about the same speed, though I climb much faster. I don't think his diet is helping him."

Dennis Culley: "I'm lucky. I'm still young enough [31] that I can just about eat whatever gets in my way, and not pay for it. But that's also partly because normally my body just craves what's good for it. My wife fixes a wide variety of typical-American high-in-protein foods, but I crave enough carbohydrates to keep my diet balanced. And as for on-the-bike nutrition, I go with Ultra Fuel, a high-calorie drink, so that my hydration and calorie needs are met at the same time."

Tom Hooker: "Nutrition is a matter of individual choice, and so, what is your dietary plan of attack? Keep something in your system, and never overeat. But I may not be the best one to answer this one. I'm very lucky and can stomach almost anything (think billy goat). During Team RAAM, or a 200-mile plus ride, the use of supplements helps. I used Cytomax mixed with a bodybuilding protein powder; trying to find something that tastes good all the time is tough. We also drank a lot of Ensure on RAAM, quick, easy, lots of calories."

Cavett Miller: "I'm definitely in the minority on this one. I'm almost 53, and people are always complimenting me on my physique and appearance, saying I have the body and age of a 30-year-old. I tell them this comes from cycling, God, genes, who knows? But they always want to know what I eat. My response is I have a high-fat, high-protein, high-carb diet. In other words, I eat anything and everything, because cycling keeps my metabolism so high I burn it all. I drink whole milk, bologna sandwiches for lunch, lots of red meat and potatoes for dinner, eggs and sausage for breakfast. But I also eat salads, vegetables, bananas, and apples. A couple of hours after dinner, I usually eat a big bowl of rich ice cream, or a microwave bag of extra butter popcorn, and sometimes both of those. I believe my relatively high fat diet helps in keeping me young looking, although of course the general public can't do this for health reasons. But I also believe God designed the human body for hard work, and since I have a desk job, cycling is my form of hard work."

IN CONCLUDING OUR chapter on nutrition, it is important to appreciate one significant reason why we bike in the first place. As a veteran mountain biker once joked at the start of a 24-hour race, "It's not that I'm a glutton for punishment. It's that my gluttony needs punishing."

High and Dry in Utah: A Dehydration Tale

SIX-hundred miles into a 1,500-mile bike trip from Berkeley, California, to the Grand Canyon and back, we made a mistake. It was July. Me and my old college pal, David Farber from Chicago, the guy who actually introduced me to bicycling several years earlier at the University of Michigan, were angling southeast across the bottom section of Utah, near Zion National Park, where it connects to Arizona. Relying on directions from a local gas station owner, we took one of those ill-advised, Hollywood B-movie shortcuts through a barren swatch of desert landscape. A barely visible squiggly line on the map indicated Utah Hill.

That morning started like a lot of our other mornings—with me going 11 mph while David, a faster cyclist, was miles ahead and far out of sight. The temperature began to climb from the 80s, to the 90s, to the low 100s. It wasn't even high noon. The traffic was nil along this lonesome cracked and potholed road. The climb up Utah Hill was not steep—just a long, steady grind of perhaps seven or eight miles.

It's peculiar how thirst and greed are so intertwined. Impulsively, I had quickly drained my two water bottles, even though the water tasted like hot tea if the tea leaves were made from plastic. Now I was out of water. *Where's the damn summit?* I demanded to know. I continued cycling, but began to feel lightheaded. I stopped and wrapped my head with a T-shirt. Looking over to my right, the landscape was all scrub, gravel, and rocks. This was nature's chewed-up parking lot from hell. And complete silence. It was as if the desert was deliberately mocking me with its hushed stillness that roaringly crashed against my hot skull. Yet I had to keep moving, because salvation would only arrive at the crest of Utah Hill, not before. I rode for several more minutes, feeling increasingly woozy, with my bike weaving erratically since it was impossible to keep a straight line. I was riding like a drunk—what a delicious irony here!—because I needed a drink . . . of water. With my sense of balance almost gone, I was now barely able to keep the bike upright. My best hope was to flag down a passing vehicle. If one would ever come.

Standing in the middle of the road, like a sentry to my uncertain fate, I never once blamed the desert for my weakened, dehydrated state. It had been my idea to take the shortcut in the first place.

About 15 minutes later, an RV came barreling down Utah Hill. I motioned it to stop. Or rather it had to brake, because I wasn't budging from the middle of the road. The water gods had listened to my liquid whispers. I asked the driver if he had any water or juice. As he handed me a plastic container of water, he said, "Your friend, back there, also stopped me and said, 'If you see another cyclist, can you do me a favor and see if he is okay?'"

Recharged and refreshed, I got back on my bike after topping off both water bottles. I wasn't taking chances. With my H_2O mojo back, I powered up the remaining climb like a new man. When I reached the crest of Utah Hill, I saw my friend sitting in some shade.

"I thought you had died back there," he remarked.

"So did I," I replied. *—BK*

John Sinibaldi

HAMMERING TOWARD
ONE HUNDRED

John Sinibaldi is unlike your normal retiree. He's got a full head of mostly dark hair. His eyesight is perfect (although his hearing is slipping in his left ear). He hasn't had a cold or flu since the Nixon administration. He works in his immense garden for hours every day, shoveling dirt, pruning trees, toting jugs of water. He's up at five every morning. He talks fast—and moves fast. He rides a bicycle five days a week, 30 miles per day, 7,000–8,000 miles per year, and can still crank it to 30 mph. In short, John Sinibaldi is what we all want to be when we grow up.

And, oh yeah, there's one more thing: nearly 500 cyclists turned out to ride with him on his birthday in 2003—the year he turned 90.

Sinibaldi, Brooklyn-born, New Jersey-bred, and a resident of St. Petersburg, Florida, since 1975, is the grand old man of American cycling. A member of the 1932 and 1936 Olympic teams, he set a record for the 100K Time Trial of 2:25:09 in 1935 which stood for 50 years before it was broken. After not riding for nearly 30 years, he unretired in his 60s and won 14 national Masters time-trial championships, including 2003, when he rode 12.5 miles in 47 minutes and 8 seconds (16 mph) to win the 85-and-older division at the USA Cycling National Time Trial Championship. He was inducted into the U.S. Cycling Hall of Fame in 1997. His multigenerational riding buddies at the St. Petersburg Bike Club call him "The Legend." Still spry and limber, he can jump into the air and touch his toes—literally jumping for joy.

What is Sinibaldi's secret to a long, active life? Here's what he told Bike for Life's Roy Wallack during their interview on March 9, 2004: Ride your bike like crazy. Hope for good genes (he has two sisters in their 80s). Grow and eat your own vegetables. Eat red meat only when it's on sale. Listen to classical music. Avoid television. Read the newspaper every day and do the crossword puzzle. Go barefoot most of the time. When you find a gear you like, stick with it. And get your rest on the bike while you climb the hills.

I BOUGHT MY first bicycle in 1928, paid $25 for it. It was a secondhand one, but pretty good. I was 14. I never rode a bicycle before in my life, but a friend of mine who rode said, why don't you try it? And I did—and liked it.

They said I was always a good athlete, but I never considered myself that before the bicycle. I was short, undersized—about 5-foot-4. I didn't really become full-grown (5-foot-11) until I was almost 20. But on the bike, it just came. I never got tired, that was one thing. And the others did.

I STARTED SCHOOL in 1918, something like that. But in 1921, my father was laid up in bed, somehow he got better, and then we migrated to Italy. Vice-a-versa. Since I couldn't speak Italian, I lost all my education, and had to repeat grades all over again.

It was right after the war [World War I], and there was no work there. So my father left us to get work. I went to school, but also had to have a job on the side.

Then we came back to the United States, so I started all over again at 12 years old. They put me in 1A school [first grade]. Imagine, me, that age, with all the little kids? Heh! So I never had no education. I went to school two more years, then I quit.

At 14, I lived in Jersey and was working in New York in a factory. I was a laborer.

How could I be an athlete? You couldn't be an athlete at that time unless you went to school, and—you wouldn't believe it, but it's the truth—the only people who finished high school were the ones that their parents either had a business or were well-to-do, like they were doctors. But the poor class never finished school. He quit when he was of age. He was allowed to quit at the age of 14. You couldn't afford to go to school.

Spending $25 for a bike was a lot of money, but I was working in New York, making a big salary. Oh, big! I was making $20 a week moving sheet metal. That was just before the Depression hit. After that, when Roosevelt got elected, they passed what they called the NRA [National Recovery Act], and I was making $13 a week.

Immediate Success

ANY TIME I had time off, it was on a bicycle. It was so much fun. At night, when I came home from work, right on a bicycle. I never owned a car, so I never drove. I took a trolley or subways to work. We lived in Union City—where the Lincoln Tunnel comes out on the Jersey side. Soon as I came home from work, we'd eat, get on the bike, and put in 40 miles. Every night.

We'd go up to the New York state line and back. Lotta hills up there. You go all the way up, then go down to the Hudson River and back. It was like a big rollercoaster. It was nice.

We did it for fun, but it was good training. Soon, we joined the North Hudson Wheelmen and we were training with the pros. They treated us nice. They were human beings—not snobs.

I got into racing when the guys told me to. The club had races on a cinder track.

They found out I was better than the other ones, so they began to give the other ones a head start.

The first entries in my scrapbook are about 1930—the first time I rode big races. I rode two big ones—one in 1930 and one in 1931. I was still underage. I became 18 in 1932. That's when I won the big ones [laughs]. That's when I started winning 'em all. As a matter of fact, the first four races in '32, I won 'em. A 100-mile race, a 62.5-mile race, they had a 50-mile race, and then there was a 25-mile race on Coney Island. That was a big race, what a mob. It was a flat course. Only 25. The shortest race I ever rode.

At that time, cycling was the biggest sport in the United States. Not football, not baseball—cycling was it.

It was the greatest sport. Those six-day races in New York—oh god, it was mobbed every night. A two-man team race that goes on 24-hours a day for six days. They keep going around, one of the two team members on the track. They cover around 2,500 to 3,000 miles in that week.

I never did those, because they were only for pros. I never turned professional, but I used to beat all the pros. All the kids I grew up with became pros, and I beat 'em all [laughs]. The pros made good money. They were paid higher than baseball players. But I enjoyed the sport so much being an amateur, believe it or not, that I never turned pro. There's no fun in pros. It's a money affair there. The fun disappears.

At the time, I was doing piecework; it was manual labor. They wanted me to ride the six-day races. One of my friends, he was a pro, he said, "No, you're too young for that." At which he was right. To turn 18 as a pro, it would've been bad.

People ask me a lot: Any regrets, not

BIKE FOR LIFE

turning pro? No, none, never did, never came to me, no. And every time I look at what I won, I've won it all by myself. Nobody helped me: no combos, nothing. All clean. That's how I rode, and I enjoyed it.

The pros was a bad vibe. And some of them did drugs. There were different drugs than today—what you call "uppers." But they didn't die young. They lived to be an old age. Today, bicycle racers reach 40 and they're dead. No, I didn't like that kind of a life. There was no fun in it.

Sports at that time was a fun life. You went to the Olympics, and everybody was a friend there. Not like today, where all the sports people seem to hate each other.

1932: Olympics, Jim Thorpe, and Hollywood Parties

I QUALIFIED IN the New Jersey state elimination. It was tough. Then there was a section elimination, and then they had the final in California—in San Francisco. We rode out there by steam train—that was nice.

California was the most beautiful place. I was gonna retire there because it was so beautiful. Never seen a place so beautiful.

Funny thing, three of the four Olympic qualifiers were from our one club in New Jersey—the North Hudson Wheelmen. Otto Ludecke, Frank Cano, and me. Charley Morton was from California—no, that was '36. The fourth rider was—I don't remember—from California. He was a good rider. Rode in the '28 Olympics.

The week after the trials, we went straight to the Olympics camp. A 500-mile train from San Francisco to Los Angeles.

When we got to the Olympics camp, a woman came around and said to Otto, "I'm your matron. I gotta take care of you. You're underage." He wasn't 16 yet. He lied about his age to get in to the Olympics [laughs].

A sad thing: One day when we were at the stadium [Los Angeles Coliseum], there were two people standing outside, and it was Johnny Weismuller trying to get Jim Thorpe into the stadium to see the games. Thorpe was banned from the games. He could not go in. We had seats for all of 'em. We had 5,000 seats in there. Johnny was trying to get him in, but it didn't work. Thorpe played professional baseball for money. That was the rule. [Thorpe, a Sac and Fox Indian, played in the minor leagues before winning gold medals by huge margins in the decathlon and pentathlon in the Stockholm Olympics in 1912. He was stripped of his medals the following year.]

We were right there, walking in. They [Thorpe and Weismuller] were right there, standing outside. If I would have known about it, I would have taken my jacket off and give it to him, and he coulda got in that way, with the athletes [laughs].

The Olympics was pretty private. I mean, there was very little media coverage. They never even knew we existed; we never met any media.

But we did meet Joe E. Brown, the famous comedian. He made a movie, too, The Six-Day Rider. He was very interested in us. We met him twice. When we went to Germany [in 1936 at the Berlin Olympics], he was there again. He ate with us at the same restaurant in the camp.

We met a lot of people. We were guests all over, which was very nice. To give you an idea, all the movie stars invited us to their parties. Don't remember who they are. All of 'em dead now.

I do remember one guy, James Agony, with the hatchet nose. He was an official at the bike races at the track they built right inside the Rose Bowl in Pasadena.

We had an official representative

BIKE FOR LIFE

assigned to manage us, but the guy couldn't tell us anything. We were self-coached. We knew all the rules. We went through all that at home.

No one told us what to eat. In my time, there was no special food for athletes. We ate a lotta pasta, beans, a lotta bread. And no liquor. It was Prohibition times, but we never drank liquor, anyway. Very little soda. We had some ice cream and different things. But as far as food, meat very little, and a lotta fish. Fish was cheap back then. Only the poor people ate fish at that time. Today, only the rich people eat it. Ha ha.

We didn't do any warm-up, like these people do today. Stretching? Massage? We never did those things. We'd warm-up in the race. Don't worry about it.

We were fast then. I'd say we could pedal faster than the guys today, even though we only had one-speed bikes, that's all. There were no problems with that. The derailleur was rare in '32, as far as I know. I rode a single-speed. When we went down big hills, we didn't let them [people with freewheels] coast. We pedaled hard so they had to pedal to stay with us. So they couldn't rest, believe me. *[Note: The freewheel and a rudimentary derailleur had been invented earlier in the century, but the modern dual-jockey wheel/parallelogram design didn't arrive until Tullio Campagnolo's Gran Sport in 1951. Riders in Sinibaldi's era either used a simple fixed-gear or a two-sided-hub wheel that had a freewheel for descending/climbing on one side and a fixed gear on the other for riding the flats. Races were often won by the speed at which a rider could dismount, loosen the wing-nuts on the hub, flip the wheel, and reset the chain.]*

I only participated in one event in the '32 Olympics—the 100-kilometer road-race time trial, 62-and-a-half miles. We didn't compete on the track—there were four events: four-man pursuit race, 1 kilometer time trial, a two-man event, mass sprint, and a two-man tandem—because the guy that represented us wouldn't let us. We did go on the track for training, though. We rode a four-man pursuit race against the U.S. team to train them, and after three or four laps we caught them. So they weren't that good.

I didn't do too good in the time trial. I was riding good. I drank something that didn't agree with me. Something in the bottle. I still did it in two hours, 40 minutes. It was pretty fast, but I still coulda done much faster that day. According to the reports, I was in second place halfway. But when I drank, that was the end. No medal.

A New Record, Moonshine, and the 1936 Olympics

MY EMPLOYERS HAD agreed to give me a leave of absence to go to California. I went back to work after the Olympics, getting $7 a week. It wasn't enough, but it was all I was used to.

In 1933, I rode a half a year. I won my first two races, and then I fell and hurt my back. Did not ride at all in '34. They repaired my back with a new operation, a spinal fusion. But I came back in '35 with a steel brace—and was faster. Better than I was when I was younger!

I did the metric 100 [100 km] in two hours, 25 minutes—took ten minutes off my old best time and set a new record. In fact, in 1975, I was talking to a girl at a supermarket checkout line who was reading *Bicycling* magazine. She turns to me and says, "Hey, your record from 1935 is still alive." *[Note: It was finally broken ten years later.]*

I won quite a few races at that time. Nobody could beat me, actually. Oh god, everybody wanted my wheel. If there was a pack ride and I came up there, everyone moved aside so they could get on my wheel and at least they'd get second. "That's a good wheel to get on," that's what they'd all say. They all knew it.

I was doing nothing different. I ate the same thing as I always did. Always working the same. I always went to bed early. I never went out, gallivanting like they do today. Or drink. That was bad. One of our pros used to say "don't smoke—it's no good." Things like that we didn't do. Anything that was bad we didn't do. Anybody who tells you to "drink beer, it's good for you" is crazy.

I didn't drink alcohol at all. We made it and sold it, yes. My mother used to make liquor during Prohibition. I used to deliver it. Drink it? No.

I really wanted to go to the Olympics again. It was 1936, and I was still young yet. In fact, I wanted to go to three more. There was nuthin to it [making the team]. Like going downhill. I finished in a tie for second to qualify.

The trip was by ocean liner, which was good. You didn't have to go by train. When I went by train to California, I didn't have the money. I sat for four nights and four days on that train. It was a long haul, believe me. But the ship, the *Manhattan*— it was a nice, beautiful ship. We were all together, all the athletes. Everybody knew everybody. It was lots of fun.

Media coverage of the '36 Olympics was exactly the opposite of 1932. Lotta coverage. Met a lotta great people. Lotta reporters. Not like today, though. No TV.

There was a grand total of six cyclists on the team, four on the road team, two for the track. Two from the North Hudson Bike Club, one from Chicago, one from California.

Once in Berlin, few athletes had full access, but we had to train and rode all over the city and the countryside. Nobody stopped us and asked anything. It was wide open. It's hard to say about what went on afterwards with the Holocaust; the problem wasn't obvious to us. They already told them [the Jews] to leave, and the rich ones did. The poor ones, it wasn't so easy. There were no signs, no graffiti.

I did see [signs of] underground bunkers. They were preparing for war, oh yes. All the roads were dug up. Everything was going underground. We went out riding looking for planes, but we couldn't find them. They had put the hangers underground. It was real advanced, everything.

As for the people, they seemed free. Every night, beer gardens all over the place, they're all out there drinking beer and everything after work. Young people, old people. You couldn't tell they were living under the Nazis. Everybody was working. Germany was booming.

.

IN THE 100K road race [the first Olympic mass-start race, rather than a time trial], the first hill we come to, somebody goes down and takes 25 of us down. We fell at the bottom of the hill. Imagine getting started at the bottom of a hill. By the time we got up, the pack was far away. So we chased 'em. A guy fell in front of us and takes us down again. And we get up again and it was four of us chasing. We went down four times, including one at the finish, too. Four spills. I finished way back.

We also rode the four-man team race at the track. Rode against Netherlands. They

BIKE FOR LIFE

shoot the gun, we went off, and we started to chase them. We went harder, and caught 'em and passed 'em. Then we slowed up. Since we won, the next day we went back to go against the other team, and got a shock: we were told we were disqualified for going too slow. We didn't have a fast enough time.

The international rules were based on time—but we didn't know that. In the U.S., you catch the team, and the race is over. When we caught the Netherlands team, we thought we were finished. We would have been way up there in the qualifications. But nobody knew.

When I came back from Germany, I got on a bike right away, within a week. The '40 and '44 Olympics were canceled due to the war. The 1940 Olympics was supposed to be in Japan, but Japan invades China and they call it off. But then they moved it to Finland, and Russia invades Finland. So that was called off.

I tried to qualify for the '48 Olympics, at age 34. I qualified for the state and even the sectional. At the sectional, I went down into a hole, broke my wheel, but then got a wheel off somebody and went out and caught the pack and qualified.

I was hurting so bad in the finals in Milwaukee, a 130-mile race. It had been a week since the sectional, and I wasn't healed [from the fall]; my ribs were separated. After 90 miles in Milwaukee, I went to the front, then quit. I couldn't breathe. Oh god, it was brutal! I thought I would heal. But ripped-up ribs take a long time to heal. At least I quit from the front.

After that, in '49, I quit for good. I got married. That ends the racing.

By then, in the races, I was getting the prize for the oldest rider. I wouldn't take it. At that time, they didn't have no Masters,

or I'd have kept cycling. I rode a little bit after that, then I stopped for 30 years.

Retirement, Family Life, and Rebirth as a Legend

[Sinibaldi's 48-year-old son and frequent riding buddy, John Jr. interjects here] You didn't stop riding completely, Dad. I remember when we lived in Butler, New Jersey, my dad taking out a track bike off hooks in the garage, maybe once a month in the summer. Early in the morning—6:30 on a Saturday, we'd hear the garage door open. We'd still be in bed. He'd be back 8:30, 9 o'clock. Then he'd go out into the garden. Dad has two passions in life. He loves to ride and he loves to garden.

He didn't talk about the old cycling days hardly at all to us kids. Dad didn't talk a lot growing up. I first heard the stories when I was 12, at Lenny Conditi's funeral in 1966. All the guys standing around. All the stories started with "remember the time John was in the lead; remember the time chasing John; remember the time John won that; no matter what we did, when John showed up, we knew we'd all be racing for second." Even though we all knew Dad was in the Olympics, it wasn't until then that I recognized just how good my dad was. It wasn't until he retired, when I was an adult, that I began to really hear my dad's stories.

I KEPT IN shape by working in the shop—which was heavy work. Sheet metal is heavy; everything you lift is in the hundreds of pounds. Eventually I tried three, four different jobs and became a sheet metal mechanic. After all those years, I retired in 1975 getting $6 an hour. I was a top-paid man [said sarcastically].

At home, I worked in my garden. A huge garden in New Jersey. Did everything by hand. Turned all the dirt by hand.

When I retired and came down here to Florida in 1976, one day I took the bike out for the heck of it. That was the beginning; I went by a library and I saw a bunch of people standing there with bicycles. It was the St. Pete Bike Club. They said, "We go out every Sunday."

That's what I wanted to hear. I had somebody to go out with.

I was 62. Some of the club riders were pretty young, so it got a little rough in there. A few of the 20-year-olds were pretty fast. They rode me hard. But after a month or so, I kept getting better until I became the fastest rider.

I was the fastest rider of that club until I was 77. I could go out there and do almost 30 miles an hour. When I was 75, I lapped everyone at the Sunshine State Games criterium in the 65-plus and 55-plus age groups, and rode with the 45-year-olds. I won a $25 preem that year, but I was worried about accepting it because I was afraid they'd take away my amateur status.

Riding Secrets: Rest on Climbs, Stay Cool in Underwear

I ride five days a week. I try to ride around 150 miles per week—about 30 miles each time. I take Mondays and Thursdays off. I gotta do my laundry, gotta hang the pots outside, gotta do shopping. I work harder now than when I was working. I don't get done till 7 o'clock at night, usually.

What do I think of Lance Armstrong? He's a good rider, no getting away from it. He's a type like I am: he rests when he's going uphill. That's when I do all my resting—uphill.

On the flat, everything goes pretty fast. But on the hills, everybody slows up. So that's when I'd rest. Three-quarters of the hill I'd rest, and the last quarter I'd take off.

Armstrong didn't see me do it, but he got the same idea somehow [laughs]. When you can rest on the hills, believe me, you've got it.

As for gearing, I believe in leverage. I don't shift gears. I ride in the big ring, but I also ride with the big ring in the back [gears]. To have it in the small gear in the front and the small gear in the back—there's no leverage there.

I don't ride in a faster cadence than anyone else nowadays. It's a relaxing ride. I go 18 to 20 miles per hour. Maybe up to 25 mph, I can hang right there in the middle. I can still hit 30 mph in a sprint once in a while.

I definitely have declined, I can tell. Believe me, there are times when I feel older than 90.

A turning point was when I got slowed down by an accident when I was 77, my last crit. I broke my back, fractured several vertebrae. Took a long time to come back. While I was healing, I found out I had colon cancer. Luckily, I recuperated very quickly. In fact, I won another gold medal while on chemo at the national championships that year.

I don't do weights. Nothing. No other exercise besides cycling and gardening. I garden four to five hours a day, and it's like a combination weights and stretching routine. All by hand. I can stand straight up and touch the ground with my hands.

I ride a Kestrel [200SCI], and here's how I got it: I was going to do the '94 Race Across America ten years ago on an over-70 team. My wife wasn't pleased about that. A week before the race, they said they didn't need me. But two months later, in the mail we get a brand-new Kestrel frame. Kestrel had sponsored the team for five riders. We hung a Campy record group on it. Probably put 7,000 to 8,000 miles a year on it for the last six to seven years. Probably

BIKE FOR LIFE

got 50,000 miles on it. *[Note: The Kestrel was wrecked when Sinibaldi was hit by a car in April '04; now he rides a steel frame he had in his garage.]*

I use an old pair of Adidas cycling shoes, about 20 years old. Off the bike, I never wear shoes—just to weddings and funerals. Everything I do, I do barefoot. So my feet are wide. None of the cycling shoes fit. I got my Adidas for half-price because the guy couldn't sell 'em, they were so wide.

I use toe-clips like in the olden days. I like the pull-on straps. I wear a helmet. Didn't for a long time. It was compulsory to wear a leather hair net when I raced.

I used to ride those 100-mile races without drinking a drop of water. I don't sweat much. It takes me all day to finish a water bottle.

I have one secret: wear a shirt under your jersey, no matter how hot it is, wool, anything. It'll get damp right away, and you will never use any sweat anymore. It'll keep you cool all summer, and you won't dehydrate. Like these runners that take everything off, the girls who have just a bra on, they dehydrate. They look dry. But they dehydrate, because the sun just dries them right up. If they were covered, they wouldn't have to drink.

Back when we rode a 100-mile race, who's going to give us water when we're riding from one city to another?

As a matter of fact, the old-timers all used a shirt under a shirt. When you see these guys today with a plastic jacket, they are dehydrating so fast. In other words, you go to Africa or Egypt, or any of these Arab countries, ask these guys to take that white shirt off—that sort of dress they wear—and they got a woolen shirt underneath it in the desert.

Diet Secrets: Soup, Veggies, Gardening, and No Restaurant Dinners

"What do you do that keeps you so young?" everyone asks me. It's what I *don't do* that's healthy. Not drinking, not smoking. I never smoked when I rode. I smoked a few cigarettes a day and a pipe a bit after I retired from bicycling for about 20 years. Then I quit in the '60s.

I'm a soup and vegetable man. Four or five different soups I make from scratch. A meat soup with ham. A vegetable soup. I have a ten-gallon pot. I throw in chickpeas in the water. Then rosemary. Garlic. Pepper and salt. On top, I put a half-inch of olive oil. Then I let it boil. It becomes a soup. It's beautiful.

I grow everything from peanuts to pineapples—three rows. In fact, I roast the peanuts myself and grind them into peanut butter. I make my own pasta, tomato soup. I grow cabbage, strawberries, kale, carrots, corn, parsley, cauliflower, onions, Swiss chard, parsley, fennel, rosemary, and one 50-foot double row of garlic. I have pecan trees. All on an oversized lot in St. Pete—a 50 by 90 plot.

I bake my own bread—eight to ten loaves every couple weeks. Sometime I make pizza from scratch when all the guys [from the bike club] come over here. I make my own pasta sauce and pasta.

My diet hasn't changed much over the years. Chicken. Liver. Whatever is on sale.

I don't eat too much meat, only when it's on sale. I eat fish when it's free. I won't pay for it. My social security is under $2,000 a year, so how can I buy it? I eat corned beef and eat it with cabbage and salad. I'll save the juice and use it three times. When the corned beef is left over, I'll make corned beef hash. Every once in a while—maybe twice a month—I'll have red meat, a hamburger.

Not much chicken, either, really. The Atkins diet—all beef? No, no, that's bad. If you must eat beef, always make it well done, never rare. And don't eat anything fried.

I'm afraid to eat energy bars and gels. Any of that kind of food is something artificial; it doesn't sound right.

The best advice? Do all the right things. In other words, do all the things you hate to do, and do them right [laughs]. Do the things you say, "I don't wanna do this, I don't wanna do that." You find out that you live longer. It's important to eat the right things, and keep away from the restaurants a little bit. You're not gonna buy something you don't like at a restaurant; you're gonna buy something you like, and most of the time, it's no good for you.

We go to breakfast at the Gold Cup Coffee Shop three times a week with the club. Lot of the riders are overweight, but the stuff they order is unbelievable—fried eggs, fried hash, fried sausage. I eat a muffin. Or at home, a nice big bowl of oatmeal with raisins and milk. I have a tea on the side. I don't drink much coffee.

For lunch today I had a big cabbage soup, which had all the vegetables in it you can think of. And some chicken stock. For dessert, a slice of pineapple. Tonight, I may have an oversized bowl of oatmeal for dinner; that tastes good at night.

Don't eat a big meal before you go to bed at night, like these guys go out to eat at 7, 8 at night. You're not going to get rid of it; it's going to just sit there in their stomach.

And be busy. I've always got something to do. If I keep moving, I like it. If I sit down, no good.

The Best Memory in 90 Years

MY BEST RACE was a 100-mile race in New York in 1933. It was raining all the night before. I had wooden rims. I put shellac on the rims and used one brake. The race started at five in the morning. We had to take the ferry to the 59th Street bridge. But when we got there, there's nobody there.

"They're all gone," someone said. "You're too late."

We got the highway number, ran to a garage station and got a can of grease, because it was raining hard. We greased up our whole legs to keep us warm in the rain—just like the people who swim across the English Channel.

We chased and chased and chased. We came to a 90-degree turn around a corner, and I applied the brake—it grabbed on and pulled right through the wheel. I jumped off the bike and bent the brakes out to make room for the [out-of-true] wheel, so I had no more brakes. Freewheel and no brakes. A 100-mile race!

Finally, after 70 miles, we caught the group. The last 30 miles it was up-and-down, up-and-down. We're going down a hill, and here we have another 90-degree turn; I had no brakes. So I jammed into the back of two riders; I grabbed one guy on one side and the other guy on the other, no hands on the handlebars, and make the turn.

I tell you, I got gray hairs that day. Maybe 15 miles from the finish, I took off, took two guys with me, and that was the end. I won it. It's late. No brakes. It's raining.

God, was I riding good that day.

THE ANTI-AGING GAME PLAN

Want to stay young and injury-free at 40, 60, or 80? Hint: Do more than ride

O NE DAY IN *the winter of 1997–1998, my bathroom mirror stopped me cold. Staring back was something so unexpected, so scary, that my every thought was suddenly dominated by one haunting image: the desperate, dying Wicked Witch of the West in* The Wizard of Oz, *shriveling into nothingness while screaming "I'm m-e-l-l-l-t-t-i-n-g!"*

It was my body. In the three months since I separated my shoulder at La Ruta de los Conquistadores—the crazy-hard 250-mile Pacific-to-Atlantic mountain-bike ride across Costa Rica—it morphed from "young" to "middle-aged." Squared pecs had became shadow-casting man-breasts. A once-flat stomach now dripped over my belt. Without any upper-body exercise—the swimming, rowing, racquetball, and push-ups that had fairly preserved my old collegiate wrestler's physique—gravity attacked. Despite 90 days of five-days-a-week Lifecycle-riding, my torso was reverting to its true 41-year-old self, like a butterfly going back to a caterpillar. It was more than a blow to my vanity; it was a visual warning: for lifelong fitness, cycling isn't enough.

Fact: After age 35, flexibility naturally decreases, VO$_2$ Max shrinks, and muscle mass shrivels—even in a cyclist's legs. Shoulders slump and posture corrodes. At any age, periods of inactivity cause a pronounced "de-training" effect. If you don't fight back with almost-daily aerobics and regular weight lifting and stretching, you could someday become one of those super-heart-rate 72-year-old cyclists who fall and break a hip because you lack the muscular strength and flexibility to react quickly when a car cuts you off. Add the risk of osteoporosis (see chapter 9), and your plan to roll into the sunset might be completed in a wheelchair.

Ironically, I'd been writing about this stuff for years. But since 1998, I've been living it—cross-training, stretching, working on my posture, and lifting weights for 45 minutes in the gym at least twice a week. It's a hassle; you have to work harder to stay fit as you age. But it's paid off. Pushing 50, I feel almost as fit as I was in my 20s. And I'm not melting quite so fast anymore. —RMW

In September 2004, three-time national mountain bike champion Tinker Juarez rode 213 miles in a day, good for his second straight silver medal at the World Solo 24 Hours of Adrenalin Championship in Whistler, B.C. He was 42. At the same event, Canada's Lesley Tomlinson, a two-time Olympian, rode 180 miles to win the women's race for the second time. She was 43. In Athens a month earlier, Jeannie Longo-Ciprelli of France pedaled in her sixth consecutive summer games. She was 45. At the 2003 world track championships in Manchester, England, Vic Copeland, an optometrist from Rancho Bernardo, California, was named the "Outstanding Rider in the World Over 35" for winning all four of his age-group events—the 500 and 2,000 meter time trials, points race, and matched sprints. He was 61 (see sidebar, this chapter). And then there's John Sinibaldi Sr., of St. Petersburg, Florida, who can be found hammering group rides at 18 miles per hour three times a week. He's 91.

Genetic freaks or paradigm shift?

Mostly the latter. Today, thousands of people over 40 are proving that high-level fitness is not merely the province of the young anymore, and that longevity isn't simply based on lucky chromosomes. The path to a long, fit life is simple: *keep training*. This rule is not cycling-specific, but a baseline for all aging athletes trying to keep the pace.

Researchers are finding that years of hard training in any or many aerobic and strength activities can keep you young. They've discovered that the old rule-of-thumb that we annually lose 1 percent per year in aerobic capacity (**VO$_2$ Max**) and muscular strength after age 30 or 35—only applies to the sedentary; active people who maintain high training levels can cut the

decline by half, or two-thirds, or more. "What we thought was aging was really just inactivity," said athletics and aging researcher Joel M. Stager, PhD, professor of kinesiology and director of the Human Performance Laboratory at Indiana University.

Does this mean that if you keep working out, you'll stay 25 forever? That it all comes down to "Use it or lose it"?

To a point. Keeping "young" involves more than time in the saddle. It involves a time-consuming, carefully balanced strategy that supports, protects, and replenishes several systems of the body, in addition to VO$_2$ Max, that deteriorate with age and neglect. Here's what goes wrong.

"By your mid-30s, most people still look young, but are already experiencing the Big Three of aging: deteriorating lean muscle mass, worsening posture, and crumbling joints," says Robert Forster, whose Santa Monica, California, physical therapy practice is the unofficial meeting hall for West Los Angeles' broken-down triathletes, adventure racers, and gym rats. "Age-related decline hits sooner than you think."

Way sooner. According to Robert Wiswell, PhD, associate professor and expert on aging and exercise at the University of Southern California Department of Biokinesiology and Physical Therapy, the typical man starts experiencing osteo-arthritic changes (loss of smoothness) in his joints by his 20s, loses a half-pound of muscle per year by 35, and has been shrinking in height since 18 due to postural changes.

"The bad news is that you can't stop the decline," says Wiswell. "The good news is that you can slow it down and get injured less by thinking long-term."

A long-term anti-aging workout plan is part physical therapy and part cutting-

THE ANTI-AGING GAME PLAN

edge exercise research, heavy on weights, hard aerobic workouts, stretching/flexibility drills, and recovery. Initially, it would baby your knees and shoulders with a lengthy, joint-lubricating warm-up. Next, it would keep your heart strong and VO_2 Max high with hard efforts in your cycling and other aerobic activities at least a couple of times a week, with active recovery or cross-training in between. Finally, you hit the weight room twice a week, avoiding extreme ranges of motion to protect connective tissue, building up vulnerable and neglected muscle groups, then hammering your muscles with heavy weights and a blistering pace. The result: you revive flagging fast-twitch muscle fibers, snap a slumping spine to attention, expand your capillary/oxygen processing network, and flood your bloodstream with youth-maintaining hormones. The workouts use jumping jacks, stretches, and the same weight machines and free weights you know and love, but require you to think—to protect your body with restraint and discipline before pushing it. No more winging it. All workouts fit into a logical, never-ending plan.

"Of course, it takes a lot more time to do all this stuff—time a lot of people with active social and work lives don't have," says Wiswell. "On the other hand, don't wait until you're 45 or 50 to integrate some of these elements. By then, you may have already done irreparable damage to your body, and will be functionally much older than you ought to be."

In other words, if you want to ride a century when you turn a century, start now. Here's a guide on how to maintain and protect the five main problem areas of aging: VO_2 Max, strength, joint integrity, flexibility, and posture.

• PROBLEM 1 •
Declining VO2 Max/Aerobic Fitness

SOLUTION: Train frequently and rigorously, lift weights, cross-train, and integrate cycling into normal life activities.

Jack LaLanne turned 90 on September 26, 2004, and was popping up everywhere from the *Howard Stern Show* to the *Today Show* to the *Tony Danza Show* to share his secrets. The fitness guru is known for chair push-ups and swimming handcuffed across San Francisco Bay on his birthday, not cycling. He doesn't have a PhD, like Joel Stager. But the overriding message he's promoted since the Depression remains the same and applies to anyone seeking longevity and fitness. "Don't stop working out," he told anyone who'd listen. "Inactivity kills your body."

Heed Jack's words. It's a fact: the more you do nothing, the more you fall apart.

Past age 30 or 35, the heart and the other elements that contribute to VO_2 Max start slipping about 1 percent a year in sedentary people. The arteries and capillaries shrink and provide less oxygen and nutrients to muscles and cells; so do the mitochondria cells that convert oxygen to energy and the muscles they move. It's a classic double whammy: a reduced volume of blood is pumped to shrinking muscles that are less capable of transporting its oxygen, nutrients, and lymphatic waste products. The effect: you produce less aerobic energy than before, so you can't ride as fast or as long—or recover as quickly.

Studies have shown that an aging heart weakens for two reasons: Maximum heart rate (its highest possible beats per minute) declines about one bpm per year with age,[1] and maximum stroke volume (the amount of blood in one pump of the heart) also decreases.[2] The muscles' oxygen-processing ability slips because muscle mass shrinks, capillaries become less numerous, and mitochondria become less dense.[3]

If you want to slow or even reverse the VO_2 Max decline, act like Jack. Jack up the intensity, lift weights, and don't stop, ever. At the same time, don't forget antioxidants and certain other supplements; over the last decade, many respected medical researchers have concluded that they help limit free radical and hormonal damage caused by hard training (see sidebar, page 108). Here are the details.

Solution 1a:
Keep training—hard

Message read on www.cyclingforums .com:

> I'm 40, started riding almost 3 years ago, and always finish in the top 5–10 percent of any event I ride in regardless of age. I attack every hill and pass a lot of younger riders regularly. On flats I can hold my own and can sprint up into the 32 to 39 mph range. Since I'm older and closer to death I take every ride seriously. I train like there's no tomorrow. How many 23-years-olds can say the same? —Rickw2, Arlington, Texas

Rickw2 is doing the right thing. Hard workouts can limit your deterioration to half the rate of the average person. Or more.

Numerous studies of runners and swimmers (there are few of cyclists) found that older athletes who maintain vigorous endurance training experience a VO_2 Max decrease of .05 percent per year[4]—half that experienced by sedentary adults. That's an average; some see almost no ill effects of age at all. A landmark 1987 study by Dr. Michael Pollock, director of the Center for Exercise Science at the University of Florida, studied two dozen 40-year-old Masters champion athletes in several sports in 1971 and 1981. His findings: the VO_2 Max levels of hard trainers barely declined at all in a decade (just 1.7 percent), but the results for those who slacked off in intensity declined an average of 12.5 percent. Low-intensity training did not increase capillary density.[5]

A study in *Swim* magazine that tracked Masters swimmers over a 15-year period reported similar results: the onset of VO_2 Max decline was delayed from age 25 to the mid-30s, deterioration was almost "imperceptible" into their 40s, and it didn't reach 1 percent per year rate until swimmers hit their early 70s. Compared to nonathletes, who lose 25 percent of their physical capacity by 50 and 50 percent by 75, competitive age-groupers who swim an hour a day declined only 3.5 percent by 50 and 19.1 percent by age 75. "Another way to look at it," said study author Phil Whitten, PhD, "is that a 70-year-old competitive swimmer will have the strength and vitality of a 'normal' 45-year-old." The key, he says: never let yourself get out of condition.

Question: Why the decline at all? Why can't you maintain the same VO_2 Max with hard training? Answer: Unfortunately, training apparently has no effect on one factor—the decrease in maximum heart rate.[6] However, the other factors—declines in heart stroke volume,[7] density of capillaries and mitochondria, and even creatine phosphate[8] can be reversed quickly with high-intensity exercise, with levels eventually potentially matching those of similarly trained younger athletes.[9]

Bottom line: in theory, an older adult who trains at the same volume and intensity as a younger adult should be capable of very similar performances. Only the natural decrease in heart rate and consequential reduction in VO_2 Max stands in the way of letting you stop time in its tracks.

Solution 1b: Lift weights

Strength training boosts more than your strength, reflexes, and vanity. Bigger muscles expand your aerobic engine by processing more oxygen. Studies have proven that strength training builds up VO_2 Max by increasing the density of capillaries and mitochondrial enzyme activity.[10] See the next section, below, for the strength benefits of weight lifting and the ideal lifting strategy.

Solution 1c: Cross-train like crazy

Daily high-intensity riding is hard on any body—young or old. Moreover, it's hard to find time to ride a bike every day, period. If you skip several days in a row, a "de-training" effect starts to set in; skip three weeks, and your hard-won aerobic fitness is largely lost. By 12 weeks, you begin to lose musculoskeletal resiliency—the strength of your joints. By six months so much joint strength, muscle tone/strength, and aerobic capacity is lost that you're back to being as unfit as someone who's been sedentary for years. The point is that long periods of inactivity—usually caused by busy lives, bad weather, and injuries—are to be avoided. And the easiest way to keep active is by broadening your athletic portfolio. Mix in running, swimming, rowing, the elliptical machine, jumping rope, Salsa aerobics, VersaClimbing, or aerobic dance. Try the Trikke, the radical three-wheeled sensation that delivers a total full-body aerobic workout (*Bike for Life*'s Roy Wallack did the 2004 Long Beach Marathon on one in 2 hours, 13 minutes). Water-run in the pool with a flotation waist belt and resistance boots. Play your nephew one-on-one in basketball and win on pure hustle. If it gets your heart rate up and keeps it there for a while, it qualifies as cross-training.

You see, your VO_2 Max isn't particular about what aerobic activity you choose to develop it. Cross-training helps your body tolerate hard workouts, and can't be beat for convenience. Two straight days of hard cycling is tough on your body, but one day of hard cycling followed by a hard swim session lets your legs recover as it works your upper body, while both blast your heart and lungs. Going on a business trip? Running shoes and swim goggles tuck into a suitcase. Tweak your knee on the bike? Kayak for a couple of days. Can't ride due to early nightfall or a January blizzard? Snowshoe or cross-country ski. Mixing up different activities—including road cycling AND mountain biking—keeps you motivated, breaks up your routine, and helps maintain wintertime fitness. As Ned Overend proved in his phenomenally long, successful off-road career (see interview at the end of this chapter), other sports not only don't hurt cycling, but provide variety that keeps you from getting bored with it.

Cross-training shouldn't be seen simply as a welcome off-season break from the saddle and something to set aside when springtime rolls around. Because it works all the muscles of the body rather than just a specific group, cross-training yields a smaller chance of chronic injury over the long term than any one single sport. And in the big picture, cross-training makes you fitter, enhancing VO$_2$ Max by developing oxygen-processing ability in all muscles of the body, not just the ones in your legs.

"The definition of fitness is that it takes less effort for your body to do the same amount of work," said Dr. Herman Falsetti, an Irvine, California, cardiologist and consultant to the 1984 Olympic cycling team. "And if your body is fit all over—not just one part of it—your body's work goes that much easier."

Solution 1d: Integrate cycling into work and family time

If playing with the kids, spending time with the spouse, and a thousand other things eat into your riding time, get creative. Do errands on your bike. Commute to work. Ride to family get-togethers. Buy a trailer, a trail-a-bike, or a kid-friendly tandem so you can combine babysitting and riding. With these items fairly cheap (a Raleigh Companion tandem is under $700—what some triathletes will pay for a wheel), you are shortchanging yourself without them.

The Anti-Oxidant "Cocktail" to the Rescue
Vitamins C and E can help reduce illnesses resulting from hard training

THERE is a downside to regular hard exercise that you can easily minimize. In 2004, Dr. David Nieman and colleagues at California's Loma Linda University verified what marathon runners and endurance cyclists have long suspected: a long, arduous event or a day of sudden, hard training puts them at increased risk of illness and infection. Immune cells aren't weakened for a long period of time—21 hours in the case of Nieman's study—but that window is enough if you catch a chill or interact with someone who has a cold. An earlier study by Nieman of 2,000 Los Angeles Marathon runners found that those who trained 60 miles per week were twice as likely to get sick in the two months before the event than those who trained 20 miles per week. Bottom line: your immune system, like your muscles, adapts to hard training but also is initially weakened by it. So take care immediately following a hard workout.

Besides covering up and resting, antioxidant vitamins can help mitigate the short-term effects of hard workouts—and longer-term damage some think may be caused by hard exercise. Dr. Kenneth Cooper of the Cooper Aerobics Center in Dallas, who invented the term "aerobics" in the 1970s and was the leading advocate of "the more, the better" school of thought, now believes that more than an hour per day of aerobic activity increases production of "free radicals," substances that can "oxidize" (damage) muscle tissue, particularly that of the heart. According to Cooper, the solution to this is regular doses of an "antioxidant cocktail" of vitamins C, E, and beta-carotene.

It's like Rust-Oleum for your body

Free radicals are natural by-products of oxygen processing that, under normal circumstances, the body holds in check. Technically, they are unstable oxygen molecules (unstable because they lack some electrons in their outer core) that are constantly shooting about crazily in your body, crashing into, sticking to, and "oxidizing"—sort of rusting—other particles and tissues. This oxidation eventually can cause cancer, coronary artery disease, and other problems. Before they get out of hand, however, the body dispatches built-in "antioxidant" enzymes to mop up the "oxidation" caused by these excess free radicals. Unfortunately, your body can get out of whack; the antioxidants can be overwhelmed when free radicals multiply in response to pollution, cigarette smoke, food contaminants, depression, and excessive exercise. "They begin to run wild," says Cooper, "successfully attacking healthy as well as unhealthy parts of the body."

Since the publication of his 1994 book, *The Antioxidant Revolution,* Dr. Cooper has advocated the use of a supplementary therapy based on consumption of vitamins C, E, and beta-carotene, antioxidants that bolster the body's natural free radical fighters. Vitamin C promotes cell growth, healing, and immunity, builds collagen, reduces risk of some cancers and cataracts, and may lower cholesterol levels and increase immunity. E is a blood-thinner that helps form red blood cells, reduces damage in muscle cells, protects against heart disease, and boosts immunity. Beta-carotene, the best-known of the substances that makes the yellow and orange color in apricots, sweet potatoes, and carrots, lowers the risk of cataracts, heart disease, and lung and other cancers. Taken together as a group, this "cocktail" protects muscles by keeping cell clumping, vessel clogging, and plaque formation in check, repairing cell membranes, and preserving them from rotting. Cooper claims the cocktail should be your main weapon in a war against a host of other age-old afflictions: cholesterol, heart attacks, strokes, cataracts, some cancers. It even fights premature aging, he says.

If you regularly work out hard for an hour or more a day, the latest research indicates that you need to take in far larger amounts of antioxidants than you can probably get from diet alone. Fifteen or 20 servings of fruit and vegetables per day may get you enough vitamin C and beta-carotene, but E is another story. It would take eight cups of almonds to get 400 IU of E, the amount Cooper recommends for a moderate male exerciser in his sixties, like himself. It would take over fifteen oranges to get 1,000 mg of vitamin C and two or three carrots to get 25,000 IU of beta-carotene.

Dr. Cooper promotes a **four-step antioxidant plan** that includes supplements, moderate—not extreme—exercise, a low-fat diet, and limited environmental exposure:

1. **An antioxidant "cocktail"**: Amounts for an active 50-year-old woman are 600 IU of vitamin E, 1,000 mg of vitamin C, and 50,000 IU of beta-carotene. If you are male or a more active woman, increase to 1,500 mg vitamin C and 1,200 IU of E. A Tufts University study found that 800 IU of E reduced the amount of exercise-induced free radical damage in muscle cells; there is evidence that higher doses fight cancer, Parkinson's, Alzheimer's, and heart disease. Nobel Prize winner Linus Pauling went to his grave at 93 believing we should take 200 times the RDA of vitamin C (12,000 mg per day).[11]

   Note: In late 2004, controversy over vitamin E erupted when researchers at Johns Hopkins, analyzing 19 clinical trials conducted in the last decade, warned that amounts above 400 IU per day may increase the risk of mortality. Numerous critics, however, noted bias in the analysis, which ignored hundreds of studies showing longevity benefits from vitamin E consumption as high as 2,000 IUs daily, and included a high incidence of chronic disease among the studied patient groups. The Johns Hopkins report also made no reference to a 1996 study of 11,000 elderly people from the National Institute of Aging that found markedly lower death rates for vitamin E users. Adding vitamin C cut fatalities even more, it added.

2. **Limit consecutive days of hard-core, high-endurance training**, which produces an abundance of free radicals. Cooper and other researchers have found a correlation between those with a history of marathon running and cancer and heart attacks.

3. **Eat a low-fat diet,** featuring whole (non-sliced) fruits and raw or steamed vegetables. Sliced fruits lose vitamins when they are cut open and exposed to air; veggies lose vitamins when cooked or canned.

4. **Limit exposure to radiation**, electromagnetic fields, and pollution, all of which expose you to free radicals.

Over time, the news about antioxidants keeps getting better. Recent studies have shown that making the "cocktail" a daily habit may be a good idea whether you exercise hard, easy, or not at all. A 1999 study even indicated that it can have an immediate protective effect against a fatty meal, making your task literally this simple: before you pig out on a Big Mac and fries or a couple of slices of double-cheese pizza, knock back a C & E cocktail—or a least a couple of oranges and a swig of wheat germ oil. That's advice derived from a study by Dr. Gary D. Plotnick, a professor of cardiology at the University of Maryland School of Medicine, who subjected twenty test subjects to a combination of vitamin supplements, low-fat meals (Kellogg's Frosted Flakes, skim milk, and orange juice) and high-fat meals (McDonald's Egg and Sausage McMuffins and hashbrown patties). He found that pretreatment with vitamins C and E may indeed be akin to temporarily spraying Teflon on your tubes.

"Maybe McDonald's should serve McVitamins, too," he concluded to *Bike for Life*.

While Plotnick warns that taking C and E is "no magic bullet"—a meal high in fat has other detrimental effects such as obesity and diabetes—his findings were clear: protected by the vitamins, the inner lining of blood vessels stayed unchanged. By contrast, the vessels of test subjects who did not take the vitamins became "impaired" (and therefore open to a fatty buildup) for a full four hours, the length of time it takes a fatty meal to digest.

Incidentally, the finding that high-fat meals impaired vein wall function for four hours raised Dr. Cooper's eyebrows when *Bike for Life* told him about Plotnick's study. "That may explain why heart attacks and angina often occur just after a meal," he said.

• PROBLEM 2 •
Muscle Mass Wastes Away

SOLUTION: Pump weights fast and heavy. Then recover.

Weight lifting is underutilized by cyclists, and even scorned by some. "My legs get plenty of work already," some say. "Bulky arms and chest will hurt me on the hills," say others, noting that Lance Armstrong didn't win the Tour de France until he lost 20 pounds of upper-body muscle mass as a result of his cancer treatments. But from a pure health and longevity point of view, big, strong muscles are more functional and safer than smaller, weaker ones. They help aerobic performance by increasing your oxygen-processing capacity and provide the strength to push through headwinds and up hills. Which is why it is mildly upsetting to discover that muscle mass, like VO_2 Max, also disappears at an average rate of 1 percent a year beginning in your 30s. And why it is downright scary to find, as researchers from Johns Hopkins and Boston Universities did in 2002, that *power naturally falls off far faster than strength as you age.*

The rapid drop-off in power is a big deal. It can cost you your life.

That's because power is defined as the ability to use your strength quickly, to respond to changing situations fast. Power gives you instant reaction, the ability to make the microsecond adjustments that often are the difference between success and failure—avoiding a fallen tree branch on a backcountry road; jumping a rock on a 30-mph downhill; swerving out of the way of cars that suddenly turn in front of you. Power is a key to survival.

Trainers have known for years that explosive weight training is necessary to keep pro athletes at the top of their game. Michael Jordan observed a rigorous explosive lifting program after age 30, as do many of this era's older pro athletes. What we didn't know until recently is that this power training is vital for average folks to *maintain* their speed and power—especially as they age. In other words, there is a very good argument for everyone to be weight training like professional athletes—especially after 30 or 35.

Examples: A 40-year-old racquetball player might still be able to bench 250 pounds like he did a decade ago, but because his power is down 5 percent he can't quite retrieve that shot in the dead corner anymore. Further along the age continuum, the power loss accelerates. A 50-year-old man may still be able to climb the same hills on his mountain bike about as fast he did 20 years earlier, but wipes out more on the descents because his muscles can't react to obstacles as quickly. A 75-year-old man might still give you an iron-grip handshake, since his strength still may be 80 percent of what it was decades earlier. But since his power is down to 50 percent, he might just lose his balance when he gets up from a table, fall, and break his hip.

Bottom line: lifting weights is good for everyone, every age. But for maximum benefits—to stay on top of your game—you gotta hit *heavy* weights *fast* and *frequently.* Here's how to best stop muscle mass decline as you age.

Solution 2a: Hit fast-twitch fibers with fast contractions

You may have heard of "super slow" weight lifting, whose proponents touted amazing health benefits from short

How Jack's Shooting for a Century

WE are aware that Jack LaLanne isn't actually a cyclist. But when the subject is anti-aging and longevity and fitness, it's hard not to pay attention to a man whose favorite line, repeated again on his ubiquitous 90th birthday television appearances, is "Dying would ruin my image." Jack's image hasn't changed in his tenth decade of life, and neither have his eight rules for a healthy life.

1. Exercise vigorously—at least twice a week with weights, plus water exercises.

"What helps you get out of a chair or go up and down stairs? It's muscles, right? These old people—they quit doing things. They sit on their big fat butts, thinking about what they used to do, and pretty soon their muscles atrophy."

2. Exercise during commercials, if you have to.

"People say 'I don't have time.' What a lousy excuse! You can do all this stuff while you're in your chair during the commercials while you're watching television."

3. Change your exercise routine every thirty days.

"You've got 640 muscles. They all need their share of work."

sessions of agonizingly slow lifts; hundreds of copycat magazine articles promoted it in the early 2000s. Well, forget it. To restore size and power, do what every pro and college trainer tells his athletes: go "super fast." A 2002 Boston University study led by Roger A. Fielding, PhD, found that rapid contractile movements, such as a speedy upstroke on a leg extension, will quickly bring back your thick, powerful "fast-twitch" muscle fibers. These short, bulky fibers, unlike the smoother, longer, aerobic-oriented "slow-twitch" fibers, will wither substantially by age 50 and can virtually disappear in old age without stimulation. On the bright side, the lack of fast-twitch fibers doesn't hurt you as much in pure endurance activities, which is why many marathon runners and cyclists have done well into their late 30s and even 40s. On the flip side, the rapid fall-off in fast-twitch fibers severely impacts reaction time. That's why you're a step slower on the basketball court at 35—and may fall and break your hip while vacuuming at age 70.

Among his test group of 73-year-old women, Fielding found that super-fast contractions brought similar strength gains as regular-speed contractions, but stimulated far greater gains in fast-twitch fiber volume and peak power output. "But why wait until 73?" he told *Bike for Life*. "In younger people, they'll come back even faster."

Note: Don't forget to hit the triceps, the muscle on the backside of the upper arm, as it is predominantly (90 percent) composed of fast-twitch fibers, says Michael Bemben, PhD, director of the Neuromuscular Research Lab at the University of Oklahoma. Also, pound calves and forearms, which wither quickly for another reason: they're routinely stressed less than muscles nearer the body's core.

Solution 2b:
Spike growth hormone levels with heavy, no-rest training

Human growth hormone (HGH) is the body's fountain of youth, promoting lean muscle mass, body fat reduction, youthful skin, thick bones, strong connective tissue, and deeper sleep. Unfortunately, your body's production of HGH tumbles after your mid-20s, some say by as much as 24 percent per decade. Your body produces about 500 micrograms of HGH a day at age 20, 200 mg at 40, and 25 mg at 80. Beginning in middle age, men lose 5 pounds of muscle per decade. Result: you may weigh the same at 48 as you did at 18, but your body composition is more fat, less muscle.

The FDA approved injections of artificial HGH in 1996, but slowing the slide that way is controversial due to numerous side effects (see HGH sidebar). Fortunately, however, you can increase the frequency and amplitude of HGH "spurts" naturally through lifting weights. The method is simple: three sets of 8 to 10 reps to failure (the point at which you can't maintain form), with no more than a minute's rest between sets.

This intense sequence of lifting may seem difficult, but it is doable by structuring the workout in pairs of non-overlapping exercises, such as push-pull or upper-lower. An example of push-pull is following a bench press, which works the chest, with a complementary oppositional exercise like a seated row, which works the back. The chest rests as the back is worked, eliminating downtime.

"This method floods your muscles with lactic acid, which cues the pituitary gland to secrete growth hormone," says William Kraemer, PhD, of the University of Con-

4. Avoid indulging in bad habits.

"When you get your dog up, do you give him a cup of coffee, a doughnut, and a cigarette? People think nothing of giving themselves that for breakfast, and they wonder why they don't feel good."

5. Always have goals and challenges.

"Never be satisfied—ever. You know, I've won all these physique contests, and I've broken all kinds of world records and been very successful financially, but I've never been satisfied. The minute you get satisfied, you get complacent."

6. If man makes it, don't eat it.

"If you go into McDonald's to get a hamburger, some of these hamburgers are 1,200 to 1,300 calories. That's all the calories you need for the day. And how many people eat that, plus milkshakes and all the rest of the junk they eat, and they wonder why they're fat?"

7. Eat vegetables and fruits.

"You've got to get at least five or six raw vegetables every day of your life. You've got to get at least four or five pieces of fresh fruit every day of your life. And you've got to eat whole grains."

8. Keep up on current events.

"Keep your mind active. I read everything from the Bible to the *Enquirer*."

necticut, a leading HGH researcher. "Just cut out the talking and work out for at least 15 minutes to maximize the spurt."

Solution 2c: Ease into it and build in recovery

Ironically, while you need more intensity with age (to produce HGH and fast-twitch fibers), safety requires you to take it easier: use lighter weight on your first set (to warm up), take more recovery time (rest and sleep) between workouts, and gradually build up to heavier workouts over time. Since muscle fibers need at least 48 hours to recover from a hard workout, don't lift two days in a row. In fact, alternate heavy and light workouts. "If you're 35 or more, make every second workout a 'recovery workout' (below 80 percent of max), and every fifth week an easy week," says Dan Wirth, president of Sierra Fitness Health Clubs of America and a former University of Arizona strength coach.

Solution 2d: Periodize your weight lifting

To prevent gradual decline, Wirth and many other coaches promote cross-training and "Periodization"—working muscles with different weights and reps every couple of months.

Ironically, while the Periodization program *Bike for Life* described in chapter 1 applies the same principles to aerobic cycling training, Romanian coaching guru Tudor Bompa actually developed the

---

Aerobic Training Exercises Your Mind, Too

AEROBIC fitness does more than strengthen your heart, increase lung capacity, build your coordination, and ward off heart disease, diabetes, and other killer diseases. It can also help you handle stress better, ward off infection, and even make you smarter—or at least keep you from getting dumber.

In two studies released in the September 2004 issue of the *Journal of the American Medical Association,* mild exercise was found to trigger the release of naturally produced chemicals that both protect brain cells and keep them performing at top speed, helping to delay onset of dementia and Alzheimer's disease.

Harvard School of Public Health researchers found that older women who walked at a leisurely pace for two to three hours a week performed much better on tests of memory and cognitive thinking ability than inactive women. And there were greater benefits for those who like to work out longer, like cyclists. Women who walked at least six hours a week had an additional 20 percent reduced risk of performing poorly on the same tests.

A second study showed that exercise could help protect against Alzheimer's. A University of Virginia group found that sedentary elderly men who walked less than a quarter mile per day were twice as likely to develop Alzheimer's as those who walked over two miles per day.

As for other benefits of aerobic fitness, some speculate that it may help you cope with stress better. That's because the rapid circulation of blood nutrients nourishes the brain, putting it on a higher functional level. And it's generally accepted that a fit body's ability to ward off infections is enhanced and its sex life improved.

Periodization concept for strength training. He noticed that muscles "learn." As you get stronger, a movement that initially took ten muscle fibers to move soon takes nine fibers, then eight. To keep firing all the fibers, you need to change your routine. At a macro level, lift heavy weight and low reps for a month, then switch to light weight and higher reps. At a micro level, change technique. Do bicep curls, but change your grip from underhand to overhand. Instead of a military press machine, find a wall and do handstand push-ups. Change brands of machines; the Universal incline-press machine involves slightly different biomechanics than the incline press on an Icarian.

• PROBLEM 3 •
Deteriorating Joints

SOLUTION: Warm up, cool down, avoid risks, build up weak spots.

Muscles can be rebuilt, but joints aren't so lucky. Microthin synovial membrane, already a tissue-thin lining that covers bone ends with lubrication slicker than wet ice, gets thinner and worn with age. Meniscus cushions in the knees get ripped. The humerus dangles precariously from the cavity of the shoulder blades, making the shoulder prone to impingement and

Injecting HGH: High Price for Eternal Youth

HOPING to reverse the muscle mass shrinkage and body fat increases associated with the drop-off in human growth hormone after your teens, researchers first harvested HGH from cadavers, then began manufacturing a synthetic variety for clinical use 20 years ago. To build strength and recover faster from training, competitors in a variety of sports began to use it instead of anabolic steroids, which do the same thing but are readily detectable in drug tests. Because HGH is produced by the pituitary gland at the base of the brain, it's difficult to prove whether it has been taken artificially. At the 2004 Tour de France, cyclists were not yet tested for HGH, because it had not yet been given full World Anti-Doping Agency approval, but athletes were tested for it for the first time during the Athens Olympics.

Today, injecting human growth hormone is a rising industry, with an estimated 100,000 Americans spending up to $1,000 a month loading up on the latest fountain of youth dream. But does it actually delay aging? And is it safe? Although 8,000 physician members of the American Academy of Anti-Aging Medicine now treat *Back-to-the-Future*–minded patients with HGH, the Food and Drug Administration approves its use only to treat severe hormone deficiencies in children and adults. There are associated risks if taken by healthy aging adults, according to a study on aging recently published in the *Journal of the American Medical Association.* Researchers discovered that men who received HGH injections exhibited signs of diabetes or glucose intolerance. Other side effects included fluid retention, joint pain, and symptoms of carpal tunnel syndrome.

Bottom line: "HGH should not be handed out like candy at these anti-aging clinics," said Dr. S. Mitchell Harman, formerly of the National Institute on Aging and now the director of the Kronos Longevity Research Institute in Phoenix, Arizona.

BIKE FOR LIFE

rotator cuff injuries. Blood, barely able to penetrate joints due to lack of capillaries in tendons and ligaments, delivers fewer healing nutrients with age. What to do?

Solution 3a:
Extensive warm-up

Do you really have the time to do a 15-minute warm-up?

"The question is, do you have time not to?" asks Rob Bolton, a certified strength and conditioning coach at U.C. Santa Barbara who advocates "functional" fitness, the popular movement advanced by Vern Gambetta, currently New York Mets director of athletic development, that sees muscles as links in a "kinetic chain" that must be worked out together, not in isolation. "No matter if you're young or old—but especially if you're old—you need that long to gradually increase your heart rate, get synovial fluid lubricating knees, elbows, and shoulders, and work up a light sweat, indicating your body is ready for action. Don't lift or run or ride without lubing the joints."

Bolton's warm-up includes body-only moves and light weights.

It starts with five minutes of jumping jacks, then systematically hits all joints from top to bottom: neck rolls, shoulder shrugs, alternating arm circles, hip circles, trunk rotations (hands on hips, rotating in circles), leg swings (side-to-side, like windshield wipers, and forward and back, like kicking a soccer ball), knee bends (put hands on quads, to avoid overloading them), and "old school" knee circles.

Next up are core-focused single-leg balance exercises. Reach forward, back, sideways, and 45-degrees with the opposite foot, then do the same thing with arms extended straight up. Follow that with five minutes on the Lifecycle or elliptical and quick stretching to avoid cooling down. Then proceed to regular weight program.

Solution 3b:
Strengthen high-risk areas

Rotator cuff exercises: Since injuries to the shoulder are the most common in sports, strengthening the four rotator cuff muscles that stabilize it is critical. "Unfortunately, it's not so easy," says physical therapist Robert Forster, "the cuff gets little blood flow and is invisible to the naked eye, so it's ignored, under-strengthened compared to the glamour muscles, and subject to tears."

Three exercises strengthen the rotator cuff. Starting with two- or three-pound weights in each hand, do three sets of 10 to 15 reps twice a week.

Work the *supraspinatus,* which helps the deltoid raise the arm to the side, by raising both your hands straight out. Hit the *infraspinatus* and *teres minor,* which pull the arms downward (as in a pull-up), by lying on your side with elbow on your hip, then pivot your arm upward.

To work the *subscapularis,* which assists inward arm rotation, pull surgical tubes sideways across your body, like windshield wipers.

Lower back and transverse ab exercises: A lifetime of sitting tightens the lower back's spiny erector muscles and weakens the transverse abdominus, the deep abdominal muscles that draw the belly button to the spine. Strengthening and stretching both can improve posture and eliminate back pain.

Back extension: Lying belly-down, raise your head and upper back to work the spiny erectors. Caution: don't hyperextend.

Dying bug: Laying face-up with arms at side, press the small of your back to the mat, tighten your core by making a "pssst" sound. Then raise and lower opposite legs and arms at once without moving the spine. Reverse.

Transverse abdominus (TA): Standing with light dumbbells at chest level, twist side-to-side as you draw a sideways figure eight.

Cross crunches: Fold left leg over right knee and cross over with elbows to hit TA, intercostals, and obliques.

Solution 3c: Avoid extreme ranges of motion in at-risk joints

Most trainers and therapists nowadays warn against extreme ranges of motion for all weight exercises, regardless of age, due to potential joint injuries and lack of functional benefit. At extreme ranges, dips, push-ups, and flys can jeopardize the humerus/shoulder joint, which is supported only by tendons and ligaments. General rule: to avoid rotator cuff injuries, keep your elbows visible in front of the body. Many trainers have banned the military press for its injury risk and lack of function. To guard the knee joint, avoid deep squats and the first half of leg extensions. And don't go too far on back extensions.

Rob Bolton even warns against the apple pie of the weight room, the bench press. "You can't avoid pinching your shoulder joint on the bench press because it inhibits the scapula [shoulder blades]," he says. "The scapula is pinned between the bar and the bench, causing the humerus [upper arm bone] to grind into and overload the glenohumeral joint. Besides that, it doesn't train you for anything in real life."

He favors pulling exercises in general and replacing the bench with a standing cable machine press, which frees the scapula and requires hip, stomach, and lower back to stabilize the body.

Solution 3d: Cool down with a recovery spin and stretching

"After lifting, your capillaries are dilated and pooling with lactic acid," says Bolton, "so jump on an easy cardio machine to pump it out. The bike allows you to slowly take your heart rate down to 90 bpm."

Elasticity of tissues drops with age; instead of bending and stretching, they break. "So stretch more and avoid injuries that are hard on these tissues," says physical therapist Forster.

Solution 3e: Baby your knees

Running is a fantastic cross-training activity for cyclists and very important for preventing osteoporosis (see chapter 9), but hard on knees and ankles. Forster's recommendation: shorten stride length and pick up cadence. "Go for 180 steps per minute—like the Road Runner," he says. "It greatly reduces joint strain because it puts your body weight directly over the landing point, not behind it." In terms of heart rate, the overall effort is no greater, because the faster turnover—a third more than normal—is balanced by the shorter strides.

• PROBLEM 4 •
Loss of Flexibility

SOLUTION: Stretch a Lot

If you wonder *why stretch?* you may need a different perspective. "The real question," says Bob Anderson, "is *why get old?*"

Anderson is the author of *Stretching,* widely known as the "bible" of flexibility. "Stiffness really has nothing to do with age," he says. "If you keep stretched, and keep active, you feel young—no matter what it says on your driver's license." Anderson lives his words. On the early fall day in 2004 that *Bike for Life* caught up with him, the 59-year-old had just returned from a "typical once-a-week" mountain bike ride of 5½ hours, 52 miles, and 6,500 feet of climbing. He says he rides 25 to 30 hours a week in Pike National Forest trails near his Colorado home, packs 138 pounds of "pure muscle" on his 5-foot-9 frame, looks and feels far younger than his years, and has a resting heart rate in the 40s. "Most of all," he says, "I try not to whine, because no one listens."

The world has listened, however, as Anderson has spread the stretching gospel. Two key points to remember: tightness is the rare malady of aging that anyone— athlete or couch potato—can completely reverse. And for cyclists and other athletes, the immediate benefits of stretching and ridding yourself of this tightness are too good to pass up:

1. *Faster speed,* due to more efficient bio-mechanics.
2. *More force,* due to the increased leverage of lengthened muscles.
3. *Faster post-ride recovery,* due to speedier outflow of waste products and correct muscle shaping.

For an example of flexibility's benefits, look at one pair of muscles: the hamstrings. Flexible hams yield more power by (1) allowing further extension of the quads and (2) allowing a dropped-heel pedaling position, which allows fuller use of the powerful glutes.

The Connective-Tissue Skeleton

Flexibility is defined as the ability to move joints freely through a wide range of motion, according to the American College of Sports Medicine. It may be best illustrated by those who don't have it—the elderly. "They walk like they are old—totally stiff," said Anderson.

That's because their connective tissue— the white, glistening sheaths of collagen that surround and shape bundles of muscles and, when condensed, become tendons— is tight, which makes their muscles tight. For that reason, the real focus of stretching is not the muscle itself, but what Bob Forster calls "the connective-tissue skeleton" that gives shape to our bodies.

"You stress this 'soft skeleton' every time you work out, and your body then lays down more connective tissue haphazardly, making you tight and imbalanced," he says. "So the goal of stretching is to remodel it into a functional pattern—to remodel your infrastructure."

Cycling, given its unnatural position, lays down connective tissue in such a way to leave your biomechanics inherently imbalanced, according to Forster. The bent-over riding position shortens the hip flexors. Abductors become weak due to the lack of lateral movement—what you'd get from playing tennis or basketball. The quads and hamstrings get short, squat, pumped, and tight from working so much. The neck muscles get tight from holding up the head at an unnatural angle.

"Chronically tight muscles, left unstretched, will adapt to this position," says Forster. "That will alter joint mechanics and increase the potential for injury." To lengthen, relax, and ultimately strengthen the muscles and correct cycling-caused biomechanical imbalances, you must stretch them.

Stretching Rules

- ▶ If possible, stretch "passively"—while lying down on the floor. Generally, it's harder to relax a muscle while stretching under tension.
- ▶ Be in a position where you can breathe properly.
- ▶ Use the "subsiding tension principle": move slowly into the stretch and allow for tension to register before adjusting intensity.
- ▶ Never reach over to touch your toes from a standing position. The lower back is concave; this move makes it convex. "Your back ligaments are already stretched out by cycling, and they don't need to be stretched more," says Forster. "A guy with a discectomy isn't finding enlightenment."
- ▶ Go slow. Rapid stretching can stimulate the muscle to tighten up.

When to stretch

- ▶ *As part of your warm-up*—within 45 minutes of a workout or race. Use a five-second "release" to prepare the muscle to perform in its normal range of motion. Don't hold it any longer. You do not need permanent elongation at this time.
- ▶ *Within 45 minutes after a workout,* while warm. At minimum, do a release. A longer session aids circulation and recovery, flushes lactic acids out of the system, corrects gross imbalances and contracture, and effects permanent architecture changes.
- ▶ *Before bed*, which promotes a functional remodeling of connective tissue to create a stronger infrastructure.

Bob Anderson's Top Ten Stretches for Longevity

The latest edition of Bob Anderson's *Stretching* is 223 pages long and filled with drawings of nearly 1,000 stretches. The author recommends that you find four or five that "really help you" and do them several times a day, including before bed. *Bike for Life* asked him to recommend ten basic stretches to start with that'll help maintain range of motion from toe to head. Here they are:

1. ***Ankle Rotation***

   The ankle is important for overall flexibility. "Nothing says 'old' like a stiff-ankled walk," says Anderson. To keep it loose, sit on the floor with legs spread, then grab one ankle with both hands and rotate it clockwise and counterclockwise through a complete range of motion with slight resistance provided. Rotary motion of the ankle helps to gently stretch tight ligaments and improve circulation. Repeat up to 20 times in each direction. Do both ankles.

2. ***Sitting Calf and Hamstring Stretch***

   This movement stretches the lower leg's rear muscles and the area behind the knee.

   Sit upright with one leg straight ahead and the other leg bent at the knee, with its foot bottom flat against the other leg's inner thigh. If you are not very flexible, point the toes toward your body, and lean at the waist toward the extended foot until you feel a stretch in the back of the knee. Hold this position for 10–15 seconds.

   If you are flexible, assume the same position but reach out with the same-side hand, grab the back of the toes, and pull them toward you. Keep the head up and back as straight as possible.

"People say, 'Oh God, I can feel that one!'" says Anderson. "They're surprised that they feel that tight."

3. **Opposite-Hand/Opposite-Foot Quad Stretch**

Lying on your side, hold the top of your right foot with your left hand and gently pull your heel toward your buttocks. The knee bends at a natural angle when you hold your foot with the opposite hand. This is good to use in knee rehabilitation and by those with problem knees. Hold for 30 seconds, each leg.

4. **Spinal Twist (lower back and hamstrings)**

Although Anderson warns that this stretch is difficult for the average person to do, it is highly beneficial for cyclists' backs, which are subject to very little movement.

Sit on the floor with your right leg straight ahead. Bend your left leg, cross your left foot over to the outside of your upper right thigh, just above the knee. During this stretch, use the elbow to keep the left leg stationary with controlled pressure to the inside. With your left hand resting behind you, slowly turn your head to look over your left shoulder, and at the same time rotate your upper body toward your left hand and arm. This should stretch your lower back and side of hip. Hold for 15 seconds. Do both sides.

5. **Groin and Back Stretch**

This comfortable stretch is an easy, safe way to stretch an area that is often tight and hard to relax: the groin. It also flattens your lower back,

helping counteract a hump. Lie on your back with knees bent, soles of feet together, and hands resting on stomach. Let the knees hang down toward the floor, the pull of gravity stretching your groin. By contrast, people often sit up and perform a groin stretch by leaning forward with a rounded-back torso that is hard on the back ligaments.

6. **"Secretary Stretch" (lower back and hips)**

Great for cyclists and people with sciatic pain, start this stretch lying on your back with knees up in sit-up position. Interlace your fingers behind your head and lift the left leg over the right leg (like a secretary would). From here, pivot your left leg to the right, pulling your right leg toward the floor until you feel a good stretch along the side of your hip and lower back. Stretch and relax. Keep the upper back, shoulders, and elbows flat on the floor. Hold for 20 to 30 seconds. Repeat stretch on the other side.

7. **The "Saigon Squat"**

"If I had one stretch to do, this would be it for keeping overall muscle and joint flexibility," says Anderson. "It's the most natural position in human history—squatting to relieve yourself in a floor-pit toilet." The squat stretches everything from the midsection down, including the ankles, Achilles tendons, groin, lower back, and hips. Anderson is fond of pointing out that it taxes humans much more than the seated-position Western toilet, which is why countrified Asians often have better postures and livelier steps than their occidental counterparts.

THE ANTI-AGING GAME PLAN

The squat is simple to perform: with your feet shoulder-width apart and pointed out to about a 15-degree angle, heels on the ground, bend your knees and squat down. Hold for 30 seconds. If you have ultra-tight Achilles, can't balance with flat feet, and generally have trouble staying in this position, hold on to something for support. If you have knee problems, discontinue at the first sign of pain.

8. **Williams's Flexion Hamstring Stretch**

Considered very relaxing and safe after a ride or a run, this easy stretch is great for pelvic flexibility, hip flexors, back, and circulation (since it gets the foot above the heart).

To do it, lie on your back, keep back flat, and draw one knee in to your chest by pulling it in from the back of the knee. Repeat with the other leg. For variation, pull the knee toward the opposite shoulder.

9. **Elongation Stretch/Total Body Relaxer**

This nearly flawless post-exercise stretch feels good, stretches many muscles—abdominals, intercostals, top of the foot and ankle, back, and more—and is particularly good for cyclists, whose sport bends them over. "No one's ever criticized it," says Anderson.

Lying down flat on your back, make yourself as "tall" as possible, straightening arms and legs and pointing toes and extending fingers. Stretch and then relax. Hold for 5 seconds. For variety, stretch diagonally, extending opposite arm and leg.

10. **Triceps and Tops of Shoulders**

Anderson calls the upper body "a storehouse of mental and physical tension" caused by cycling as well as non-athletic pressures, such as getting yelled at by the boss at work.

With arms overhead, hold the elbow of one arm with the hand of the other arm, gently pull the elbow behind the head and push it down, creating a stretch. Do it slowly. Hold for 15 seconds. Do not use drastic force to limber up. Stretch both sides. You can do this stretch while walking.

Anderson suggests that a cyclist take the stretch further by placing the back of the head against the bent elbow and bending to the opposite side. "This counteracts the cycling position and keep cyclists standing straight up as they age," he says. "It's especially helpful for men, as we tend to get tighter with age than women."

• PROBLEM 5 •
Slumping Posture

SOLUTION: Straighten Yourself Out Before You Ride or Lift Weights

Lifting weights when you have bad posture is akin to "building a Ferrari on a bent chassis," according to postural therapist Patrick Mummy of San Diego–based Symmetry, who provided the back straightening exercises described in the "Biker's Back" section of chapter 8. That 12-exercise routine is an antidote to the slumping, hunching posture that he says is often first apparent by age 35. The exercises will stretch the hip flexors to restore the correct pelvic tilt, reposition the shoulders back, and equalize the hips to restore bilateral symmetry.

"Step one of any anti-aging maintenance program by definition must be posture," Mummy says. "Otherwise, everything you are doing to build yourself up is reinforcing the problem." Perform them twice daily in the order presented, especially before any weight or aerobic exercise. At one to two minutes each, the dozen exercises you'll find in the sidebar in chapter 8 should take 10 to 15 minutes.

Profile: Vic Copeland and the Fountain of Youth

The secrets of the world's greatest over-35 bike racer

VIC Copeland, a 62-year-old optometrist from Rancho Santa Fe, California, is officially the world's greatest old cyclist. His coach, Eddie B, says he could have been another Greg LeMond had he started the sport in his teens. At the 2003 World Track Championships in Manchester, England, when he won the 500-meter time trial, the 2,000-meter time trial, the points race, and the matched sprints (the same four events he swept six years earlier in slower times), the UCI named him "Outstanding Rider in the World Over Age 35." Pretty good for a guy who got into cycling because he wanted to take it easy.

"'How did this happen?' I often say to myself," says Copeland.

It starts with innate talent. As an athlete, Copeland had excelled in everything he'd tackled since grade school—football, basketball, track. He was a fast learner, too. In 1982, as a recreational runner who rode his wife's clunker bike and dog-paddled on the swim ("I grew up in Kansas," he explains), he finished dead last in his first triathlon, the United States Triathlon Series (USTS) San Diego race in Torrey Pines. Two years later, he won his age group. But after doing five Hawaii Ironman triathlons from 1983 through 1987, including setting a personal record (PR) of 11:00:09 in 1986 at age 42, Copeland walked away from the sport he loved. In 1988, with his kids entering their teens, he and his wife, Joyce, concluded that triathlon was taking too much time away from the family.

"I had to get into something less all-encompassing," he said. "I thought cycling was something I could do to keep in shape." Talk about an understatement.

One day, while Copeland was riding with the same bike club he'd trained with during his triathlon years, they challenged him to do a cycling race. He finished fourth . . . and the rest is history. He hired Eddie B (profiled in an interview at the end of chapter 7) when the legendary coach moved to nearby Ramona. At the 1988 nationals, he won the criterium and took two second places and a third on the track. By the mid-1990s, Copeland was known as the Mark Spitz of age-group cycling, scorching the record book with 14 national records in events ranging from the kilo to the road race. At age 49, going against 20-year-olds, he placed eighth overall in the kilo at the Olympic trials. At 50, he set a record for the 35-year-old age group.

How does he explain his success on the bike?

"Besides good genes, the Ironman," he says. A naturally fast sprinter, Copeland says that his long-distance Ironman training taught him how to hold his sprint speed longer than most—

a theory he says is borne out by the exceptional performances of Australian track sprinters, who do a lot of long-distance work earlier in the season.

The result? "The younger guys would be ahead of me in the first half of the kilo, but their speeds would drop off the second half," he says. "My speed stayed the same, so I'd win in the last half." Records that Copeland set range from the shortest to the longest: the kilo (1 kilometer; 1:07) and flying-start 1k (1:02), both in 1993; standing-start 3k (3:38) in 1996, the tandem 40k (48:18) in 1996, and the flying 200 meter (11.5 seconds) in 1995.

Initially, Copeland got a lot of attention for his exploits ("After all, I have no hair," he says, referring to his shiny dome), but his age soon became a non-issue to his opponents. "Occasionally, somebody would come up and joke, 'Hey, I've got 20 more years to get as good as you.'"

Cycling success became a family affair for the Copelands. Son Zack won the Junior National Championship on the track one year and was on the national team; father and son both competed for a matched-sprint slot at the 1992 Olympic trials but never met head-to-head, because Vic didn't survive his qualifying round. (Zack missed the Olympics by finishing fourth.) Daughter Joannie, then 16, set a world junior record in the 1k in 1992 and won the criterium nationals the next year; she finished high school in Colorado Springs because she was a member of the U.S. Junior National team. Both gave up cycling in college and haven't looked back.

Told that Eddie B said Copeland was born with as much talent as LeMond, Copeland says he's never dwelled on what might have been. But the numbers don't lie: his record 1k time in 1992 would have won the Olympic Gold in Tokyo in 1964. His reaction? "If I did it at age 49, certainly I could have done it age 21."

Copeland's greatest challenge today will be slowing himself down. He was faster than ever at the U.S. National Championships in Colorado Springs in August 2004, winning four gold medals and setting two world records in the 60–64 age group, but later had a scare. At the U.S. Road Championships, he got faint as he went into atrial fibrillation, a rapid-heartbeat condition that prevents blood from circulating through the upper chamber of the heart.

"It's caused by my training—and is triggered by riding hard," he says. "I can go to 87 percent of my maximum heart rate of 160, but can't go anaerobic. At 90 percent or above, which is what you have to do to win races on the track, will be trouble."

While Copeland trains these days at under 85 percent, he's mulling his next move. "Maybe I'll go back to triathlon," he says, coming full circle. The long, slow rides that took him into cycling, so long abandoned, are starting to look pretty good again.

Training Tips: How Copeland Did It
1. **Hammer and recover:** Coach Eddie B only lets Copeland do two days of intensity a week. "Eddie holds me back," he says. "He says that high intensity raises the acid level in the blood, and that you need longer, slower rides to renormalize you." Copeland rides two hours a day, indoors on a trainer and outdoors at the track at San Diego's Balboa Park.
2. **No mega miles:** "It becomes comfortable to take long, slow rides—but that only trains you to go long and slow," he says. "And they leave you too tired to go fast." During his

triathlon days, while his competitors were biking 500-mile weeks, Copeland logged only 150 miles.

3. **Specificity:** "I break an event down into each segment. If a bike course is hilly, I'll train by doing hill repeats over and over and over."

4. **Visualization:** Psychologically, Copeland begins his preparation the day before the race. "I try to act as if I've already won the race, in the way I talk to people and act. It creates a winning attitude." Additionally, he visualizes important moments of the race itself, so his race reactions and strategy will be automatic.

5. **Resistance training:** Copeland does not lift weights, but for two years has used a one-of-a-kind bike trainer invented by his son in which the pedals turn backwards with resistance. "It increases the stress on my muscles in a cycling-specific motion, yet doesn't stress me cardiovascularly."

6. **Mind of a champion:** "I always had confidence, and Eddie B liked that," he said. "Eddie is not interested in you as a rider unless you're highly motivated already—somebody like Lance Armstrong, who'd ride himself unconscious. I've never seen Eddie once push people to ride harder. He wants a mental champion who he can mold."

Ned Overend

THE GRAND MASTER OF BALANCE

In September, he's working the Specialized Bicycles booth at the Interbike trade show in Las Vegas, kneeling down, putting shoes on the feet of retailers as if he's a high school part-timer working at Foot Locker. In March, he's in Washington, D.C., in a three-piece suit, lobbying Colorado congressmen for the passage of bicycle-friendly legislation. One moment, he's on the podium at an XTERRA race, the next promoting a local mountain bike event, the next flying to California to participate in product planning meetings at one of the world's largest bike manufacturers. At 49, mountain bike icon Ned Overend, inducted into the Mountain Bike Hall of Fame in 1990 and the U.S. Bicycle Hall of Fame in 2001, told Bike for Life's Roy Wallack in their interview on April 10, 2004, that he's superfit and busier than ever. Heading into his sixth decade, this son of a diplomat who was born in Taiwan and raised in Ethiopia and Iran seems to barely have time to think about the six national mountain bike championships, the three UCI World titles, and the two XTERRA off-road triathlon titles he's acquired over the years. Aging glacially has always been the modus operandi of the down-to-earth superstar still known as "The Lung" for his prodigious climbing ability. Back in 1988, battling Ned for the national title, a young competitor remarked with relish, "He's 34 and won't be riding much longer." Overend didn't bow out of mountain biking for another eight years, then was a full-bore off-road triathlete until 2002—several years after his young rival retired.

I GOT MY first road bike in 1973 when I was in high school. While running on the cross-country team, a Dutch teammate of mine got me a Crescent, a double-butted European road racing bike which had Campy components on it and sew-up tires. I ended up doing the Ironman Triathlon on it in 1980.

It was Bob Babbitt's idea to do that. [Note: Babbitt is now the editor/publisher of *Competitor* and *City Sports* magazines.] We met at a rock-climbing class when I was going to San Diego State and he was a teacher. We started doing some runs and 10k's together and ended up getting a house down at the beach. He read an article in *Sports Illustrated* about the 1979 Ironman and said, "Let's do this." I did it because it was in Hawaii and I'd never been.

Yet even after doing the Ironman Triathlon, I still wasn't a cyclist. I didn't really become one until I moved to Durango and started riding in the mountains here. By 1982, I'd done more triathlons, but what really got me into road racing is the Iron Horse Bicycle Classic, a huge event here in town. It really gave me an appreciation for how important events are for getting people involved in the sport. The Iron Horse is an epic. It's only 50 miles, from Durango to Silverton, but it's over an 11,000-foot pass. Everybody in town knows it, because it's a huge race every Memorial Day weekend. Everybody wants to do it—even, to this day, my 13-year-old son and his buddies do it on their downhill bikes, because they don't know any better. Iron Horse piqued my interest in road racing.

For me, road racing was more exciting than triathlon—more neck-and-neck. Whether it's a criterium or road racing, the excitement of racing in a pack is incredible.

I did quite well quickly. In '82, I was a Cat 4 [Category 4, beginner-level racing]. In '83, I was a Cat 1 doing the Coors Classic, riding for 7-Eleven with Andy Hampsten—on the same Crescent bike I got back in high school. In '84, I started racing mountain bikes, and I was good right away—took second at my first national championship that year at Lake Eldora to Joe Murray. It may seem like a rapid rise, but I had the background: before cycling I raced motorcycles and was an accomplished mountain runner. In high school, we had the one of the best teams in Northern California. I won several mountain runs around here. Indian Pass. Kendall Mountain. I did the Pikes Peak Marathon—finished second place twice. So the fitness and skills were there.

I didn't plan on being a pro mountain biker. Actually, I had switched from being a car mechanic/carpenter to a bike shop mechanic so that I could be a pro triathlete or road racer. But while I was in the bike shop, I saw these Specialized Stumpjumpers come through. I thought, "Man, this is a great idea! We've got great trails out here." When I found out about the mountain bike racing series, I called Schwinn, because we were a Schwinn dealer. And they said, "Yeah, we want to do a mountain bike team. Let's do it." At first, they just picked up my expenses and I'd get a performance bonus plus prize money. So I worked a variety of jobs. I worked at Pizza Hut, Subway, things like that in the off-season. Eventually came the salaries—started $10,000, plus bonus. I kinda rode the wave from there.

My first national championship was in 1984. I remember being in the parking lot with almost no other cars there. We're wearing jeans and T-shirts; I really didn't have a logo. We are shaking the hands of the promoter and it is snowing. There is

nobody but us left there. Those are the early days of mountain biking.

Contrast that to 1990, when I won the World Championships—and helicopters are flying around. I've been to races in Spain where there were literally 40,000 spectators. Where you could not walk out of a protective compound to go into the crowd to sign autographs, because there'd be almost a riot.

I had switched to Specialized after I won the national championships in '85, '86, and '87. The meteoric rise in the sale of mountain bikes was on. Mountain biking became a UCI-recognized event. Europe really came on board when car sponsors came in and the big salaries started. No more working at Pizza Hut.

Banishing Burnout with Variety

I THINK IN 1987 someone was interviewing [John] Tomac [two-time world champion] when he said, "Ned is 32 already. So I doubt he'll be riding much longer." Like I was going to be out of there and he was going to be racking up some championships. Well, I retired from mountain biking as my main job in 1996. I wasn't out of there quite as quick as he thought I would be [laughs].

If someone had told me in 1985 that in 1996 at the age of 40 I was going to miss making the Olympic team by one spot, I would have thought that was absurd.

I get asked a lot how I stay so fit at my age. What I manage to do even now is maintain an enthusiasm for racing and riding hard. I think my approach is really important: cross-training and not being obsessive.

Back in the early days when I was battling Tomac, he'd put in 30 percent more miles than I would. He'd come out of the winter months strong. At the Cactus Cup,

BIKE FOR LIFE

the first big race of the season in March, I would get my ass kicked. It would almost be embarrassing. I couldn't finish in the Top 5 in the Cactus Cup, even when I'd come off a year when I won the world and national championships.

That's because I would back off in the off-season. I'd get in the weight room. I'd do some cross-country skiing. I'd do some running. I'd do some swimming. And I'd really back off on the cycling.

I'd start up later in the spring and I'd kinda build through the summer. So that by August and September, the most important races—the National Off-Road Bicycle Association (NORBA) nationals and the World Championships—I would be fresher than these guys. There's nothing that gets your enthusiasm going like winning, like improving. There's a lot of guys whose best performance was in the Cactus Cup in March. What would be more depressing than having the races get more and more important as your fitness plateaus or actually goes down?

It happens to a lot of athletes. They overtrain. They are too excited. They are super serious and they get obsessive about it.

What saved me is that I don't have the appetite for putting in huge miles. I didn't have the attention span. Another thing was that I was actually building a family from the late '80s on. I had two kids at home, and the idea of riding five hours and lying on the couch for the rest of the afternoon didn't really work at home. My wife wasn't going to accept that.

The formula I'd use for getting off the bike in the winter was going Nordic skiing and trail running. I think a variety of sports keeps you healthier from an injury standpoint. Overall it makes you a better athlete and gives you more longevity.

I have tremendous respect for guys like Tinker [Juarez] who do 24-hour races. I know they are going long and hard the whole time. That's why it does not appeal to me at all. I know for a fact that 24-hour races will accelerate the aging process. And I'm getting old fast enough as it is.

Post-40: Taking on New Challenges

I RETIRED AT 40, but didn't stop mountain bike racing. There were always a bunch of races that I wanted to do. But because racing was my job, I was locked into the NORBA national series and the World Cup series, with a lotta traveling in Europe and going to Japan every year. So now I was able to focus on some of these events that I missed, like the Wamagans, a classic race in the Midwest. And I wanted to get into some of these off-road triathlons which were just starting up.

In 1996, the year I retired from the World Cup circuit, they had the first XTERRA Triathlon Championship in Maui. I can guarantee you, because it was in Maui, I was going. My wife was okay with that. "We're all going," she said.

Off-road tris [triathlons] fit in really perfectly with my whole training philosophy. Turns out in that first one I ended up getting third to Mike Pigg and Jimmy Riccitello, a couple of accomplished triathletes. I knew I could improve a bunch in the swim and the run.

Specialized covered the expenses for me, which was a risk because there was no press that year. But it was on ESPN, and I ended up I getting considerable press over the years. Huge press. *USA Today* wrote articles on it, so Specialized was happy. If I can examine an event to see if it's got any value, I can do it.

It's great to have new challenges. That is one of the great things about triathlon.

BIKE FOR LIFE

Trying to be efficient in the swim. Trying to develop leg speed in the run. You have to do it all. As you get older, you do it with an eye towards not getting injured. Because I constantly go from one little overuse injury to the next. That's one thing I think runners and triathletes do more than cyclists.

As you get older, you can't ignore a tight hamstring. You can't ignore a pain in your shoulder. You have to start getting massage, physical therapy, stretching. As you get older you have to pay close attention to nutrition and hydration. If you're going to be successful as an athlete, you have to pay attention to all those things.

I still eat a lot—I'm a skinny guy, 135 to 140 pounds, and never had a problem with weight—but my diet has changed as I got older. In the old days I would maybe restrict the amount of fat I would take, which I think was probably a mistake. I think it's probably more important to restrict the simple sugars and still get quality sources of protein and fat. For recovery, you need protein. In the old days, I didn't care about protein that much. Just a pound of pasta. But now I also make sure I'm getting some lean sources of either dairy or meat. I take pretty complete vitamin and mineral supplements. I'm more careful to replenish after a hard workout with a four to one mix—four carbohydrates to one protein.

I'm a stickler on it. But it's got to taste good. I don't like to spend a lot of time using up calories for food I don't enjoy eating. So sometimes I'll do things like Ensure, the old-people drink. It has a four to one carbohydrate to protein mixture. They also have a buncha vitamins. And it tastes good.

The Atkins diet is too strict on the carbohydrates. You need more fuel. I'm looking at a can of Slim Fast here. Thirty-five grams of sugar and 10 grams of protein.

Huge variety of vitamins. It's a premium milk chocolate shake. That's the important thing, I think. And I've always done that. You know. A diet I enjoy. If you put all the work in to burn those calories, you should enjoy the replacement of 'em.

I work out every day if possible. In 2002, I did a ton of XTERRAs [off-road triathlons]. Last year, I was involved in this Muddy Buddy duathlon series, helping promote it. Specialized was a sponsor of that. I think it's great entry-level way to get people who aren't involved in mountain biking in the sport. Because of my recent travel schedule—a week in D.C., a week of product meetings in Morgan Hill—I find that it's hard to carve out time and train for the different sports of triathlon. You don't have the time or the energy to swim, bike, and run. Hopefully I can hit an XTERRA at the end of the year. But I'll always still train.

I'll do two workouts a day maybe two or three days a week. I have a lunch hour ride at Specialized. That's a 45-minute hammer session. So I'll do that and I might run for 45 minutes after the meeting.

The Ultimate Tip: Don't Fall

YOU RECOVER FROM injuries a helluva lot slower when you're older. So a good rule is: don't get injured. In my career, I've had no broken bones. I did break a couple fingers. But never broken a big bone. No collarbones. I'm really knocking on wood now.

I've been a good faller. I'm looking at my elbows and hips; I've got scars all over me. I've gone down at 45 mph on a road bike. I had one of my worst crashes ever last spring at one of the club rides. We were going like 30 mph on a slight downhill and there was a chunk of wood in the road. I was about five guys back. And nobody pointed it out, because they were all attacking and going so hard. And I pegged the thing and knocked my hand off the bar. That was ugly. I went face first into the pavement and rolled over on my back and slid down the road on my back. Crushed the helmet. But I was all right. My neck hurt for a while. I've been lucky.

On a mountain bike, a lot of injuries happen at slow speed. You don't get time to get your foot out of the pedal. You come to a technical section, your speed slows to zero, you don't make it over this little log or through these slippery rocks, and you start to fall over. Now, if you can balance, if you've practiced doing a track stand—which everyone should do—you can avoid falling to start with. You have this little extra second or fraction of a second where you can clip your foot out and put your foot down. Most people can't balance when they're falling over. Other people break collarbones. . . .

A key: knowing how to set up your pedals. Set them up correctly, so they aren't sticky, so you can get out easily. Clean out the grit—it gets in your pedals and really changes the amount of release tension it takes. People can't get out of the pedals in a crash. That's a dangerous situation.

And when you do fall, minimize impact. Instead of sticking my arm out, I'll just fall and let the handlebar with the bar end on it hit the ground and let the pedal hit the ground first and then I'll let my body hit the ground with a little less impact. We used to actually do drills in the late 1980s—the teacher was a Polish guy named Andre Modgeleski, a truck driver in Colorado Springs who was a buddy of Eddie B in the old country. We had a camp and we'd do some tumbling. We'd have mats on the floor and you'd jump, tuck, and roll, and figure it out. You'd never stick

a straight arm down. You'd put your hand down and immediately pull it in and tuck.

Look how much an injury like that would set someone back. Just look at [Australian pro rider] Cadel Evans—three broken collarbones last year. Here's someone who has a tremendous amount of talent. Two years ago [2002] he was in the pink jersey, leading the Giro—made him a huge amount of money when he signed his next contract. Since then he's been unable to finish any important tour. He hasn't made it very far into the season without getting injured. He's going down in crashes and busting his collarbone.

Beyond Riding

A LOT OF times riders' main passions are just racing. But I gotta say, I love the R&D [research and development] side of it. And the equipment. I'm an equipment geek, ya know? I've got five road bikes in my garage and I'm a mountain bike racer. I've got like seven of my old mountain bikes at the Mountain Bike Specialist bike shop—from early hard-tail suspensions to one of the first Epics in prototype form. They actually have a museum for it. They've got Greg Herbold's old bikes, and Julie Furtados. . . . A lot of people thought I was in business with [owner] Ed Zink just because I had so much stuff hanging down there. Not really. Better hanging down there than in my garage.

I have a unique relationship with Specialized, really my only employer. I am standing in Durango, where it's important for me to be able to stay for training and racing, while Specialized is in California. I don't really have a title; I'm involved with R&D and product development, especially cross-country suspensions and shoes and tires. I'm involved with promotions, and

BIKE FOR LIFE

with advocacy, and sales as far as dealer relations. When we do a product launch to the media, I'm there for that. I ride with the dealers and explain the product to them and things like that.

My current job started evolving when I was still riding. It's been 15 or so years now I've been an employee. As I was racing, I gradually got involved in dealer PR [public relations]. I'd go to the bike show and meet a lot of dealers. And as I would travel around the country racing, I'd dicker with them, get to know them on a personal level. At the same time, I'd get to know the magazine people, because they'd be covering the races, so it was kind of a natural transition when I got more involved with product development. Which was also happening while I was racing, because the Specialized racing teams have always had an influential role in product development.

The Bigger Picture
In March 2004, I was a delegate at the Bicycle Summit, an annual summit meeting in Washington, D.C., for 350 bicycle advocacy groups. We do workshops, learn about the specific issues before the senators and Congressmen, how to lobby them as a constituent, a business owner, a taxpayer.

Greg LeMond was there last year. It's always nice to have a recognized name, a world champion. Also, since I'm a citizen of Colorado, I went with the Colorado delegation. We talked to four representatives and both senators.

I think I had an impact. Senator Allard went to school at Durango High. My poster was hanging up in her history classroom. So she was excited. We took a picture together. I'm gonna sign it and send it to her. Stuff like this. But—okay, granted, yeah this is Ned, the World Mountain Bike champion, XTERRA champion—but if it doesn't go beyond that, it's only got limited value. What pulls more weight is the fact that I am involved in fundraising, in the local trails plans, and advocacy issues for mountain and road biking; that I'm a local business owner in Durango [Bouré Ridge Sportswear]; that I'm involved with a local bike dealer [through Specialized]; and also on the board of the Iron Horse Bicycle Classic. We put on the race on Memorial Day and we put on the NORBA Nationals—the national finals last year, and a World Cup before that. These are the kind of things that really speak to the politicians.

It gets attention when I say, "Hey, these events take in a million dollars in May with Iron Horse, then another million dollars in August with the NORBA Nationals, and get international media that brings Europeans here all summer long as a destination bicycle trip." They buy bikes, they're in the hotels and restaurants, taking raft trips. Millions and millions of dollars are generated by these events beyond the events themselves, giving notoriety to the whole Four Corners area. And these senators and congressmen understand that. They know how important cycling is as far as a tourist attraction to Colorado.

If you're just there as a do-gooder, talking about cycling only for its health benefits, you're not gonna get too much attention. Yes, there is Senator Oberstar from Minnesota, and senators in Wisconsin and California and Vermont who are avid cyclists themselves. So they are going to support it because they realize how valuable it is. But for most of them, we go in with a several-pronged attack: the money cycling brings to the state, this whole obesity issue, and health.

I'll tell ya what feels good is when they build a county road in this town and they put a three-foot shoulder on it. In Durango, it's better than most towns, because we have so many people involved in cycling living here. Here, the public works guy for the city calls the cyclists in and says: "How can we help you guys out?" They'll paint stripes to create narrow lanes in town to make a wider bike path.

Oh, I mean we got money to improve a dedicated bike path along the river. But when you get out into the county, it's a whole different situation. It takes more to get shoulders on the roads, and we don't have a captive audience like we do with the city government. That's where we need to work next. But like I learned in racing, it's early in the season. We'll get stronger as time moves on.

BIKE FOR LIFE

6

BICYCLE SEX

Cycling and impotence:
easy solutions to an (un-)hard problem

"The sex is out of this world. My wife jokes about my prowess." —Mike Miller, 53, an 8,000-miles-per-year rider, August 2004 (*Bike for Life*, chapter 12)

19 percent of cyclists who had a weekly training distance of more than 400 km (250 miles) complained of erectile dysfunction. —2001 study of 40 German cyclists by Dr. Frank Sommer

When I'm not riding, I'm with Jody, providing her with endless sexual pleasure. —Dan Cain, 46, a 20- to 30-hour-per-week mountain biker, September 2004 (*Bike for Life*, chapter 12)

Frequent mountain biking may reduce fertility in men, according to an Austrian study. Of 55 avid mountain bikers who each rode at least 3,000 miles per year, an average of two hours per day six days a week, nearly 90 percent had low sperm count and scrotal abnormalities, about three times that of nonbikers. Researcher Dr. Ferdinand Frauscher, a urology-radiology specialist at University Hospital in Innsbruck, suggests the cause is the frequent jolts and vibration caused by biking over rough terrain. —Presentation at Radiological Society of North America, December 2002

Riding a bike may substitute for Viagra in some men with weak heart muscles, according to Dr. Romualdo Belardinelli, director of the Lancisi Heart Institute in Ancona, Italy. "Cycling improves your sexual function," he said. Questionnaires given to 29 male heart patients and their sex partners showed the men who rode had better erections compared to the study's non-exercisers. —November 12, 2001, American Heart Association conference in Anaheim, California.

Men should never ride bicycles. Riding should be banned and outlawed. It is the most irrational form of exercise I could ever bring to discussion. —Dr. Irwin Goldstein, 1997

When you graph the impotency rates of cyclists against the general male population, cyclists were half as likely to suffer severe impotence and one-third as likely to suffer any form of impotence. —Charlie McCorkell, owner, Bicycle Habitat bike shop, New York City, at New York University School of Medicine Conference in December 2000

Fourteen of 15 members of the Marine Bicycle Patrol of the Long Beach, California, Police Department, who each ride six hours a day, five days a week, complained of genital numbness during or after their rides. While none experienced impotence, Rigiscan erection monitoring devices measured a one-third reduction in erection quality and duration during sleep. The police were advised to study the feasibility of switching to nose-less bike seats. —National Institute of Occupational Safety and Health, May 2001

Blood supply to the penises of healthy men, which fell by two-thirds from normal when they sat on a bike seat for three minutes, increased to 110 percent of normal levels when they pedaled in a standing-up position for a minute. —"Pressure during cycling," BJU International, April 1999

I'd often measure my rides two ways: total elevation gained, and degree of numbness in my crotch. Numbness was good, a barometer of a solid training session. Since it unnumbed quickly, and my plumbing never malfunctioned, why worry? Then came the 1997 article in Bicycling, and things changed. I didn't stop riding, but took a few precautions: Got a new saddle, a new bike fit, a habit of standing up more. Given what we know now, it's dumb to be numb. —BK

It's the debate that still has legs, though the passion that the controversy once aroused has ebbed. "We don't see guys walking into our stores like we used to, all worried and inquiring about becoming impotent from cycling," says Mike Jacoubowsky, co-owner of Chain Reaction Bicycles of Redwood City and Los Altos, California. So does this mean men shouldn't be concerned about their plumbing? Does it mean that the famous (or infamous) 1997 article in *Bicycling* magazine that started the "cycling-causes-impotence" firestorm was wrong—or that its lessons have been forgotten?

What's the truth about the bicycle-impotency issue?

The truth is that we don't know what percentage of cyclists are impotent, but that it's probably higher than the percentage of runners and swimmers who are impotent. On the other hand, it's certainly far lower than the percentage of the general population that is impotent.

We do know that there is some undefined risk of impotency in cycling, but not for the vast majority of riders, as an alarmed cycling community came to believe after the aforementioned *Bicycling* article and subsequent airing of a similar story on ABC's *20/20* program. We do have a good idea of who are the bike riders most at risk of impotency: ultra-distance riders who've logged 200-plus miles a week for years.

One such rider is the courageous 50-year-old *Bicycling* magazine editor who revealed his impotency in an essay in the magazine; he'd averaged 14,000 miles per year for seven years, much of it in the aerobar position, while training for cross-state records and team Race Across America events. That rider, who asked not to be named here, deserves our thanks. By personalizing the issue, he emboldened other cyclists to seek help and motivated the bike industry to do three things: **make safer bike seats, pay more attention to proper bike fit, and do a better job of teaching sex-safe riding technique**.

Bike for Life strongly advocates that those precautions, spelled out in detail later in this chapter, be observed by *all* cyclists, regardless of mileage. Here's why:

1. *You never know.* As you'll see below, although numbness indicates temporary (and generally non-damaging) obstruction of blood vessels and nerves, problems can arise as megamiles add up over the years. But given variations in anatomy, riding style, and vascular resiliency, impotency has occasionally occurred in lower-mileage riders, too.
2. *Taking precautions is cheap and easy.* It's like putting on sunblock,

said one man; the small inconvenience is worth the off-chance it'll stop skin cancer (impotency).
3. *You're rewarded with super sex.* Sex-safe cycling does more than preserve your sex life—it upgrades it. Numerous studies indicate that cycling, like all aerobic activity, stokes the libido, enhances endurance and power, and supercharges the duration and quality of sex.

ANATOMY OF A SQUISHED VESSEL

To understand why numbness and impotency occur in the first place, and why no cyclist should ignore it, let's go back to Anatomy 101: sitting on a bike seat *improperly* can put unusual stresses on the perineum, the soft area between the base of the penis and the anus that houses the nerves and two main blood vessels responsible for an erection. When you sit straight up, as you do in a flat desk chair, your weight is focused on the pelvic bones known as "sit bones." But when you lean forward on the nose of a narrow bike saddle, your weight shifts forward and between these sit bones—directly on the delicate perineum.

"When a man sits on a bicycle seat, he's putting his entire body weight on the arteries that supply the penis," says Dr. Irwin Goldstein, director of the Boston University Medical Center urology department and the featured player in the storied 1997 *Bicycling* article that broke the cycling-impotence connection. Although he'd studied bike-related impotency for years, Goldstein suddenly became the issue's "founding father" and an overnight media sensation. He was assailed by the bike industry as a scare-mongering, publicity-hungry opportunist who shamelessly preyed on male rider's fears. Unrepentant, he asserted that probably 100,000 male cyclists in America have problems with impotence, that no one should ride a bike for more than three hours a week, and that the ideal bike saddle would be "shaped like a toilet seat."

This wasn't wild speculation, Goldstein explained, but a sober analysis of anatomy: from a study of 100 impotent patients, he had determined that it only takes 11 percent of a person's body weight to compress the perineum arteries, causing a 66 percent average reduction in penile blood flow when subjects were on a skinny bike saddle. Sit on those arteries enough times, compress it, rub it, flatten it out, accumulate scar tissue in the artery wall, he explained, and eventually it will become like a soft-drink straw you chew on—permanently narrowed and squashed.

"For cyclists who put in many miles," he says, "it's a nightmarish situation."

•

How nightmarish? Try *Friday the 13th* grab-your-private-parts nightmarish. Just ask reporter Joe Lindsey, who visited Cologne, Germany, in April 2004 to write an update of the impotency issue for an article in *Bicycling*'s January 2005 issue, "The Hard Truth." Lindsay was invited on the trip because an earlier article he wrote about the damage done by the impact of mountain biking (excerpted in the lead at the beginning of this chapter) got the attention of Roger Minkow, who had gained fame as the designer of a popular anti-impotence saddle. The two of them traveled to the University of Cologne's Poliklinik for Urology to meet with Dr. Frank Sommer, who would be conducting the first study to measure actual blood flow among cyclists while they pedaled.

Sommer, 37, so respected that he was named the Minister of Health for the European Union earlier that year, had already conducted a 2001 study in *European Urology* that opened eyes: he found that 61 percent of 40 healthy German bike riders had numbness; worse, a fifth of those with over 400 km of weekly mileage complained of erectile dysfunction (ED). He later surveyed 1,700 German cyclists and found similar problems.

Technically, Sommer explains, the problem is low penile oxygen retention, which causes increased collagen development. "That's very bad for the penis," he told *Bike for Life* in a telephone interview on April 20, 2004. "Over the long-term, you will lose elasticity. You will lose capacity of getting blood into the penis and holding it there. If you have sexual arousal, your erection won't be as good."

"Of course," he adds, "this is a very long-term problem. This takes many, many years of riding before you find this problem." Mountain bikers are not immune, Sommer said, but for a different reason: trauma. "Shock waves to the perineum from impact can damage arterial vessels, which leads to restricted blood flow," he says.

In April 2004, Sommer was the first to apply an oxygen-saturation measurement device to penile blood flow. He tested about 20 saddles on dozens of German amateur bike racers and triathletes. The results from his breakthrough study—in which Joe Lindsey was a participant—basically confirmed Goldstein's assertions and should serve as a wake-up call to riders who haven't gotten the message yet.

A View from the Bike Shop

The type of saddle is often not the main villain. It's a combination of tilt and the drop from seat to handlebar that makes the difference.

by Mike Jacoubowsky

MUCH as we'd like to sell zillions of new saddles, in most cases the saddle itself is not the problem. It's more how one sits on the saddle that is at issue here, and it really doesn't matter whether you've got a $10 stock seat or the fanciest $100 aftermarket urologist-approved model. If you're not set up correctly on the bike, you're going to have potential for problems down the road.

The first place to start is the tilt, or angle, of the saddle. In almost no case is it a good idea to ride with a saddle that's tilted up at the front! This focuses the pressure on exactly the wrong areas. As you slide forward on the seat, you're essentially driving your most delicate parts (and the ones that could cause problems down the road) into the nose of the seat.

So do you want the seat "down" at the front? That's not a good idea either, because you're going to spend the whole ride pushing back from the handlebars, creating a lot of tension in your arms and shoulders. A level saddle is the best bet.

What if a "level" saddle causes discomfort? Then it's definitely time for a different saddle. You need to be able to distribute pressure across a wide area, and the only way you're going to be able to do this is if the saddle's level. If this gives you problems at the front of the saddle, then you might look into something with either a cutout or soft layers of foam and/or gel in the appropriate location.

But there's more to it than just saddle tilt. If your seat is well above the level of the handlebar, then you're going to be rotating downward over the front of the saddle, once again bringing the wrong areas into hard contact with the seat. This, I believe, is the number one reason for saddle-related male problems.

Specifically, note the difference in height between the top of the saddle and the top of the handlebar. For a smaller road bike (up to about 54 cm or so) try to keep this difference to 5 cm (2 inches) or less. For a mid-sized road bike (up to 58 cm) a difference of 6 cm (2.5 inches) is acceptable, and for larger bikes, try to avoid greater than an 8 cm difference (3 inches). The issue here is that as the difference becomes too great, the rider is rotating his midsection downward over the front of the saddle, bringing undue pressure onto exactly the wrong areas. In my opinion, this is far more likely to cause a problem than a saddle!

Why would anyone want a stem so low that it might cause such trouble? Primarily for aerodynamics. Lower stem equals less torso and head up in the wind! Triathletes in particular go to great trouble trying to achieve the most aerodynamic position possible, and even serious recreational riders get into aerodynamics as well. But hear this, and hear this clearly. If your saddle/handlebar differential is beyond the recommendations above, or if you're feeling any discomfort in the saddle area, try raising the stem a bit. If this makes cycling more comfortable, your stem was low enough to potentially create serious problems down the road.

Something else to consider. The way you ride might make all the difference in the world. Most injuries don't occur instantly, but rather over a long period of exposure to whatever's causing the problem. If your riding style is such that you sit endlessly on the saddle and never stand up or stretch, you're much more likely to have problems. The best way to combat this is to regularly take a break from the grind and stand up for a bit, take a breather, stretch a bit, and then get back in the saddle. Wanna hear a secret? If you do this on a regular basis, before you start to experience a sore tail end, you'll go a lot farther without pain than you would otherwise. Anyone who has miles on a tandem knows this to be true! Even when you're feeling great, you still need to take breaks once in a while, and you'll feel a whole lot better for a whole lot longer.

Cyclists most at risk are those living in flat areas, since it's unlikely they'd find many "natural" excuses to get out of the saddle and stand for a bit. On the other hand, those living in very hilly areas are more likely to find themselves alternating between sitting and standing as they climb.

But what about mountain bikes? Different issues are found here since, in general, mountain bikers don't ride in such an aerodynamic (low) position on their bike, and the frequent need to stand up reduces the likelihood of problems caused by staying in the same position for long periods of time. More likely to cause problems on a mountain bike would be impact with the top tube in the event of a crash . . . this can really hurt! Nevertheless, it's still possible that an overly aggressive riding position (such as that found with a tall rider on a small frame) could cause trouble.

Finally, it's all about common sense. If you're uncomfortable on your saddle for any reason, seek the advice of a competent shop or experienced cycling friend! And don't be quite so willing to sacrifice comfort in a quest for absolute speed.

Mike Jacoubowsky is co-owner of Chain Reaction Bicycles, Redwood City and Saratoga, California

As Lindsey told *Bike for Life*, he had the ride of his life in Dr. Sommer's small, bare-bones lab—and it wasn't pleasant. In fact, it was unnerving. Yet, for some unexplained reason, his confession never made it into the magazine. Here's what Joe told us:

"It was definitely a weird, funky situation. On the head of your penis, they taped a little centimeter-long capsule filled with water; it was the size of a watch battery. It measures oxygen saturation, which is directly correlated to blood flow. Sommer was the first to figure out this relationship.

"As you ride, a digital readout appears on a small screen in front of you. To get a good comparison, we were measured beforehand, while standing there, not on the bike. My raw number was 37, a measure of capillary density. Everyone's raw number is different, but whatever number you get is your 100 percent. All the subsequent on-the-bike numbers will be compared, in my case, to 37.

"The on-the-bike test is just seven minutes long, which in itself is limiting, considering that cyclists ride a lot longer. After all, you never know what'll happen after an hour or eight hours.

"The first test was on my Fisik Alliante saddle, the one I've used almost every day for two years. Pedaling on the bike for a minute, my number drops off the cliff—to 6 (from 37)! I've lost 85 percent of my blood flow! [That wasn't so bad, actually. In his *Bicycling* story, Lindsey reported that another subject lost 95 percent of his blood flow.]

"Now I knew from watching a previous test subject that your number initially drops way off and then slowly comes back. Not all the way, but it tops out after about four minutes. Okay, cool, mine's coming back, we're on schedule, I thought. But after four minutes, I'm bummed. It didn't come back much—just to 10 or 12. I've still lost 70 percent of my blood flow!"

Lindsey was surprised to find that there is no correlation between comfort and blood flow. "I'm sitting there looking down at the seat I rode Montezuma's Revenge on because it is so comfortable—and I'm thinking, 'What's scary is that it *is* comfortable—and reducing my blood flow to a trickle!'" he said.

There were several problems with Lindsey's test that he says might have skewed the results. "My set-up was wrong. The bike that they had there was too big for me and didn't have clipless pedals. Could it have affected the results? And Sommer, who administered the study, told me, 'Stay calm, don't affect the test by thinking about it.' But inside my head, I was thinking, 'That's crazy—I'm not thinking about *anything else!'*

"I was tested on three other saddles. They got progressively better. The last was best. I had 100 percent blood flow on the Specialized Body Geometry Road Pro saddle. Guess what I'm riding now?"

According to Lindsey, Sommer and Minkow ultimately concluded that no saddle can completely eliminate compression, and that numbness generally starts when there is 50 percent blood flow reduction for an hour or more. Minor blood flow reduction—10 to 20 percent—is no worry; that's about what you get sitting on an average desk chair.

MAKING A BETTER BIKE SEAT

Today, many manufacturers offer an "open-wedge" bike seat, which features a deep cutout extending from the rear to the center or front of the saddle that is designed to eliminate the seat's contact area with the perineum. The paradox is that it owes its existence to Goldstein. On the one hand, he was attacked for his anti-biking message and research, which to many seemed contrived and lacking in scientific rigor; yet on the other hand, his conclusions sparked a new growth industry in anatomically contoured seats.

"Dr. Goldstein is the man that we kind of love for what he did for our sales," says Paula Dyba, the marketing director of Terry Bicycles, which had been making bikes solely for women for nearly two decades when the impotency wave hit in 1997. Several years earlier, Terry had debuted the Liberator, a unique women's saddle with a hole cut out from the front section of it to relieve female chafing. (See sidebar for genital numbness in women.) "The idea was comfort—nothing medical, just comfort," she said. "We got laughed at. Some people called it a 'toilet seat.' Then, surprisingly, we started getting calls—and orders—from men."

Some of the calls to Terry were laughable. "One woman called to say that her

Saddle Numbness vs. Impotence

BIKE FOR LIFE queried participants on several Internet cycling newsgroups for their views regarding saddle numbness and impotence. Here's a representative sampling of replies:

I have had considerable trouble with saddle comfort and numbness; particularly on long rides, and have tried almost all saddle types. Standard flat, noseless, split, holes in the middle; you name it! All with little relief. The best seems to be a split V saddle made by Specialized. It has a wide V split from the back foreword, and has a raised rear. The rear supports my sit bones; and when I push back on it, it raises the center of my bottom and relieves the pain. The only trouble is that this puts too much weight on my arms, and I can't sustain this for long (especially on my road bike; on the mountain bike, the more upright position helps produce a natural rearward force). I need to have a nose, and rest my mid on it for much of the ride; hence I hurt and go numb. I end up moving around a lot toward the end of a ride, and push back as much as possible.

Yes, I experience numbness any time I ride over 150 miles in a day, the numbness goes away in a day. No problems with impotence. No, I haven't seen a urologist. As for how I deal with saddle issues: Be one with the bike. My bicycle is adjusted perfectly to my body. My pedal stroke is so smooth, my body so motionless, because everything is just so, to the millimeter. An added benefit is that no matter how far I ride. I don't need Advil. Saddles are a very individual preference, as everyone fits their bike differently. I spend most of my time on long rides in aerobars, with the center of my crotch at the tip of my saddle. Thus, I use well-padded shorts (Performance Elite) and a saddle that's light but has a well-padded nose (Terry's Fly).

Except for the longest events (over 500 miles) generally no problems; over 500 miles, crotch and hand numbness. So far, impotence only has been a temporary condition. Haven't seen a urologist. Erection function is not what it used to be but not sure if its cycling related or normal age/hormone condition. Saddles used: Brooks B-17 Champion Special (for over 500 mile events). Also have a bike with a Avocet O2-40 men's road model (the wide men's model). I use these seats because they work. I don't use chamois cream of any sort.

I am always struggling with comfort after 1.5 to 2 hours. But mostly in the sit bones area (I'm 155–160 lbs.). I have tried many, many saddles. Cutouts don't seem to make much difference. I've never had a lot of numbness problems, just here and there. On any quality saddle, it's been a non-issue. I seem to do best on a lightly, but softly, padded saddle, no cutout needed, with slight curve to it. The Fizik Aliante seems best so far. The Arione, flatter and firmer, was awful. The supposedly great for private area circulation Specialized Body Geometry Pro wasn't too bad, but padded thickly and too firmly for my rear end. I have had no issues with the private equipment's function. But then, like I said, my issues tend to be with the duff/saddle connection, not up front. For example, the aero position is actually more comfy than a more upright one.

My saddle gives me numbness but only on time trial efforts. Long rides no pain, no numbness. The numbness that I do have during time trials doesn't seem to affect me after I get off the bike.

Give up sex? Never. One thing does need to be mentioned on this issue that is often not addressed. If a man has an enlarged prostate for whatever reason, leading to pressure on the urethra and pudendal nerves, that will certainly make any saddle numbness and pain worse.

17-year-old stepson had penile numbness from riding—and she had to massage it for 45 minutes," said Dyba.

"We couldn't claim that we stopped impotency—no saddle can. But we can claim comfort. We began working with the Italian seat maker Selle Italia to make a Liberator for male riders. The seat was designed to shift the rider's weight off the perineum, and has a long groove down its middle and is hollowed out in front. The seat became our number-one selling product that year because of the hysteria over impotency. It grew the saddle business phenomenally. And sales stayed that way until 2003. Sales only dropped off because so many imitators have been coming into the market."

One of those imitators was Specialized's Body Geometry, a narrow saddle with a V-shaped wedge cut from the rear. It was developed by Roger Minkow, a Napa Valley doctor, ergonomics researcher, and spine center founder who had invented and successfully marketed lumbar-supportive airline pilot's seats. "I started riding a bike in 1997," he told *Bike for Life*. "Soon after that, I saw Joe Kita's article, 'Are You At Risk?' the famous article in *Bicycling*. Within three weeks, I designed a bike seat with a cutout wedge—which I thought was a big improvement over the hole in the Terry saddle, since men need the pressure relieved further back. I sent it to the *Bicycling* editor [with the impotency problem]. And soon after that, I got a call from Specialized's president, Mike Sinyard. 'I'd like you to help us,' he said.

"Sinyard is a visionary. He smelled that this was a good opportunity. He brought me to the company. There was resistance from all his people, but he said we need to do this. Sinyard backed the ergo-seat project even when his own dealers rejected it. They would send the product back."

But in September 1998, a year after the *Bicycling* impotency article, the magazine published a product review of the Specialized seat and gave it five chain-rings, the best rating. Sales skyrocketed. Soon, Diamondback, Avocet, Serfas, and other companies started manufacturing seats designed to not compress the perineum. Millions sold. Men were obviously not taking chances.

To further test the Specialized seat, Specialized consulted with Dr. Robert Kessler, professor of urology at Stanford University Medical Center in Palo Alto, California. In March 1999, Kessler recruited 25 cyclists, each of whom regularly rode at least six hours weekly and had suffered from perineal pain, numbness, and erectile dysfunction. After each used the new wedge seat for a month, Kessler found that 14 had complete relief, nine had almost complete relief of their symptoms, one had partial relief, and one indicated no change. He presented his findings at the 1999 annual meeting of the American Urological Association.

Dr. Goldstein maintains that even open-wedge seats offer little insurance and assurance and favors "wide, noseless seats that force you to actually sit, not to straddle, because the weight is borne on the ischial tuberosity and not on the perineum." Since this is an impractical solution for most cyclists (the nose is used for control and balance—without it would be like trying to drive a car using only your legs instead of the steering wheel), the open-wedge seat has emerged to grab a sizeable chunk of the saddle market among concerned cyclists.

This isn't to say that the only option for diminishing numbness is to buy an expensive wedge saddle. Which one would work for you depends on your anatomy, and everyone's is different. A few quick adjustments to your riding style and equipment (see next section) will help take care of that.

• BIKE FOR LIFE'S •
12 ANTI-NUMBNESS TIPS
Does the Right Seat
Cure Numb Nuts?

Goldstein, who considers cycling a hazardous avocation, says cycling would be dangerous even with a foolproof seat, since you can still get injured by falling on the top tube. But Sommer, who raced bikes in his early 20s as a time trialist, believes that "cycling is a very healthy thing. But you have to do proper precautions to avoid any health hazard and sexual dysfunction. I think a good seat is very, very important. Nonetheless, for the sexual health, you also need good technique."

If you want to ride as much as you want, while being able to happily perform that other type of riding in bed, follow these twelve basic rules.

The Obvious One

1. **Stand up!** Getting off your butt is remarkably effective, the easiest, most effective antidote to ED. Occasionally rise out of the saddle. Stand for a one-minute interval every five minutes—even on stationary bikes. One study showed it restored 110 percent of blood flow to the undercarriage. The highest propensity for cycling-caused ED is among those riders who stay glued to the saddle hour after hour, consumed with achieving perfect aerodynamic form or lost in thought.

Type of Saddle

2. **Firm, not soft.** "A hard saddle supports the sit bones while leaving the perineal area untouched. "I have some

patients who like a soft, cushioned saddle very much," says Sommer, "but despite their comfort, they still have diminished blood flow. That's because the padding compresses as the rider's weight sinks into it, pushing very hard into the perineal area, reducing blood flow."

3. **Concave, not dome-shaped.** "A rounded shape that peaks in the middle is the absolute worst," says Sommer. "A flat or concave saddle stays out of your way."

Saddle Adjustments

4. **Level the seat; do not tilt up.** All seats instantly compress arteries and nerves when pointed up. Stick with horizontal, or drop the nose a few degrees to raise the perineum.

5. **Lower the saddle to eliminate rocking.** Rocking side-to-side means the saddle is too high and you are likely grinding across the perineum with your body weight. A check: make sure knees are not fully extended at the bottom of the pedal stroke.

Other Riding Techniques

6. **Sit back.** "If you sit back on the wide part of the saddle so that you are actually on the sit bones, the ischial tuberosity, you'll be fine," says Goldstein. "Of course, that's not the usual case. If you lean forward on a seat with a long, narrow nose, all bets are off." The narrower the saddle—and the more cutouts—the smaller the surface area and the more pressure on the perineum.

7. **Alter riding position frequently on long rides.** "This gives your penis a chance at good oxygenation," says Sommer. "If you are bending forward in the racing position, the blood flow is very, very, poor." If you start feeling numb, immediately change position and give the aerobar a rest.

8. **Use legs as shock absorbers.** While mountain biking over roots, train tracks, or curbs, stand out of the saddle and use legs as shock absorbers. This minimizes harsh vibration and trauma to penis and testicles.

Workout Tips

9. **Strengthen legs.** "Although pro cyclists did not volunteer for my saddle test, I have made an assumption that their strong legs may help prevent numbness by lifting them up from the saddle," says Sommer. "Strong legs let you keep your whole weight off the saddle, and only use the saddle as a guide."

10. **Stretch the hamstrings.** Loose hamstrings allow you to sit back in the saddle easier and utilize your glutes.

Other Tips

11. **Padded short and gloves.** The padding cushions and spreads the contact area with the saddle, while bike gloves allow more weight to be put on the hands (and off the seat).

12. **If in doubt, go recumbent.** 'Bents place the rider in an aerodynamic, feet-forward lounge-chair position that is fast, comfortable, and causes virtually no blood loss. The wide seat and full back support put no acute pressure on the pelvic region.

Viagra: Getting It Up . . . the Hill

VIAGRA certainly lays claim to a charmed life. After first being developed for potential use by heart patients, the drug was later discovered to help men cope with erectile dysfunction. The luck continues. According to a recent German study of Swiss and German mountain climbers published in the August 2004 issue of the *Annals of Internal Medicine,* sildenafil (the generic name for Viagra) allows the body to better tolerate the lack of oxygen at high altitudes. Research tests were conducted on 14 climbers (two women) scaling Mt. Everest; popping those pills allowed them to better deal with hypoxia—lack of oxygen—which causes altitude sickness, by opening up veins and arteries in the lungs, much in the same way that it affects blood flow to the penis.

So the obvious question: Can Viagra reverse impotence caused from biking?

In a *Los Angeles Times* interview, Dr. Hossein A. Ghofrani, assistant professor at the University of Giessen in Germany and research team coleader, said that he has considered the use of Viagra in sports. "It could potentially also be seen as a performance enhancer, though it remains to be seen whether sildenafil can increase cardiopulmonary exercise capacity in healthy athletes operating at sea level."

Ghofrani didn't, however, think it would improve lung function in healthy athletes in normal conditions, because their lung and blood vessels are dilated already and dilate more with exercise. However, he notes that it has been shown to improve performance in horses. Race horses sometimes suffer lung bleeding and edema after races due to severe pulmonary hypertension, which sildenafil appears to alleviate. Ghofrani does not recommend its use for the majority of people in any setting, however. For one thing, it seemed to exacerbate headaches that occur often at high altitudes."

For the time being, however, Viagra is not currently banned for use by Olympic athletes. Yet try to imagine the following fictitious scenario: we're at the 2004 Tour de France and it's the morning of the brutal Alpe d'Huez time trial stage. Team trainers instruct riders to take Viagra with their breakfast. "Getting it up" takes on a new, nonsexual meaning.

But what about the average cyclist who finds himself flatting in the bedroom? He's worried about performance in the sack, not finding a competitive edge at altitude. Here, Viagra succeeds.

"It maximizes the sexual response," says Dr. Irwin Goldstein, head of the urology department at Boston University of Medicine, "by preventing enzymatic hydrolysis or degradation of the message that keeps the muscle relaxed. So it maximizes sexual response. So whatever blood can get in, can get in. And people can sustain the erections better. So they will get a more rigid, better quality sustained erection. But is it the exact same as it was before? As rigid as it was before? Not necessarily."

CONCLUSION: Put Bike-Impotence into Perspective

Several years ago, Goldstein and his colleagues at Boston University compared the rates of sexual and urinary dysfunction of 738 members of a bicycling club and 277 members of a running club who did not bicycle. Their research, presented to the American Urological Association, discovered that the level of moderate-to-complete impotence in cyclists was higher than in runners by a factor of *four to one*. Those didn't seem like good odds if you were a betting man.

What got clouded in the public reaction to Goldstein's study is that as a group, *male cyclists experience less erectile dysfunction than the general male population*, where ED is approaching epidemic proportions. According to the *Los Angeles Times*, there are 30 million American men estimated to have at least occasional problems getting and sustaining an erection, although less than 10 percent seek treatment. Sales of anti-impotence drugs like Prozac, Levitra, and Cialis have skyrocketed. Just the marketing budgets for these magic bedroom pills approach $100 million annually.

So, while cyclists get a free pass in the plumbing department when statistically compared to sedentary nonathletes, they are worse off when compared with their aerobically fit conterparts: runners and swimmers. Bikers, plain and simple, are high-risk candidates within the general aerobic athletic population. That, at least, was Goldstein's most potent warning, and one that generated stacks of hate mail sent to his clinic by outraged (aroused?) cyclists.

For that reason, many of Goldstein's peers still consider the whole issue overblown. "It's safe to bicycle. That's an easy one. This whole [cycling impotence] thing is really out of proportion," said William D. Steers, chairman of the urology department at the University of Virginia School of Medicine in Charlottesville. "In China 90 percent of the male population cycles, and they don't seem to have a problem maintaining the population. The cycling-impotence question has diverted attention from behavioral factors—like smoking, overeating and inactivity—that are far riskier to male reproductive health. I find it disconcerting that attention to unhealthy behaviors hasn't been raised, when a healthful activity is getting this huge scrutiny."

Goldstein, hailed by many in the bike industry for calling attention to the problem ("We've changed everything for the better because of him," said Minkow), remains unrepentant.

"What is amazing about the bike industry," Goldstein told *Bike for Life,* "is that it's like the tobacco industry in how effectively the health risks are denied and hidden. The thought that you can have numbness and accept that in the hands and legs and wherever else you guys get numbness, and recognize that exists in the penis, and then be blind to the fact that the nerve and artery are within millimeters of each other. You can cause permanent injury to either of the structures' nerve or artery. It can happen at any one time in any one acute fall. So, I see it in non-bikers. I see it in weekend warriors. I see it in novice riders. I see it in kids riding for the first time. I see it in stationary bike riders. Any person who bears his weight on his perineum puts his penis at risk. It is not complicated."

Goldstein's Boston urology clinic is a revolving door of concerned riders. "Our

BIKE FOR LIFE

clinic sees many, many bike racers," he says. "I have so many patients who come here and say there can be no letters; there can be no notes taken. They tell me, 'If my sponsor ever found out I was here, I would lose my sponsorship. And that is my life.' The fear of being exposed is huge. Or even worse, we have all these men who go on these charity races like the Jimmy Fund in Massachusetts for children's research. Every year we get half a dozen men coming in the office with incidents following that ride. One fellow said, 'If someone would have told me that the act of raising the $2,000 would end up hurting my body, I happily would have given it to them out of my own pocket and not ridden. Because now I have impotence. It's not going away. I have numbness. It hurts. Why didn't anyone tell me this?'

"Luckily for a substantial number of people, the situation can go away. But not for everybody. There are permanent irreversible erectile dysfunctions that happen. We have treatments. Viagra, Levitra, Cialis can help these men and many do use it. They have diminished blood flow. They're just like a guy who has high blood pressure and diminished blood flow."

Despite this anecdotal evidence offered by Goldstein, just how many riders actually visit his clinic? Is he perhaps stretching the truth regarding bike impotence? "Our clinic sees something like 80 men and 40 women a week," he responded. "It's about 3,500 men and 2,000 women a year."

And what percentage of them are bike riders?

"Let's look at a typical day of treating patients at my office," he suggested in response. He randomly chose the previous Friday, April 9, 2004, and began reading aloud entries from his appointment book:

ZD, 68-year-old man with prostate cancer. He is not a biker.

RW, 44. Biker erectile dysfunction. Numbness. Pain in penis, erection to hard 60 percent rigid. Tenderness in alcox canal.

PW, 71, since hernia surgery erectile dysfunction.

SF, 27, sport soccer cleats. Like bike riding but not exactly.

AL, 36, lifetime premature ejaculation. Mountain bike rider.

CP, 74, diabetes hypertension high cholesterol, smoking. Not biker.

ED, 42, England. Bike rider thirty years. Decreased libido: Decreased erections.

MB, 61, ED, five to six years incidence always low libido. Heart disease, high cholesterol, depression. On anti-depressive medication

MS, 44, pain in penis after using penile enlargement device.

MW, 22, blunt trauma—fell on plastic bike seat.

RC, 54, neuropathy, disabled depression.

AC, 49 decreased libido, decreased erection.

Out of 12 patients, three were actual cyclists. At that rate, over 1,000 cyclists per year visit Goldstein for sex-related issues. Is cycling the cause of their problem? How many more across the country, out of 50 million Americans who ride for fitness, have problems?

No one has a clue. But with cycling participation numbers remaining stable, it indicates that the vast majority of male cyclists either don't have the problem or prefer riding over fornicating.

BIKE FOR LIFE

Having fathered the bike impotency scare, it's doubtful that Goldstein will one day back down from his claims that erectile dysfunction and cycling go hand in hand, though he cagily admits that, "Some of my best friends are bicyclists. I am not a poison to the industry. I am simply pointing out what is intuitively obvious sitting in a chair and seeing patients day in and day out. It's not that complicated."

Neither are cycling's myriad of health benefits—or the methods needed to minimize its sexual problems. Yes, a male cyclist can experience a wide range of problems, often undiagnosed until it's too late. But to millions, Goldstein's cure—abstention—is worse than the disease. Especially when less radical solutions are so rational and accessible.

Women Cyclists and Sexual Dysfunction

WOMEN owe a huge debt to the bicycle. But like men, they aren't immune from the wrath of the bike seat.

When the cycling craze first hit in the late nineteenth century, women saw this newfangled transportation device as a way to finally assert their independence and freedom to travel unhindered, without a chaperone. "Bicycling has done more to emancipate women than anything else in the world," asserted turn-of-the-century suffragist and women's rights leader Susan B. Anthony.

Not everyone agreed with this pro-feminist sentiment.

The medical profession was particularly alarmed by the prospect of women cyclists taking to the streets. According to Ellen Garvey's book *The Adman in the Parlor, 1880 to 1910,* "Anti-bicycling doctors said it would be sexually stimulating—and that was dangerous to good Victorian women and to their marriage prospects. One doctor warned that the saddle could 'form a deep hammock-like concavity which would fit itself over the entire vulva and reach up in front, bring[ing] about constant friction over the clitoris and labia. The pressure would be much increased by stooping forward, and the warmth generated by vigorous exercise might further increase the feeling.' He reported the case of an 'overwrought, emaciated girl of 15 who stooped forward noticeably in riding, and whose actions strongly suggested the indulgence of masturbation.'"

If the bike were viewed as some kind of sex toy, then what did it say about women who liked to bike? Were they loose, licentious, and sexually impure? Several bike manufacturers attempted to circumvent this overwrought and ill-formed perception by coming up with new types of saddles with crotchless designs. Furthermore, "manuals and catalogs instructed women to ride decorously: sitting upright (none of that pressing forward on the saddle), and not too fast," writes Garvey. In 1880, the Cycle Touring Club of Great Britain, for example, admitted women as full members, but the club refused to allow women's racing for several decades. The reasons cited for this ban: propriety and female physiology.

Now, over a century later, the issue of female physiology has resurfaced, but for a different reason: to investigate whether biking leads to declining sexual performance. Instead of causing sexual stimulation, medical researchers are now examining whether cycling leads to sexual dysfunction.

As you might expect, Dr. Irwin Goldstein is front and center on the issue. "We now see anorgasmia—difficulty in having an orgasm—as the primary complaint of bicyclists," Goldstein told *Bike for Life* in March 2004. "A lot of women who like horse riding have the same problem. Do other doctors make this connection? I'd have to say it's growing knowledge."

He's right. A study in the *Clinical Journal of Sports Medicine* (October 2001) reported that women cyclists experience vaginal numbness, inability to have climax, and limited blood flow to the clitoris.

Another study, published in the *British Medical Journal* (2001), reported findings conducted at Brugmann University Hospital in Brussels that looked at six women, ages 21 to 38, who had a unilateral chronic swelling of the *labium majus* after a few years of intensive bicycling—an average of 250 miles per week. "All six had typical unilateral lymphoedema, which was more severe after more intense and longer training. The position of the bicycle saddle, the type of shorts worn, and the women's perineal hygiene were optimum. There was no family history of lymphoedema in any of the women, nor any common factor that might explain it."

Obviously, riding 250 miles every week is something very few women do, but what about the rest of the female riding population? How many miles, at what kind of intensity, or for how long before pelvic numbness, clitoral and labial lacerations, even inability to orgasm start to arise?

Hoping to take this growing knowledge and quantify it with scientific data and testing are urologynecological professors Dr. Kathleen Connell of Yale University Medical Center and Dr. Marsha Guess of the Einstein College of Medicine, who are jointly studying sexual dysfunction among women riders. In May 2004, *Bike for Life* spoke by phone with Dr. Connell, just back from a meeting of the International Mountain Bike Police Association in San Antonio where they had conducted testing on female police officers.

"The National Institute for Occupational Safety and Health was doing male erectile dysfunction research and wanted us to do the female side," she said. Collaborating with NIOSH's Steve Schrader for this government-funded project, Connell's group recruited competitive cyclists from Central Park, since there aren't many female cyclists with the NYPD. They used runners as controls.

"We've contacted bike clubs, handed out fliers in the park on the weekends to attract willing subjects, and paid $50 to each volunteer," she says. At press time, they'd collected data on over 50 people. The findings: "Women are telling us that they have numbness in their pelvic region if they ride too much."

According to Connell, major problems in the women tested are chafing, numbness ("riders were saying 'we know we're *in the zone* when we're numb'" she said), and chronic swelling on external genitalia—the labia. "Some women feel numb after two hours of riding because the pudendal artery—same as males' perineum artery—gets flattened. Many branches of the pudendal blood vessels go to the urethra, clitoris, and vagina. Putting proximal pressure there affects blood supply.

"We're also looking at which seat designs are the best. The cutout seats with the hole are good for some women, not good for others." Why? The labia are very thin. They may fall into the hole.

If the hole doesn't work for all women, what does? What should women be concerned with? "A combination of things," Connell replied. "How a person rides—leaning forward or back. Tilting the nose down a bit helps. I'm guessing better-padded seats. It may come down to riding style and proper fit—seat, handlebar height. Our study is investigating these things."

One of the difficulties Connell's team has faced is a natural reluctance by woman riders to discuss the subject. "There's still a taboo in women talking about this," she said. "Lots of Central Park riders didn't want to talk. They were embarrassed being approached by strangers asking about sexual function. Still, there is a paucity of data on this topic for women." Cyclists were asked to fill out a questionnaire and then ride in the lab while attached to a specially designed sensation measuring device for the pudendal nerve.

"We are looking at vibration and tactile sensation," she said. If numbness or decrease in blood supply is detected, "we suspect a lot of the damage is temporary. Though occupational cyclists—women police officers—are more at risk because they have 30 pounds of equipment strapped on them."

Does this mean that cycling may interfere with women cyclists' ability to obtain orgasms? Will the Big O turn into the Big No? "I'm hoping we don't find sexual dysfunction—just discomfort," says Connell, who plans to study this subject for the next several years. "I don't want any hype. I just want to determine how to make riding safe and comfortable for women. I don't want to say, 'Women can't cycle.'"

Mike Sinyard

FIGURING OUT THE FUTURE

The Henry Ford of modern cycling—or the Thomas Edison? Time and time again, Mike Sinyard has identified a tiny, under-the-radar trend, mass-produced it, and improved it somehow. In 1980, after six years of importing European components, making touring tires, and tiptoeing into bike manufacturing with several racing and touring bikes, his Specialized Bicycle Components changed the bike world. Sinyard took a new invention for off-road riding called the mountain bike, then offered by a couple of local Bay Area custom bike makers, and retooled it for the assembly line. He was stunned when 450 Specialized Stumpjumpers sold that year and abruptly changed the direction of an industry. Before long, his small Morgan Hill, California, company had become a colossus, and it stayed that way by pouring millions into mountain bike racing and developing some of the leading dual-suspension designs over the next two decades. All the while, Sinyard didn't ignore dedicated roadies, who he felt were asking for street bikes with more comfort. Over the last few years, adopting the mantra "Comfort Equals Performance," Specialized has pushed the development of a new generation of comfort road and racing bikes to address the needs of an aging enthusiast base who are a lot like him: over 50 and still hammering. In his case, as he told Bike for Life's Roy Wallack in an interview on March 26, 2004, it's over 200 miles per week during long road and off-road rides in the coastal mountains of the Bay Area.

I GREW UP in San Diego on a little farm with 1,000 chickens and rabbits; my mom sold the eggs in the front of the house and my dad was a machinist, and he could fix anything. I was very close with my dad. He never made much money; he used to say, "It doesn't matter how much money you make, it matters what you do with the money you do make." Our house stuff was good because he could make anything. We always had a great big shed in the back where we had a ton of old materials, something you could beat into shape. My dad was always the guy who'd walk around and find a bolt on the ground. And he'd pick it up. He'd go, "Hey, I might be able to use this!"

I was seven when he bought me my first bike at the Goodwill. It was a girl's bike—one of those where somebody had painted the whole bike and tires with a spray can. So we fixed up that bike and I rode it around. As for being a girl's bike, I didn't know much difference. The step-through frame made it easy because it was so big, with 26-inch wheels. Just a few turns of the crank and you were flying on this big ole thing. So that's how I started riding. I really used to love it. In fact, as a kid, sometimes I would have some of the neighborhood guys over, we'd get up in the middle of the night and go riding. At night you feel like you're going so fast. We'd sneak out all the time to ride the dirt roads through the canyon. In daylight, we'd make dirt jumps and wooden jumps. I loved that.

Then it just really developed. A lot of working on bikes. My dad got bikes, fixed 'em, I painted 'em, and we would go to the flea market. So that's really how it started.

I almost cannot remember a time when I wasn't intrigued with bikes. There probably was a little time in high school when I had a motorcycle and thought a bike was a little bit pedestrian. That lasted for a year or two. But then I went back to the bike. I used to take bike trips with friends. And then when I went to college [San Diego Mesa College, then San Jose State] and I didn't drive a car around, I really became connected up with bikes again. Out of college, I wasn't into racing but I had a nice road bike—a Peugeot U-08 which I took apart and painted. A ten-speed—two in the front and the freewheel in the back. That is when I really began to appreciate high-quality bikes. My specialty was long-distance riding—the double-centuries and stuff like that. I was okay at those kind of things, and sort of had to be. Because out of college I sold my van, and I went seven years with no car at all.

When I was in school and a little bit after school, I made a living by fixing old bikes to sell at the flea market. I put an ad in the paper. One ad. And I'd make it a little bit generic: "Nice bike completely rebuilt. Real reliable. Call." I wouldn't list the price and I had about twenty bikes. They'd call and I'd say, "Well what are you looking for?" I'd have probably a bunch in progress and maybe five or six that were already done. If somebody wanted something else I could whip it up.

These were pretty basic bikes—kinda college bikes. And I couldn't really afford the more high-end bikes. But as I got nicer bikes I realized there was a great opportunity for high-end bikes. At that time, in 1969, 1970, there weren't really high-end parts available in the U.S., except for a few shops that imported directly. So I said to myself, "Hey! When I get out of school, I want to go over to Europe and meet these really great companies that make these products." Most people in the U.S. weren't

aware of those companies. At that time, when you went around in cycling shoes and black shorts, you looked like a dork.

The Big Score in Italy

I WAS SO sick of school. So I went to Europe. Rode the bike around a while. Went to the Oktoberfest. Partied up a little bit. I met this one guy who had a bike shop in Holland. And I went there—just outside Amsterdam. Worked in the bike shop for a couple weeks. Fixed some flats and partying. What a life! Can you imagine working in a bike shop in Amsterdam when you're like 23 or something? Then I rode all the way from Amsterdam down through Barcelona. Over to Bonn. Three months. Only spent $350, because I usually slept outside. Had a fantastic time. All self-contained with a sleeping bag and everything.

And then I went to Milano, stayed in a youth hostel and met a woman. I said I was really into bikes. She goes, "Hey, I met Gino Cinelli before." I said. "Wow! Let's go over there!" I had $1,500 in travelers checks that I got for selling my Volkswagen van. I bought a suit, so I wouldn't just look like a bum. And I went over there and I said I was pretty impressed with their products, their philosophy, and what they had done. And I told Gino that I knew many of the high-end riders in the U.S. and there was a big demand for high end products. He said, "Sure, we'll sell ya." And I thought, *I can't believe he would sell me.*

So that was it. I bought those products. And once I bought that, you know, I came home immediately. I primarily bought Cinelli handlebars, which were in short supply. I shipped them home. That was the start of it

And I thought, *Wow, this is great. Now there's access to all these great parts.* I called a lot of the bike shops I knew when I got back. I said, "Hey, I got these great parts." They said, "Where'd ya get that? You steal it?" I said, no, I had contacts in Italy. And then essentially the stores bought those products, and I had a lot of the dealers pay in advance.

I decided to call the company Specialized because I always admired the Italian companies that were really the artisans. *Artigiani,* they call 'em—really focused on doing beautiful work And in Italy they say "Spe-ci-al-eee-zed." Which means you are really into it. I thought that's the right name for us. I didn't check trademark or anything. I didn't want to call this Mike's Bike Stuff. That's lame.

Soon, I was importing all those products from Italy when the idea to make my own tires came up. I was importing some Italian clincher tires that were terrible. They would always get bubbles and snake and stuff like that. I told the factory. They said to me, "You must be doing something wrong. Nobody else has a problem with these at all." At first I said, "Well, maybe that's right." Then I thought, *These guys are pulling my leg!* And I say, "You know what? I am sick of this. And I'm not going to sell products that have this kind of quality." So then I started looking. I'm going to make our own tires.

People know us for the mountain bike. But the tire thing was kinda what Specialized was initially known for. It was the tires that really kick-started the company.

I was 25. I got a little experience with manufacturing about that time when I met Jim Blackburn, a really famous designer now known for his racks. He was doing a master's thesis at San Jose University on how to design and develop a product and take it to market. I was selling Claude

Butler European racks. And he says, "Man, I could make a better one than that out of aluminum." I said, "Great! Let's do it. I'll buy the first hundred."

So, I just knew there was an opportunity to make a great clincher tire. I was riding 300 miles a week and I knew other people that were, too. I intuitively knew what would be right on the product. I looked around the world and found the best manufacturer for tires in Japan. I dunno if I want to mention the company. We got the tires and we got started really selling a lot of tires. The company really started taking off. Then the guy from the tire company in Japan came over to visit me—and he said, "Geez, this guy is operating out of a shed. He doesn't even have a typewriter!"

Yeah, I was working in a shed at this trailer that I lived in. It was an 8- by 35-foot trailer. And all the products, when I get 'em, I just store 'em under the trailer until they were sold. I would usually sell out of everything in a couple days and get another shipment.

No creature comforts. I put it all back into the product.

A bigger, rival bike company in Los Angeles got the Japanese company to cut me off. But then I found another Japanese manufacturer that was even better that would listen to my requirements more. I would say that I definitely learned a lot from the different cultures. From the Italian culture and then probably the most from the Japanese.

I really respected the Italians' passion and dedication to the product and design. Everything with the Italians is about how it looks. And what I learned from the Japanese was attention to the smallest, smallest detail. No detail was too small.

I made quite a few trips to Japan—that's what really got the company going at that time. Sometimes we get these big shipments of tires in. So many tires I couldn't store it in the warehouse. Just had the container there for a couple days until we sold 'em all.

It Reminded Me of Being a Kid

In 1976 we made our first bikes: a sport-touring frame called the Sequoia, and the Allez road bike. The Sequoia, which was really received well; it fulfilled a niche that wasn't being addressed. Classic Italian road racing geometry, but you could ride it on rough roads. You could ride it all day long. Nothing else like this—halfway between a clunky touring bike and a road bike.

I was hooked into the mountain bike early because I supplied tubing, lugs, and fittings and all kinds of components like Briggs and TA cranks to builders like Tom Ritchey, Steve Potts, and Breezer. All these guys. Then I said, "Gee, you know? I see a way we could make, you know, a better mountain bike that uses all the latest technology."

In 1978, I had a Ritchey mountain bike—the one he and Fisher made. Riding it, I said "Man, this is fun! Road bikes are okay. But this is great!" I used to be an off-road motorcyclist, too. So it reminded me of that. It reminded me of being a kid.

One thing made me realize that this is going to be really something. I was riding around on a street where I lived in San Jose, and I saw this older gentleman walking along. He waved to me; I went over there and he goes, "Wow! What kinda of bike is that? I remember riding bikes on dirt roads!" You could see this guy's eyes light up.

Then, a few minutes later, I saw these kids, and they go, "Whoa! That's really cool!"

So, I go, you know, "Man, this is it!" Because it relates. The old people like it, and the young people like it. It's really the fun bike for everybody.

I had a guy working doing designs for me, an engineer/frame builder, Tim Neenan, who was famous for Lighthouse bikes. Tim told me that he had ideas how to do a bike differently—even lighter, more of a road bike geometry and clearance. In a few months we had prototypes. Then Tim left and Jim Vers came in and made the bikes even lighter.

As we readied the bike, the issue of the name came up. We were sitting around and said, *Hey what should we call it? Well, it's fun. It's kinda funky. Kinda like . . . ? The Off-Roader? No.* So I said, "Hey, how about Stumpjumper?" At first it sounded pretty funky. But, hey, why not? We want something that's fun. And just like when we picked the name Sequoia, it kinda conjured up an imagination.

The Stumpjumper was really the first mountain bike available in the bike shops. I think that is kind of our claim to fame. It was the first one that really defined the category. But yeah, when I first came out with it at the 1980 bike show and took it around, most of the shops went: "What is that? What are you doing with a big kids' BMX? Man, we're only interested in adult bicycles."

I said, "Well this is an adult bike. C'mon, let's go for a ride. I'll show ya."

Our slogan was "The Bike for All Reasons." And, ah, the concept. I even thought we should include it with poison oak medicine and a snake bite kit *[laughs]*. 'Cause I thought that makes it sound fun. Just the fun of it.

The beauty of it is, everything about bikes historically has been defined from road bikes—from Rome. I said, "Hey, this is the one that is defined from California." We can make our own parts. We can define it as we want—use our creativity. We could make tires. Search around and find motorcycle levers from Italy. We made the Stumpjumper tire. The handlebar. The stem. Fork. We used a lot of touring components. Like Mafac brakes, TA cranks, Jerez dual-part derailleurs.

I didn't know if it would take over cycling. But I knew this had huge, huge appeal. This is more than just riding. This is a lifestyle. Kinda like surfing lifestyle. 'Cause I was a surfer for years in San Diego. I felt this is like surfing because it has a whole lifestyle with it. I thought, *Hey, I dunno how big it's gonna be. And it doesn't matter. But I'm into it—personally.* I may be riding every day and every weekend go for some crazy long ride through the woods.

A lot of those people who ran the shops at that time didn't ride. Some did, usually the people in the stores. Most just said, "We don't want this."

Four hundred and fifty Stumpjumpers sold that first year, 1980. It was fantastic. The Sequoia and the Allez were 100 or 200 units. The Stumpjumper was like "Whooh!" We had no idea how big that was. Everybody who didn't want 'em before now said, "Hey, we want it! Immediately!"

In 1981, everybody had 'em. And a lot of people didn't really think about how to make 'em; they used plain-gauge steel. The forks were bending [chuckles].

Our first bikes had no frame failures; they were overbuilt, 36 pounds or something. They totally held up. Ritchey probably made the lightest ones. But where we added value was in bike parts. We were the first to use the **quick-release** [QR] hubs.

Everybody was using the bolt hubs. Everybody worried QRs won't be strong enough. And our engineer Jim Vers said, "It is *stronger*. The hollow axle is stronger!" Then we changed the wheels to 32-spoke, down from 40. We had the capability to make prototypes right there—and Jim would make a bunch of different ones that we could test and compare quickly.

From there, the mountain bike took on a life of its own as a whole new sport. You look at the first poster we put out for the Stumpjumper, and we show people are just riding along in tennis shoes and ragged pants and no helmets or anything. So from there, the whole thing of enhancing the whole ride. The gloves. Shorts. Shoes, and all that stuff. For quite a while we didn't go so much with the Lycra stuff, even though we were road riders. We just didn't. It was kind of a rebellion, if you will. Against the road bikes. So they really developed into different groups. The road people and the mountain bikers.

Mountain bike people were open to anything. Probably too much, because a lot of stupid things have been put out. We put out our share, like the Umma Gumma tires. Really soft rubber for super traction. A great idea. But it was too soft! It wasn't tested enough. The rubber just kinda melted.

We tried lots of different things. In 1985 and 1986, we came out with the Rock Combo—a cross between a mountain bike and a road bike. Basically a mountain bike with **drop bars**. We said, "Hey, this is what everybody wants!" Now people say, "Aw, that was such a great bike! Kinda like the Edsel."

We had the Expedition bike around 1984. Kind of a full-on touring bike with all the wiring inside. Four water bottle fittings. Like a Winnebago bike. That did pretty well during the touring period. Then it just kinda died out.

An Everyman Mind-set

I WAS ALWAYS interested in those different areas, because I was never a hot racer. I'm just kinda interested in a lot of different areas. By the 1990s, the Sequoia and the Expedition faded out. I was kinda sad to see those go. But we brought the Sequoia back as a comfort bike. And maybe the Expedition will come back as a bike you could jump out of an airplane with a parachute, then go live in the woods or travel across the country with. Yeah, that's the idea. I like that.

Not being a hot racer gives you an open mind, I think. Because if you're a hot racer, you have a hard time seeing why somebody would want a Sequoia bike with a higher **headtube** and things like that. They can't get their mind around it. Those types at a bike shop won't bring in that bike, right? They'll say, "Hey, nobody asked for it."

Just like nobody was walking into bike shops asking for a mountain bike. You can't define the world based on the past.

Our philosophy is to make the bike as if it was a custom bike—but make it on a production basis. It was the concept I started the company with. Make bikes for the way you ride. That's what we did with the mountain bike. And that's what we did with the Sequoia and the Allez. And I think essentially that is what we did with the Roubaix—a performance road bike loaded with comfort features. Now some racer people might be kind of scared away from a bike with a tall headtube and shock absorbing forks. They go, "Oh, that is too pedestrian for me." But, you know, it's not. . . . People are really loving that bike.

The Roubaix is a natural. The old road bikes used to have a quill stem which you could pull way up, which you can't do with the Ahead stem. The Ahead is lighter and perceived as the current thing, but you lose all the adjustments it used to have. Lot of times people who are riding a bike care more about how they look. But common sense eventually rules if you go out on an event ride and look at how people ride. People on the floor in the shops know. Sometimes friends and neighbors help them get set up on a bike, and it's not right. I could easily see this problem. Well, it is just logical. Andy Pruitt [director of the Boulder Center for Sports Medicine] had a lot of influence on us. "Raise the head-tube!" he said.

It's basically ergonomics. Even look at these guys who are riding in the Tour. They are riding in a much more upright position. Look at Lance and the position he has. A lot more upright than they ever had. So, I just thought this was logical. And now that we made the Sequoia, that thing really resonated with people well. In fact, half of our customers probably are women. I think there is an opportunity for the Roubaix and the Sequoia to expand people's ability to ride—just like the mountain bike did.

Our latest idea is an aluminum handlebar with a rubber sleeve in it to absorb shock.

I like to go on these real long rides—seven hours. And go over dirt roads and stuff. And, sure, you can do it with any bike, but if you have something that works better, why not? I'd say that the biggest addition to comfort and performance is suspension for mountain bikes. Why not a fully suspended or fully damped road bike? It solves a real problem.

Getting older, I can relate to other people who are older. And I can also relate to people who are just coming into cycling. That is the thing that sometimes we just don't think about. Like, how can we get these other people into cycling? And not making the bike so intimidating. Make them more comfortable. If you're more comfortable, you can go a lot harder and faster. For Specialized, that's the real opportunity.

Ramping Up His Own Fitness

THE LAST COUPLE years I've put extra effort into really trying to be fit. I just wanted to change the level I was at, and I'm kinda pleased and surprised with myself. I was staying at the same level, and wanted to improve. I've always ridden five to six days a week, probably about 200 miles, Now I do yoga; we have an instructor come in here—it's a nice complement to riding. The way you're bent over and yoga stretches you all out. For the last two years, I've lifted weights in the gym probably four days a week. If I miss a day I feel bad. I just feel mentally bad. Because it makes me feel so good. I got some advice from John Howard and Andy Pruitt about position—I was too far back on my seat. You need an expert to give you some tips. I eat healthy. No particular diet—lot of vegetables, olive oil, a bit of pasta, regular vitamins. No big deal. Exercise really changes your metabolism.

I've really worked hard and can feel the difference. That's the great thing about cycling: what you put in, you get directly back. That is so different than other things in life, which are very confusing—there's not a direct correlation. But this is a direct deal.

What would be the ultimate goal in life? It is, like, you know: great family, being healthy. But you see some of these 80-year-old guys in Italy? On Sunday morning they're out riding on these real cool bikes. I mean, that's the goal, to be healthy like

that. And helps ya keep perspective. You go for a long ride and you come back and you have a full glass of juice. It's like the best thing ever.

As far as endurance, I'm probably better than I was even 15 years ago. And I just kept working on it. I kinda surprised myself in a positive way. I can go for a 100-mile ride and I'm not that tired.

I'm 54 and a half. I feel 30, mid-30s maybe. I do feel healthy. I feel like even if I am doing things or I am traveling time zones, I don't have any problem. Even riding with the guys around here, can I go as fast as they can? No, I can't. But I probably never could.

It's a shock when you meet people who stopped doing activity once they got out of college. So it's probably been a long time since maybe they even sweated. If they ask me how to get into cycling, I say go and find somebody to get you comfortable on the bike, then go at your own speed just like you were going on a walk. That is one way to think about it. If you were going on a walk, you could go out and walk for two, three, four hours no problem. Well, think about a bike the same way. Don't push the big gears. Spin. Get set up right. Drink a lot of water. Take a few energy bars or something with you. And that is a wonderful way to start. Once you start doing that, it's huge.

People don't have to feel like they have to compete. Just do your own thing.

This whole thing with obesity and kids. Whew. I was maybe too hard-core with my kids. But I said, "Hey, that Nintendo and all that shit? No way! You're not going to have that stuff. Go outside. Get outta the house. Let's get out on our bikes!" Make it a family focus thing. If the parents are healthy, the kids are like the parents, right?

Around Christmastime in San Diego, I was riding along with a guy—a good, competitive rider around 35, 38, who told me that he only started riding five years ago. Before that, he was overweight and had high blood pressure and was going to the doctor to get this blood medicine. And he told me, "Nothing was working. And my car was out of commission. So for like ten days and I had borrowed this guy's Rockhopper to ride back and forth to work. And I kinda started liking it. And then it just built from there. Now, I've never been happier in my life. I never have to go to the doctor, and my pulse rate is down to whatever. I am hooked."

·

THE SAME WEEK I was riding down there and another guy out on that ride said to me, "You from Specialized? Well, you won't believe this. But I used to be addicted to drugs. I wasn't proud of that, but it's a fact.

Then I got this mountain bike a couple of years ago. Look at my shoulder. I got a tattoo of your bike! A Specialized! Now I'm a fanatic. I plan all of my vacations around the bike. I'm not a superstar. But I'm not bad. And I changed my whole lifestyle."

Those kind of stories are all over. I have one myself—it's about how I got into long-distance riding. In college, I broke up with this girlfriend who I had lived with for four years—so I was really upset about it. One day I just took off and rode from San Jose and I said, "I think I'll go to the beach." I never rode that far, ever. I thought, *Shit, I could do that. That is no big deal.* Through that process of working this thing out, I went for these real long rides. I got stronger and stronger and I just couldn't believe it. I was always into bikes, but I was never into going very far. Never had ridden 100 miles in a day. But all of a sudden I went that far, and when I came back, I was clear-headed. I was proud of what I did. I was getting fitter. And that was the real turning point in my life.

BIKE FIT: THE FOUNDATION

*Proper set-up for comfort, power,
and injury prevention*

At mile 100 *I felt a twinge, but didn't have time to worry about it. At 200 miles it became pain, but I was in a groove and couldn't break my momentum. At mile 375, teeth clinched in agony as the needles under my kneecap pierced every pedal stroke, I checked into the turnaround point of the 1999 Paris-Brest-Paris, the quadrennial 750-mile randonee from Paris to the Atlantic Ocean and back. And I didn't check out. For the first time in my life, I "abandoned" (as the French call it) a bike event. Either that or risk permanent damage to my knee.*

On the train back to Paris, I was struck by the irony: I was much fitter now than in 1991, when I completed P-B-P an hour under the cutoff in 88 hours and 55 minutes. But maybe I wasn't as fitted to my bike. Instead of using the bike and shoes I'd trained on for years and completed all the brevets (qualifiers) on, I'd come to France with all-new equipment I hadn't used before. Later back home, checking it against the old gear, I found that the new bike's seat was set up an inch lower, the handlebars an inch higher, and my left cleat was slid back toward the arch and slightly crooked. Roughly two inches of deviation from my correct position wrecked the event I'd trained two years for. —RMW

"I was suffering out there today," you might hear a cyclist say. "Suffer" is an odd and venerable term, strangely specific to cycling, that can have a range of meaning, good and bad. Your long-term cycling health may well depend upon creating the basic foundation that will make all of your suffering good suffering. That foundation is proper bike fit.

Usually, suffering is defined as good pain—when everything's working at full-speed efficiency, when your lungs are heaving and your legs are churning, and you're joining the company of the cycling gods as you push to the lactic-acid boundaries of your very being. In other words, good pain = high performance, when man and machine are indistinguishable, working as one, suffering from the joy of muscles fatigued by working at peak efficiency.

Then, there's bad pain and suffering, like my knee in P-B-P, which indicates that something is wrong. Bad pain is when your knees, back, wrist, hip, hands, or crotch hurt, when your toes tingle, or all of the above hurt, when you get the nagging feeling that you're working against yourself. Bad pain is a double whammy: bad pain = fatigue-unrelated pain + poor performance. Bad pain can have many causes, but often at its root is poor alignment. Ironically, there's a relatively easy fix for that: proper fit. But bad pain is too often tolerated, confused with good pain.

• FITTING BASICS •

"Strangely, people check common sense at the door when it comes to riding a bike," says Paul Levine, owner of New York–based Signature Cycles and the director of the famed Serotta Fit School. "There is a huge misconception among cyclists that there needs to be some level of discomfort for them to assume that they are riding well—that you actually need to be locked into a bad position. This is dead wrong. You should be comfortable on a bike. And comfortable means that your weight is distributed as evenly as possible over your back, butt, shoulders, arms, and hands so that no one muscle or joint is overly stressed."

In other words, a bike should fit you like a glove. It should bring about good posture. If it doesn't, if it isn't properly aligned with your body mechanics, peak performance will never be realized, and energy will be wasted due to inefficient transfer of force from you to the pedals. You won't be as stable, or breathe well, or digest calories well. And as you expend precious energy compensating for the stress of your body holding itself incorrectly on the bicycle, you will put yourself at risk for aches and pains and injuries that are completely unnecessary.

Over the last decade, Levine has gained a reputation as the "Fit Guru," a name he recoils from but won't deny. One of the most sought-after bike fitters in the country, he saw firsthand how changes in position caused changes in power output for several thousand riders while conducting SpinScan analyses for CompuTrainer in the 1990s. Now he's so busy giving $200 bike fits to wealthy buyers of $7,000 custom Serottas (which he sells more of than any bike shop in the country) that he didn't have the time to schedule a *Bike for Life* interview for a week.

What does the right fit actually look like on a bike? If bike fit seminars and magazine articles have left you bleary-eyed and befuddled with angles and percentages, consider this Levine advice, which *Bike for Life* considers the simplest, most understandable description of the proper overall posture on a bicycle:

The proper posture to have while seated on a bicycle is like sitting on a chair that you know is about to be pulled out from under you. This leaning forward, **neutral spine** position not only supports the weight of your torso with your quadriceps and hip flexors, but activates the core muscles that provide a stable platform for the athlete to become more efficient. The neutral spine position also rotates your pelvis forward, relaxes your shoulders, and opens up your air passages. It also puts you in the best position to produce power from your gluteus maximus—your butt.

Note: The butt is the cyclist's great ignored power source; tapping it gains you a stunning supply of mainstream power on par with that of the quads. To find out why, see Step 4 below. In addition, a proper fit that activates your glutes can play a large role in reducing injuries to the back and knees (see chapter 8 for more details).

To understand the benefit of "sitting at the edge of the chair" consider what follows if the opposite occurs, if your pelvis is rotated backward: the pelvis essentially rolls up under your chest cavity—preventing the bottom of your lungs from fully expanding, rounding your spine, and pushing your shoulders farther from the handlebars. In turn, this tenses your shoulders, narrows your breastplate, and further restricts your airflow.

Cycling posture/alignment hinges on three connection points: seat, handlebars, and pedals. "If they are not all aligned together," says Levine, "the body tries to adapt, which leads to injuries and less power output."

Everyone is different, he says, and exact measurements are dependent upon comfort and a computerized power-output analysis, but certain basic rules apply across the board.

THE FOUR-STEP FITTING APPROACH

Nothing about the Serotta fitting method used by Levine and others seems unconventional. The process isn't much different than what most fitters (like Victor Larivee,

see sidebar) have been doing for years.

Step 1: Shoe/pedal interface: cleat at the ball of the foot

Clipless pedals, in widespread use among enthusiasts, increase efficiency by allowing the rider to make better use of the entire pedal circle, but have also been blamed by many for the increased incidence of knee pain. This can be avoided with proper cleat positioning: mounted directly under the ball of the foot and angled to match the rider's stride type. First, the ball of the foot: "People typically set the cleat of their clipless pedals too far back toward the heel—ultimately leading to numb foot, tingly toes, and inefficiency," says Levine. Nearly all bike fitters agree that maximum power is derived when the ball of the foot—the outermost protrusion on the inside of the foot—lines up with and pushes directly though the centerpoint of the **pedal axle**.

Not all fitters agree exactly where the ball is, however. Levine says this point is the second metatarsal phalange joint, while Andy Pruitt, director of the Boulder Center for Sports Medicine, says it is the first metatarsal. If you have lost your dog-eared copy of *Gray's Anatomy* and don't know a metatarsal from a metrosexual, heed the advice of Levine's fellow Serotta School practitioner Christopher Kautz, co-owner of PK Racing Technologies, who says if you must err on cleat placement, err toward the front of the shoe. Doing so gains you a mechanical advantage.

"The foot is a first-class lever arm for the calf muscle, and by locating the cleat forward, you effectively lengthen the lever and allow for more force production," Kautz says. In other words, a forward-placed cleat lets you push the pedal harder.

As for the angle of the cleat, common sense rules. Ride like you walk. If you walk pigeon-toed, point the bike shoes in; if you walk with toes pointed out, you'll ride the same way. Otherwise you will be fighting your body's natural movement and range of motion.

Step 2:
Ideal saddle height:
hips don't rock, legs don't straighten

"When people come in to see me, their bike seat's all over the place," says Levine. "As a general rule, if it's too low, you'll get pain in the front of the knee. If it's too high, there's pain in the back of the knee. And if it's tilted back, you get serious back pain." Here's why:

A low saddle results in excessive bend of the knee at the top of the pedal stroke, causing the underside of the patella (kneecap) to jam into its tracking groove in the femur (thighbone). So instead of tracking smoothly in the groove, cartilage rubs on cartilage. On the other hand, a too-high saddle leads to knee pain on the back side of the leg, because the excessive reach over-stretches the hamstrings. It also leads to a loss of power, as the patella becomes a less effective fulcrum in the leg's lever system.

What's too high? There are many formulas, but the best one may be common sense, says Levine. If your hips start to rock slightly from side to side as you pedal, or your toes begin to point down, or you feel discomfort in your crotch, you're too high. Lower the saddle a few millimeters at a time until these symptoms disappear. From a profile view, your knee should have a slight bend at the bottom of the pedal stroke.

Step 3:
Ideal saddle tilt and fore/aft:
little to none, slid back

How much should you tilt your saddle?

All fitters recommend that the saddle should be near level—no more than 3 to 5 percent tilt up or down. A down-tilted saddle (back is higher than the front) slides you forward, compromising handling and comfort. This tilt can irritate your crotch and put too much weight on your arms, hands, and front wheel. An up-pointed saddle (front higher than back) changes the curve of the lower back, risking lumbar pain, and smashes against the delicate blood vessels and nerves of your crotch, risking numbness and erectile dysfunction. The flexed lower back position often leads to **creep**, a stretching of the ligaments that can lead to sudden instability and injury (see "Rules for Triathletes and Time Trialists" below). Another problem with flexed lower back muscles, according to Chris Kautz, is that they turn off your gluteal muscles, forcing the quads to do more work. The right amount of tilt is ultimately determined by comfort and a computerized analysis that identifies maximum firing power.

As for the saddle's fore-aft position, beware sliding it too far forward; the Serotta school says that'll force the quads to do too much work. Here's the rule: at the 3 o'clock position on the crank circle, your foot should be horizontal. The reason: the foot can push straight down on the pedal at 3 o'clock, momentarily giving this position maximum potential power. There is also a safety benefit; if your seat is too far backward or forward, it tilts your foot and can lead to injuries and chronic pain, according to Andy Pruitt.

Describing the process used to find correct fore-aft positioning is rather technical,

Case Study: The Fit Got Him Fitter

LAST year, Javier Saralegui used to dread the 54-mile ride from Bridgehampton, New York, to the tip of Long Island and back with his brother-in-law, Melchior Stahl. "I'd come back from the ride and feel like my neck was broken, like someone took a two-by-four to it," says the president of the online group of Univision, the Spanish-language network. Then he saw the Serotta Legend titanium bike in an *Outside* magazine article titled "The Best Toys in the World," called the company, and was told, "Go see Levine."

"It changed my life," says the 45-year-old father of three.

Levine asked Saralegui his goals, where he rides, what surfaces he rides on. He put him on rollers and on a Computrainer, analyzed his form, and put him on the fit cycle. He made him stretch for half an hour. After four hours, Levine looked at him. "You say you want to be superfit, to ride with your brother-in-law, but I don't know how serious you are," Levine said. "This is an animal sport, and I'm going to give you an animal bike. I'm going to give you a Ferrari; what you had before [a LeMond] was sporting goods."

Then Levine looked Saralegui in the eye. "But it isn't the bike," he said.

Saralegui did start stretching, as Levine advised. In fact, he started taking Pilates. He got more flexible, and began riding with his heel lower, too. But at first he would have argued that it *is* the bike.

"Suddenly, everything was 100 percent different," he says. "I'm a different rider. No neck pain at all. Less fatigue. Now I use a lot less energy to go the same distance. Today, I just did a 54-miler and don't even feel it; in the past, I'd be in the Jacuzzi and telling you to call back. Right now, if you were to say, 'let's go for a 20-mile spin,' I'd say, 'Let's do it.'

"The new bike doubled my mileage, upped my comfort, upped my power. I don't cramp up anymore. The Napeek stretch, where you're in the **drops** for a half-hour against 25 to 30 mph headwinds, doesn't kill me anymore. Going to Montauk used to be a once-a-summer ride. Now it's once a week. I don't even see it as being a hard ride. Now I lead my brother-in-law. I ride all day with my heart rate between 155 and 170 beats; before, I couldn't hold it for more than a few minutes. Look at the real numbers on my Computrainer: it used to be 160 to170 watts for a 90-minute ride; now it's 190 to 200. On the road, I ride now at 24 to 25 mph, compared to 18 to19 before. The next level above me are guys who don't have jobs."

"The new bike gave me a new sense of power," says Saralegui. "For the first time, I feel myself using the glute, a huge muscle. Another big thing: the calf works more.

"I'm manic. I started tennis ten years ago and now I'm an 'A' player. I started surfing a few years ago and I'm good at that, too. But I've always been into cycling—just not like this."

Saralegui's fit took four hours and cost $500. The bike was upwards of $7,000. "But maybe Levine was right," he said. "It's flexibility. It's motivation. It's the fit, the efficiency. It's not the bike."

so skip to Step 4 when your eyes glaze over. All fitters make use of a plumb line (a string with a weighted end) to check that there is a vertical line-up between the knee and the pedal axle. Traditionally, the plumb line is dropped from the *tibia tuberosity*, the bump below the knee, but Serotta fitters believe that the unnamed soft hollow just behind the kneecap on the lateral side better indicates the true function of the knee joint. Pruitt says all that is too complicated; just drop the plumb from the front of the kneecap.

Step 4: Upper body position— comfort is king

Handlebar height is the least "scientific" part of the fitting process, according to Levine, because it's all about one thing: being as comfortable as possible in a variety of positions for a couple of hours at a time.

"A lot of people tell me that they've never been comfortable on a bike, and that's a shame," says Levine, "Unfortunately, that's because recreational riders often imitate professional cyclists, whose handlebars are typically set very low for aerodynamics. The pros have a high tolerance for pain; regular people don't." In other words, Levine says forget rules and forget aerodynamics; upper body comfort is king. The biggest cause of back pain is a too-low handlebar. Don't copy other people. And don't mess with the saddle.

"An indicator of poor bike fit for a road bike is when you can't comfortably ride in any of the handlebar positions, including the drops," says Levine. "It usually means the handlebar/headtube is too low and/or the stem and top tube are too long for you." Road bike handlebars are designed to allow the rider to take advantage of many positions, allowing the use of different muscle groups and aerodynamic positions. Not surprisingly, the most common request asked of bike shops by bike buyers, whether they are newbies with $300 **hybrids** or veterans plunking down thousands for exotic custom machines, is this: raise the handlebars.

You simply shouldn't be riding in pain or in a stretched-out position that hurts your hands. You shouldn't be riding humpbacked. You shouldn't get numb hands—suffered by 20 percent of riders. You shouldn't look like a silhouette of the letter "C." You should be riding with a neutral spine.

One problem often leads to another: to reduce pressure on the hands, people automatically roll the pelvis forward, causing the neck to hyperextend.

The spine is considered neutral when the muscles around it are relaxed, not in tension. Levine says that when a bike takes you out of neutral, it's because the handlebars are in the wrong position—usually too far away and too low.

Q: How high to raise the handlebars?
A: Higher . . .

"A good start for recreational riders is to match seat height and handlebar height," says Levine. "Performance riders can drop the handlebars 3 to 4 centimeters [about 1⅛ inches to 1⅝ inches]." In practical terms, the handlebars should be high enough so that a road bike rider can ride most of the time on the hoods (the rubber covering the top of the brakes) with arms in a shock absorbing position. For most people, that's a revelation. "You should ride 80 percent of the time on the hoods, 15 percent on the top of the bar, and 5 percent on the drops," says Levine. The hoods are very practical; from there, you can shift, brake, and instantly jump into the classic out-of-the-

BIKE FOR LIFE

saddle climbing position. Biomechanically, the hoods are the most comfortable, natural place for riders to put their hands, because doing so reduces the risk of carpal tunnel syndrome and puts the wrists in a neutral "handshake" position: thumbs pointing forward, wrists turned vertically.

In this position, says Levine, you should not be riding with straight arms. The upper arm should be at a 90° angle to the torso, with a slight bend to the elbow and the wrists not hyperextended. "The bend helps turn your elbow into a shock absorber; without it, the shock runs all the way up to your shoulders and neck," he says.

. . . but not too high.

Although high handlebars are a good thing, too-high handlebars are not. "The 'comfort' fit that brings your back almost perpendicular to the ground is okay for casual, flatland riding, like at the shore, but it'll cost you power and discomfort, especially in the hills," says Levine. Here's why: the largest muscle group used for cycling is the gluteus maximus, the butt, and it is not called into action until the hip is flexed at an angle of 45° or less. Very high handlebars do not allow this.

Example: Sit with your back straight up in a chair (a 90° angle), then try to stand out of the chair and notice what direction your back moves. It moves about 45° to your hips for the gluteus maximus to activate and raise you out of the chair. "Pretty cool, huh?" says Levine. "Now try getting up without leaning forward. It's extremely difficult. Welcome to the 'comfort' position. Try climbing hills in this position, and your wrists and neck start to hurt."

The reason for this, he explains, is that you can't stop your body from naturally wanting to lean forward as you climb, just like getting out of the chair. However, since the handlebars are too high and close to your chest, your leaning body puts excessive weight on your wrists. This is why a too-high bar is as bad as a too-low bar.

Q: What about mountain bikes and hybrids?

A: The same handlebar rules apply on **flat-bar bikes**, including cruisers. Your elbows should be naturally bent outward, serving as shock absorbers. To lessen the potential of carpal tunnel syndrome, nearly all fitters recommend that you *add barends,* short, 90°-angle handlebar extensions that, like hoods on a road bike's drop bars, provide a comfortable "handshake" riding position.

Q: What adjustments should older riders make?

A: It is important to note that flexibility—range of motion of your hamstrings, hip flexors, external hip rotators, and back—also plays a major role in handlebar placement. Paul Levine likes to use the example of two identical twins: a flexible one who does yoga and can bend over with legs straight and put his palms on the floor, and a couch potato who can only reach his knees. The flexible twin will need a longer top tube or stem and can ride in a lower, more aero position, while his stiff brother will need a shorter top tube, a shorter stem with a positive rise, or/and a headtube extension.

Aging has a similar effect. An adult's inevitable loss of flexibility after age 35 forces him/her upright. Given the vast increase in the number of older riders today, it is no surprise that one of the hottest new bike categories is the comfort road bike, which is characterized by a taller headtube and softer seat. Formerly limited to custom bikes, particularly from Serotta, taller front ends are now showing up on production bikes like the Specialized

Roubaix line. Personally championed by Specialized founder Mike Sinyard (see interview in chapter 6), these bikes include a number of novel, shock absorbing inserts throughout the frame, specifically placed to add comfort for older riders.

Q: How wide?

A: The accepted rule is to match handlebars to shoulder width. Don't go wider; it's not aerodynamic (it increases the rider's frontal surface area) and encourages a sagging between the shoulder blades. In the long run, this will lead to neck and shoulder pain. Too-narrow bars can lead to more nervous steering, and, hence, to loss of comfort. But they do not inhibit breathing, as many think. That's good news for those who use aerobars for aerodynamic positioning, like triathletes, time trialists, and even bike tourers.

RULES FOR TRIATHLETES AND TIME TRIALISTS:
Watch your back

Brace yourself for the world's simplest triathlon advice: don't stretch out. Wind tunnel tests prove that being narrow on a set of aerobars is more important to aerodynamics than being low. A too-low position hurts performance, because it encourages a humped back, not the flat back that gives the glutes a solid platform from which to fire. More importantly, a low position is uncomfortable and harmful to your back.

"It is not surprising that there is a much higher incidence of herniated disks among time trialists and triathletes," says Dr. Pam Wilson, a Duke University biomechanist and bike position researcher who treats many cyclists and runners, teaches clinics with seven-time national champion Karen Livingston, and consults frequently with Levine. "Beware the curved, humpback position you get when stretched out on low handlebars. The hump causes 'creep' hysteresis, a permanent lengthening of the spinal ligament that breaks down the integrity of the bonds."

Avoiding creep, which has long been an issue among people who sit at a desk all day, is easy on a bike: adjust aerobar armrests as high and far back as possible. Upper arms should be near-vertical, with elbows lined up just ahead of the shoulders.

Two warning signs of poor bike fit for a triathlon bike include (1) the inability to maintain the aero position throughout the ride without straining your neck, lower back, or shoulders, and (2) sitting on the nose of the saddle and constantly readjusting your position. Remember, the goal is to stay in the aero position! All the work you do to get an aero position doesn't do any good if you're not in it. Again, keep in mind that the optimal time trial position is probably not the most aero, but is the one that finds the best balance of aerodynamics, power, and efficiency.

Despite the relatively straightforward rules about handlebars and comfort, a final comment is in order: the bike industry doesn't make raising or adjusting handlebar height easy. Although pre-1990 bikes came with threaded steerer tubes and "gooseneck" stems that could be easily raised by loosening a quill, they were replaced by fixed-length systems that don't adjust. Today, you must buy a new "riser" stem, or acquire a whole new bike, like those from Giant's compact road bike line, that come standard with adjustable stems. Don't be surprised if you have to go back to the bike shop several times to get your handlebar height issue resolved most comfortably.

GOOD FIT, GOOD RIDING

Poor bike fit is like having a tire out of alignment on your car: you don't get a smooth ride, and you start seeing unusual wear patterns after a while—aching knees, back, neck, butt, and feet. A proper bike fit is the absolute first step you need to take to assure more comfort and power, reduce fatigue, and gain precise handling. If you buy a new bike, get a fit. If you feel pain on your old bike, get a fit. If you've never been fit, get fit. Because until then, you aren't as efficient as you could be, and may waste time and money trying to remedy your aches and pains.

The Bike Fit Process

Two hours with a fitting master

"I'M going to give you an extra 15 miles tomorrow," boasted jumpsuit-clad Victor Larivee, beaming with the conviction of an Old World craftsman. Any cycling aficionado knows that proper bike fit aids performance, minimizes injuries, and can counter biomechanical inefficiencies, but few seem as, well . . . *fitting* as Victor.

Seating his subject in a platform-mounted shoeshine-type chair, Larivee strips off a sock and begins probing and poking the bare foot, beginning yet another of the two-hour fitting sessions he performs over a hundred times a year at his small Bicycle Workshop bike store, an institution in Santa Monica, California, for the last 20 years. Some Westside bike shops offer fitting services, but few can match the sheer number of contraptions Larivee uses to make sure that his customers ride in the most efficient and stress-free biomechanical position. "Hey, a lot of 'em know how to do this, but not enough to make a science out of it," he said. "Remember, I do this for a *living*."

The 15 extra miles Larivee promises come from finding the rider's neutral position on the bike. "Everything I'm about to do will simply be duplicating your natural gait—that's your neutral position. It's where you're most efficient," he explained. Does that mean that if you walk like a duck, you should also ride like a duck? "Yeah—that's right. I like that," he smiles, dedicated teacher to eager student.

Custom-molded orthotic

Larivee starts off a fitting by making a custom heat-molded Superfeet brand orthotic of each foot, both of which are worn inside cycling shoes. "This stabilizes the foot, giving you more power," explains Larivee. In a static situation like cycling, where the feet themselves aren't moving, a foot will automatically collapse on the downstroke, dissipating your energy. The orthotic keeps the foot arched and aligned in its own neutral position—putting 100 percent of your power through the pedal. Also, it maintains the neutral position by allowing the natural tilt of the rider's feet.

Cleat positioned so you pedal through the ball of the foot

Next, Larivee slips a cycling shoe on the foot, pokes a rod tipped with wet paint through a hole in the shoe, and performs one of the most critical tasks in a fitting—finding the ball of the foot. "The ideal situation in cycling is to have the center of the knee driving straight through the ball of the foot, which then should drive directly through the pedal spindle," he explains. Larivee redrills holes and moves the cleat fore and aft until it is over the ball of the foot. Then, to make sure the knee is directly over the ball of the foot, he uses a plumb line to position the saddle back or forward.

Matching leg lengths

Next, the rider lies on his back and Larivee measures the legs from the top of the thighbone (femur) to the heel. If one is any more than a half-inch longer than the other, he builds up the bottom of the cleat to make up the difference. Normally, there is no surprise involved here. "People know when they're that far off."

Neutral rotational alignment

At this point, orthotic in shoe and cleat in place, the rider goes to his own bike, which has been placed on a stationary trainer. Larivee hauls out a small, square steel box with two rods—one red, one white—sticking out of its side. This is a **RAD**, or Rotational Alignment Device. The angle of the cleat is adjusted until the two RAD rods stay parallel through several rotations. At that point, the pedal stroke matches the rider's natural walking gait—the long sought-after neutral position.

Proper seat height

While the rotational alignment is being done, Larivee is also adjusting the seat. Using a pivoting ruler called a gagiometer, the seat is either raised or lowered to give the leg a slight bend at the knee—about 30°—in the bottom pedal position. This position is not only the most efficient for riding, but also puts the least amount of stress on the knees.

Comfortable handlebar height

The final step is the least scientific. Larivee adjusts the handlebar stem for the best comfort of the individual rider. "This is the only time I let your brain tell me what to do—not your body," says Larivee. As a general rule, performance riders ride with handlebars parallel or just below the seat height. Riders with shorter torsos—especially women—can use a longer stem to keep them from having to reach too far.

The fitting just described took the fast-working Larivee about two hours. He charges $75 for a fitting and $125 for the Superfeet orthotic molding. "People who've been sent by other shops never complain about the price," he said, "but the people who call up on their own freak out. They have no idea of what's involved."

Incidentally, Larivee's fits have gotten faster over the years. "More older people are riding today, which is why back pain is the biggest complaint I hear—bigger than knee pain," he says. "If the guy who comes in for a fit is 35 or older, I won't just raise the handlebars. I'll say, 'You want to ride faster than you've ever ridden—with no back pain ever again? Try a recumbent.'"

Then he points to his showroom. The inventory at the Bicycle Workshop, once composed entirely of exotic foreign road-racing bikes, is now 90 percent recumbents. "One ride and they're sold," says Larivee. "But that doesn't mean a 'bent [recumbent] rider doesn't need a bike fit. His feet, legs, and knee are just as at-risk, although the upper body gets a break."

Fresh from the fit, I headed down the Venice bike path feeling great. I didn't expect to be on a recumbent, but it felt so darn comfortable. No trace of the bad knee. No numb hands or numb nuts or aching back, either. I rode noticeably faster in the bike's low-slung aerodynamic position. I enjoyed the attention, too; dozens of beachgoers stared, smiled, and waved at me, as if I was riding a bike from another planet. Damned if I didn't ride an extra 15 miles more than I'd planned. *—RMW*

Eddie B

THE WORKAHOLIC POLE WHO CHANGED AMERICAN CYCLING

"We had a complex about the Europeans, with their three lungs, four hearts, and five legs," said three-time Tour de France winner Greg LeMond. "Eddie B helped us get over that."

With that introduction, Edward "Eddie B" Borysewicz (Bor-say-vich) stood up to a rousing ovation at the Endurance Sports Awards dinner in San Diego in February 2004. On stage he was greeted by LeMond and all eight members of the 1984 U.S. Olympic team, whom he had coached to a record nine medals, including four gold. They had come to honor Eddie and to participate in a cycling fantasy camp that raised money for the reconstruction of Eddie's home, which was destroyed in a massive San Diego fire several months earlier. For the moment, Eddie was living in an 8-by-10-foot pool house.

"He was the John Wayne, the catalyst," said 1980s star Alexi Grewal.

"He took us young cowboys, and made us real cowboys," said LeMond.

In the 1970s, the U.S. Cycling program was in shambles and the sport underdeveloped. then Eddie B defected to the United States from his native Poland in 1976 and resuscitated the team with his common sense and Eastern Bloc training methods.

In Poland, Eddie had won two junior national championships, two national championships, and was awarded the highest sports award in Poland, the "Special Champion in Sport." Damaged by aggressive treatment of a misdiagnosis of tuberculosis, he began preparing for a coaching career in his twenties,

earning a master's degree in physical education, physical therapy, and coaching. he went on to coach a leading Polish trade team and 30 national and world champions, including bronze and silver medalists at the 1976 Olympic games. soon thereafter, he defected to the U.S. to head up the United States Cycling Federation [now USA Cycling] as coach of the U.S. National Team. During 12 years of coaching, his American riders won thirty world championships, nine olympic medals and fifteen Pan-American medals. In 1988 he left the USCF and with investment banker Tom Weisel created the Subaru Montgomery team, which later became Montgomery Bell and then the U.S. Postal Service Team.

Throughout his coaching years, Eddie B developed and coached some of America's greatest cycling stars, including LeMond, six-time tour winner Lance Armstrong, Olympic medalist Steve Hegg, and six-time world champion Rebecca Twigg. Since 1996, Eddie has been running training camps in Ramona, California; his clients have included many national and world Masters medalists. Speaking with a thick Polish accent and ungrammatical English, Eddie B was interviewed by Bike for Life's Roy Wallack on March 9, 2004. Variously described as "blunt-spoken," "really tough," and even "cold" by his adoring riders, the intense Polish immigrant put performance first and America squarely on the world's cycling map, where it has been ever since.

FROM YOUNG AGE, I read everything. I read the Italian Coni Blue Cycling Book. Later I read papers from the Polish Sports Institute and from the Soviet Sports Institute. So maybe my fate to coach.

I was born in Poland in 1939, on the Nemen River on land that now in Belarus. Before World War II, Stalin take eastern part of Polish country. In fourteenth century Poland was the biggest country in Europe, did you know it?

Cycling was a big sport in my country when I grew up. I was good at cycling almost all my life—but was a better runner. I run very well, 400 meters excellent. At age 17 I run 51 seconds with no training. I have natural stride.

The coach even take me to national team. Then he give me a racing bike for fun, to help run training, because he knew I was crazy about cycling. So, I start to compete in bike races. First year I race in 30 events. I was double junior champion in 1958 at age 19.

My progress stop when I go into military. I supposed to be privileged in sport, to go to Sport Battalions like other athletes, and continue training, [but] wasn't allowed to do athletics for one year because my father was anti-communist. They didn't do me any favors. They made it hard for me. Did not to do any training at all for cycling.

My club and my federation really fight for me. After one year, I move to a regular division, where was a little sport program. But when I there just for a few months, everything canceled because of Cuba problem [Cuban Missile Crisis]. East Bloc forces went on alert. We have to send bicycles home and are regular soldiers again.

Nothing about the military helped my cycling. I did a lot of cross-training on my own. Everything I can to keep in shape. It was like being in prison; I do what I have to do.

Fate Intervenes

At 21, one season after getting out of military, I was already on national team again. I start winning races. Everything incredible. Then my cycling career was change by a doctor decision.

In an exam, doctors discover I have a little point under my left collarbone they think is indication of contact with TB. The doctor thinks this is a new thing, because nobody sees before. I spent four months in the hospital. This guy screwed up my career.

I probably had TB when I was little boy during the Second World War and my body just took care of it. But it left a little scar, like scar tissue. Like a little bean you can't see on the X-ray when my arm hang down, but is visible when I lift my shoulder high.

So here I am, winning races and making national team, one of the strongest guys, achieving all my dreams. Then I go into the hospital for four months, and in two weeks I might have killed myself. I was very depressed. So I don't talk to anybody. Even right now hard to talk of this, because it touched my heart.

Half season after hospital, I am back to national team. I am good again. But I know I am not going to be as I was. Because after 100k when I was on the break, I used to get better and better. Now, after hospital, I have pains with my liver.

So, at 22, I know my future. I love cycling so much, but I'm not stupid. I know my best thing is over. So I start went to Academy Physical Education and I change my goal, because I know I am not going to be world champion. But I am going to develop world champions.

I rode very well for three years more as member national team. I did well at nationals, and I compete with our national team in different countries. I wasn't a good climber, like when I was junior. I was different guy after the hospital; I pick up like 25 pounds and only lost 15 or 10. So I become heavy guy, muscle guy. In team time trial I was excellent. Also in crit and classic races that did not have hilly stages. I didn't make selection for some stage races with one-third mountain stages. I did pretty good on the road—a few times top-20.

I was two-time national champion of the track and national champion of the road, but I not make any progress. So I study hard.

I kept riding until I was 29 only because I love cycling—and the life. I was amateur by license, but of course I really a professional. I rode bike for very good money, for a communist country. So I had very good life and I do what I like to do: pursue my physical education studies. I graduate Academy Physical Education. Next, I graduate special after physical therapy and coaching school. I spent 22 years in school. Results always "A."

Coaching Career

WHEN I WAS 29 to 30 years old, I plan to race two, three years more. One Sunday, I won a classic race. On Monday, I am called by secretary from office of chief of sport this region, and told please come to see. When I come, he told me name of some person who is president/CEO of different club. "That is your new boss," he said. "Excuse me if I don't understand it," I say. "Please just do," he said. And that is it. He tell me I have to work. So I have to quit being a bike racer.

He told me I now head coach of different club.

I not afraid at all. I was coach even in my last years of competitive cycling.

My nickname as bike rider was Professor. Two reasons: One, I only guy with master's degree. Two, I always thinking. My friends ask many times for advice, even when I still a bike rider. I always analyze.

My generation was exactly similar like in United States. No professional coaches, only ex-bike riders, with no education. That eventually changed in Poland; now you can be only coach if you have get a master's degree in PE [physical education], two years after graduating coaching school. Besides studying, I listen old guys. I try to learning from everybody and I read every book. Anything that can help me. That was my second education. By this experience, learning a lot, learning hard way.

A good coach is combination of things learned in school and developed on your own. You have to always think, "I am . . . teacher." I know cycling because I race hard and many years and successful. School is important too. Both things together and not other things. You must really be dedicate. You must love. You must be passion. Okay? Impossible different.

It takes much time, this passion. During our divorce my ex-wife said, "We weren't married for 21 years because he was on the road 255 days a year."

Now always I lecture. I tell people, "Don't be crazy and be imbalance with work and family." Because family is very important and I miss this. I have two nice, smart kids and I have good relations with my ex. But I was a divorced single guy at age 55.

Coaching Philosophy

COACHING PHILOSOPHY FOR me is: you must be educated. You must have cycling [experience]. Not necessary best in country or best in the world. But you must have professional experience. That help. Bigger that help. Many times superstars cannot be coaches. I don't know superstars can be coaches. Because these guys have no education and think what is good for them must be good for everybody. So for me cycling experience, practical experience very important. Education very important. And next self-education. You must know how to use this university stuff in practice.

My own experiences as a cyclist taught me a couple simple truths: Hard work is equal important as rest. You must work very hard. And you must rest well. You have to relearn how much is too much.

People absolutely don't rest enough. Rest is ignored. It is key.

And so is analyze [-ing]. I check my pulse all the time after two years racing. There were no heart rate monitors then. I was only guy checking pulse in two positions, horizontal and vertical [standing and lying down]. Both are important. Vertical can be horizontal same. For example 42 and 42. But usually vertical was, 55 for example, always higher.

I taught myself to take pulse. I always talk to doctors. I gauged my fitness by my pulse. In my time on the national team we have always a blood pressure check, a pulse check, weight check, urine check. Nurses did it; it was expensive, took much time, very complicated. So many different things can be checked. For me, pulse is simple and very good. That's enough for me. We can't do everything.

The pulse is a simple, accurate gauge. On day before race [Saturday], pulse should be low, perfect. On Sunday in morning, will be higher from adrenaline. After race on Sunday your pulse is [naturally] high; when was hard race, my pulse must be up. Monday pulse always is higher. Tuesday it is still higher than normal, but going down. Wednesday almost perfect. My philosophy is day after race is easy recovery ride. Second day after race [Tuesday] is a test to see how you feel. Do light warm-up, then speed work—jumps or sprints. If feel weak on the second sprint, do not any more sprints that day. If feel good, do more. Depends on my feeling.

The coaches did not tell me to do this. They had us doing a regular workout the day after a race. I was one of first to say we need a recovery day after hard workout.

And I was first guy in Poland to have a longer **crank arm**. We all used 170 mm steel crank arm. It was primitive; we used hammer to change them. On visits to France, I discovered aluminum crank arm. Every year, when I'd go there, I'd always collect money beforehand from riders and go to bike shops to see latest stuff. One time when I said I wanted aluminum crank arms, shop owner say, "Which price?" I was surprised. This was first time I heard of different prices and sizes. I picked up a 170 and told him that this size was normal for us. So he recommend me a 172 and a half. I say, what else do you have? He say 170, 172½, and 175.

"Give me 175," I said.

"No, no," he said. "This going to be *grande problema*."

I was always the thinking guy. Longer crank arms will give me advantage in climbing. So I stuck to 175. We argued. I took the 175s and a bottom bracket home on Friday, put them on, then go to the big classic race on Sunday: 240k, 250 starters.

After 50k, only 14 guys were left. It was the crosswinds—in Poland, there is a lot of crosswind, "devil wind," we say. But I outsmarted devil, I thought. After 50k, I passed everybody. Oh, so smart! My crank arms—wonderful! They work! At 50k, I'm not usually trying to win. I usually take over after 100k. But now I jump after 50. And it is not long before I have a cramp. And I lose.

BIKE FOR LIFE

I said, *My God! Uh oh!* I was one of seven guys to finish the race. I always finish first, but now I was the seventh. I rode cramped all the way. The hardest race in my life. I knew the problem was not the crank arm. The problem was the big change. The Frenchman in the shop was right. Change crank arms for 2½ mm. But not for five. It was a very good lesson I learn. Something I pass on to my students.

Coming to America

WHEN I WENT to United States I never believe I am going to be coach.

I did not come here for coaching. I quit cycling just six, seven months before. I get divorced because of cycling. I was workaholic. That's my problem. I work from 7 [AM] to 11 [PM]. You know in Poland, I was full-time professor in University of Poland. I teach PE and physical therapy, was a full-time coach, and head coach of club. I was national coach for juniors. And I was tour guide for some times. I was incredibly busy. And I threw out my first marriage by being workaholic. So in 1976, I say no more cycling in my life!

At that time, I already I develop world champions. Olympic medalists. I was most successful coach in Poland by results. So I say, "Good-bye sport!" Unfortunately, I have this sport in my blood. After break of ten months, I met [U.S. cycling director] Mike Fraysee and I see what they got in U.S. He offers job and I back to coaching again.

Main difference in the way I coach: I am not a guy who tell you how many repetitions you have to do. I explain how you have to train and how hard you have to train. So you make decision of one more repetition or not. Because you are the captain of your body, not me. And always I explain what's going on. I always honest with my client.

Client must come to my place. I never ever coach anybody by Internet I never see. People offer me more money. I say: Sorry, thank you, good-bye. I have to see this body. And I have to set up position on the bike. I have to talk about life, training, recovering, nutrition, discipline, and on and on. Okay? And for me is very important self-discipline. Not discipline. I never ever check riders 10 o'clock is in room?

If you ride for me, I need to know about him. I have to see him on the bike. I need to see his VO_2. I have to see his blood. Next we can start program. And I push him to the max. Because only push hard and recovery well you can produce. Always I am monitoring his training.

When you racing once a week, I always explain to riders four different training days. Monday is *recovery* ride, Tuesday is *testing* day—sprints, so I can see how my recovery is going. It is going to give me information about what kind intervals I'm going to do next day. Wednesday is *super-hard training*—intervals, maximum, harder than race! That's maximum. My intervals, my philosophy is different than other people. Some people for me don't know what they are talking about. Must know what is different between sprints and intervals. Absolutely big difference. Thursday is *endurance*. Friday is recovery day. Saturday is a warm-up day. And you ready. Sunday is race day.

Recovery ride means you riding when you want it, with who you want it, how you want it and where you want it. Everything what you want it. Important is even with who you riding. Where you riding. In other words, I say you riding bike with good rpm, with gears you not feeling you pushing pedals. You listen the bird. And looking like grass growing. Or ride on the beach and see nice jogging women. Look at the scenery, Okay? Heh heh. For how long recovery ride depends on who you are. Everyone is riding differently. Professional rider is two hours. An amateur, about hour. And that is individual. When he don't like to ride after 30 minutes, he feel bad, psychology bad, go home. Try afternoon maybe for another half hour. That's fine too.

The second day [after the race or hard training effort] is "testing day"—you are testing myself with speed work. Testing day means testing your performance. Testing who you are. How you recover. It's a two-hour workout. In this plan, many coaches follow me. After all, I am in this country 20 years. Before I come to this country, I learn only one thing about American sport cycling: LSD—long slow distance. More you are riding, the better you are.

For touring, LSD yes. For recreation, LSD fine. But not for competition. Speed work, intervals, endurance, and recovery—is necessary for Americans to be good. You must have a balance. Americans were not doing speed work before me. Nothing was organized. It was really wild in cycling.

Here's how to do a test: warm up for 15 to 30 minutes depends on who you are. Then maximum strength about 50 seconds—where you pushing body to the max. Your heart to the max. Blood pressure to the max. Maximum acceleration and hold. And always your legs feel like table legs. Before you do again, allow full recovery. Your pulse going the same level as when you start ride bike.

Sprints and intervals are different thing. My God! Sprints are 15 seconds. Intervals different—there is five different kinds of intervals. Is different for crit, is different for time trial, is different for hill climbing. Different for road race. And only big difference is time, is speed and recoveries. Because with sprint, recovery is maximum. Speed is not important. In interval, speed is important. Because you must simulate race.

My philosophy is two days after a race and two days before a race I always [use the] same training principles. How many days I have between races [and the two-day cushion on each side of them] is how many days I really train. I have one day I combine intervals with endurance. When I don't have more than four days [to train], that is recovery stuff.

I dunno what U.S. cyclists did before me. But my program become very detailed. For two years, I work with Ed Burke [University of Colorado professor and prolific cycling health writer] who die unfortunately last fall. Every Friday, we fly to different place around the country and do clinics for 100 to 150 people. And I give always 40 pages information about cycling. My ex-wife say why I don't give one page to marriage?

His Stars and His Health

MY PROGRAM WORK for everybody to get better. First you need the right position on the bike. Next, knowledge to make you better. But not anyone can be champion. Need genetics. LeMond was 16 when I met him. He had incredible body and personality; I immediately say "this guy can be world champion." One of the best I've work with. The natural athletic body. Without it, cannot be a world champion. I gave him the structure. Now only ones like LeMond I meet are older. Vic Copeland, doctor from San Diego, we work together I dunno how many years, ten, fifteen. Was just marathon or triathlon racer when we met, not so great. In two, three years with me, began winning. Now, he is not beatable. Not

BIKE FOR LIFE

touchable. He is better than younger guys. Mr. Tom Weisel, [former] CEO and owner Montgomery Securities [he sold it—Ed.], is another incredible athletic body. Too bad we cross each other not when he was 16, like LeMond. He was already 45. After one year he won national champion. He win five times national champion. He becoming world champion in Masters category. He or Vic could have been another Greg LeMond.

I love cycling and always will, but only ride three or four times a year. I swim every day, but it not like going out for a two-hour ride. That makes you feel so good and sleep so deep. Had two bikes on the porch of my home in San Diego that burned down in the fire [of 2003]. Too busy. But after the fire, LeMond sent me his stationary bike. I put it between the pool and the sliding door, so I am forced to ride it.

I'm 65 now, alone. Twelve years divorced. My grandfather lived till 90 and had all his teeth. The swimming keep me with 50 heart rate, 110/70 blood pressure, and 140 cholesterol.

American people eat too much. I eat six times a day fruit and vegetables. My biggest meal is lunch, like in France. Noon to 2 o'clock. They got it right. When you eat too late and go to bed, that's how you store fat.

I worked so hard. I wanted to make better team to win Tour de France. Now I coach six hours a week in the velodrome and three hours on the road on Sunday. Otherwise, I worked on my house farm— three horses, 50 chickens, cats, dogs. I dream of riding three times a week. I always said I'd ride tomorrow, but tomorrow never came. When my home is rebuilt, I will ride again.

8

PREHAB

*Prevention and rehabilitation of cycling's two
biggest injuries: cyclist's knee and biker's back*

JULY 26, 2000, *Day Five, TransAlp Challenge:* "*Vhy do you alvays do zat at ze check-
points?*" *asks a German mountain biker. He's curious as to why my partner, Rich White, and
I are tossing a Frisbee back and forth at Forcella Ambrizzola, elevation 7,268 feet, the highest
stop on this grueling eight-day, 400-mile race across the Alps.*

"*It's a natural way to stretch and strengthen your core,*" *explains Rich.* "*Since cycling is a linear activity—that is, you move forward with virtually no twisting movements—your back is the
first thing to go. It gets weak, stiff, and subject to strains. Throwing a Frisbee requires a transverse
motion that works your abs and the muscles around your spine, protecting you from a bad back.*"

*I'm dumbstruck. For years, I'd viewed Rich simply as a witty bike shop manager, not a quasi-
physical therapist. Throwing a Frisbee actually helps to cure "biker's back," one of the most widespread maladies in the bike world? Crazy, but . . . logical. And to think, all this time, I thought
we were just having fun.*

•

*May 4, 2002, Day Three, TransGabriel Challenge: Rich and I have just finished our hardest-ever
ride, a self-mapped, 125-mile mountain bike expedition across the length of the San Gabriel
Mountains. We think we might be the first bikers to have conquered the fabled "Roof of L.A.,"
the immense wilderness just north of Los Angeles where motorcyclists scream around isolated
mountain roads and serial killers dump bodies. Our route had 25,000 feet of climbing and
only two remote water spigots. We each lugged camping gear and three gallons of water in
60-pound trailers.*

I trained hard for the TransGabriel, which we designed as a training ride for the first-ever TransRockies Challenge in Canada in August. Every weekend for months, I climbed hills for hours. My bike fit was perfect. But at ride's end, my knees ached; two weeks later, I dropped out of a double-century at mile 96, hobbled by clicking/scraping sounds and excruciating pain. Something was wrong; this was no mere muscle strain. I stopped riding. I canceled on the Trans-Rockies. Six months later, I had an operation on a torn meniscus. Two years later, my bad knee still wasn't right and the good one hurt.

Back in 2000, I was the first person to complete the TransAlp and La Ruta in the same year. I felt indestructible. But by early 2004, after therapy and a dozen doctor visits, I could barely ride, or run, or sometimes even walk.

Cycling is famously easy on knees, yet knee injuries dog the sport, due to poor bike fit and overuse. The former zapped me at Paris-Brest-Paris in 1999; the latter got me at the TransGabriel in 2002, when I'd been in shape, but hadn't trained pulling a 60-pound trailer, like Rich had. Moral of the story? It's not just "Use it or lose it." It's "Overuse it and lose it," too. —RMW

One works too little, the other too much. Those reasons, and more, are why physical therapists say that the back and the knees, respectively, are the two biggest problem areas for a cyclist.

"Knee pain has been the number-one problem in cycling for years, but back pain is catching up fast as the cycling population ages," says Andy Pruitt, director of the renowned Boulder Center for Sports Medicine in Boulder, Colorado. Studies have shown knee injuries to be the most common overuse injuries evaluated in sports medicine centers, and can occur in over half of the participants at endurance events.

Generally, "cyclist's knee" arises from too much of a good thing. Pedaling a bike, normally so benign an activity that cycling is the preferred rehab therapy for knee injuries from other sports, can be a source of injury through sheer repetition. Since an average cyclist can turn the crank 5,000 times an hour (around 83 rpm), the smallest misalignment, whether anatomic, technique, or equipment related, can lead to dysfunction, impaired performance, and pain. Moreover, even with perfect alignment, cycling's gentle efficiency encourages overdoing it. On the flip side, "biker's back" is the result of inactivity—first, of the sedentary lifestyle that keeps modern humans, athletic or not, seated most of their lives, and second, by the standard cycling position, in which the spine stays hunched over and virtually immobile. Underworked and stretched-out, back muscles become too weak to do their job of maintaining your posture and spasm in pain.

As you saw in chapter 7, proper bike fit can eliminate many knee and back problems. But fit is only a necessary first step, on its own not enough to reverse the misalignment caused by years of accumulated injuries, age-related muscle decay and inflexibility, ingrained bad habits of form, over- and underdevelopment of certain muscles, plain old overuse, and off-the-bike inactivity. In other words, if you have a history of training improperly on the bike, and your body is weak, tight, out-of-balance, and generally neglected off the bike, you're a ticking time bomb. Just one

$$\bigodot\kern-0.9em 8$$

PREHAB

ride too hard and too soon, and the nagging twinges you've shrugged off for years could explode in knee and back pain bad enough to keep you off the road for weeks or months or longer.

To make sure that doesn't happen, to roll through your 60s, 70s, and 80s on a bike saddle, not a wheelchair, this chapter watches your back with several detailed, straightforward programs of on- and off-the-bike stretching and strengthening that can restore a natural, balanced posture. To protect your knees, it provides a common-sense "overtraining-avoidance" checklist, recommends specific stretches and weight lifting to keep the knee on track, discusses specific supplements, preaches self-discipline to monitor and throttle back training loads, makes sense of the evolving science of proper riding technique, and even suggests that you relearn the way you ride.

The prevention and rehabilitation of cycling injuries are two sides of the same coin, which is why we call this chapter "Prehab." For long-term cycling health, you can't start it too soon.

· 1 ·
Cyclist's Knee

Some people call it "cyclist's knee." Some call it "the overuse syndrome." Doctors officially call it patellofemoral pain, a burning sensation that occurs between and around the patella (kneecap) and the femur (thighbone). But the most succinct explanation of cycling's most common malady that I've ever heard came from Greg Stokell, a longtime manager of the SuperGo bike shop in in Santa Monica, California: "Macho-itis."

"No matter the terrain or the wind or how out of shape they are, these people say, 'Pain isn't gonna stop me—I'm not gonna downshift,'" Stokell would say. "And their connective tissue screams, 'No!'"

In theory, cycling is not hazardous to your knees. One reason that the sport has grown so popular over the last 30 years is that it improves fitness in a "joint-friendly" manner (i.e., without the repetitive, 5 to 6 Gs of joint-impact forces associated with running). Overall, cycling is considered to be much less injury-producing than running, and many runners substitute cycling for running workouts in order to give their legs a break and recover more completely between running sessions. "Knees don't have to be a problem in cycling. In fact, it's so stress-free that we put people from other sports into cycling for rehabilitation," said Gail Weldon, a Los Angeles physical therapist.

Nonetheless, knee pain happens in cycling. "And when it does, it indicates that you are doing something wrong," says Weldon. "That's why any problem a cyclist has with his knees was probably avoidable—and generally fixable. Even hill climbing is no problem—as long as you have the strength and conditioning."

That's it in a nutshell: if a proper bike fit and, to a lesser degree, proper training and technique (chapters 1 and 2) don't help you avoid knee pain or rehab it, you're probably overdoing it. "Overuse" injuries result when the chosen volume or intensity of training causes damage to tissues that are not adequately repaired during a training cycle. Cyclists feel the pain if they ride too long, too fast, too steep, too soon without sufficient warm-up or base of training. That's why overuse injuries are especially prevalent early in the season, after months of winter inactivity. "They haven't done anything at all, then they go on a full-day ride on a Sunday," said Beverly Hills chiropractor Russell Cohen. "And we see them in the office on Monday."

Hard-core racers are no different than average Joes. "Most injuries I see are from competitive cyclists who come back too soon," said Jim Beazell, chief physical therapist and professor at the University of Virginia-Health South physical therapy clinic in Charlottesville. "These people are too gonzo—they ride 100 miles the first weekend without training." That tendency has been encouraged by the growth of ultra- and cross-state road rides and 24-hour mountain biking events in the past decade.

Cyclist's knee doesn't discriminate by age. Older bodies aren't as strong and flexible as they were when they were 16 or 17, so they get hurt if they don't warm up enough and allow time for recovery. Yet youthful vigor can create problems, too. Although stronger and more flexible, younger riders get hurt because they go harder and longer.

Bottom line: beware overuse. Ride too hard too fast, and something's gotta give. Often, what'll give is the weakest link: the knee.

WHY KNEES ARE AT RISK IN CYCLING

The knee is one of the body's most vulnerable junctures, and extra-heavy demands can overwhelm it. Acting as part hinge and part pulley, the knee extends and flexes the leg by functioning as a juncture of our biggest bones and muscles: the thigh's quadriceps and hamstrings muscles, which respectively straighten and bend the leg, plus the thighbone, the shin-bone, the kneecap, and the calf muscle. All of these are strapped together by a criss-crossing latticework of tendon, ligament, and cartilage.

"The knee is a relatively unstable connection in which bones can be easily displaced, which is why it has the most stress and abuse potential of any area of the body during athletics," explains Peter Duong, PhD, an anatomy instructor at Indiana State University. "Even though bicycling, unlike running, is a non–weight bearing activity and has little lateral motion, it generates forces in the area between the kneecap and thighbone that can actually amount to several times the body weight."

For a cyclist, knee pain is most often manifested in two conditions: *patellar tendonitis* and *chondromalacia*. The most common is the former, which refers to a strain of the tendons, the tough fibers that attach the quadriceps to the kneecap and the hamstrings to the shinbone. Tendonitis is painful, but quickly and easily fixed with rest.

Chondromalacia, burning pain that occurs between the patella and the femur, occurs less frequently than tendonitis, but is far more serious. For some rather complex reasons, to be described below, including too-hard training, poor alignment, and natural overdevelopment of one side of the thigh muscle, the kneecap can get pulled off its track during the leg extension, tearing up some cartilage in the process. Initial patellofemoral pain can be severe, but often occurs after cycling rather than during the ride. Further agitated, it can become chondromalacia, a painful, almost audible grating sensation with every stroke that can't be completely rehabilitated. Chondro is permanent damage and usually leads to arthritis. It is to be avoided at all costs.

Below, more details about chondro and tendonitis, and a plan to deal with them.

Tendonitis

Patellar tendonitis, the most common cycling knee injury, is the inflammation of the tendon structure that surrounds the kneecap and connects the thigh's quadriceps muscles to the lower leg. Having been repeatedly stretched beyond its capability by overuse, the tendons become inflamed and enlarged by microtears that heal as scars. Swelled up, the tendons now move with increased friction and pain. According to Andy Pruitt, patellar tendonitis shows up as a burning pain in the front of the knee, below the kneecap, while pedaling or walking up or down stairs. It hurts to the touch and may, he said, "squeak like a rusty hinge."

Patellar tendonitis occurs more frequently in cyclists than other tendon damage for a simple reason: the quads are the prime movers in cycling (that is, for those who haven't yet discovered the power of the butt muscles—see "Butt Power," later in this chapter). The contraction of the quads pushes the pedals down. Push them too hard, too often, and you get pain in the tendons and within the knee joint. Of course, fitness is relative; what's too hard for you in March may not be what's too hard for you in July. As you'll see below, knowing where you stand fitness-wise is a key to staying injury-free.

Causes and Solutions

Most of the time, tendonitis is caused by too-high training volume and intensity for underconditioned and understrengthened tendons. But other issues also play a role. To help avoid tendonitis, we've outlined its causes and effects in the table below.

TENDONITIS AVOIDANCE PLAN

Cause of the Problem	Solution
A. Lack of conditioning	Off-season weight training; SAID Principle (gradual buildup); Periodized training plan; 10 percent increase rule
B. Sudden, overly hard efforts	10-minute warm-up; spin in low gears
C. Underlubrication of the joint	Same as above
D. Cold weather	Knickers and tights; gradual warm-up
E. Tight hamstrings	Stretch before, during, and after rides; massage afterward
F. Too-low seat	Raise seat

A. CAUSE: Lack of conditioning

Tendons, like the muscles they are attached to, strengthen over time with training. And, like muscles, they become strained when a rider increases mileage drastically and/or uses too-high gears. But tendons tend to get strained more. That's because they don't have a good blood supply as muscles do, so they take longer to build up and repair.

SOLUTION 1: Weight-train in the off-season

Strengthen knees and the quadriceps muscle before serious training begins with leg presses, squats, bench step-ups, bicycle leg swings, knee extensions, hamstring curls, stair climbing, and very small amounts of cycling against high resistance. Weight-maintained tendons will not fatigue as quickly when riding begins. (See the "Lift Weights"section of chapter 1.)

SOLUTION 2: Use the SAID principle, maintain an off-season base, start gradually

For decades, athletic trainers have sworn by the SAID principle—Specific Adaptation to Impose Demand. "Tissue and ligaments actually get stronger with stressful activity," explains Jim Beazell.

"That response is there in your body. If you don't abuse it—meaning adding more stress gradually—you'll be okay."

Starting slowly strengthens most structures involved in cycling: muscles, tendons, and ligaments—everything except bones (see chapter 9). Once body structures are strengthened, they can handle high training loads.

"We didn't have many injuries at this level, because all the connective tissue had been strengthened," said former U.S. national team coach Dan Birkholz. "Once in a while, we'd get a little tendonitis when a guy hadn't been working out for a while, then would jump back in too quick."

Generally, cycling trainers promote a 10 percent rule: don't increase the duration or intensity of their training by more than 10 percent a week. Some trainers and physical therapists are even more conservative, recommending maximum weekly increases of only 5 percent. "That's why it's important to keep some sort of base in the off-season," said Jenny Stone, a former USCF athletic trainer. "You won't have so far to come back."

Ultimately, the most foolproof tendonitis-avoidance method may be to follow a "Periodized" training program, like that described in chapter 1. Periodization, honed by East Bloc strength coaches in the Cold War era and now a staple for all types of athletic training, carefully stairsteps athletes up to performance peaks through successive four-week training blocks. In a methodical sequence, it focuses on incrementally building strength, endurance, and speed, preparing the body to handle larger loads without injury.

Incidentally, the "gradual increase" rule also goes for terrain. Start off your training on flatter surfaces first. Don't do a 50-mile cross-country trip through the mountains right away. Don't pull an 80-pound trailer over steep hills for 125 miles if you've never ridden with one before.

B. CAUSE: Sudden hard efforts and impact

According to Pruitt, tendonitis can appear with sudden, high-stress actions, including hard sprinting, big-gear climbing, and off-bike activities like hard leg presses, squats, or jumping.

SOLUTION: 10-minute warm-up; low-gear spinning

Apply the "start slowly" rule to the beginning of every ride, not just the beginning of the season. A good analogy is starting a car. Any mechanic will tell you that you "shock" your engine and reduce its life by instantly zooming away when the ignition is turned; any motor will last longer if you let it warm up for 60 seconds in the driveway, allowing it to coat its pistons and other moving parts in a soothing oil bath before hitting the freeway. An easy five- to ten-minute warm-up in lower gears does the same thing for your body, calmly priming capillaries to open up and begin distributing blood throughout the muscle and the heart to increase its workload. The result: you don't go anaerobic, your knees smoothly transition into action, and tendons don't get stressed.

C. CAUSE: Underlubrication of the joint

Muscles and tendons aren't the only things that are ill-prepared for sudden increases in stress; you can also exceed your body's ability to lubricate the joint itself. To keep the bones sliding easily against each other without rubbing, the knees manufacture their own lubricant, called synovial fluid. Like any manufacturing plant, the synovial membranes scale down production during periods of inactivity. That's why, if you lay off all winter then go all-out on the first day of spring, your knee will be underlubed.

"If the biomechanics of the rider are okay, the problem is one of overstressing the structures in your joint," said Beazell. "It's like the bearing surfaces in an axle: if they're not greased or lubed, they'll break down. Same thing in a joint." Beyond the fact that the joint itself can suffer significant injury without lubrication, the tendon must work harder to overcome the added friction in the joint.

SOLUTION: Ride in low gears and spin

Rapidly pedaling in lower gears puts much less stress on the joints than slowly pushing large gears. Big-gear pushing exacerbates all other problems. Spinners generally don't get much patellofemoral pain.

D. CAUSE: Cold weather

Riding in the cold without adequate covering also restricts lubrication. Blood vessels constrict, shunting blood and oxygen away from surface areas—like the knees—to the vital organs. All knee structures, including the synovial membranes that lubricate the knee, will be undernourished. That's why the knees ache after a cold day.

SOLUTION: Cover up

Ride in knickers or full-length tights to keep the knees' joint lubrication mechanism warm enough to maintain flow to tendons and muscles. Doing so even makes riding in the dead of winter knee-safe. "There's no such thing as bad weather—only bad clothing," says fabled Minneapolis bike messenger Gene Oberpriller, who for years rode every winter day in temperatures as low as 40°F below

with a 70°F below windchill. Oberpriller is to cold-weather bike clothing what Imelda Marcos is to shoes. Of course, it takes him 20 minutes to put his clothes on. In the winter, he wears fleece-lined tights over his regular padded cycling shorts, making them easy to strip off when it warms up. And when the cold is combined with a stiff wind, Oberpriller slows down. "Windchill increases exponentially," he says. "Stay under 22 mph or in your middle chain-ring."

E. CAUSE: Tight hamstrings

The range of motion of the leg on the downstroke is limited when the hamstrings are tight, compressing the knee. The hamstrings, actually three separate muscles at the back of the leg that connect the pelvis to the back of the knee, serve to bend the knee—the opposite function of the quads. If the hamstring muscles are tight, the quads and tendons have to work harder to straighten the leg on the downstroke. (Note: Tight hamstrings also have highly negative effects on the back and all-over bike fit. See chapter 7 and the "Back" section later in this chapter.)

SOLUTION 1: Stretch hamstrings before, after, and during the ride

Stretching should be an integral part of cycling. Before a ride (cold stretching, contrary to some reports, is completely safe), it prepares your body by getting nutrient- and oxygen-packed blood flowing to all parts of the muscles and tendons. Spend additional time stretching in the morning, as muscles tighten during sleep. They are naturally more stretched-out in the afternoon or evening after daylong movement. Stretching after a workout helps restore ("warm down") the body to its normal state by reelongating exercise-tightened muscles and blood vessels. Stretching speeds the inflow of blood—and the outflow of exercise waste products like lactic acid.

What is the correct way to stretch the hamstring? According to physical therapist Bob Forster, whose Phase IV High Performance Center in Santa Monica, California, specializes in cycling, triathlon, and running training, all stretches are safest if performed on the ground. The hamstring is stretched by sitting with the left leg outstretched and the right bent so that the bottom of the foot is wedged against the upper inside of the left thigh. Slowly reach for your outstretched toes and lower your upper body by bending at the waist, keeping the back as straight as possible. Don't move fast; that will stimulate the muscle to tighten up. Also, don't hold the stretch for more than five seconds; that leads to permanent elongation, not the goal here. Do this stretch several times, then switch legs.

Note: Avoid the old-fashioned hurdler's stretch, in which the foot of the bent leg is placed straight back under the glutes. That puts too much pressure on that knee. (For a full ranges of stretches, please see chapter 5).

Ideally, cyclists should stretch not only before and after riding, but while they ride, as muscles and tendons tighten. But you don't need to get off the bike. If you just climbed a hill, for example, you can stretch in the downhill and the flats. Here's how: while coasting, stand and press the heel of the lower leg down, then arch your pelvis toward the handlebar.

SOLUTION 2: Massage

Often overlooked, sports massage, like stretching, helps you loosen and rearrange muscle sheathing and helps bring oxygenated blood back into your muscles.

F. CAUSE: Too-low seat

Riding too low or too far forward in relation to the pedals is how millions of recreational cyclists unwittingly stimulate overtraining. A low seating position causes the knee to flex more, generating more stress and rubbing of the quadriceps tendon against the thighbone. It forces the rider to push the pedal at a less efficient angle—and to work tendons and quads too hard.

SOLUTION: (Surprise!) Raise the seat

Sit high enough on the bike to give only a slight bend to the knee—about a 30° angle. This is the most efficient, least stressful position.

What to Do Once Tendonitis Strikes

1. *Back off:* No need to stop. But at the first sign of tendonitis (i.e., pain and swelling) you must shift into "active rest." Cut mileage by 50 percent, pedal easily, avoid hills, and eliminate all interval training. There's no need to stop altogether if you coordinate the "active rest" just described with icing, stretching, re-strengthening, and perhaps ultrasound and anti-inflammatory medications. In one study of cyclists with patellofemoral pain, 80 percent of symptoms were alleviated by use of those simple, traditional treatments.[1] Warning: Do not immediately return to the same training load as before; that will probably bring the pain right back again.

2. *Ice the area:* "Ice is the miracle treatment," says Forster. "It blocks pain and reduces many aspects of an injury, including spasms, inflammation, and swelling." How ice works may surprise you. While pain is a good thing—it is a protective mechanism that creates

increased muscle tension that limits movement—the swelling that comes with it can do more harm than good, especially for an athlete who needs to recover fast.

"Swelling occurs when the body dumps a large quantity of water in the area, which has the unfortunate effect of stopping blood flow," explains Forster. "So we have to out-think the body—and limit the inflammatory response by immediately applying ice to minimize the swelling. This causes an initial vasoconstriction, which pushes out fluids." When the ice is removed after 20 to 30 minutes, the veins open up, the flow is reversed, and the body sends blood, not water, flooding back to the area.

Andy Pruitt recommends that a two-step icing process be used three times per day until the tendon feels healed. He says to place crushed ice or small cubes in a Ziploc plastic bag and place it atop a washcloth laid across the affected tendon. The cloth protects the skin from damage. After 15 to 20 minutes, remove the ice pack for half an hour, then reapply. Rub raw ice on the affected area with a gentle massage motion, but you must stop after about five minutes, when the skin gets numb. Pruitt says you may speed the tendon's recovery by performing cross-friction massage (rubbing across the tendon fibers with your thumb for ten minutes) before reapplying the ice.

3. **Whirlpool treatments:** Whirlpools bring more blood to the injured tendon by vasodilating and massaging tissues, while microstimulation speeds the healing of injured tissue.

4. **Activity modification:** Avoid situations that put extreme stress on your tendons, such as squatting, lunging, leg press, stair climbing.

5. **Continue stretching:** It will not disrupt healing if limited only to the pain-free range of motion, says Forster.

6. **Take aspirin:** To relieve the inflammation, most RPT's recommend aspirin, taken at a rate of six or eight each day.

7. **Heat and cover:** Before riding, increase blood flow to the area by applying products like Ben-Gay or Icy Hot, says Pruitt. Then shield the injured tendon from cold wind with leg warmers or a coating of petroleum jelly.

Chondromalacia

Chondro-(cartilage) *mal-*(bad) *acia* (softening) is bad news. It refers to the shredding, softening, and wearing away of the cartilage on the underside of the patella between the kneecap and the thighbone. A burning sensation that occurs between the kneecap and the thighbone, chondro occurs less frequently than tendonitis, but is far more disabling. Tendonitis responds to rest, but the tissue damaged in chondromalacia doesn't quite return to normal—ever.

One look under a microscope explains why. "In a normal knee, the kneecap should slide on your thighbone as smoothly as two ice cubes against each other," said Beazell. "That's because the patella is surrounded by shiny, super-smooth hyaline cartilage, which is meant for gliding. But with chondromalacia, the cartilage gets frayed. In its bad stage it looks like kelp hanging off the back of the kneecap."

Chondromalacia is painful; extending or flexing your knee may include a grating or crunching sensation that can sound like the crackle of Rice Krispies and feel as painful as being raked by shards of broken glass. You especially hurt when pushing big gears or when climbing or descending stairs, and may feel aching and stiffness after sitting. If you feel any symptoms resembling the above, don't wait to have it checked out. Chondro is difficult to rehab and portends a future of arthritis.

Why Chondro Happens:
Lateral Tracking of the Kneecap

If "know thyself" is the key to self-enlightenment, "know thy anatomy" may be the key to understanding and preventing chondromalacia. The hyaline cartilage that Beazell just mentioned gets torn up when the kneecap doesn't track evenly where it should: in the groove at the end of the thighbone, which is formed by its two ball-shaped knobs (the same shape you see on a chicken drumstick bone). Although the front of the kneecap is flat, the back part—the part you don't see from the outside—is V-shaped, so it can slide smoothly in the thighbone's groove throughout all ranges of a kneebend.

Two groups of muscles are involved in moving the knee: the quadriceps, found on the front of the thigh, which straighten the leg and extend the knee as it flexes; and the hamstring, on the back of the thigh, which bends the knee back as it flexes. In bicycling, the quad pushes the pedal down while the hamstring pulls the pedal up.

The quadracep, or "four-head," is made of four separate muscles that all begin up at different points ("heads") on the hip and attach together at the bottom of the thighbone at the knee. When the four muscles contract, the patella is pulled up and the knee straightens out. If you hold your leg out straight and flex your thigh, you can see three of the quad muscles—the *vastus lateralis,* on the lateral (outside) of the leg, the *vastus medialis* on the medial ("middle" of body or inner) thigh, and the *rectus femoris* in the middle. You can't see the *vastus intermedialis,* which is underneath the other three, around the femur.

The problem, "lateral tracking," occurs when the kneecap comes out of the groove on the outside side of the leg. This has the same effect on your knee as a car tire that is out of alignment: it wears the cartilage out in one spot.

Out of its track, all the pressure of the cyclist's pedal stroke is focused on only one small part of the kneecap, instead of distributing it evenly and painlessly over the entire kneecap surface. The cartilage is scraped at that point and chondromalacia begins.

Runners, because of the weight-bearing pounding their knees take, have far more trouble with chondromalacia than cyclists (so much that it's commonly known as "runner's knee"). But what bicycling lacks in quality of stress, it often makes up for in quantity. "Cyclists spin at a fast rate," said Beazell. "80-rpm bicycling legs are extending and flexing twice as fast as a guy running a four-minute mile—and you can ride at 80 rpm for hours." As a result, biomechanically imbalanced cyclists can put a little bit of stress on a specific area of cartilage repeatedly for a long period of time—maybe 10,000 revolutions on an average three-hour, 40-mile ride. The problem may not surface at low riding levels. "A lot of people can get away with a little biomechanical inefficiency at lower workout levels," Beazell adds. "But when you increase in intensity, it really shows up."

Getting Your Knee Back in the Groove: A 4-Step Strategy for treating chondromalacia

Ask any physical therapist about "curing" chondromalacia, and you'll get a look of resignation and a variety of answers, none of them good. You can fix the problem, limit the damage, and even rebuild the knee a bit. But the truth is that once chondro strikes, the knee will never be as good as it used to be.

"That's because the hyaline cartilage [that was ruined] replaces itself with a lesser grade of cartilage," says Beazell. "It fills in with fibrocartilage, which isn't as good—and can be ruined even easier." Surgery is iffy; radical pain-reduction methods that attempt to smooth the frayed cartilage through arthroscopic "patella shaving" surgery or rapid-flexing, tissue-sanding Cybex isokinetic exercises are not well regarded or considered effective.

In spite of its poor prognosis, chondro doesn't have to be a lifelong curse that stops you from riding. *Bike for Life* has identified four steps that can help you stop it and mitigate its past damage.

1. ***Get a proper bike fit*** and compensate for physical abnormalities such as leg length differences.
2. ***Reposition the kneecap.*** Many believe that cycling has a tendency to overstrengthen the lateral side of the quadriceps muscle, pulling the kneecap to the outside; therefore, that part of the quad must be stretched while the opposing, or medial, side is strengthened. At last resort, "lateral release" surgery can loosen the lateral pull.
3. ***Butt-centric riding.*** There is strong evidence that proper riding technique and strengthening the butt muscles also play a surprisingly large role in rehabbing chondromalacia. A glute-centric riding style not only can cut knee injuries by reducing valgus (side-to-side knee movement) and internal pressure on the knee joint, but gives you more power and endurance.
4. ***Joint-building supplements.*** There is strong evidence that glucosamine and chondroitin can help rebuild the joint.

Following is a more detailed description of the steps you can take to help the kneecap get its groove back.

Step 1: Get a proper bike fit and gear down

Since chondromalacia is considered an overuse injury, the first stage of its rehab sounds a lot like the strategy for tendonitis: stop riding, correct your position, and resume riding at a radically reduced level. In the short run, rest will stop further damage and allow some healing. You can fix abnormal biomechanics through correct bike fit, paying particular attention to seat height, says Pruitt. (Too low, and it puts shearing force on the back of the kneecap; raise it to the point where you start rocking, then lower it just enough to stop the motion, he says.) Then avoid or gear down your training to the point where you can ride with no pain, and gradually ramp up. Because the kneecap cartilage is left permanently weaker after chondromalacia, the rider should be careful to spin in lower gears in all future riding. "It doesn't mean you'll have to hitchhike up hills or ride in a 42–19 (an easy gear ratio) for the rest of your life," said Beazell. "Just be smart in your training—and keep aware of the SAID principle."

Step 2: Reposition the kneecap

If the above doesn't work—indicating that you have biomechanical problems that have led to severe lateral tracking of the patella—quickly take deliberate steps to reposition the kneecap by addressing biomechanical abnormalities, strengthening one side of the leg and stretching the other, and, as a last resort, undergoing minor surgery.

Address biomechanical abnormalities:

There are micro-stresses between the kneecap and the thighbone in nearly everyone. But the more imbalanced a person's biomechanics, the shorter the time period before cartilage irritation arises. A good bike fit will take care of bicycle and equipment settings (saddle height, cleat position, cleat type, and shoe type) and abnormal forefoot and rear-foot alignment. But what about something natural, like leg-length discrepancies, excessive feet pronation (duck feet) or supination (pigeon-toes), flat feet, bow legs, and knock-knee?

"Any of those may cause problems, but over a quarter-inch difference is a red flag," says Santa Monica, California, bike fit expert Victor Larivee. "A cyclist puts stress on his joints when he doesn't ride in his 'neutral position,' or natural gait, and leg-length differences beyond one-quarter inch are not considered neutral. The short leg must be raised to match the other, either through shims under the cleat, a lift on the pedal, or platform shoes."

Strengthen the inside thigh muscle (VMO) and stretch the outside leg muscle (VL) and the illio-tibial (IT) band:

Some researchers believe that the motion of cycling—a straight-ahead leg movement rather than the centered, in-line footprint of running and walking—has a natural tendency to cause an imbalance in the thigh muscles, which can cause lateral tracking of the kneecap. This imbalance is the overdevelopment of the muscle on the outside of the thigh compared to the one on the inside. Bike racers are famous for having huge quadriceps, the group of four muscles on the front of the thigh that extend the leg, but cycling apparently causes the one on the outside, the *vastus lateralis* (VL), to become much bigger and stronger than the one on the inner, or medial, front of the thigh, the *vastus medialis* (VMO; technically the muscle is called the *vastus medialis oblique*).

According to a study completed for the book *Physiology in Bicycling*, a seminal overview coproduced by a prestigious Danish sports-research institute and the U.S. Cycling Federation, the VL and the gluteus maximus (the large buttock muscle) are heavily involved in pushing the pedals down at peak force, but the VMO is not. That is understandable: Put your fingers on the VMO as you sit on a chair and straighten your leg; it does not flex (stiffen) almost until the leg straightens, which *should never occur* in the pedal stroke. Although the study was of track racers, the researchers found a similar recruitment pattern in recreational riders.

Why is this a potential problem? The overdeveloped VL, now relatively stronger than the VMO, can exert a strong pull on the kneecap that can tug at it laterally. You know the rest: when the difference between the strengths of the VL and VMO is great, the kneecap can be yanked sideways, lateral tracking begins, and the underside of the kneecap begins scraping valuable cartilage away from itself and the end of the femur.

Does this mean that a lateral tracking of the patella is unavoidable in cycling? Not necessarily. "After all," said Beazell, "If the lateralis always got stronger than the medialis, then why is it that every Tour de France rider doesn't have a patella lateral tracking problem?" Why some biomechanically sound cyclists get lateral tracking of the kneecap and others don't isn't clear. Natural overdevelopment of the VL in cycling is a fact; concluding that this causes knee pain isn't.

Still, if you have problems, many agree that it couldn't hurt to do two things to stabilize the kneecap: strengthen the inside muscle of your quad, the VMO, to pull the kneecap back in line, and stretch the outside of your leg, which can help loosen its outside pull on the kneecap.

A. *Build up the VMO (vastus medialis, the inner-thigh quad muscle)*

   Get familiar with the leg extension machine, because you'll be using it a lot to prehab and rehab lateral tracking problems. During the exercise, keep your toes pointed out to the sides as if you have duck feet, then complete the exercise to full extension. Bring the bar straight up with your leg at full extension. While this exercise works the entire quad, it specifically targets the VMO. Like the pedal stroke itself, standard leg extensions don't fully extend the leg, somewhat ignoring the VMO. Lift heavy weights with low reps to build strength and size.

B. *Loosen up the lateral pull on your kneecap by stretching the VL and IT Band*

   VL Stretches

   ◗ **Standing quad stretch:** Stand on one leg, grab the opposite foot or ankle from behind, and pull it up toward the butt. Put your knees together and push your hips forward. Hold on to something until you can balance free-standing.

   ◗ **Prone quad stretch:** Lying on the ground facedown, pull one foot up behind your butt, and slowly raise your leg off the ground.

   ◗ **Kneeling quad stretch:** Kneel on one foot and the other knee, keeping the knee far in back of you. Calf should rest flat on the ground. Push your hips forward.

   ◗ **Side quad stretch:** Like a standing stretch turned horizontal, in this stretch you lie on your side with the bottom arm outstretched past your head, with knees together. Then pull your top leg behind your butt, and push your hips forward.

   ◗ **Tensor fascia lata stretch:** Lie on your back with knees bent and arms out wide. Cross your legs and use the top leg to push the bottom leg over to the side. Take your legs over until your opposite shoulder starts to come off the floor; you should feel the stretch on the outer thigh/hip area.

   IT Band Stretches

   Some think that a tight illio-tibial band is more responsible for lateral tracking of the kneecap than an overdeveloped VL. (I found that IT band stretches provided immediate relief for my lateral tracking problems—RMW.) The IT band is a wide sheath of tough, fibrous connective tissue extending on the outer side of the thigh from the front of the pelvis's iliac bone (the crest of the hip) to the top of the lower leg's tibia bone, just below the knee. Flexible only at the hip, it feels like the thick, old-fashioned leather belt barbers sharpen their blades on.

- **Crossover bend:** Stand erect, move the left foot to the right of the right foot, thrust the left hip out sideways and tilt your upper body to the right. If you can't balance, extend your left arm against a wall or chair or other stable object. You'll feel the IT band stretch from the hip all the way down the length of the thigh to the knee.
- **The lazy leg stretch:** Lie on your right side at the very edge of your mattress so that your butt is almost falling off the edge (as you are facing the middle of the bed). Let your top leg (left) fall behind you and over the edge of the bed. Let the weight of your leg stretch your hip. Repeat on the other side.
- **Hanging crossover:** Lie on the floor on your back with your body in a T shape, with arms spread wide and legs straight forward. Then lift your left leg up one foot and move it sideways over the right leg, until it is suspended at a right angle. All the time, keep your arms outstretched and back as flat on the ground as possible. Let gravity pull it down toward the ground; hold for a minute. Repeat on the other side.
- **Roller massage:** Lying sideways on the floor, roll back and forth over a 6-inch diameter Therapy Foam Roller ($20 at fitness stores) from hip to knee. "It'll hurt at first," says Bruce Hendler, owner of the Ath-

letiCamps cycling school in Davis, California. "But there is no better way to loosen up the IT band—especially as it gets more rigid down toward the knee. It's a cheap private massage." Hendler believes the majority of knee problems, from tendonitis to lateral tracking, are related to tight IT bands.

Stretch Tight Adductors

A *Bike for Life* test in June 2004 directed by Christopher M. Powers, PT, PhD, director of the Musculoskeletal Biomechanics Research Laboratory at the University of Southern California Medical Center in Los Angeles, led him to speculate that tight adductors (the upper inner thigh muscles) and/or weak external rotators may help lead to knee cartilage damage. Stretching the adductors and strengthening the rotators may help prevent the kneecap from rotating (and therefore coming out of track) during the leg extension portion of non–weight-bearing activities such as cycling.

Adductor Stretches

- Sit up with the soles of your feet together. Using your hands, push your knees gently apart to the floor, stretching the groin area.
- Sit up with legs straight out and as wide as you can get them, stretching the groin. Support your body with hands behind you.

Step 3: Butt Power

Utilizing your glutes during pedaling—often not even done by the best riders—is not only a superb way to generate power, but the safest, too. Glute-centric riding eliminates valgus (inward knee bend) and excessive side-to-side swinging of the knee during the downstroke. And gives you more power and endurance.

Many racers almost seem to touch the top tube with their knees as they ride, pushing inward to get leverage as they set up their downstroke. Some believe that riding with the knees angled inward is aerodynamic. Pictures of the pros in such a position inspire amateurs to ride the same way, effecting a figure-eight motion from the hip down when viewed from the front. But pedaling this way is not a good idea. It is inefficient and can lead to injuries.

"Valgus—an inward bend of the knee, increases lateral force on the kneecap and is known to lead to knee injuries," says USC's Chris Powers. "The knee should stay in the same plane during the pedal stroke, like a piston in an engine."

In fact, the proof that valgus leads to injuries is well documented. One study found "excessive side-to-side swinging of the knee during downstroke in more than 80 percent of cyclists with patellofemoral pain."[2] The late Ed Burke, PhD, a prodigious ultra-cycling participant and University of Colorado researcher who wrote extensively on cycling biomechanics, found that of "cyclists with no patellofemoral pain, most had a linear pattern of downstroke, with little mediolateral deviation."

Another nail in the "valgus-is-bad" coffin is the common knowledge that females' natural valgus makes them more predisposed to lateral tracking problems and chondromalacia than men. Wide hips cause the thighs to bend in, the knees to

come together, and the lower leg to bow out, creating a lateral pull on the patella.

A cure for valgus in male riders and narrow-hipped women is both simple and complex: use butt power—a full utilization of your gluteal muscles while riding. An accurate fitting that aligns hips, knees, and ankles theoretically eliminates valgus and puts the rider in an efficient position that yields more power. Specifically, this correct position—a hip flexor angle under 45°—forces you to make more use of the huge, powerful gluteus maximus muscles, which are routinely underutilized in cycling.

"After a fit, so many people call me and say, 'Wow, I can feel my glutes working—I've never climbed a hill so fast,'" says Pam Wilson, a biomechanist who provides the EMG studies used by Paul Levine of Signature Cycles (featured in chapter 7). "When you aren't fit correctly, the glutes are turned off and you focus too much on your quads."

Everyone, regardless of injury, should use a glute-centric pedaling technique; it yields reduced valgus, more efficiency, and less potential for injuries. But achieving that ideal form requires more than a perfect bike fit; it requires a change of mindset, of changing your thinking from quad-centric to glute-centric.

The importance of the oft-ignored butt to pedaling power led *Bike for Life* to conduct original research with Dr. Powers, the USC biomechanics lab director. Time-in-motion biomechanical mapping we conducted at his Los Angeles lab in June 2004 found clearly that seated pedaling, focusing through the butt muscles, not the quads, reduced valgus and side-to-side rocking, and kept the back flat instead of bowed (therefore reducing the risk of back pain).

Our own anecdotal road tests and Comp-uScan lab tests measuring watts and heart rate showed that glute-centric riding had near-identical wattage and heart rate levels to quad-centric riding, but with less perceived exertion. As the gluteal muscles become conditioned to the new motion, we found that our endurance increased. In other words, if you completely rethink your riding technique, focusing on initiating the pedal stroke with the butt muscles, you can ride stronger longer, because you spread the workload over more muscles. Reeducating yourself may be the most difficult aspect of butt-centric riding. But it is too beneficial to ignore, especially if you want to be riding a bike at 90.

Step 4: Joint-Building Supplements– Glucosamine and Chondroitin

"People over 35 should baste themselves in the stuff," said Andy Pruitt in the November 2003 issue of *Bicycling* magazine, another believer in the power of glucosamine and chondroitin, three-decade-old supplements viewed by some as miracle joint-builders and arthritis fighters. Are G & C the real deal? Although not backed yet by long-term studies, the supplements have delivered significant pain relief in numerous short studies. We at *Bike for Life* first heard about the pair in 1999, when many riders trying to qualify for that summer's Paris-Brest-Paris endurance ride were swearing by it, claiming it relieved aching in their knee joints brought on by the challenging 200k, 300k, 400k, and 600k brevets.

Cartilage, like bone, is living tissue— always wearing out and reforming. Glucosamine and chondroitin are thought to speed the formation of new cartilage "building blocks." Glucosamine is a precursor to a molecule called a glycosaminoglycan, which is used in the formation and repair of cartilage. Chondroitin is the most abundant glycosaminoglycan in cartilage and is responsible for the resiliency of cartilage. The effects appear to be dramatic. Studies found that arthritis patients experienced more pain reduction when taking G & C for one to two months than those receiving a placebo.[3] Moreover, the improvement was similar to that of the leading arthritis treatment, nonsteroidal anti-inflammatory medications (NSAIDs), while providing better long-term protection of the cartilage surface without its increased risk of side effects, such as gastrointestinal complaints and bleeding. Also, short-term studies have shown chondroitin and glucosamine alone to be effective.

If taking G & C are so good, why isn't everyone doing it, you ask? Well, the lack of a long-term study has delayed its acceptance as a primary treatment plan for osteoarthritis, and the lack of regulation of the supplement industry has others worried about quality. Still, glucosamine and chondroitin look promising at this point, and should be considered mainstays in the medicine cabinet of any serious cyclist with some knee pain.

Step 5: Go Under the Knife

Surgery is a last-ditch option if the four steps above fail to get the kneecap tracking correctly, but it's far from a sure thing. Surgical procedures for lateral tracking include the following:

▶ *Lateral retinacular release:* This arthroscopy involves cutting all the lateral structures from the patellar tendon to within the muscle fibers of the vastus lateralis. Results: Fairly good if done in conjunction with a post-operative rehabilitation program.[4]

▶ *Dynamic realignment:* Counteracts the lateral pull by strengthening the medial pull of the VMO through transfers of muscles or tendons. Results: Iffy, and rehab is quite slow.[5]

▶ *Washing out the knee* (arthroscopic lavage): This simple procedure can have a profoundly positive effect on knee pain. Potentially, it can remove small particles of cartilage that produce synovitis.

How to De-slump Your Posture
Ten exercises to straighten out your crooked body and end back pain.

IF you've got a bad back and you don't have a major weight problem, chances are that poor posture is the cause. "The slumping and hunching that first becomes noticeable in your 30s causes poor athletic performance, restricts your breathing and digestion, and is the basis of most injuries and joint diseases like arthritis," says Patrick Mummy, president of Symmetry, a unique pain relief clinic based in San Diego. "And cycling makes it worse; it reinforces a bad habit." Fortunately, like misaligned wheels on a car, bad posture is fixable. Symmetry, a leader in the relatively new field of postural therapy, prescribes custom stretching and strengthening exercises that are designed to get your posture back to where it was when you and your back were bomb-proof: age five.

"Chest out and proud. Butt high and back. Shoulders square. Body balanced front-to-back, side-to-side. This is perfect, symmetrical posture—and it starts to degrade the day you go to kindergarten and begin sitting at a desk all day," says Mummy.

Crouched forward to write and type, sitting hunches the shoulders forward. It angles the pelvis up, changing its natural 10° forward tilt to something closer to zero, or level. The result: hip flexors shorten, the back is pulled into flexion, and the lower back muscles are overworked and strained. Eventually, most sedentary adults develop what Mummy calls the "Suck 'n Tuck": butt drawn in, belly pushed up, shoulders stooped forward, diaphragm collapsed, and lower back flattened—a backache-ridden, constricted position that squeezes lungs and intestines.

Over the years, good posture is further corrupted by leg-length discrepancies, accumulated injuries, right- or left-hand dominance, and repetitive motion activities like hitting a tennis ball (which can cause a side-to-side torso tilt that puts one shoulder higher than the other). "Then add sports activities that train you to be imbalanced," says Mummy. "A common one is overemphasis on chest presses over pulls in the weight room. Another big one is cycling."

"Over time, your body mimics the activity," he says. "Whereas basketball or soccer uses your body functionally in its natural state, with your pelvis as the center of gravity, cycling removes the pelvis from the equation. Leaning forward to the handlebars, your back is now the center of gravity, the tie-in between the upper and lower body. Cycling trains you to take the shape of a C; so off the bike, your back struggles to keep you upright."

According to Symmetry, undoing the damage isn't as simple as going to a chiropractor for an "adjustment" that temporarily pushes a vertebrae this way or that; for cyclists, it requires a complete overhaul of your body's misaligned and out-of-balance muscles and daily exercises before, during, and after you ride.

The process at Symmetry (undergone by Roy Wallack) begins with two full-length photographs of your body—straight-ahead and profile. After noting your points of deviation from the ideal form of a five-year-old (shoulders and hips should not be tilted, and head, shoulder, hips, knees, and ankles should be in a vertical line), Mummy prescribes a series of stretching and strengthening exercises that will restore the balance. The exercises are not easy and don't involve lifting weights (Mummy is against pumping iron until you've straightened your posture; to do otherwise is akin to "building a Ferrari on a bent chassis," he says.) Some people see immediate improvement; others take months. Asked to provide exercises for this book, Mummy initially hesitated; he designs exercise regimens specific to individuals. But eventually he did agree that a series of general exercises, described below, can help anyone at risk for a bad back, including all cyclists.

"Hypothetically, do them before, during, and after you ride" he says, "But especially before. You brush your teeth at the beginning of the day. You need to start any activity in a balanced body position."

Symmetry Posture Fixers

While Symmetry designs custom posture-rehab programs, Mummy believes a generic anti–suck 'n tuck strategy would go a long way toward eliminating biker's back. The strategy will stretch the hip flexors to restore the correct pelvic tilt, reposition the shoulders back, and equalize the hips to restore bilateral symmetry. At one to two minutes each, the 12 exercises below should take ten to fifteen minutes. Perform them at home or in the gym in the order given and as often as possible, especially before any weight or aerobic exercise.

1. **Static Floor**

    Purpose: Relaxes and evens spine and spiny erector muscles to prepare for exercise.

    How to: Lie on back, calves flat on seat of a chair, with thighs bent, legs 90°, arms out to side, palms up. Sink into floor and breathe through diaphragm. Tighten abs for one second at end of exhalation.

2. **Crossover (piriformis stretch)**

    Purpose: Removes pelvis elevations, untwists the hips (evens right-left bias), and indirectly repositions shoulders.

    How to: Lie on back with arms out at 90° angles, knees bent, and left foot on the floor. Cross right ankle to left knee and rotate right foot and left knee to floor as one unit until right foot is flat on floor. Look in opposite direction and press right knee slightly away, feeling stretch on outside of right hip. Hold one minute. Repeat in opposite direction.

3. **Cats and Dogs**

    Purpose: Old yoga pose restores natural tilt to pelvis by aligning it with the spine.

How to: Starting in bent-knee push-up position, pull chin to chest while pushing low back to ceiling, then look up to ceiling and allow back to sway and shoulder blades to pull back and together. Keep a constant, smooth motion, not allowing your body to move forward or backward. Repeat 10 times.

4. Extended Floor Position

Purpose: Dramatically tilts the pelvis forward and pulls the shoulders back by putting the spine in "traction."

How to: From Cats and Dogs position, walk hands forward 4–6 inches and place elbows where your hands were, positioning hips in front of knees. Let back sway, shoulder blades collapse together, and head drop. Hold this position one to two minutes.

5. Arm Circles

Purpose: Strengthen shoulder girdle and reposition shoulder blade back.

How to: While kneeling on floor, raise arms straight from side as you squeeze shoulder blades together. With palms facing down, rotate arms in 6-inch circles; then switch to palms facing up.

6. Shoulder Rotations

Purpose: Stretches and repositions shoulders.

How to: Sit in a chair with knees bent at 90° angle and hips rolled forward to create an arch in the lower back. Place knuckles on your temples, pivot arms inward until elbows touch, then raise arms up if you can.

7. Overhead Extension

Purpose: Reposition shoulders.

How to: Standing with fingers interlaced, push palms up and away from body toward the sky until straight. Pinch shoulder blades together, look straight up, feel arch in lower back, and hold.

8. Sitting Torso Twist

Purpose: Transverse stretching of the back.

How to: Sit on floor with legs straight, put hands behind back. Bend left foot on outside of right knee. Place right elbow on left knee. Sit up as tall as possible by arching low back. Pull left shoulder back and twist torso, looking back over left shoulder.

9. Triangle Position

Purpose: Lengthen and unkink torso.

How to: Standing against a wall, with the right foot perpendicular to it, rotate the left foot so that it is perpendicular to the right and 3 inches away from the wall. Take a large step sideways out with the left, keeping it 3 inches from the wall. Holding arms horizontal at sides, tighten quads, and keep both glutes and shoulders on the wall as you rotate and lower the upper body from the waist toward the left foot. Slide down until right glute starts to come off the wall, hold position and stretch right arm directly vertical.

10. Wall Sit

Purpose: This is the glue that holds all the previous exercises together, lowering your center of gravity back to your pelvis and changing your posture from a bow to a straight line. It lowers center of gravity by strengthening pelvic muscles and quads that have become so weak that they can no longer hold your spine and legs together as one unit.

How to: With lower back pressed firmly against a wall, slowly walk your feet away and slide down until the knees are bent at a 90° angle. Keep weight on heels. Increase the length of time you hold the stretch to 60 seconds. Repeat five times and do two or three sets.

While stopped mid-ride at a 7-Eleven . . .

In the middle of the ride, while everyone else is sitting on the curb guzzling a Big Gulp, spend four minutes fixing your posture. Do three of the exercises described above: Sitting Torso Twist (1 minute); Triangle Position (1 minute); and Wall Sit (1 to 2 minutes). This loosens your transverse (twisting) plane, your frontal (side-to-side) plane, and reemphasizes the sagital (straight-ahead) plane in a positive way.

• 2 •
Biker's Back

Cycling News item, July 8, 2004: "McGee Packs It In" "Bradley McGee of www .Fdjeux.com abandoned during today's stage of the Tour de France. The Australian rider had been having a very good year, and was a favorite to take the prologue, but he's been suffering from back problems since the Tour started, problems he blamed on planting some olive trees at his new home."

•

Since bikes were invented in the late 1800s, the number-one complaint from the people who rode them was knee pain. "But there's been a paradigm shift in the last decade or so," says Andy Pruitt of the Boulder Center for Sports Medicine. "With the aging of the cycling population, back pain is now rivaling knee pain."

At a meeting with a bike manufacturer in 2002, Pruitt brought in a chart showing that the growth curves of two cycling trends now meet—baby boomers and high-

performance. His point: forever-young boomers are still pushing the big ring, but they're also pushing 50. And that means that they are subject to some of the same middle-age medical conditions that dog their non-cycling peers. Topping the charts: back pain.

The fact that back pain is now number one is no surprise considering that it's America's equal-opportunity affliction, similarly affecting blue- and white-collar workers, athlete and couch potato, Colnago connoisseur and Huffy puffer. Endemic in our sedentary society, back pain leads three-quarters of the population to seek medical attention at least once in their lives and up to 10 million people to miss work every day. Back pain is undoubtedly exacerbated by cycling, which keeps your body seated and back bent over, humped, stretched out, virtually frozen in place, and, in the words of John Howard, "stuck in a strange semi-fetal crouch found nowhere else in the athletic world."

The result: the key support beam at the bedrock of your body's stability is weak, tight, and ready to blow. When it does, you have been officially introduced to the condition known as "biker's back": pain in the muscles along the spine, pain in the area just above the pelvis, and pain between the shoulder blades.

Howard reports that more than half of the students at his cycling school complain about biker's back. He personally understands the pain; he's had it ever since he began riding in an aerobar tuck in the late 1980s.

The seeds of biker's back, however, were sewn not the day you bolted an aerobar to your new high-performance carbon-fiber dream machine, but about the time that Dad bought you your first $39 two-wheeler from the local hardware store. Yet the bike itself wasn't the problem; going to kindergarten and sitting all day was.

"Your postural decline starts at age five, when you stop running around all day and begin slumping, hunched over a desk," says Patrick Mummy, whose Symmetry Pain Relief Clinic in San Diego has developed a reputation for curing near-hopeless back pain cases. A lifetime of sitting—while doing homework, driving, cycling, surfing the net—stoops shoulders, shortens hip flexors, draws the butt in, and flattens the lower back. The result, says Mummy: a constricted position that squeezes lungs and intestines and both weakens the lower back and makes it work harder. By age 35 or 40, this weakened posture may lead to the dull agony or debilitating flare-ups of biker's back.

Back pain is no mystery if you understand the lower back's anatomy: five lumbar vertebrae bones separated by discs of hard cartilage, each with a soft, watery center called a *nucleus pulposus*. The spinal cord ends in this region, and exiting between the bones and the discs are a series of nerve roots that can become compressed and inflamed through degenerative changes in the structures. When the body is bent forward and the spine rounded (the opposite of its normal concave profile), the back wall of each disc stretches and its front wall contracts. This pushes the soft *nucleus pulposus* toward the back wall of the disc, where sudden twisting and turning motions over time can tear, rupture, or "herniate" it. When that happens, the *nucleus pulposus* can rupture through these tears, irritating or pinching the nerve roots when they emerge between the vertebrae, thus causing low back or leg pain.

Bikers shouldn't ignore biker's back. It's a fact: a nonrecumbent racing bike forces riders into a bent back position that can harm discs, already at risk by years of sitting. Failure to adopt lifestyle changes, alter your bike position, and follow a regimen of specific strengthening/stretching exercises can end one's cycling career and lead to irreparable damage to the lower back.

The incidence of biker's back is even driving product changes in the bike industry. For years, custom builders like Serotta have been swamped with orders for bikes with taller headtubes and higher handlebars, which allow aging enthusiasts to ride with a more erect torso. Specialized got wind of the trend and in the fall of 2003 introduced the Roubaix, a high-end production road bike that, like the pricier Serottas, featured a taller headtube. Adding to the comfort, the Roubaix includes "Zertz" elastomer shock absorbers in the frame, seatpost, and fork.

Of course, riding more erect on a new bike that'll cost you thousands is not the only way to fight biker's back. At most, new hardware is the first step of an evolving plan that includes strengthening your back and core muscles and making other surrounding muscles more limber; eventually, that will allow you to resume or maintain a high-performance riding position without back strain. Here are the details of the *Bike for Life* "Banish Biker's Back" plan.

13 WAYS TO BANISH BIKER'S BACK

1. *Raise the front end*

Beware the low handlebars of triathletes and time trialists. Beware the curved round hump in your back. From a performance standpoint, it does not provide a good core stabilizing anchor. And from a biker's back standpoint, the hump is terrible for the spine. It causes spinal creep or hysteresis, a permanent lengthening of the posterior spinal ligament, hastening a breakdown of the integrity of the bonds that hold the vertebrae together. It is not surprising that there is a much higher incidence of herniated discs among time trialists and triathletes than for normal cyclists.

The quickest and least expensive way to get immediate relief from biker's back is to simply raise the handlebars of your existing bike, either by rotating the bar upward, raising the stem, or buying a taller stem. An adjustable stem may be ideal, allowing you to exactly dial in the most comfortable height as you develop improved ranges of strength and flexibility over time. The added height, which you can also achieve by buying a bike with a shorter top tube and/or taller stem, will minimize the unhealthy convex curve of your back and the pressure it puts on your discs.

On the other hand, be aware that an upright position can compromise your power. As discussed in chapter 7, the Serotta Fit School believes that an angle greater than 45° between back and seated hips will not activate the glute, which will cost you power and increase knee strain. That's why an adjustable stem is a good hardware choice; you can lower the handlebar height as you use some of the following tips to become more limber.

2. *Straighten our your body first*

"What good is it," asks Patrick Mummy, "to stretch and build big, beautiful muscles on top of a bent frame?" His Symmetry Pain Control clinic uses a number of unique exercises to straighten out your body. (For a detailed all-body Symmetry posture plan, check "How to De-slump Your Posture" in this chapter.)

3. *Address leg-length differences*

Pruitt reports that laboratory studies have shown that leg-length inequality is the most common cause of back pain in cyclists. For those with a difference of 5 mm or less, Pruitt moves the cleat on the short-leg side forward by 1 to 2 mm. If the difference is 6 mm or more, he recommends that you have a shoe-repair shop place a shim between the shoe sole and the cleat.

4. *Stretch hamstrings, hip flexors, and glutes*

When the three aforementioned muscle groups tighten with age, they cause a number of secondary problems: the quadriceps are forced to push harder to extend the leg, tiring them and stressing the knee joint, and the difficulty in bending at the waist puts pressure on the back to bow. A humped back is bad; it can squeeze the discs.

Fortunately, tightness is one aspect of aging that is easily reversed. Do not start a ride without stretching; even cold-stretching is safe, according to physical therapist Bob Forster. Occasionally stand up to stretch while on the bike, and especially stretch after the ride, when the muscle is warm and the sheath that surrounds it is malleable.

Hamstrings stretch: Lie on your back with your knees bent. Grab one foot with your hands and pull the leg straight up. Then straighten the knee as much as you can, stretching the hamstring.

Hip flexor stretch: Kneel with one foot forward, keeping the front knee at a right angle and the other leg behind your hips. Keep your upper body upright. Tilt your pelvis back, tucking in your stomach and squeezing your gluteals. You should feel the stretch strongly in your hip flexor.

Note: Never do a standing toe touch. Stretching the back by bending over and touching your fingers to the ground causes a stretching of the back ligaments, which can cause injuries. Whenever you stretch your hamstrings and calves, lie on the ground to avoid adding tension, keep your head up, and focus on bending at the waist and keeping the back flat. See the Symmetry stretches in the sidebar below for safe back-muscle stretches.

5. Strengthen core muscles

Blame a lifetime of sitting for tightening the lower back's spiny erector muscles and weakening the transverse abdominus, the deep abdominal muscles that draw the belly button to the spine. Strengthening and stretching these both can improve posture and reduce back pain.

Back extensions: The erector *spinae* lines on each side of the spinal column become weak and tight through lack of use, especially if your only athletic activity is cycling. They strengthen quickly with back extensions, which can be performed at home by lying belly-down, clasping your hands behind your neck, and simply raising your head and upper back off the floor. At the gym, find a padded bench that gives you enough clearance and has a way to anchor the feet, then clasp hands behind the neck and bend at the waist up and down in a smooth, controlled motion. Over time, hold small weight plates (e.g., 2½, 5, or 10 pounds) behind the neck for added resistance, but be careful not to go overboard.

Transverse abdominus (TA): To work these stomach muscles, used in twisting motions, stand with knees bent and light dumbbells at chest level, and twist side-to-side as you raise and drop your arms while drawing a sideways figure eight.

Cross-crunches: Fold left leg over right knee and do a crossover sit-up, touching elbows to knees to hit TA, intercostals, and obliques.

Dying bug: Lying faceup on the floor with arms at side, press the small of your back to the mat, tighten your core by making a "pssst" sound. Then raise and lower opposite legs and arms at once without moving the spine.

6. ***Activate and strengthen the glutes***

Those glutes again. You already know from the "Cyclist's Knee" section above and the preceding "Bike Fit" chapter that the underestimated, underutilized butt muscles become major contributors to cycling power when you have a proper fit. But you may not realize that this power derives from the key role the gluteal muscles (gluteus maximus, medius, and minimus) play in maintaining an upright posture and extending the trunk, all of which serves to prevent back pain. As *Bike for Life*'s biomechanical analysis with USC's Powers showed, initiating the pedal's power stroke with the glute not only lessens valgus (the inward drift of the knee while pedaling) and enhances core stability (minimizes side-to-side rocking), but it effectively straightens the back. Glute-focused pedaling clearly lessens the hump that characterizes quadriceps-focused pedaling. For that reason, insufficient recruitment and strength of the gluteus maximus may increase the risk of back injury.

Two exercises to improve the gluteus maximus's ability to support the extension of the spine are the "bridge" and the "wood chop":

The bridge: Lying on your back with knees bent, draw in the lower abdominals and curl the butt off the floor, lifting the hips until the knees, hips, and chest are in line. Hold this position for ten seconds, squeezing the glutes to support the bridge position, holding the pelvis level, and keeping the lower abs drawn in. Do 10 reps, build up to 2 reps of 60 seconds, then try a one-legged bridge, lifting one knee up in the air.

The wood chop: This is a dynamic exercise where the gluteals must work to extend the trunk from a flexed position. Standing with feet at shoulder width with knees slightly bent, hold a weight in two hands above your head (10 to 15 pounds for men, 5 to 10 pounds for women) and act as if you are wielding an ax to chop wood. Bend from the waist and bring the weight down between your legs, not bending the knees any further as you bend forward. At the bottom, draw in your abdominals and squeeze your glutes for support before returning upright to the start position. Straighten up in the correct sequence: extending your lower back first, then bringing your shoulders up, and finally lifting the weight above your head. Begin with 2 to 3 sets of 10 reps, building up to 20 reps.

Hip flexor stretch: Because inflexible hip flexors can cause an excessive pelvic tilt, which inhibits the gluteus maximus, they must be stretched (see 4, above).

Additional Back-Saving Tips:

7. **Change position**

    Move around on the bike to take pressure off your back. On long rides, change hand positions and stand up for one minute of every five. Stretch out, scooch here and there. Standard road bikes allow many different positions—drops, hoods, top of the bar. For the same reason, bar-ends on mountain bikes are a good thing. On long climbs, slide around from the front, to the middle, to the back of the saddle.

8. **Go swimming**

    In several ways, swimming is a near-perfect cross-training counterpart to cycling, because it fills in the latter's deficiencies. Where cycling bends you over and generally leaves you stiff, swimming stretches you out and makes you flexible. Where cycling is all legs and linear, a swimmer's upper body delivers 70 percent of his or her power, and the pronounced hip-twist on every stroke works the core ab, transverse abs, and back muscles ignored on a bike. Swimming travels well, unlike bikes; packing a pair of goggles helps a bikeless cyclist maintain cardiovascular conditioning on the road. Of course, you may want to pack a pair of running shoes, too. In the first sentence, we put the "near" in "near-perfect" because swimming, like cycling, lacks the weight-bearing and impact that helps build bone. You'll need running and weight lifting for that.

9. **Do push-ups**

    A good set of push-ups a couple of times a day can help save your back, according to Julie Bookspan, MD, a Philadelphia orthopedist who has helped the U.S. military develop back-friendly exercise programs. The key is keeping a straight back. Perfect form in a push-up is the same as perfect upright posture. Bad form—too much arch—can resemble bad posture. Good push-ups train you to hold good posture in life, cutting the risk of back pain.

    Incidentally, push-ups are better for your back than bench presses, according to Michael Clark, CSCS, PT, and president of the National Academy of Sports Medicine, because they build your entire muscular support system. In particular, push-ups develop scapular and rotator cuff muscles that stabilize your shoulders far more than presses do.

    Finally, mix push-ups in with your bike rides. We've used them as pre-ride warm-ups on cold mornings, to revive from a long 7-Eleven Gatorade break, and to shake off a chill while waiting for slower partners at the top of long hill climbs.

10. **Protect your back all day**

    Incorporate back-friendly behavior into your normal life. For instance, don't bend over to lift something up; squat and use your legs. Drive a lot? Strengthen your core muscles while seated in your car with this "red light" ab workout, invented by Carol Ross, a Venice, California, chiropractor: When you come to a red light, hold your abs to a count of three. Do it at every red traffic or taillight, and soon you will be giving your body a subconcious cue: when it sees red, your stomach contracts. "One of my clients told me that he contracts when he sees his boss's red tie," says Ross. "He also said that one girl in red thought he was making a pass at her."

Jim Beazell takes Ross's tummy tightening a notch further, recommending that you tuck your abdomen anytime you sit or stand. Positioning is important, too. "Try sitting with your knees lower than your hips," he said. "This will straighten up your spine."

11. *Consider a recumbent*

"Instead of fussing over tall, back-friendly handlebars and glute-strengthening exercises, just test-ride a recumbent," says Victor Larivee. "You won't go back to your old bike." Larivee converted his Bicycle Workshop in Santa Monica, California, from racing bikes to 'bents a decade ago, when the baby boomers began hitting 40. Comfort—i.e., relief from back pain—brings them in, but aerodynamics makes them believers. Recumbents own many bicycle speed records; as it turns out, a well-fit 'bent puts riders in the ideal, glute-centric position for generating power. Your back—and other parts of your body—will thank you.

12. *Go dancing*

A 2004 study in the *British Journal of Sports Medicine* suggests that dance training may help athletes alleviate back pain. Swedish researchers had 16 elite cross-country skiers take dance classes six hours a week for twelve weeks, while ten skiers served as controls. The dance exercises included ballet, modern dance, and jazz, with the aim of improving balance, coordination, muscle flexibility, and agility. After three months, the dancing skiers showed improved spinal flexibility, better posture, and greater range of motion in their hips. And while the dancing didn't necessarily make them better skiers, four of the six who had previous back problems said their backs no longer hurt following the three months of training.

13. *Finally, throw a Frisbee*

The introductory anecdote at the beginning of this chapter was no joke. You may have used a Frisbee as a food tray, a makeshift sand shovel at the beach, or a water tray for a thirsty dog. So why is it so far-fetched to find that the famous flying disc can save your lumbar discs? Tossing a Frisbee opens your cycling-collapsed chest, twists your inactivated cycling trunk, works your unused transverse abs, and loosens your stiff back—the perfect antidote to long hours in the saddle.

• EPILOGUE •

At this writing in December 2004, my left knee will probably never be what it was, but there's hope. Following an X-ray in January 2004 that showed that my kneecaps were visibly pulled to the lateral side, a doctor immediately wanted to perform a lateral release surgery on the left knee, which I refused. Fearful of being sliced up without exploring noninvasive remedies, I was quite motivated to make myself a guinea pig for this chapter and have religiously tested much of the advice offered here.

Now, I stretch my IT bands several times every day and hit the leg-extension machine to work my VMO muscle at least twice a week. I take glucosamine and chondroitin every day, I begin every ride slowly, in lower gears, getting the synovial lubrication flowing in my knees. Discussions with fit experts like Paul Levine, a morning spent in USC's biomechanics lab with Dr. Chris Powers, and testing on a CompuScan Velotron with personal trainer Chris Drozd (see his cyclist's strength-training plan in chapter 1) have shown me the benefit of powering through my glutes and keeping my legs lined up from hip through knee through ball of the foot.

Results have been encouraging. From a low point in January 2004, when I literally couldn't walk 10 feet without feeling my kneecaps scraping as they slipped out of their groove, I now can run and ride normally, including 11.5 hours one day at the Furnace Creek 508 in October. When I feel pain, inevitably it is because I've neglected to stretch my IT band and therefore have not relaxed the pressure forcing my kneecaps into lateral tracking. The pain immediately goes away when I get off the bike and stretch the ITs for a minute.

I am convinced that my improvement is due to my research. As I've gained an understanding of how my body is affected by its interaction with a bike, my condition has improved to the point where I consider my lateral tracking manageable, if not cured.

Researching this chapter has also helped me in other ways. I've never had back problems, but now I do back extensions at the gym to strengthen my spiny erectors and some basic posture exercises every day to counteract the long hours in front of my computer screen. For me, "prehab" isn't just a clever word anymore. It's common sense if you want to keep all your body parts functioning correctly. —RMW

Case Study:

Phil Curry Goes Straight (His Body, That Is)

HE'S 6-foot-2, 180 pounds, with a head full of brown hair and "mega-legs" that look like "telephone poles." He's a lifelong athlete, a self-described "kick-ass rider," a widely recognized merger and acquisitions expert who hammers 6,000 miles a year at a relentless 20 mph clip and says without hesitation that he can "power-sprint with elite racers." People are shocked to find out that San Diego investment banker Phil Curry is 63; the grandfather of three hardly believes it himself. He would probably think he was 35 if it weren't for his memories of The Back.

"It started around 1997 or 1998," he says. "And within a year it was bad enough to take me to surgery."

It was a pinched vertebra, an unusual problem for cycling. The pain went down his right leg from his groin into his right knee. "I couldn't ride without pain," Curry says. "I'd go out on the bike, take a ton of ibuprofen, and pedal until it crippled me up. Finally, after doing a century in 1999, I said this is it. I need help."

Curry sought medical attention from everyone: acupuncturists, physical therapists, sports medicine docs, and chiropractors. He even got epidural shots. "Nothing worked," he said. "Then I ran into a rider who said, 'Go to Symmetry.' Patrick [Mummy] took one look at me and said that I was 'crooked.' I thought, *yeah, sure.*

"But I couldn't argue with the photo."

The Photo—the famous Symmetry Polaroid. Two of them, actually, full-frontal and profile, overlaid with a drafting grid of horizontal and vertical lines. The photos showed Curry's shoulders shifted to the right, his midline off-center, and his hips a mess. Instead of a normal 9° forward cant, one tilted 6° forward and the other tilted 2° backward. He was, indeed, crooked.

Mummy's Symmetry Pain Relief clinic has made its mark by straightening the crooked. To restore the natural 9° cant of Curry's hips, Mummy prescribed a 20-minute sequential routine, which Curry performed before and after each ride. The six exercises, a personalized combination of yoga and isometrics, included the following:

1. **Backdrops**: Lie on the floor on back with legs bent at a 90-degree angle and resting on a chair for 5 minutes. This relaxes the back and prepares it for further exercises.
2. **Sit-ups in that position**
3. **Block and strap:** With a block placed between the knees, do 50 crunches; with a strap around the ankle, squeeze the knees together and push out at the ankles.
4. **Strap and block:** reverse of #3: Place block between ankles and do 50 crunches; place strap around knees, put ankles together and try to spread knees.
5. **Pelvic thrust:** With the block between the knees, thrust hips upward.
6. **Quad stretch:** 50 sets.
7. **Wall sits:** Standing with back flat against a wall, slide down to where your thighs are parallel to the ground. You look like a human chair.

"I did them religiously, and felt some improvement. My body was straightening out, but I still had pain," Curry said. Turns out that he was too far gone already; a disc was pushing into the nerve, and required a lapendectomy, the cutting away of a fingernail-sized chunk of vertebrae to relieve the nerve. That helped somewhat; within several months, the Symmetry protocol brought the back to 100 percent pain-free for the first time in years.

"I've been bulletproof ever since," says Curry. "And as long as I maintain the exercise regimen, I'm confident that there is no chance I'll go under the knife again."

Now, whenever Curry stops to get a Coke at a 7-Eleven, he drinks it while doing a Wall Sit. "I get the funniest looks from other bikers," he says." "What the hell is wrong with you?'" they say. "'You think you have an imaginary chair?'"

The exercises have paid off in other ways, too. "My wife says I'm an inch taller and I walk straighter," says Curry. "And I've become somewhat of an expert on posture."

"Cycling throws your body off balance," he says. "On a road bike, your whole pivot point is your lower back. You develop humongous quads, which get out of balance and overpower your pelvic girdle area. Your hamstrings get tight and pull your spine, so you have to stretch them."

Bottom line: Curry's a Symmetry lifer. "This stuff's not snake oil," he says. "I don't understand acupuncture, but I understand this. I understand the picture of the five-year-old boy, the way we used to be. The exercises Symmetry gave me are making me younger every day."

Jim Ochowicz

THE ORGANIZATION MAN

Friends and former teammates know the former Olympic cyclist and founder of 7-Eleven and Motorola pro cycling teams simply as Och. It sounds like "ouch" but with a long "o." Longtime followers of bike racing know Jim Ochowicz as the pioneering go-to guy who helped sucessfully lead the Americans' mission to race across the pond. Back in the 1970s and early 1980s, during the pre-LeMond era, the U.S. was considered pretty much a joke when it came to European racing. Ochowicz was instrumental in changing that impression and reality as racer-turned-sports director. As he told Bike for Life's *Bill Katovsky in an interview on March 5, 2004, it all happened because he loved cycling and needed to find a way to make a living from it after his racing career was over, His storied resumé, which includes induction into the U.S. Cycling Hall of Fame in 1997, is still growing adding USA Cycling board of directors president and team men's road coach of the U.S. Olympic bike racing squad in 2004. These days, the American racers, helped along by Lance Armstrong's Tour de France streak, are now a dominant fixture in Europe—much to the chagrin of the French, German, Italians, Spanish, and Dutch. Off the bike, Ochowicz is a vice president at Thomas Weisel Partners and Merchant Bank in San Francisco.*

MY DAD HAD raced bikes before World War II. I figured that out when I was about twelve. He had a box of medals on his dresser. I had a regular ten-speed and started racing around a circular driveway at the cemetery after school with my friends. And I wanted to really try to do it at a much bigger level. So I started riding to bike shops and looking at photos of real racing bikes. I bought a Schwinn Paramount with my paper route money. I started racing in 1966 on the track in Kenosha [Wisconsin] and then Milwaukee. I was 14 and got second in the nationals on the track. Then it was just full gas. I started speed-skating in the winter, because I lived in Milwaukee, to stay in shape, so I became a speed skater as well. But my primary focus was on the bike.

I was 20 when I made the U.S. Olympic team in 1972 in team pursuit on the track. And did it again in '76 on the track. Those things were the highlights. At the time no Americans were in Europe racing. A group of us—John Howard, Mike Neel, Dave Chauner—decided to go to Europe and we'd try racing together. And we did pretty well. We did the Milk Race [Tour of England] a couple of times and we won some stages. Then Greg LeMond came along. By that time I was transitioning out of the racing part of it, I was getting into sports management. I got married and I had a daughter and couldn't afford to race anymore. So I needed to get into the real world of making a living. And I got a chance to get into sports management by being the manager for the U.S. Speed Skating team in '79 and '80. And of course those were golden years of U.S. speed skating.

Off to Europe with Roll, Hampsten . . . and Armstrong

AFTER THOSE OLYMPICS, my plan was to try to find a sponsor like a European pro cycling team and develop a generation of racers that hopefully we might get to Europe one day and race as a team. And this kinda came on its own. Because when we met up with the Southland people at 7-Eleven, they had just made a commitment to Peter Ueberroth to be an Olympic sponsor. They got the sport of cycling and didn't know anything about it. We walked in the door about a week later. At that point, historically, Americans hadn't won a medal in cycling at the Olympic games since 1904. So these were the 1984 Olympic games and in L.A., and we felt with the right funding, we could find the right athletes, develop them, and win some medals. And that's what happened.

It was then time to decide what's next. And for me what was next was not gearing up for another Olympic games, but going over to Europe and seeing what we could do in the pro ranks. So, I talked Southland into backing us financially. We went to Europe, and the very first race we entered, Trofeo Laigueglia, was the kickoff race of the Italian season. Ron Kiefel won. And nobody had ever heard of us before. And he beat people like Francesco Moser and all the world champions.

We did that spring campaign and we got invited to the Giro d'Italia. We didn't have enough riders, so I recruited Andy Hampsten out of his tour of Texas that spring. We got Bob Roll on. We brought Chris Carmichael in. And we went to Europe and did the Giro. And won two stages. So we were off and running. That set the stage for me to go back in July and meet with Tour de France officials for the first time, convince them to have an American team in the Tour. And so in '86, the first American team raced in the Tour, and in that process we were building another generation of cyclists with a developmental team that we started. And the second generation was started in 1991 when we recruited Lance Armstrong.

Certainly Greg LeMond can take a lot of credit for creating awareness for the sport of cycling. It was televised. We were winning races. People were interested. And for enthusiast cyclists it was a great opportunity to be able to enjoy it from another perspective rather than seeing just Europeans racing. There was an American presence. Lance took it a giant step forward in '99 when he won the Tour. Because he just didn't win the Tour like everyone else won the Tour. He won the Tour having had cancer. And that was a unique story and a miracle, if you want to call it that.

The first year he rode as a pro, he won a stage in the Tour de France. He was the youngest rider in history to win a stage in the Tour de France. And a month later, he won the World Professional Road Championships. So you're not talking about somebody who wasn't already a very accomplished athlete right from the start. Physiologically, I don't know if anybody is fitter than he is. He's got a great will and determination. He has a winning attitude. He's got a work discipline. All the things you need to be a champion. He was just too young to win the Tour de France in those years and too inexperienced. He still needed to understand what it means to go up the Alpe d'Huez. To understand how big the Tour de France really was and how important it was in an athlete's career to do well there. We focused on the things we could focus on with all of our athletes during that time. Unfortunately, Lance got cancer and we stopped having a team at the same time. And he had a few years with nothing really happening. But all along that I believed that he could win the Tour de France. I believed he could win anything he wanted to win. Once he decided he wanted to do it.

The number one thing is, he definitely has the biggest engine. Nobody can push the kind of wattage he can push on the bike and sustain it for as long as he can. We've had some very accomplished athletes in our organization over the years and I've known a lot of very good athletes. But I've never seen anybody like him. So, starting out that's a huge asset. The second thing is, I've never seen anybody who can train as hard as he can train day after day after day. When he trains with the team, everybody has to take a rest day to stay up with him. He just keeps going all five days. The rest of the guys have to take a day off. He can go and go and go. That is one of the things that makes racing for him not that hard. Until he wants to make it hard. He determines when the race is going to be difficult. And he has done that because he has trained harder than anybody else and is better prepared. Those were some of the things we tried to get him to learn. For example, before we did Tour of Flanders, we'd spend two or three days out there working the Tour of Flanders course. Knowing where the left turns were. The right turns. Uphills. Downhills. Pavement. No pavement. Whatever. And he does the same thing before the Tour de France. Preparation is a big part of being able to compete at that level. And he does it more than anybody else.

Training in Your 40s and 50s

AT ARMSTRONG'S AGE, if you have an injury or illness, you can take time out. I think you can come back up until the age of 32 or so. At 34, it'd be a lot harder to come back. I'm 52 years old. Actually I can ride as many miles as I used to. When you're in your 40s you can probably do the most training. Your body can really take it. I think you can put in a lot of hours. And you can do it in a bigger gear. If you have the time, you can just do a lot more. The question is *consistency*. You can't do this for three months and then stop in three months and then come back and do it again for three months and then stop for three months. You need to have consistency. Consistency means you don't have breaks for more than two to three weeks where you're not going to do biking stuff, or some other kind of similar substitute. Like cross-country skiing in the winter or maybe ice skating or running.

I think you can train a lot when you're in your 40s. In your 50s, you can maintain some high level. At least I can. I feel like I can maintain. You're not as strong. No matter what you do, you won't be. But you learn to survive out there by knowing when you can make efforts and when you can't make efforts. I'm not a good climber. But I gotta climb a lot because I live in San Francisco. I ride with people who are better than I am. I don't count miles. I count hours—about 14 hours a week. Which isn't a lot. But it's enough. Because I do more than half of it really fast. Really fast means really fast *for me*.

I don't get any injuries. Never a bad knee. Never a bad back. I do stretching. Sit-ups, push-ups. Not a lot. A little yoga. If you do 15 minutes a day, that's enough to keep some good flexibility and keep sort of a body balance going.

The older you get, the more you have to consider nutrition. The difference between the nutrition I am looking at and the kind of a nutrition a Tour de France rider is looking at is like day and night. They need to have a very bland strategic diet during and around the Tour, because they need a massive amount of calories and they need to digest that food. And so nutrition to them is a totally different story than to somebody who is just a recreational rider. We can still indulge ourselves with something you may not want on a plate of a Tour de France table. But it is not going to be far off. I am pretty conscientious about what I eat and how I eat it. I follow a low-carb, low-fat diet. I take supplements. Just multivitamins. And try to watch my blood for cholesterol.

You can't deviate too much with diet in professional cycling because of the fact they have to eat so doggone many calories. And it can't be substituted 100 percent of the time with bars and gels and liquids of a sugary nature. We used to race with a bottle of water and a bottle of Coca Cola. That was it. Maybe a sandwich. Or a cookie. You could get cookies then that were wrapped individually. Stick 'em in your pocket so they didn't get all messy. Even today, if you go to the Tour de France there are some riders who just can't eat all that stuff. They can't stand all the sugar content and they get bad stomachs. So there are still people who eat sandwiches or paninis. It's not the fruit. You need some substance to swallow so you think you have a full stomach with food in it, and it can't just be gels and GUs and electrolyte drinks.

Time management is another important aspect of my life. My job is consuming, as most everybody's job is. I've always been pretty good at time management. It's learning how to fit an hour or two hours into a day so that I can maintain a reasonable level of fitness in a sport that I like. So that's not an easy thing to do, particularly if you travel a lot. But I make efforts to accommodate that even in my travels. I bring a bike a lot of times with me. I throw it in a canvas bag. Drag it to the airport and throw it on the plane and put it together and ride if I can. I do that whether I'm going to L.A. or to Zurich, Switzerland. I guess I'm a little more fortunate than the average person because I can keep a couple of bikes around the country. I keep a bike in Austin at Lance's garage—he has a couple of Trek mountain bikes and three or four road bikes. I got a bike in Europe in Eddy Merckx's garage in Belgium. I just go to Eddy's and go for a ride.

The Joy of Wheel-Sucking

I HAVEN'T RACED since 1980. But I like going fast. I find it more fun. I am just competitive. We do races every Tuesday and Thursday down in Palo Alto. Now, they are not official races. But they're races. People meet in Palo Alto. We do a loop. It's an hour-fifteen, an hour and twenty minutes. Everybody goes flat out. Fifty, sixty riders. I'm the oldest dog on the ship you know? All I got to do is finish and I've accomplished something. I know how to ride a wheel. So I can wheel-suck really good. Survival is probably my forte right now. Because it is fast for me—and hard. But I enjoy it.

We got a guy riding with us right now who just started riding about a year and a half ago. He was a four-minute-miler in college. Went to work, didn't do a lot of athletics. Then got hooked on the bike— and he is a really strong bike rider right now. He is dedicated and can train hard. He's got a big engine. So my advice to him starting out is take it slow. Build a base. He had to work really hard for about six months to build a really reasonable base of miles. Then he started transitioning and developing a little bit more speed, little more style, changing his training program a bit. More from just long slow miles to a little more fast short-interval training. And today, he's still getting better.

BIKE FOR LIFE

The first thing I'd tell people, don't just get on a bike and go as hard as you can. You've got to learn to discipline yourself a bit. Build a base. And you've got to have someone good—a personal trainer, or someone who knows how to race. Learn about bike handling. And drafting and positioning and riding in an echelon. Do all the things that make riding a bike a lot more enjoyable.

This is true even for recreational riders. I see groups of five, ten, fifteen riders, groups of forty to fifty riders out on weekends around where I live. And they're all in a big bunch. When you're in a big bunch, you better know something about wheels. What side do you sit on? How close do you get? Those are all just basic needs that every cyclist needs to know. Even at any level, whether you do charity rides or centuries, it's important to know the basics of riding a bike. It's not just how fast you can go. It's how fast you can go, but with a lot more thought put into it.

My middle daughter, 20, trains for speed skating on a bike. She was on the Olympic team in Salt Lake City for speed skating. Then my 15-year-old son just got his first brand new bike. An Eddy Merckx. And we'll be doing some riding this summer. You know, my father never rode with me. He took me to the bike races. But we never rode a bike together.

Even in this complex world with so many choices, riding a bike is still a lot of fun and interesting. It's an interesting sport for recreation, and because of one's ability to go fast, you have the ability to stay in good fitness and relatively injury-free. It's one of those sports that when somebody does fall upon it or happen upon it in some way, they fall in love with it. That was my case.

CYCLING AND OSTEOPOROSIS

How to fight the scary—and until-now unknown—
link between biking and bone thinning

I N THE SPRING *of 2003, while researching tandem bikes for one of my L.A.* Times *sports gear columns, I called Rob Templin, an old friend of mine who worked as a sales manager at Burley, a leading tandem and recumbent maker in Eugene, Oregon. I'd known Rob since 1988, when he was one of the top-seeded competitors in that year's Race Across America (RAAM), which I was handicapping for California Bicyclist magazine. A longtime bike racer, Templin never won the agonizing, near-sleepless 3,000-mile race from California to the Atlantic Ocean, but finished second once and four times overall. He then went on to make a career with Burley, which allowed him to pursue an all-bikes-all-the-time lifestyle. He rode 400 miles per week by riding to work every day, taking extra time off in the slow winter months for Southern Hemisphere tours, and representing the company at dozens of cross-state events and endurance rides, such as the 1993 Davis Double Century, which we rode on a tandem together. (The guy's an engine with legs; I'd never ridden a ten-hour double before or since.)*

"How's it going?" I asked when he picked up the line.

"Oh, not too good," he replied. "I've got osteoporosis."

Shock. Silence. Templin was 47, an age when most men don't show any bone loss at all. Most noncycling men, that is. —RMW

Cycling and osteoporosis seem like strange bedfellows. Superfit humans with powerful hearts and legs like steel rods—oddly coupled with wimpy, brittle skele-tons that turn them into broken hips waiting to happen.

Rob Templin surely didn't expect it. Yes, he had always been skinny—bony, really—but lots of hard-core bike people are. He was an aerobic animal, superfit in every way. Or so he thought until he got a call the year before from legendary two-time RAAM winner Pete Penseyres, who was participating in a research study being conducted by a professor at San Diego State University.

Dr. Jeanne Nichols, PhD, a professor of exercise and nutrition and a serious cyclist, was conducting bone density studies of veteran bike racers and endurance riders. Ultimately, she examined the bones of 27 Masters racers and endurance riders, like Penseyres and Templin, who had an average age of 51.2 and had trained an average of 12.2 hours a week for 20 years. Her study, "Low Bone Mineral Density in Highly Trained Male Masters Cyclists," was published in the August 2003 issue of *Osteoporosis International*. And her conclusions, communicated in an article by this coauthor published in the March 2004 issue of *Bicycling* magazine, would stun the bike world: **Anyone who rides a bike as his or her main form of fitness is risking osteoporosis.**

If the idea of fit men with thin bones seems oxymoronic, it may be because osteoporosis has always been considered an "old ladies' disease." Four out of five victims are women, whose bone thinning begins at menopause; the "change" causes women's bodies to stop producing estrogen, which helps absorb and store calcium. In 2002, the National Osteoporosis Foundation reported that 44 million Americans over 50 had elevated bone thinning, with full-blown osteoporosis striking 8 million women and 2 million men. In 2004, the surgeon general's report said that half of all Americans over 50 would soon be at risk for osteoporosis.

The disease is blamed for about 1.5 million broken bones a year, including debilitating fractures of the hip and back that leave victims wheelchair-bound. Estrogen and other supplements can help prevent bone loss after menopause, although they do not reverse bone loss.

Men are lucky—their bones naturally have a higher bone mineral density (BMD) than women and usually don't begin to show signs of osteoporosis until 20 years after them.

In Nichols's study of 27 male riders, however, two-thirds showed at least "osteopenia," moderate bone loss. Four of those had severe bone thinning, or osteoporosis. The test group's average hip and spine bone densities were 10 percent lower than a control group of similar aged, moderately athletic noncycling men.

When I remarked to Nichols that 10 percent didn't seem like a big deal, she was aghast.

"Clinically, 10 percent thinning is significant—not good—almost frightening," she said. "Because at age 50, average men have *no bone loss at all.*"

The thinning of hip bones and lower spine early in life is indeed scary, as it accelerates a huge quality-of-life issue by several decades. "Ten percent bone loss today will lead to a much higher than normal fracture risk as they age," explained Nichols. "The debilitating bone fractures that normal men become susceptible to in their seventies and eighties may happen to these superfit guys in the next few years."

In fact, during the time of the study, one participant, a 51-year-old ex-racer and personal friend of Nichols, fell while riding and fractured his hip.

At Penseyres's urging, Templin visited San Diego in April of 2001, met with

Nichols, and spent 16 minutes in a Dual X-ray Absorptiometry (DXA) bone-scanning machine. Nichols's study measured the densities of the lower spine and hips, the areas at much greater risk (along with forearms) of orthopedic fracture among the general population than other parts of the body. The hip, in particular, wears away quicker than other spots because of a high concentration of trabecular bone, the softer inner bone, compared to the tougher, outer cortical bone. The DXAs also yielded a total body bone density. (The clavicle, probably the most frequently fractured bone among cyclists, was not studied. Nichols and others we spoke with, including Conrad Earnest, PhD, resident cycling expert at the Cooper Institute in Dallas, put most of the blame for collarbone fractures on the trauma of falling, with bone thinning playing a minor role, although growing with age.) Generally, the experts agreed that one can infer from the hip and spine whether the entire skeleton is thinning.

The results of Rob Templin's DXA scan left him woozier than a sleepless crossing of Kansas at 4 AM. His lower vertebrae and hip bones were only 75 percent the density of those of a normal person his age, equal to those of a person twice his age. At a time in life when most men's bones are still robust, Templin's skeleton was literally wasting away.

Templin was the worst case of all the 27 test subjects. But not all of his bone thinning could be pinned on cycling, Nichols guessed. Some of it could be partly blamed on his daily habit of drinking two liters of cola, which is laden with phosphoric acid, known to leach calcium from bones. Cola drinking (one of many risk factors for bone loss—see sidebar at the end of this chapter) probably explains why DXA scans of other mega-mile riders' bones, though alarming, weren't as bad as Templin's.

Pete "Half-Million Mile" Penseyres, 58, who has ridden 500,000 lifetime miles in his cycling career, was found to have borderline osteoporosis at his spine and hips. Despite his extreme mileage, his bone thinning was surprising given his weekly consumption of two gallons of milk and several quarts of ice cream. Dairy products are loaded with calcium, a known bone builder. It was the same story for Don Coleman of San Diego, 42, an amateur racer since his teens, who had borderline osteoporosis in his spine despite his love for milk, cheese, and ice cream.

Among the most surprised of the test group was Dr. Bob Breedlove, 51, who had osteopenia despite a lifelong regimen of weight lifting, another known bone builder. "I was stunned," said Breedlove, an orthopedic surgeon from Des Moines, Iowa, who set a transcontinental tandem record in 1992 and the transcontinental age 50-plus record in 2002. "I thought I'd test normal. I used to run marathons, have no family history of osteoporosis, eat five helpings of dairy a day, and for decades have been lifting three days a week from September through March."

As surprised as many of the test subjects were, many bone researchers were not completely surprised by the results. Although Nichols's study is one of the first to specifically examine bone density in elite male cyclists (most seem to examine women and other sports), the topic has long been in the news, ironically associated with *younger* riders. A 1996 study in *Sports Medicine Digest*, "Rapid Bone Loss in High-Performance Male Athletes," discovered massive bone loss in the vertebrae of four Tour de France racers during the event's three-week time period. In 2000, England's Chris Boardman, the famed Tour rider and Hour Record holder, retired because of osteoporosis at age 32. Women aren't immune, of course. Former NORBA star Tammy Jacques, now 35, blames her retirement on osteoporosis (see sidebar). Pro mountain biker Sally Warner, 33, a University of Washington PhD who published a 2002 study that showed mountain bikers have thicker bone density than dedicated roadies, was found to have just 83 percent of the spinal bone mass of a normal female her age.

If you're a little spooked by findings that seem to cut, uh, a little close to the bone, join the club. In Nichols's opinion—a controversial opinion that is now being hotly debated—bone thinning goes beyond racers and extreme riders. She says average cycling folk are at risk, too.

"Even if you aren't a hard-core racer or RAAM rider, you still are at risk if cycling is your only athletic activity," she says. In other words, it doesn't matter whether your thing is mountain biking, road riding, or spinning, or whether you do it 20 hours a week or two hours a week. If all you do for fitness is pedal a bike, Nichols believes that you are at risk of wasting the foundation of your body—your skeleton—and turning yourself into a broken hip waiting to happen.

Nichols admitted to Bike for Life that this conclusion surprised even her. Although she knew from existing research that non-weight-bearing activities like cycling and swimming don't cue the body to strengthen bone like impact activities such as running do (more on this later),

she assumed that hard-core cyclists would certainly have much better bone density than found in same-aged nonathletes. "But instead of having similar bone densities, it turns out that the bone health of the cyclists, as a group, was actually worse!" she said.

The bottom line? "A recreational cyclist who rarely does other sports has the bone density of a nonathletic couch potato and is most likely on the road to moderate to severe osteoporosis," Nichols says.

It is important to note that none of the national bone experts Bike for Life contacted were willing to endorse that conclusion. "This is a good study," said Dr. Felicia Cosman, clinical director of the National Osteoporosis Foundation, after she obtained a copy of it at our request. "But given that it is not longitudinal [a long-term comparison with several measuring points], includes no dietary assessment, and has no similar studies of recreational cyclists or couch potatoes to compare it against, you can't generalize it to the general cycling population."

After all, Cosman pointed out, there are other causes at play in bone thinning (including heredity, body type, and diet; see "How to Build Bone" sidebar, below). And most of us haven't trained 12.2 hours a week for 20 years.

Even so, logic seems to indicate some level of risk for tens of thousands of century riders, long-distance tourers, dusk-to-dawn mountain bikers, four-day-a-week spin-class junkies. "Big-mile enthusiasts ought to know about this," says Breedlove. "If you're regularly in the saddle for long stretches, it makes sense that some of what happened to us could happen to you."

Profile: Tammy Jacques Is Boning Up

WE live in an era when women in their 40s are discovering their athletic prime. In 2004, forty-four-year-old Leslie Tomlinson won her second World Solo 24 Hours of Adrenalin Championship. In 2003, 45-year-old Pam Reed won the Badwater 135 Ultramarathon run from Death Valley to Mt. Whitney for the second year in a row, again beating all the men. In 2004, Tatyana Pozdnyakova, a 49-year-old Ukrainian mother of four, won the L.A. Marathon. That's why it seemed odd to many that Tammy Jacques, one of America's top mountain bike stars of the 1990s, retired in 1999 at the ripe old age of 32.

"I didn't want to. I was just reaching my prime," she said. "But I had no choice. My bones were disintegrating. I had osteoporosis."

Jacques was a natural athlete who experienced one athletic success after another. She was selected for the Maine state gymnastics team at age ten, was a champion swimmer at age 14, was a competitive skier in high school, and saw instant success as a cyclist. Introduced to road cycling in her senior year of high school, Jacques found she could keep up with her male ski team friends during off-season training rides in 1989 at the University of Utah. In short order, she entered and won her first bike race, the Casper Classic, was instantly upgraded from a Category 1 to a Category 2, won the Utah state mountain bike championships, was accepted to the Olympic Training Center road-racing camp, finished in the top-15 in stage races in Europe, won the Queen of the Mountains and the sprint jersey at the Ore-Ida road race, and signed a pro mountain biking contract with Giant in 1991.

It seemed that nothing could stop Tammy. Not even a faulty hypothalamus.

For reasons doctors don't understand, Jacques's hypothalamus, a region of the brain that secretes a number of hormones into the blood, including those that lead to the release of dopamine and growth hormone, was damaged, gravely shorting her supply of estrogen,[13] the steroids that give girls breasts, wider hips, and pubic hair. Estrogen also assists the parathyroid hormone to minimize the loss of calcium from bones, thus helping keep the skeleton strong. Coupled with years of hard exercise, which drains calcium unless routinely replaced, Tammy's bones paid the price: at age 26, she had osteoporosis.

"Strangely enough, I didn't get too worried," she said. "I was young and dumb. I thought I could beat it." She took tons of calcium supplements, lifted weights, did the "full-on hunter-gatherer diet—spinach, olive oil, meat, dairy." It didn't matter. Nothing worked.

In 1995, Jacques finished fifth overall in the World Cup. In 1996, she narrowly missed going to the Olympics. In 1998, she lost the nationals on the last day due to three flat tires. In 1999, at the peak of her strength, but increasingly worried about osteoporosis, she contracted Lyme disease and retired.

"I wanted to have kids and a long, healthy life," she says. "If my bones got much thinner, it might not make that possible. Another couple of years on the circuit started seeming too much of a risk."

In October 2000, 18 months into retirement, Jacques finally got good news. A year of weight lifting and taking the bone-building drug Fosamax, which she hadn't been aware of previously, improved her bone density by 10 percent. "I was so happy that I considered un-retiring," she said. "In fact, I did come back for one race—but slipped on ice in January 2000 and broke my leg [fibula]." She previously had broken two collarbones.

Required to stop using Fosamax during her two pregnancies [she is married to former NORBA pro Rishi Grewal], Jacques is excited about the new bone-building therapies now coming on line and even is looking forward to restarting her pro career, possibly as early as 2005. "I still have the itch to race," she says. "My career was cut short. I'm 37, but that's not too old anymore. Look at Paola Pezzo, who came back [in 2004] at 38. Now, with the new [*New England Journal of Medicine*] study proving Fosamax keeps working[14] and Forteo hitting the market, there's no reason why I can't too."

• HOW BONE LOSS HAPPENS— • AND HOW TO STOP IT

Here's why pursuing a strict cycling-only lifestyle may pose risks to bones.

Bone density is affected by aging, diet, and physical activity. In young adults, 5 to 10 percent of bone is replaced every year. In a process similar to scoring a wall before applying plaster, specialized cells called *osteoclasts* prepare bone for a new layer of calcium by dissolving away surface bone and creating an indentation. Cells called *osteoblasts* then help plaster in a new layer of calcium.

As we age, however, the process slows and less of the lost calcium is replaced. But the density can be maintained and even thickened by a calcium-rich diet and two types of physical activity: on-your-feet movement that has impact, G-forces, and vibration, such as running; and any activity that requires you to overcome some resistance, meaning resistance-training exercise like weight lifting with dumbbells and weight machines or using your own body weight to do push-ups.

The rule: Anything that strengthens muscle mass strengthens bone.

It appears that bone responds to stress by building more bone. Repeated jumping and landing, and the pulling and pushing on bones from contracting muscles and tendons, forces bones to adapt to stress, just as muscles do. The stress creates small electrical "potentials" (differences) in bone tissue that stimulate the growth of new bone. Additional hormone release and the increased blood flow associated help transport vital nutrients to bones.

The results are visible on certain athletes: the stronger, denser bones in the dominant arms of tennis players and baseball pitchers and the extra-thick leg, hip, and back bones noted in numerous studies of runners, weight lifters, and volleyball players.

Impact and resistance builds bone for people of all ages. One Oregon State University study had kids jump off 2-foot-tall boxes 100 times, three times per week for seven months. The result was 5.6 percent higher bone mass in those kids than a control group who did only stretching and non-impact exercise. "That translates to a 30 percent decrease in the risk of a hip fracture at adulthood," says study director Christine Snow.

A study of triathletes aged 40-plus found that the bone-building potential of running apparently is powerful enough to

BIKE FOR LIFE

counteract the bone-losing potential of cycling and swimming. A survey by the Veteran Affairs Medical Center of San Diego triathletes who competed in the 1999 Hawaii Ironman found that female athletes who trained intensively had just as much spine and upper thighbone strength as those of older male athletes. The same bone-building triggers exist in animals, too. Sheep placed on a vibrating platform for 20 minutes for five days a week increased their hip bone densities by one-third.

For pure cyclists, however, the news ain't so good. Sports physiologists have surmised for years that cycling's seated, off-the-ground position, which eliminates weight bearing and impact on the legs, does not trigger the body's bone-building mechanism much or at all. Cycling is not alone in this regard; bone thinning is also associated with low- or no-gravity activities such as swimming or, to a radical degree, space flight. (You'd have to ride intensely for 100 years to equal the bone damage incurred on a two-month space orbit, according to Nichols.) Injured athletes also suffer bone loss from inactivity.

Despite cycling's lack of running-style, weight-bearing impact, we were not convinced that this explanation concluded the bone loss story. If you've ever ridden your bike up a hill, you know that it puts plenty of stress on muscles and tendons, and by extension, bones. Even Nichols admitted that logic dictated that the "heavy tension on the pedals while standing and climbing, especially, probably builds some bone."

After calling bone experts around the country for comments on Nichols's findings, one remark nagged at us for months. Dr. Eric Orwoll, director of the Oregon Health and Science University in Portland and one of the nation's foremost authori-ties on male osteoporosis, called Nichols's study "provocative" several times during our interview. But he was certain that undernutrition, not the sport of cycling, was the culprit.

"You can speculate all you want about cycling and osteoporosis," said Orwoll, "but get enough calcium and vitamin D and you're okay."

That's logical—just get enough calcium. But thinking about Orwoll's statement several weeks later, a lightbulb went off: getting enough calcium is not easy for cyclists.

The recommended daily calcium requirement for an average adult male, according to the National Institutes of Health and several other government organizations, ranges from 1,000 to 1,200 mg. But wouldn't this be too low if you partake in activities that burn up a lot of calcium? Even if you steered clear of eating disorders, adult lactose intolerance, or overconsumption of soft drinks (all of which lead to bone thinning), could a cyclist's calcium stores still could get hammered by the sport's unique capability for seemingly endless hours of hard training?

Orwoll, clearly not a cyclist (we could tell because he referred to them as "cyclers"), was probably not aware that cyclists can ride all day long. We know from 25 years of putting in 12-hour days in the saddle during tours and endurance events that cyclists lose tons of minerals through calorie burn and sweat—salt, potassium, you name it. After all, that's what Gatorade is all about. So what about calcium? Could it be that all that riding was chewing up all the calcium those old bike racers took in—and more?

One look at a Gatorade bottle shows no calcium among the ingredients. Calls to RAAM contacts revealed no calcium in the most-used ultra-endurance drinks. We had to go all the way back to a RAAM rider from the 1980s to find an energy drink with calcium in it: GookinAid Hydralite, now used in the tennis and rehab markets. GookinAid was concocted in 1968 by a top U.S. marathoner after he left "green puddles" in his wake (i.e., he puked) during an unsuccessful afternoon at that year's U.S. Olympic Trials.

"Turns out that you sweat out a lot of calcium," said Bill "The Bagman" Gookin. Dissatisfied with his Gatorade experience, Gookin, a biochemist, gained local notoriety by taping plastic sandwich bags to his back, chest, and armpits to gather sweat samples for analysis. "It was no surprise that sweat is composed of water, potassium, sodium, magnesium, calcium, amino acid, vitamin C, and other noxious substances. All these need to be replaced," said Gookin, who went on to ride the Race Across America with GookinAid in 1985, crossing the country in eleven days.

How much calcium comes out in sweat? Dr. Christine Snow, director of the Oregon State University Bone Research Laboratory, told us that an average-sized man engaged in intense training loses 200 mg of calcium in sweat an hour. But she said not to worry. "Twelve hundred milligrams of calcium per day [the NIH recommendation] has enough padding to handle one hour of exercise," she says.

But then we did some math. Given that cyclists can easily ride four, five, six, even ten hours per day, a seven-hour century ride could sweat out 1,400 mg of calcium—more than a day's recommended intake. At 12.2 hours of weekly training, the participants in Nichols's study lost 2,440 mg of calcium—two full days' worth a week, year after year.

With typical energy drinks containing little, if any, calcium, century riders would have to down an extra dozen servings of milk or yogurt per week on top of an already healthy diet. Otherwise the calcium they sweat out could come from only one place: their bones.

Like other bone experts we interviewed, Nichols seemed surprised and amused when we called her to share our theory that sweat loss could be a major factor in cyclist's bone thinning. She told us that her three-person medical-journal-peer review board, in addition to other bone experts interviewed for this story, hadn't considered sweat loss a factor. But confronted with the above math, and being a serious masters cyclist herself, Nichols admitted it couldn't be ignored.

"Losing calcium through sweat is a plausible explanation, but not the whole explanation," she said.

As it turns out, there are precedents for calcium sweat loss, which does not discriminate by age or sport. Robert Heaney, PhD, a nationally known calcium researcher and professor at Nebraska's Creighton University, liked our sweat-loss theory. He told us about a 1996 study, "Changes in Bone Mineral Content in Male Athletes" (*JAMA*), that documents sweat-loss-induced bone thinning among college basketball players. "But at least they had several factors to help them minimize the loss: weight-bearing vibration to stimulate bone growth, and a limited season length," he says, "Cyclists don't have either."

Beyond sweat loss and cycling's lack of triggers for bone building, bikers have other strikes against them, too. A 1998 *Journal of American Orthopedic Surgeons* report, "Exercise-Induced Loss of Bone Density in Athletes," found that female and male endurance athletes may suffer decreased levels of sex hormones, which leads to bone thinning. Also, size of bones matters. "It could be that people who like to do a lot of cycling have less-heavy bones to start with," said Orwoll, correctly surmising that many of those who are drawn to the sport and do well in it are often skinny, a major osteoporosis risk factor.

And, finally, there's the simple bugaboo of time: hours in the saddle can leave little opportunity or desire for bone-building activities such as weight lifting, basketball, or running. "Face it, it is an axiom in bike racing that 'If you're not riding, you're resting,'" says Nichols. "Fact: most cyclists hate running."

That comment reminded me (RMW) of the time I asked Greg LeMond, just back from doing the TV commentary on the bike leg of the Hawaii Ironman, if he would ever consider doing a triathlon. "No way," he said. "I find running painful." Maybe not as painful as a broken hip when you're 70, though.

THE BOTTOM LINE

"For racers and extreme riders, the evidence of bone loss is piling up," says the Cooper Center's Conrad Earnest. "For recreational riders, whom we haven't studied yet, we only know that cycling is not as good, bone-wise, as other fitness activities."

One thing we know for sure is that bone loss is difficult, though not impossible, to reverse.

Take Dr. Bob Breedlove. He's religiously following many of the bone-building recommendations listed below. He added more weight lifting to his program and more calcium to his diet (to 2,000 mg a day) while training for his 2002 transcon-tinental ride and the 2003 Paris-Brest-Paris. But he got disappointing news at his DXA scan in November 2003. Since Nichols's initial test two years earlier, Breedlove's hip bone density was down 3.7 percent, although his lower spine was up 1.5 percent.

"My radiologist told me he's seen couch potatoes with stronger bones," says Breedlove. "Of course, their cardio system ain't worth stink. So pick your poison." But he's not giving up the fight yet. After his second test, he increased his daily calcium intake closer to the 3,000 mg ceiling Christine Snow deems safe, lifts weights all year round instead of only during the off-season, and substitutes running for cycling some days. In early 2004, he began taking Fosamax, a bone-building drug.

Rob Templin, who has biked an average of 300 to 400 miles per week for the last 20 years, has been trying to bone up since he received the results of the study. Now, he takes calcium supplements daily, has upped his mountain biking from none to twice a week, and runs two to three times a week for 30 to 60 minutes. He also cut out Coke completely; he'd been drinking a case a week. He's also trying to get into a test program for Forteo (Lilly), an injectable form of human parathyroid hormone (PTH) that was approved by the FDA in 2003. It is the first drug to actually build bone—supposedly faster than Fosamax.

"I only ride 200 to 300 miles a week now, but I feel better," says Templin. "I've put on a little weight—5 pounds. And people tell me I look better." He'll know for sure next fall, when he goes back for the next of the annual bone-density scans he will have for the rest of his life.

Note: While the sweat-loss theory advanced in this chapter received a positive reaction from the bone experts *Bike for Life* interviewed, it has not been formally studied and backed up by academic research. No consensus has developed about the benefits or drawbacks of extra-high calcium ingestion. Some speculate that it may spur the development of kidney stones. Some say it can't hurt, especially since your body only absorbs one-third of the calcium you ingest, anyway. But if there is something to it, it could be another tool that endurance athletes of all types, not just bikers, can use to assure long-term health.

The Plan: How to Build Better Bones

SINCE most people don't worry about their bone density until the day they break their hip, cyclists might choose to think of themselves as lucky. Although bone thinning appears to be endemic to their sport, they have been given advance warning by Dr. Nichols's study. Given that, it probably wouldn't hurt to try what magazines have been blaring at you every month for years: get more calcium into your diet and more balance into your athletic life. Make cycling your main thing, but not your only thing. Add weight lifting, weight-bearing activities, and impact exercises. Get more dairy, cut smoking and soda consumption. With some powerful new bone drugs, it is even possible nowadays to build back some of the bone you've lost. Bottom line: the changes that cyclists need to make will not change their lifestyles much and will leave them with a stronger skeleton and better all-round fitness. They can still ride as much as they like, as long as they also do the following.

1. **Take calcium supplements:** Get at least 1,200 mg of calcium per day. The National Osteoporosis Foundation recommends 1,000 mg of calcium a day for men under 65 and 1,500 mg over 65. According to the N.I.H., less than half of men get 1,000 mg. Vitamin D intake should be 600 IU over age 70. Good supplementary sources include calcium tablets, Calcitonin (a non-estrogen hormone), vitamin D, Tums, low-fat yogurt, and raloxifene (an oral tablet that mimics estrogen in the bone but not in breasts or uterus). Help your body absorb the calcium by taking 400–800 IU of vitamin D per day.[1] Mega-milers should increase calcium load by 200 mg for every training hour beyond an hour per day.

    Note: Some research has shown that too much calcium may actually increase the risk of prostate cancer, but the vitamin D in dairy products (see below) can offset that.[2]

2. **Add dairy products:** Got dairy? You'll build bone—and lose weight, too. Add more milk (any type), yogurt, Swiss or cheddar cheese, calcium-fortified orange juice, salmon with bones, and other high-calcium products during your regular diet and post-ride refueling. Each serving contains 200 to 230 mg of calcium.

    Incidentally, new studies show that increased dairy consumption may have another benefit: weight loss. Eating an extra three servings of yogurt a day caused men in a 2003 University of Tennessee study to lose 61 percent more body fat and 81 percent more stomach fat over 12 weeks than men who didn't eat yogurt. The trick: calcium. "Calcium helps the body burn more fat and limits the amount of new fat your body can make," says

Michael Zemel, PhD, the study's author. Other recent studies back the finding: teens in Hawaii with the highest calcium intakes were thinner and leaner than those getting less calcium, and a test comparing groups of mice yielded similar results.[3]

3. **Add more protein:** Several studies show that consumption of relatively high amounts of protein (higher than the RDA) can actually improve bone status.[4] Older studies showed that additional protein significantly improves recovery from hip fractures.[5] This makes sense for two reasons. Throughout history, humans have adapted to higher rather than lower protein intake. And bones, being made up of about 50 percent protein and living tissue always rebuilding itself, require a significant amount of replacement protein from the diet.

    On the flip side, those with the lowest daily protein intake in a Tufts University study of 600 men and women also had the weakest bones, especially in the hip, thigh, and spine. In a University of California study, researchers found that for every 15 grams of protein you add to your diet each day, your bones become exponentially stronger.[6]

4. **Add more magnesium:** Magnesium may help to keep the skeletal system healthy by preventing calcium and potassium from seeping out of bones. "Magnesium is most abundant in unprocessed, whole foods—the very foods that men don't get enough of anymore," says Katherine Tucker, PhD, a Tufts University epidemiologist and professor of food science quoted in *Men's Health* magazine. Her recommendation: protect your bones by adding one serving of spinach, yogurt, brown rice, bananas, or almonds to your daily diet.

5. **Lift heavy, all-body weights:** Heavy weights, used in two or three sessions per week, put maximum stress on muscles, and, by extension, bones, cueing the body's bone strengthening mechanism. "Heavy weight shocks the muscles like running does, signaling the bones to grow," says Dr. Warren Scott, former director of sports medicine at Kaiser Permanente Hospital in Santa Clara, California, and head of the medical care unit at the Hawaii Ironman Triathlon. When muscles contract and pull, they produce electric currents in the bone tissue. Maximize the effect by lifting heavy weight—enough so that you "max out" (i.e., reach failure or lose form) at 6 to 10 reps per set for three sets. Lighter weights (sets of 11 to 20 reps) build bone slower, but also help. Do at least one set for each major muscle group (chest, back, shoulders, arms, legs); two to three sets would be more beneficial.

    "When Lance retires, he better hit the weight room," says Dr. Jeanne Nichols, author of the study that brought the cycling-osteoporosis crisis to light.

6. **Do push-ups at home:** Can't get to the gym? Try exercises that use body weight or a resistance band. Conventional floor push-ups and handstand push-ups against the wall, for example, can help strengthen shoulders, chest muscles, and triceps.

7. **Do back strengthening exercises:** Protect the lower vertebrae, which become particularly weak in cycling due to lack of movement, by working the oft-neglected *spinae erector* (lower back) muscles. At the gym, do a set on the back extension machine every time you finish doing sit-ups; the two exercises are complementary, with both being essential to balanced core strength. At home, lie on stomach, place hands behind neck, raise head and back off the floor.

BIKE FOR LIFE

8. **Get significant impact by running, hiking, and more:** Jogging, uphill and downhill hiking (especially with a heavy backpack), skipping rope, jumping jacks, stair climbing, dancing, or simply jumping up and down for 10 to 20 minutes several times a week helps jump-start bone growth with weight-bearing vibration.

    Weight-bearing exercise on the major muscle groups releases hormones that trigger bone cells to multiply as much as 2 percent a year. (Note: Swimming won't build upper body bones, since it isn't weight-bearing.)

    "The impact must be significant," says Christine Snow, director of Oregon State University's Bone Research Lab. "The vibrations of cycling aren't enough." A Johns Hopkins study, published in the November 2002 issue of the *Journal of Internal Medicine,* found that light-intensity activities like walking did not strengthen bones. A Hebrew University study found that running was the only exercise that strained the shinbones enough to strengthen them.

    Must you run a 10k to build bone? Length of time is being debated. Some studies say just a minute of impact is enough, but to be safe do 20 or 30 minutes, Snow says. An OSU study found bone density increases in postmenopausal women who jumped up and down 50 times a day three times a week and did squats and lunges while wearing vests weighted with one to ten pounds. Another study ("Good, good, good . . . good vibrations," *Lancet,* December 2001) that placed sheep on a vibrating platform for 20 minutes each day for five days a week over a year showed a 32 percent increase in hip bone density.

9. **Stand up on the bike:** Standing on the pedals loads all your weight on the legs. Many cyclists never get off the seat, especially since the advent of aerobars. Add more standing, especially during climbing, which puts very high torque on your muscles and bones.

10. **Mountain bike more:** Sally Warner's PhD study, *Bone Mineral Density of Competitive Male Mountain and Road Cyclists,*[7] found significantly higher bone density in mountain bikers, particularly in the upper body, probably due to the occasional hiking, jarring ride, and high-torque climbing.

11. **Cut back on smoking, excessive alcohol, and soda:** All of the aforementioned are known bone thinners. One study found the more cigarettes smoked, the more bone was lost. Soft drinks are loaded with phosphorus, known to leach calcium from bone. Alcohol is toxic to bones, and alcohol abuse is associated with accidental injury, nutritional deficiency, and hypogonadism. One study found that long-term hard drinkers lost almost 70 percent more bone than nondrinkers. Recommendation: swig less than 60 grams per day (less than four cans of beer or 2 ounces of hard liquor).

12. **Know your risk factors for osteoporosis:** If you're skinny, Caucasian, Asian, have a family history of osteoporosis, trained to excess as a youth (i.e., female gymnasts), and took steroids, you have a higher propensity for osteoporosis.[8]

13. **Get a bone scan:** Know where you stand, skeleton-wise. Insurance companies won't pay for the $200–250 DXA bone-density scan until men are 65 and women are 50–unless you appear to slump when you see your doctor, complain of aches, and mention that your

wife or friends say you look shorter, which could indicate premature kyphosis, a grandmotherly forward slump.

14. **Get some summer sun:** Your skin cranks up production of vitamin D and banks it for later in the year during the summer, so allow 10 to 15 minutes in the sun before putting on sunscreen, take a short walk outdoors during lunchtime three times a week with your sleeves rolled up. According to Dr. Michael Holick, a professor at the Boston University School of Medicine and author of *The UV Advantage,* chronic lack of sun exposure due to covering up and sunscreen can lead to a vitamin D deficiency that can increase the risk of bone thinning, muscle pain, multiple sclerosis, and colon and prostate cancers.[9]

15. **Try powerful bone-building drugs:**
    ▶ *Fosamax*, manufactured by Merck and approved in 1995, reverses some of the effects of osteoporosis by slowing bone-destroying cells and thus allowing more time for bone-building cells to catch up. A study published in the *New England Journal of Medicine (NEJM)* in early 2004 found that the bone built by the slower turnover was as solid as normal bone. A later *NEJM* study in 2004 found that Fosamax keeps strengthening bones for at least a decade, dispelling fears that it might eventually boomerang and start making hips and spines brittle and prone to breaking.

    ▶ *Forteo* (Lilly), a faster-acting drug, was approved by the FDA in 2003. It is an injectable form of human parathyroid hormone (PTH). Side effects include growth pains similar to those experienced by fast-growing teenagers.

    ▶ *Strontium Ranelate,* shelved for 50 years, is a "new" drug that was found to increase bone density in postmenopausal women, according to a study in the January 2004 edition of the *New England Journal of Medicine.* Mixed with water, it is a powder composed of the mineral strontium (discovered in lead mines a century ago) and ranelic acid. While Dr. Felicia Cosman of the National Osteoporosis Foundation warned that is was no better than any other bone drugs, it is noteworthy due to its easy absorption and lack of side effects, except for diarrhea, experienced by 6 percent of patients in the study. In other words, it can be taken for years without concern, a big plus considering that other bone therapies have some downside. Fosamax, a biphosphate, can cause stomach cancer. Estrogen, which keeps bones healthy, has been linked to a slight increase in stroke and blood clots and has side effects such as vaginal bleeding, mood disturbances, and breast tenderness. Raloxifene is generally free of side effects, but can cause hot flashes, leg cramps, and deep-vein thrombosis, a blood-clotting disorder. Forteo can cause nausea and cramps and is also linked to cancer in mice.[10]

16. **Take folate, B vitamins, or a multivitamin tablet:** The aforementioned work by reducing levels of homocysteine, an amino acid that, at high levels, can double the risk of osteoporosis-related fractures (and also raise the risk of heart attacks, strokes, and Alzheimer's disease).[11] A standard multivitamin, taken once a day, does the trick, according to Dr. Douglas P. Kiel, senior author of the U.S. study and director of medical

BIKE FOR LIFE

research at the Hebrew Rehabilitation Center for Aged Research and Training Institute in Boston. Foods naturally rich in B vitamins and calcium—including dairy products, broccoli and other greens, leafy vegetables, carrots, avocados, cantaloupes, apricots, almonds, and peanuts—can also reduce the risk of broken bones.[12]

Missy Giove

THE PERPETUAL QUEST FOR A "NEW 100%"

"Why are you so fast?" they'd ask. "I've got bigger ovaries than the other girls," she'd reply. A New Yorker to the core, Queens-born Melissa "Missy" Giove was always in your face and in a hurry. U.S. Ski Team at 17; downhill mountain biker at 18; World Champion at 21; first two-time World Cup season titlist (1997 and 1998); first three-time NORBA national champion downhiller (1999, 2000, 2001); first gold medalist at the first X Games; and first female pro athlete in any sport to wear a dead piranha on a necklace, sprinkle her dog's ashes in her bra, and confidently "out" herself as gay. Superlatives precede her name in every realm: most intense, most outrageous, most fearless. Her style was literally "go for broke"—nine torn MCLs, eight cracked ribs, five broken wrists, two broken tibias and fibias, two fractured vertebrae, two broken kneecaps, five major concussions, a bruised lung, a ruptured spleen, and a whole lot more. Before she retired at 30 in 2003, her multicolored shaved/dreadlocked hairdos, brash four-letter-word-laced speech, and willingness to push the envelope racked up wins at 14 NORBA and 11 World Cup races, a Reebok commercial, Letterman and Conan O'Brien appearances, more money than any other female rider, and more instant recognition than any off-roader of either sex. Belying rumors that a brain hemorrhage suffered at the 2001 World Cup in Vail left her brain-damaged, the well-educated, articulate superstar sat down with Bike for Life's Roy Wallack on March 23, 2004, at the

International Health and Fitness show at the Las Vegas Convention Center and unveiled the next move in her career: master trainer for the Trixter X-Bike, an indoor "mountain bike" with a freewheel and rocking handlebars, maybe the most unusual take on classroom cycling since Spinning. Here's Missy "the Missile," who spits words like machine-gun fire, won a race the first time she rode a mountain bike, and knows only one speed—all out.

THAT PIRANHA WAS sort of my alter ego. I was always a crazy, full-blown athlete—rode motocross from age 11 to 16, played hockey, lacrosse, skied, mountain biked in college—crazy sports that girls didn't always play often. And in my fish tank I had this piranha who I named Gonzo—because he was nuts. He would jump up out of his tank all the time. One day I came home and he had flopped out. I had a lid on it, but he popped it off. That wasn't normal for a fish. He was on the floor one day when I came home—all dried out, because I'd been away for three days. So I put him in the windowsill and dried him out, then punched a hole in him, strung some line through it and put it around my neck. Gonzo became my warrior symbol, my reminder to be crazy. I'd ride fast and he'd be flopping behind me, tagging along. During hard times, he reminded me that I needed to go a little harder.

I wore Gonzo for a decade. Ten years. When he broke, I duct-taped him up. Finally, in 2000, a friend's cat made a meal out of him.

I GOT INTO biking in 1990 at 17 and used it as cross-training for skiing. I already had the downhill skills—and the guts. At UNH [University of New Hampshire, which she attended for one year], I was the national third-ranked J-1 downhill skier at age 17 and 18—which seems odd because I didn't really like the attitude of skiing and knew I didn't want to pursue that entirely.

I was introduced to cycling on a fluke. At my grandparents' in New York, I used to hang out with this Jewish family down the street. The son, Dave, was a friend of mine, but his brother had cerebral palsy and I would play Ping-Pong with him all the time. His dad appreciated it and said, "Hey, we want to give you something for being so nice." And I said, "Well, you don't have to give me anything for being nice. I really enjoy him." But he said there were some bikes up in the attic, including one that was his grandfather's bike. So I accepted the gift and went upstairs and picked out a road bike. I had a choice of a Barry Hogan or a sea-green Falcon. I didn't know anything about bikes. I liked the color of the Falcon. It was an English bike, a 12-speed. I rode that every day for training.

My first time on a mountain bike was in a race—the beginner category cross-country race at Mt. Snow, Vermont, later that year. My friend gave me a mountain bike to win a prize for him. "You ride every day; I want you to enter this race and win me a pair of Sidi shoes and pedals," he said. "I know you'll win."

So I went out there with no training, no number plate, no helmet. I wasn't registered, hadn't paid fees. I was a vagrant in army fatigues. In the race, I kinda went crazy, whipping around, weed-whacker lines. By the second lap they pinned a number plate on me, made me pay the fee, and put on a helmet. And I won.

When it was over, I was so happy. Mountain biking was awesome. I was really taxed. That day I found my "new 100%."

That has always been a key in my life, something I now preach to everyone in my talks: find your new 100%—a challenge—every day. Age or circumstance does not matter. Every day, shoot for a new 100%, mentally, physiologically. You are only limited by your mind. Entering a new season, I would say, *last year was the maximum.* But you know what? I'll find a new 100% this year. I'll give myself better nutrition, more recovery. You will find a new 100%. But you've got to search for it. You've got to push.

So I found my new 100% in mountain biking. At first, I liked the idea of utilizing the fitness of mountain biking as cross-training for my skiing. But I jived with mountain biking much more, attitude-wise, than skiing. It was more free rein. There wasn't as much tradition in it. And I was a nontraditional person. A little bit more extreme.

I was 18 when I won my first Worlds—the junior mountain bike championship at the first official Worlds in 1990, Durango, Colorado. I entered the slalom and ended up second to Cindy Whitehead. So I entered another race at the same meet—and I ended up getting second to a pro.

I was still on a collegiate ski racing scholarship. But after another season of mountain biking I realized I was skiing to bike, not biking to ski anymore. Biking is what I loved. So I dropped skiing and went full-time biking in '91. Soon, I started training specifically for the downhill.

Fame, Fortune, and "Coming Out" on Her Own

By the time I won the Worlds in '94, I was more and more recognized, but I didn't personally recognize that I was famous. I'd talk to everybody as usual, and

every once in a while they'd say, "Aren't you that girl?" That usually was cool, but occasionally it posed a problem. One time I was in a sex shop weeding through tapes or whatever when someone came up and said, "Aren't you that girl?" And I said, "No, I'm not," and very quickly got out of there. One time, I got arrested for skateboarding illegally, and, having no ID, just gave a different name—but the cops caught the lie because they recognized me. It's weird, but it seems like all of the highway patrol know who I am—and that's actually worked to my benefit. Many times I was speeding, or driving without ID or registration, when the cop who pulled me over said, "Aren't you her? Just get outta here now," without ticketing me.

Certainly, being gay added to it [the notoriety]. I had outed myself in the *Village Voice* in New York City [in 1992] at 19 years old—way before anyone else. In 1995, when the cover story of me in *Deneuve* [now *Curve*, a lesbian magazine] hit, it was a very big deal. That was before these TV shows featuring gays came out [Ellen Degeneres, *Will and Grace*, etc.] It was more hidden. In fact, *Girlfriends* magazine just put me on the cover and named me "Athlete of the Decade" because Martina [Navratilova] and a lot of other athletes were outed, but they never came out—and I came out on my own. I was, "this is the way I am, you don't like it, oh well." It shouldn't have been an issue, but you know how society is.

Cannondale was a sponsor before I came out, but knew I was gay before they hired me. I'm definitely not going to hurrah them, "Wow, look at Cannondale—they hired a gay person." After all, I was the best in the world—why *wouldn't* they have hired me? I'm not going to give them any props for

hiring somebody gay. But later on in my career, when the company changed hands [and dropped her sponsorship in 1999], I felt like I was discriminated against.

I'm not going to live a lie. I felt like if that's my lifestyle and that's how I chose to live, it's kind of like if you're a warrior and that's your oath, then stand by your oath. Not to mention, too, that it's disrespectful to the person that you love, to hide somebody. Unless there's a true reason to do that—if it was going to jeopardize or harm somebody else, say, for instance, in a custody battle or something like that. Other than that, if you're not proud of who you are and what you're doing, then you shouldn't be doing it.

People who wanted to be my friend had to accept it because that was the reality. So you know what I got? I got a lot of the bullshit out of the way. People who really wanted to find out who I was for the right reason would talk to me, and the people that didn't eliminated themselves by not approaching me, because they were prejudiced. So in a certain sense I did myself a favor. At the same time, it's harder to live an alternative lifestyle—you definitely get a lack of support financially. I mean, if you're gay, *kettcchh* [sound of door slamming]. You hear about this issue all day long—she didn't get this, didn't get that, because she was gay. Well, you know, she also grosses $8 million a year in prize money, so it wasn't that bad.

There's a definite downside to taking a stand on anything. Like taking a stand on abortion—you'll get support from people who are for it, slammed by those against it. I'm not for abortion. But look at all the movie stars and singers like the Dixie Chicks who are catching slack for criticizing the war [in Iraq]. They are losing jobs

BIKE FOR LIFE

because of it. There are financial repercussions for taking a stand. It's like declaring a religion. You say, "I'm a born-again Christian," and you're gonna get Catholics, saying, no, no, ours is better. You take a position and you are highly scrutinized, but at the same time you do get some support. I choose to focus on the positive and on the people who supported me and try to deflect the negativity.

Hopefully, my strength in taking a stance and showing people who I am will help other people, and not necessarily because they are gay. Over the years, I've done a lot of suicide prevention talks to gay youth. Maybe a couple less people would kill themselves because of the fact of their sexuality, over something they couldn't help and wasn't a choice. For some people it's a choice, but for most people it's not—they don't choose to live a harder lifestyle.

Fortunately, it's 2004 now. It's a different place.

Crash Course in Fitness: Missy's 8 Rules

INJURIES CAME WITH the victories over the years, but you can't ride in fear. Some call it crashing—I call it R&D [research and development]. I was constantly breaking some of the things that were causing some of the crashes I was having. One time my handlebar snapped in a compression and I broke my collarbone. In 1994 I broke my pelvis in five, no, seven places. All compound fractures. Broke both my legs at one time. The list goes on. The worst was the brain hemorrhage at the Worlds in 2001. The doctors told me not to ride again, but I came back in 2003 and qualified 13 seconds ahead of everyone at the first World Cup, then got a flat in the next round. I crashed, hit the shit out of my head, and tore my MCL [medial

cruicate ligament] and PCL [posterior cruciate ligament] in the next race, but was back by mid-season. Took a fourth at the Telluride World Cup and won the nationals in Durango in my last race. So I left on a winning note.

I could have probably kept going, winning races, and been on top of my game until however long I wanted to, really. I think I am that strong mentally an athlete that I could do it until my body would say, "no you can't." But it was really a choice of respecting the people in my life, around me, because if I was going to hit my head a lot, and hurt myself real bad again, then they're the ones who are going to have to be taking care of me. And I might not know what's going on. They're the ones who are left to pick the pieces up. And I thought that was kind of selfish, because I accomplished what I wanted to accomplish and had a lot of fun doing what I did.

I'd have crashed a lot more if I hadn't worked on my strength and flexibility and good nutrition. I did and still do a lotta core workouts, so I have maximum control over my limbs. I train in unstable environments, using trampolines and stability balls. Helps your kinesthetic sense to work on flipping, landing. With a more facilitated core and balance, you can actually pull yourself out of a lot more accidents. And if you do get hurt, you get better a lot faster.

I've spent lots of time in gyms rehabbing. But I was always in the gym two hours a day, five days a week. Starting at 15, I lifted weights—dry-land training for skiing. Downhill bike racing needs a lot more upper body conditioning than regular cycling. Females especially, since we lack the muscle mass. I am naturally 120 pounds [5-foot-6], small for gravity sports.

So I work my ass off to get 15 to 20 more pounds of muscle. I can bulk up to like 140. Downhillers have to do a skill every day—either motocross or downhill or jumps. After that I'd go hit the weight room two hours. Then my ride—two, two and a half hours of intervals. Way different from a cross-country rider. They do the LSD, Long Slow Distance. Just ride; no real strength or conditioning programs.

My experience made me a natural trainer. I love being a teacher. I've added academic training. A degree from the C.H.E.K. [Corrective Holistic Exercise Kinesiology] Institute in neurological training. I'm also officially a cranial sacral therapist, from the Upledger Institute in Palm Beach Gardens, Florida.

If I had to give fitness rules to live by to someone getting older, I'd start with my old favorite:

Number 1: Find a challenge; find your new 100% every day.
Number 2: Quality, not quantity. Train smarter. When you're older, you can't hammer for a couple hours every day. So you do quality. An hour and fifteen maybe every other day. Whatever is 100%.
Number 3: Balance stress and recovery in all aspects of your life. If you are always stressed out at work and you go home and work your ass off to lose body fat, you're imbalanced. Parts of your recovery are nutrition and sleep. Fall asleep by 11:30 PM, or lose a lot of your neurological recovery and regeneration.
Number 4: Take responsibility for your own health. Everybody wants a quick answer and there is no quick answer. Don't necessarily rely just on doctors or trainers.

Number 5: Maximize workout time with functional fitness. Instead of dicking around for two hours in the gym, chatting it up, do more neurologically demanding exercises that mirror real-life movements. Rather than sitting in an ab machine, do physio ball sit-ups with a medicine ball against the wall. Take the leg press machine—is there anything in the household that requires me to move while sitting in a chair? Better: do a one-legged squat. It's functional, requires stability. It's functional fitness—good utilization of my time and energy. Do it indoors and take it outdoors. Taking a family ski vacation? Better be able to do squats—so train for them. Weights aren't necessary—do body-weight squats. Walk up and down the stairs while doing the laundry. Do step-up squats on a bench.
Number 6: Watch form. Bad biomechanics and bad form is going to alter joint mechanics.
Number 7: Work the core—front and back. With more of a facilitated functional core you'd be able to utilize your power better.
Number 8: Use your ass: "Most cyclists aren't making use of their glutes, but they are a must in downhilling, because you have to be explosive. Also, being a kinesiologist, I knew that strong glutes reduce back pain—cycling's number one injury. I set my seat back and hit the weight room for butt-building exercises, including deadlifts, the one- and two-legged squats I mentioned earlier, plyometrics. Bottom line? You've got an ass—You may as well use it. [See chapter 7 for more on the benefits of butt-centric riding—Eds.]

BIKE FOR LIFE

X-Biking into the Future

THE X-BIKE people contacted me to be the celebrity endorser in 2002. Since you can rock its handlebars side to side and coast, it replicates what happens on a real bike a lot more. That means an all-body workout—shoulders, arms, core—that regular spin bikes can't do. I was impressed.

So that's why I turned around and told them I wanted a bigger role. Wanted to train people, write training manuals, help design the program. I said I'm a high-performance kinesiologist; my thing is training and rehab. I was pre-med in college. After years of work, I got a degree from the C.H.E.K. Institute in 2002—a career move. When I got my brain hemorrhage, I decided to get some actual certification that I had been studying. Had my eye on retirement—not going to do downhill forever. I had to get started with other things.

I just kept shaking it in every direction I could. When you're into punk rock and have this image as a gonzo jock . . . I had to definitely prove what my intellectual property was worth. I said, "Look, this is what I think I can do for you. I know I can make you successful." I basically created a spot for myself. Got a three-year contract plus a six-year endorsement.

This is a perfect job for me. I love cycling. I love the gym. The X-Bike is both—a full-body workout, which I am already into because of downhilling. So I was a great advocate of the product from a personal and business level. I'm a stickler about form, and the ergonomics of this bike allow you to actually exercise in proper form. On bikes where the handlebars aren't moving, you can't move in a natural plane of motion. I think our bike is healthier in the short term and also in the long term. It trains your body to have the correct response. As a downhiller, my life depended on it! I had to train my transitionomics to kick in. Instead of going to my shoulder. I've already hit that tree.

So I love this product because it does all of that—multiplanes, proprioception, neurological training. I don't want to be limited by my equipment. This is for me. I would be involved no matter what they paid me.

Over the years, I turned down alcohol and tobacco sponsorships that coulda made me a lot of money. I'd have made so much that I probably wouldn't have had to work again. But I was more idealistic. I contributed money to Team Amazon, which was dedicated to women who couldn't get sponsorship. I gave tips to girls who wanted to beat me. In my life, I've definitely stuck to my guns.

I don't miss the back to-back races. I had a wonderful time. I got out from a full-time racing schedule at just the right moment for me—I left the sport when I was ready to move on to bigger, better things. The transition has been really smooth and easy. Besides, I still ride and motocross all the time. I'm a rider—I just like to ride. I'll ride by myself on a Sunday, go downhill or dirt jump, just free-ride—tear down mountains with no line and no trails, jumping off cliffs. We're shooting *Kink*, a video all about dirt jumping and big air. Who knows if I get neurological problems or Parkinson's when I'm older? The brain is a mystery—you never know what'll happen. I'm not being stupid or trying to kill myself. I'm just having a good time. An accident's gonna happen, or it's not. It's a little bit of roulette, but I gotta live life.

MOTIVATION AND MENTAL TRAINING

*Success through positive thinking,
visualization, breath control, training journals,
creative riding, and time management*

I
T MEANT A *pleasant break from studying. During my junior year at the University of Michigan, I often found myself neglecting my studies for a well-thumbed, oversized Rand McNally atlas of the United States. I was planning to bike solo from Ann Arbor, Michigan, to the West Coast that summer, and so I examined, state by state, possible cross-country routes that might be spidery lines on a map but would determine my lonesome highway journey. When it was finally time to begin my trip in late June 1978, I could already see in my mind's eye, no matter which route carried me west (I was still undecided), a picture of myself running in to the ocean somewhere in the Pacific Northwest.*

There was a bit of Lewis and Clark exploratory fever running in my blood. Not that I was looking for the Northwest Passage. What I hadn't anticipated was how some days, especially those lonely, hot slogs through Iowa's green seas of corn or pedaling through dusty, barren swatches of eastern Wyoming, challenged my reserves of willpower and determination. Apart from headwinds, a constant foe was boredom, of being glued to my leather saddle for hours at a stretch. The temptation to quit was strong, especially when the headwinds picked up. So I devised ways to combat mental fatigue. I broke each day into small, easy-to-achieve motivational increments: an hour ride before breakfast; two more hours before lunch; an hour break for lunch, with perhaps a nap, then three of four hours of riding before nightfall. Or I would select a town as my day's goal instead of trying to calculate how many miles were left until the next state. I kept to this schedule as best I could, averaging 65 miles per day. On those mornings when I was desperate to find an excuse not to cycle, I visualized the Pacific Ocean. Although it was weeks away, the sound of pounding surf reverberated in my head, its virtual spray brisk enough to raise goosebumps as it drew me inexorably closer.

A vision, a mental picture of reaching the continent's edge was all the motivation I needed to travel 2,800 miles to Lincoln City, Oregon, where I leaped into the waves triumphantly and screamed to the world, "I did it!" Cycling is as much mental as it is physical. Strong quads and a strong mind make an effective team if you set reasonable, forward-thinking goals for yourself, goals that test you in every conceivable way. —BK

In 2001, Emmanuel Ofosu Yeboah didn't merely see himself riding a bicycle. He visualized himself riding hundreds of miles, crisscrossing his country of Ghana. It was quite a dream for someone who'd spent 22 years on crutches due to a deformed-at-birth right leg that had a foot dangling back where the knee should be.

Emmanuel's vision—communicated via e-mail to the Challenged Athletes Foundation of San Diego—was so strong that the organization did not hesitate. They sent him money for a mountain bike, which he used with his one good leg to pedal 600 kilometers—and change a nation. Village kids ran after Emmanuel chanting his name. Radio, television, and newspapers not only wrote stories about him, but began taking up his message: that Ghana's 2 million disabled people—10 percent of the population—are not cursed, as tribal custom has dictated for centuries. Shaking Ghanian society to its core, he proved that tradition is wrong, that the handicapped are not worthless scum to be reviled and ignored and discarded, but human beings with feelings and potential to achieve.

When Emmanuel later came to California's Loma Linda University in 2003 to have his bad leg amputated and be fitted with a prosthetic that allowed him to walk and run for the first time in his life, he was asked if he would choose to stay in the United States, where life was easy. "No," he said. "I have my vision in my head. I am going back home to help the others."

Today, with the help of $50,000 in grants from Nike and CAF, he is building Ghana's first training center for the disabled. He's helped dozens of disabled get their own bikes and prosthetics. He's getting government authorities to build handicapped-friendly facilities and initiate programs to aid the disabled. And, not to be forgotten, he's cut his time for riding 56 miles from seven to four hours.

Motivation is a powerful thing. A clear picture of the future motivated Emmanuel to carry out a grandiose goal and ultimately motivated a nation to change the way it thinks. But visualization, which we will discuss in detail further on in this chapter, is just one of several powerful motivating tools that you can use to help you achieve your own health and fitness goals.

Motivation is a key component of mental training, and obviously varies in intensity and degree. Motivation is why some of us exhort "Just Do It," while others snarl "Just Screw It." After all, genes take us only so far. Talent gets us to the base of the mountain. Willpower and determination take us up the mountain. You might even say that motivation is gravity's own nemesis. Motivation works against the laws of inertia, of standing still in life. Motivation is movement toward a goal. Think of a shark—always moving forward. It doesn't have a reverse gear.

Motivating yourself is a fairly simple transaction, actually. Realizing your own potential rests with only one person—you. (For those who have a personal trainer, he or she is a mere catalyst. Sorry, *you* do the sweating, lifting, huffing, puffing, and writing the check at the end of the session.) You need to set goals, and then break those goals down into achievable increments. It's foolish, for example, to enter a mountain bike race a week after buying your first bike. The experience will be so dreadfully humiliating—crashing, being run over by other competitors—that you will feel less inclined to even ride again. The same goes for your first century. Choose one with moderate terrain. Build up your confidence level before signing up for events like California's fabled Markleeville Death Ride, with over 16,000 feet of climbing.

Goal setting ultimately can be reduced to a line from one of Clint Eastwood's spaghetti Westerns: "A man's got to know his own limitations." Two things are at play here: (1) be realistic about your goals so you don't set yourself up for failure; and (2) never stop testing, challenging, probing your own limits.

Goal setting differs with individuals. Some prefer the carrot to the stick. In other words, the "carrot" people like the satisfaction and reward of obtaining a finisher's medal or T-shirt for a job well done. Other carrots, of course, can be prize money or age-group awards! For the "stick" people, performance is often measured by competition with one's peers and by a hard-pressed, constant need to avoid finishing behind them. Even casual Sunday mountain bike rides among friends can turn into mini-tests of will—arriving at the creek first, making it to the hut before others. Oh, the ego can turn into such a fragile, delicate flower on these group rides.

Setting goals means finding the right motivation to reach these goals. It also means self-empowerment, of placing the power to realize your potential in your own hands, not someone else's. (No one else is climbing that hill, correct?) But what happens when things go wrong? What should you do about temporary setbacks in life, training, or competition, setbacks that can often take the wind out of your motivational sails? What are some effective ways to overcome frustration, inadequacy, or disinterest? How can you achieve your potential without getting bogged down in negative thoughts or wallowing in stress-induced torpor? Fortunately, in the next few pages, there are plenty of everyday strategies that can help you achieve your goals. We will look specifically at six: positive thinking, visualization, breath control, training journals, and time management.

No matter which technique—or combination thereof—that you use, just remember this simple tip: mental training is as important as physical training. Neglect one and the other falters.

· 1 ·
POSITIVE THINKING

Okay, *Bike for Life* now wants you to take this short quiz to get you well-situated in the pop-pysch realm of positive thinking. Presented here are five quotations. Read them carefully. Now *who* said all of them?

1. Believe in yourself! Have faith in your abilities! Without a humble but reasonable confidence in your own powers you cannot be successful or happy.
2. Change your thoughts and you change your world.
3. Do not be awestruck by other people and try to copy them. Nobody can be you as efficiently as you can.

4. Formulate and stamp indelibly on your mind a mental picture of yourself as succeeding. Hold this picture tenaciously. Never permit it to fade. Your mind will seek to develop the picture. Do not build up obstacles in your imagination.

5. Throw your heart over the fence and the rest will follow.

The answer is not some legendary coach or athlete. His teams didn't win any Superbowls, Tours de France, or NBA championships. The person responsible for these quotes is the preacher Norman Vincent Peale, who died in 1993 at age 95. He was best known for his book *The Power of Positive Thinking*, which sold almost 20 million copies in 41 languages since its first publishing in 1952.

Strip away the sectarian underpinnings of his self-esteem gospel, and you still won't erase the basic elemental truths underlying the power of positive thinking. Because cycling is an individual sport, it is paramount that you stay positive on and off the bike to get the most benefits— benefits that are both mental and physical. Dr. Saul Miller and Peggy Hill are strong believers in using "power words" and "power thoughts" as critical ways to keep one's self-esteem humming along in high gear. "Power words should be so strong," they write in *Sport Psychology for Cyclists*, "that they create a feeling and a picture that increases your power, direction and potential." They consider these words as part of your inner-dialogue arsenal: "tuck" to give you an aerodynamic edge on downhill; "attack" in racing; "smooth" and "flow" to help you along bumpy, rocky off-road trails. For these, or any other words you decide to choose (i.e., "fast," "alert," "power") to have maximum impact, "You have to train them into your mind in practice. That means, define and select a few key words before you go out on a ride and consciously and repeatedly use these words at appropriate times as you train until they become part of your cycling self-talk."

Power words are all part of power thoughts. They are building blocks to increased self-confidence. You can say to yourself, "I can attack this hill at my current speed," or you can adopt a defeatist attitude and say to yourself, "This hill is killing me. I can't make it." Or take the case of your first century, despite having never ridden more than 50 miles at one time. If you start harboring thoughts of shutting down at mile 50, you probably won't make it to 100. You have already made that surrender in your own mind. Maybe you are silently wishing for a flat tire or mechanical breakdown to allow a graceful exit. But if you etch the number "100" in your brain, so it seems like it's part of your DNA, you will make it to the end, past the fatigue and exhaustion. Keep that "100" flashing in your head like a Times Square billboard. Visualize what it will feel like to make it across the finish line. Think of the bragging rights you will have secured. So instead of worrying about not finishing, dwell instead on what it's like to finish. Quitting is an option only if you allow that vexing sentiment to trespass across your mental threshold. Post a keep-out sign for all negative thoughts. And consistently blaming your equipment or bike for your own poor performance is often a fruitless exercise in avoiding personal responsibility.

· 2 ·
BREATH CONTROL

To offset anxiety and to increase levels of concentration and performance, many coaches suggest using breathing and breath control as a way to gain mastery of your mental and emotional states. Who doesn't want to feel calm before a race? If you are mentally thrashing about like a skittish thoroughbred being led to the starting gate, chances are that you will have a bad performance. You have already dug yourself an emotional hole. "The best and easiest way to develop emotional control," write Miller and Hill, "is to focus on your breathing. Breathing is a process that integrates mind and body."

Rhythm and focus are the most important aspects of breathing. A steady approach will melt away tension. The next key ingredient is direction—how you direct the smooth rhythm and increased energy. And here, Miller and Hill use a five-pointed star as a handy symbol. "Allow yourself to imagine sending this energy down through your hips and glutes and quads, down into your calves and right into the soles of your feet. As you direct the energy out, say to yourself, 'I am a star.'"

Breath work takes time. Practice it in short bursts, increasing duration within reason. The goal is to put your mind and body on an equal performance footing.

· 3 ·
TRAINING JOURNAL

Cyclists can be divided into two groups. Those who use a training journal and those who don't. Of those who use a training log, there are those who fill out the pages with the care and attention of a NASA researcher, recording daily fluctuations in resting pulse, weight, moods, ride intensities, route, cadence, diet, and weather. Others just scribble down some mileage and leave the number-crunching at that. Some just tally hours. The most serious download their heart rate monitor and cyclometer information onto their personal computer. Others use online services like www.trainingbible.com that can track your daily progress with graphs.

How you use a training journal as a motivational tool is an individual choice. But the journal never lies, unless you do. It can act as your conscience. Or drill sergeant. Or your loyal companion. Just make sure that the journal doesn't take over your life, that it doesn't become more important to fill in the day's grid and boxes than it is to have an enjoyable ride. *How?* you might ask. Say that you don't want to have this week's mileage fall off from the previous week's, but you are nursing a cold and the weather is wet and miserable; nonetheless, you feel to compelled to ride those 25 miles in the rain to make the week's goal. But this ride, of course, makes you even sicker, and so you spend the next several days in bed. So let common sense be your guide, not guilt. Your journal, you will gladly discover, can be most forgiving and tolerant.

"A journal helps you grow by increasing motivation," writes acclaimed endurance coach Joe Friel, author of *The Cyclist's Training Bible*. "Motivation comes from recording successes such as training goals accomplished through higher levels of training, subjective feelings of achievement, and personal race performance records."

Another area where training journal devotees fail, in Friel's opinion, is improperly recording mental comments. "Training

BIKE FOR LIFE

and racing are usually thought of as strictly physical, deeming what's happening inside the head as unimportant. Sometimes emotions are the most telling aspect of physical performance. Mental comments should include unusual stresses in your life off the bike. Visiting relatives, working overtime, illness, sleep deprivation, and relationship problems all affect performance."

• 4 •
VISUALIZATION AND MENTAL IMAGERY

"By the time of my 1985 land speed record attempt in Utah, I wasn't at my peak anymore," admits American cycling legend John Howard in his *Bike for Life* interview. "I was already 40 years old. So I had to develop something else: mental fortitude. So as I meditated, I came to my method of dealing with the pressure—visualization. I saw image replays like a video camera in my brain. I visualized scenes of streaking above the vast, endless ribbon of salt flats, a mirage on top of a mirage, the image above me flashing in giant red numbers in the sky: 152."

And what speed did Howard's superbike reach? It was 152 mph, beating the old record by 12 mph.

What Howard accomplished in the desert is an extreme example of positive visualization. It applies to riders of all abilities or goals, from those not wanting to languish on a two-mile hill climb during a weekend ride (visualize the summit as you grind up the ascent), to focusing on your day's riding objectives before you strap on your heart rate monitor and leave home for an hour ride, or finishing your first half-Ironman Triathlon.

In their book *Sports Psychology for Cyclists,* Dr. Saul Miller and Peggy Maass Hill, refer to visualization as power imaging. "The way to achieve this is through mental rehearsal. It means practicing in your mind the things you want to do on the bicycle in competition or on a challenging ride." It's like rehearsing your role in your own movie of what you need to do. For example, they suggest these mental rehearsal skills for road riding: good form, looking ahead, elbows lowered and loose, shoulders relaxed, quickness in legs, flowing pedal strokes. To encourage your private mental rehearsal, the authors suggest these easy-to-follow pointers:

1. *Specifically define what you want:* Uncertainty leads to confusion and stress.
2. *Relax then imagine:* Whenever possible, release and breathe before putting your imagination to work for you.
3. *Stay positive:* The only value in running a negative thought or image, something that didn't work, is to determine what you can do to change it and enhance your cycling performance and pleasure.
4. *Go easy at first* instead of going hard and tiring.
5. *Be dynamic and brief:* Create imagery in your mind that is a movie, not a static snapshot.
6. *Use all your senses:* Smell the leaves, listen to the wind or birds, because this heightens mental alertness.

Putting together your own script and mentally rehearsing its details is critical for cyclists who ride safety's edge. For example, in the adrenaline-supercharged world of downhill mountain biking, races

BIKE FOR LIFE

may last around five minutes but require intense concentration and mental preparation. A stray thought, a meandering mental flicker can mean all the difference between crashing or finishing; the mind and body have to be trained to operate in total sync. Self-guided imagery is as important as the 45-pound full-suspension bike. One slip and hello ER.

World champion downhill racer Marla Streb trains year-round, three to four hours a day, so she can weather these five-minute thrill rides. She describes how she prepares for a race in her autobiography, *The Life Story of a Downhill Goddess*: "I've drawn a map during this week's practice. I study the lines of this map at night and play them over and over in my head like a favorite Django Reinhardt guitar riff so that on race day I can hit every note. Focusing on these lines that wink in and out of the blinding sun and through the black shade of trees and into the floating fog of trail dust, at 40 miles per hour I race down this mountain trail that can break bones and ruin careers."

Visualization also has a valuable place in the great indoors, where the most lethal danger is having your sweat mar the floor polish, or being bored silly by the monotony of going nowhere fast.

Spinning classes at the gym are often fun, intense, sweat-dripping bouts of camaraderie. But take your indoor training home into the privacy of your living room, and you will often find it hard to replicate the same high-powered, heart-bursting workout on your stationary trainer. Cycling coach and author Arnie Baker, MD, in his e-book, *Psychling Psychology,* offers these tips, which can often apply to spinning classes as well: "Let your mind drift. Look at your cadence. Now focus on your leg. Look at your leg directly, or close your eyes

and picture it as you pedal. Say to yourself: 'Push! Push! Push!' with each pedal stroke. Look again at your cadence. It is possible to get that cadence higher and do more work, isn't it?

"Spinning and finding it hard to maintain 100 rpm? Close your eyes. Count to 10 while pushing down on your left foot, pulling up on your right. Now switch, count to 11 while pushing with your right, pulling with your left. Now switch, count to 12 while pushing with your left, pulling with your right. Keep changing back and forth while building a pyramid to 20 strokes while concentrating on pushing/pulling, then let the pyramid decrease 20, 19, 18, down to 10 again. I find it easier to keep spinning this way. Not only that, it can take a full three minutes to do this pyramid at 110 rpm."

Baker also discusses a nifty mental imagery tip for riding outdoors if you are trying to keep pace with another rider, especially on a hill climb. "Climbing about the same pace as a rider 100 meters ahead of you on a climb? Working hard? Look at that rider? Focus on that rider. See a string coming to you. See yourself pulling that string, reeling in that rider closer and closer."

·5·
CREATIVE CYCLING

Ride like Picasso. Try treating your bike like a giant paintbrush, taking you to imaginative, creative places in the great outdoors. It's not wise or healthy to remain inside a hamster wheel cage that locks you into a rigid style of riding—same route, same speed. The bike can allow you to make connections to the world in a myriad of ways—

adventure, exploration, beauty. Unless you are a time trial specialist or elite triathlete who must train hard and fast in repetitive conditions to better gauge and monitor fitness, the average recreational cyclist can benefit by viewing the bike as a means, not as an end itself. Of course, reaching your destination is important, but you don't want to be so hard-pressed by this fixed notion that you miss out on all the interesting things you might see along the journey.

Let's face it. Many of us hate sucking wheel. We don't like to ride in tightly clumped pace lines, our front wheel inches away from the next person's rear wheel. We would go postal if we tried to emulate the U.S. Postal Team in the Tour. We would rather have other things on our mind than someone else's butt inches from our front tire. We miss the scenery—sunlight flashing through the trees, the silhouette of green rolling hills. Some of us even prefer riding alone—traveling at one's own pace. This lone-wolf attitude appeals to Cat R riders—recreational cyclists.

Rather than use a heart rate monitor or cyclometer to measure miles or fitness, use your bike to commute or go shopping around town. You'd be amazed to find out how easy it is to developing quads of steel by doing local chores or shopping at the supermarket on one of your older, heavier mountain bikes. Invest in some panniers or a lightweight, frameless backpack with upper chest and waist straps to ease strain on your lower back.

Commuting is another great way to break the tedium of training. You don't need to be a hard-core five-days-a-week bike commuter. By simply integrating just two commute rides per week, you can find yourself getting stronger on the bike; work and working out can make an ideal team. A bike commute of five or ten miles in the morning will energize you better than a jumbo latte, anyway. You'll be luxuriating in an endorphin high while your colleagues are swilling the black stuff to stay alert. The ride home will do wonders to help alleviate job stress. You don't have to worry about traffic jams, being stuck at some toll plaza, or paying for gas. You'll also sleep better.

·6·
TIME MANAGEMENT ·

What often derails motivation in a self-defeating loop of procrastination is this excuse: "I don't have time to ride because I have too much to do at work." But sacrificing the bike for the in-box or answering all those e-mails is a mistake. Guilt can easily set in on this slippery slope. Instead of riding, you find even more excuses not to get on the bike. So let's take a quick look at managing your time more effectively in the workplace. Your goal here is to pry yourself away from the desk.

"The reality is that most people don't need more time, they just need to reprioritize the time they've got," says Jeffrey Gitomer, author of *The Sales Bible* and *Customer Satisfaction Is Worthless, Customer Loyalty Is Priceless.* "The basic underlying principle of time management is 'do what's important first.' The time-management industry has complicated that principle to a fault. There's an 'A-B-C' system, a 'First Things First' system. I say reduce sales time management to one word: 'Yes.' How does it work? Simple. Devote your time executing functions and meeting with prospects and customers who will lead you to Yes. Almost everything else is a waste of time." A big Gitomer "no-no" is making personal calls at work.

Make that in-box so yesterday. Ever notice that CEOs in Hollywood movies have desks the size of aircraft carriers but with nary a scrap of paper in sight? Maybe a Mont Blanc pen holder, but that's it for the clean desk club. Learning to file, organize, and prioritize your workload streamlines productivity and saves time. You need to unshackle yourself from superfluous information and data overload, or to empty what is known as your "collection buckets," says David Allen, productivity guru and author of the best seller *Getting Things Done*, and the best way to do that is "do it, delegate it, and defer it" so long as it appears later on an action-item list.

"I manage the clock by multitasking," says super-workaholic John Duke, who rides 200 miles per week. Time is the framework for this mad maestro of multisport, who is a magazine publisher, sports marketing consultant for a large footwear company, and founder of a personal coaching and training business in San Diego. "I require at least seven hours sleep, so if it wasn't for time management, I couldn't make all that happen. I don't let minutes flit by. I don't waste time talking to my friends. I have two computers; I have a headset on my telephone so I can ignore people while I'm talking to them and work some more when they're boring me. I have a silent keyboard. I use a Blackberry handheld so I can stay in touch with e-mail while I'm traveling. I have several cell phones. I'm never out of communication."

"I only go the gym two to three days a week and I always circuit train," continues Duke. " I don't have time to go and spend two hours; I never spend more than 25 minutes. I'm an aerobic athlete; I don't need to rest in between workouts. I just switch muscle groups and I count that as an aerobic workout as well. I can do two muscle groups. The only part of my training that I consider social is when I'm running or bike riding, because a fair variety of that is at a lower heart rate and I tend to do that with people with whom I enjoy their company—and that's the entire extent of my social life."

Bottom line for the workaholic Duke: "My time is compressed. I'm trying to live three lives in one lifetime. I don't believe in reincarnation, so I've got to do as much as I can while I'm alive."

Reclaiming Your Motivational Mojo

YOU'RE stuck. Psychologically, physically, or situationally, you're in a rut, not finding the joy or challenge in your training that you once did. What to do? We asked award-winning sports journalist Timothy Carlson, longtime senior correspondent for *Inside Triathlon* magazine, to divulge some of the best pick-me-up tips he's gleaned from years of interviewing the world's top cyclists, triathletes, and runners.

Pick Your Fight: If you are big and powerful, but heavy, don't keep knocking your head against the wall of a long mountain climb. Find a nearby pool-table-flat time trial course. If you aren't fast but you can ride all day, try doing the longest event you can reach and finish it—a century ride or a double-century. If you're old and slow and your equipment is

BIKE FOR LIFE

ancient and creaky, start to follow in the footsteps of that old gentleman who has ridden his bike to the last ten summer Olympics, where he parks his rusty old cruiser with a basket for his clothes and attends all the free events, eats at McDonald's, and soaks in the Olympic spirit.

Dream Time: On a ride through the countryside, focus on the blur of covering ground and imagine you are a low-flying bird. Enjoy the technology of your steed, and then forget it is there and get lost in the beautiful Impressionistic passing of green fields, white snow patches, pointillist batches of wildflowers, and the passing herds of cattle.

Do-It-Yourself Indoor Triathlon: Let's say you are snowbound in Chicago on a business trip and cannot in good conscience dare the icy slick streets. But you are training for a half-Ironman come summer. Go to your health club. Swim 1.2 miles. Hop out of the pool, change into cycling shorts and a T-shirt and shoes. Hop on an exercycle and program it to go over several hills and cover 56 miles at over 20 mph. Then get off and run 13.1 miles on either a treadmill or cover 131 laps on an indoor 1/10-mile running track. Count your entire time—including transitions—in this do-it-yourself triathlon. Ignore all strange looks from Type-As on their hour workout break. When you are done, sit in the sauna, get a massage, then go to a fine local Mexican restaurant, suck down some margaritas and a big enchilada as a reward.

Hill Repeat: Have a steep hill you cannot get up without stopping to push or catch your breath? Or within a certain time period? Attack it once every one or two weeks. Eventually your body will improve and adapt and you will make it to the top. Even if you don't, the dream will keep you young.

Speed: Try to set your personal land speed record. Find a perfectly level stretch of road that continues for a mile. Look splendid in your most aero outfit. Pump up your tires to the highest pressure. Go at it one way. Stop. Turn around. Go at it the other way. Take the average of your two attempts. Keep track. Keep pushing the average up.

Neighborhood Fun: Have kids who are in grade school or above? Set up a bike race in your neighborhood. Spray-paint *Lance, Ullrich, Hamilton,* on the backs of T-shirts. Have parents hold out water bottles and carry flags. Have a barbeque to celebrate the winners.

Inspiration: Invest in some remastered cycling DVDs (www.worldcycling.com). Relive the final day time trial finish of the 1989 Tour de France—newly aero'd Greg LeMond tops distraught French crybaby Laurent Fignon, and the overall victory goes to Greg by a mere eight seconds. For your post-ride Sunday cool-down, there's "A Sunday in Hell! Paris-Roubaix, 1976." Watch Eddy Merckx battle competitors and cobblestones in this great Danish-produced documentary gem. Or watch that family favorite, *Breaking Away,* and work on your Italian.

Patrick O'Grady

RIDE MORE, REST MORE, WRITE MORE, DRAW MORE

No one better mocks cyclists with greater passion and twisted wit than Patrick O'Grady, a freelance writer, cartoonist, and editor whose satirical work appears in a variety of publications, including VeloNews, Bicycle Retailer & Industry News, and Bike. His cartoons are peopled with a dirt-splattered spectrum of hard-core purists, including surly, goateed bike mechanics and cross-country mud studs. O'Grady's twisted brand of humor is an aerobically inspired mosh pit bringing together the torqued sensibilties of the late Hunter S. Thompson, Doonesbury, and Mad magazine. He lives in Colorado Springs with his wife, Shannon, and their cat, Ike. For a look at examples of the bent observations Bike for Life's Bill Katovsky glimpsed firsthand during several e-mail exchanges with O'Grady in the late spring of 2004, see his Web site, www.maddogmedia.com.

MY PARENTS BOUGHT me a little police "motorcycle" when we lived in Ottawa, Canada—this heavy black-and-white garbage wagon that looked like a miniature Vespa, but you had to pedal it. I was five or six, I guess, and it immediately extended the range of my misbehavior, so clearly the law enforcement angle was lost on me. That was the thing about having a bike when I was a kid—you couldn't have a car, and being afoot greatly limited your opportunities. A bike gave you the world.

When I was in my 30s, cycling gave me back my physical and mental health. A few too many years sitting on my butt at a few too many newspapers shot my weight up to nearly 200 pounds—cycling helped me take it off, and racing helped me keep it off. Quitting the newspaper business and finding some new friends who were interested in something other than drinking until three in the morning helped, too.

I especially liked cycling because it wasn't mainstream, like jogging. Anyone can lace up a pair of Nikes, strap on a Walkman, and go tottering around the neighborhood. Cyclists were weirdos who wore tight, black wool shorts, shaved their legs, and pedaled up tall mountains. Not everybody could "just do it." Then when cycling had its boom periods, thanks to Greg LeMond and mountain biking, and it suddenly seemed that everyone was doing it, I drifted off into cyclocross, which may be the last refuge for the serious oddball. Joggers in the park give you strange looks when you run past them, wearing a bike.

When I was in my 30s and racing a few dozen times a year, I'd ride 200 to 300 miles a week and feel guilty if I skipped a day. If it was really evil outside, I'd ride a wind trainer, watching Tour de France videos and listening to the Allman Brothers. Riding 90 minutes of intervals in your living room qualifies as obsessive, I think.

When I was riding hundreds of miles a week as an adult, I swore by various over-the-counter potions—Gatorade, Exceed, what have you—but I can't credit them with any triumphs or extensions of my longevity. The few, small successes I've had as an amateur bike racer are due more to training sensibly, paying attention to what the good guys were doing, and pure dumb luck than to any combination of chemical

BIKE FOR LIFE

enhancements. The one drug I use regularly is albuterol; I've had asthma and various allergies since I was a kid.

I like to eat well, so I learned how to cook (I also buy organic meats and produce when possible, but I don't obsess over it). I take a daily multivitamin as insurance against those days where I don't feel like eating sensibly.

These days I ride less than I did in the 1980s, because I don't race nearly as much as I did back then. But I still get out for ten or so hours a week, for love and money. I freelance cartoons and commentary to a couple of bike magazines, and when you earn your living cracking jokes about something, you'd better be involved in that something. I even moved back to Colorado Springs, Colorado, from a ranchette in the high-country boondocks, because I felt I was losing touch with the cycling community. In Custer County, I *was* the cycling community.

Half-Century Mark:
Beware your inner fatso

Now, I'm bearing down on 50, my racing is limited to cyclocross, and I'm a damn sight less likely to bundle up for a slushy four-hour road ride in February or do wind-trainer intervals as preparation for a road season that I don't care about anymore. I'll go out for a 45-minute run instead, or an hour of cyclocross. Or I'll just say the hell with it and take a brisk trudge through the snow to the neighborhood liquor store for a bottle of Tractor Shed Red, which is what I did this afternoon after shoveling a block of sidewalk. Call it cross-training.

Cycling is still my primary form of exercise, and from spring through fall I'm in the saddle at least four days a week. But ride

the road when it's 18°F with the windchill factored in and the streets look like something Michelle Kwan might use for training? No, thanks. Life may indeed mean suffering, as the Buddhists say, but there's no need to get ridiculous about it.

I'm definitely less serious about training. If a group ride gets too animated for my purposes, I'm not shy about sliding off the back and doing my own ride. I'm more inclined to see training as recreation, an end in itself, rather than a means to an end. That's not to say I won't attack a group ride on a hill, or try to chase down a break when it feels right.

Recovery time has definitely become more important. I take at least one day a week off, year-round, and I mix things up a bit. Mostly I ride the road, but I also do quite a bit of cyclocross in the fall and winter, and run trails a couple days a week.

I don't have an off-season, and frankly, I don't think anyone my age can afford one. Days off, sure. A relaxing solstice season, definitely, with lots of good food and powerful beverages. But pencil in rides on Thanksgiving, Christmas Day, and New Year's Day to sweat out the gravy. Tyler Hamilton says he takes a month off once the season's over, but he's 32; if I did that, I'd wind up looking like Mr. Creosote from Monty Python's *The Meaning of Life*. It takes too long to get your form back in your late 40s. So it's best to stay on top of your inner fatso.

The most important thing is have fun on the bike. I've seen too many terminally serious types blow themselves right out of the sport trying to ride a young man's training program in middle age. For those getting into the sport for the first time, my advice is to get a decent bike and a proper fit from a local bike shop. Cycling is harder than it

INTERVIEW: PATRICK O'GRADY

looks, and it will be uncomfortable enough at first as your body adjusts to the effort. For the same reason, outfit yourself with a good pair of cycling shorts and a jersey, cycling-specific shoes, gloves, and a helmet. The shorts, shoes, and gloves cushion your three points of contact with the bike—saddle, pedals, and handlebars—and the jersey will wick sweat away from your pipes. The helmet is for when you fall off, which you will. Plan on it.

Second, don't try to do too much too soon, because you'll flame out. Start with short rides, and include at least one day of rest per week, because that's when your body will make its gains. Gradually add duration and intensity to your rides—if you ride ten flat miles on Thursday, go for twelve the next Thursday, or do ten miles on rolling hills. Once a month or so, take a few days off the bike altogether, do a couple of easy recovery rides, maybe try some other form of light exercise to forestall boredom. Then get back after it for another four-week session, gradually increasing your duration (long, steady rides) and intensity (short, harder rides). The coaches call this "Periodization," and there are plenty of books out there to give you the basics. *The Cyclist's Training Bible* by Joe Friel is a good read.

It's tough to fit exercise into a busy day, so don't neglect what my wife calls "exercise moments." Instead of driving to the grocery for that crucial ingredient you're missing for dinner, ride your bike. Ride it to the gym as a warm-up for weight lifting. Leave the car at home one day a week and cycle to work.

Finally, make your cycling habitual, something you do as a matter of course, like brushing your teeth or reading the newspaper. Take it at least as seriously as you do any other sort of basic maintenance—changing the oil in your car, mowing the lawn, whatever. If you have to cut back somewhere, cut back on your TV watching. Unless the Tour de France is on, of course.

Physical exercise greases your mental gears. If I'm struggling with a column or a cartoon, I go out for a ride, and nine times out of ten, all will be revealed. Other forms of meditation, like the Zen Buddhist *zazen*, have proven less fruitful. I still have my cushions, but I do my best *zazen* on a Selle Italia Flite saddle.

BIKE FOR LIFE

11

CYCLING PSYCHOSIS

*Cycling can help stave off depression—or cause it.
Here's how to balance the sport's
psychological highs and lows*

BEING A LIFELONG *back-of-the-pack multisport athlete, I am definitely more tortoise than hare. Oh, I will eventually force my body to the finishing line, though it might occur late at night like at the Hawaii Ironman. So it was after the second frustrating time of being unable to complete La Ruta de los Conquistadores three-day mountain bike race in Costa Rica, in 1998, when I entered a strange, troubling passage in my life. I lost interest in cycling. It became a chore to slip into my bike clothes and pedal up Mt. Tam in Marin County—which literally is my backyard. My motivation had flatted. Depression set in. I grew listless. My quads turned soft. I stopped cycling for months—for the first time in two decades.*

I thought I had sufficiently trained for the '98 race by going on numerous six-hour weekend mountain bike rides. But I was wrong; again I had underestimated the severity of this 250-mile torture test, with its 20,000 feet of climbing and 50 percent rider-incompletion rate. My Bike for Life coauthor Roy Wallack, who finished the race, was more blunt: "Bill, you didn't train hard enough. You didn't care enough." Was he right? Did I set myself up for failure? Were my goals set too high? Had I been self-destructive? Had I overtaxed my stressed-out body? Was my behavior an unconscious surrendering to psychological forces I couldn't precisely fathom? —BK

A generous portion of your brain's 12 billion neurons is being employed as you read this sentence. While the brain is a marvelously complex organ that continues to baffle scientists with its hidden mysteries of chemical reactions and physical properties involving receptors and neurotransmitters, wouldn't it be grand if researchers could isolate and identify all our mood genes? Would this help us better understand our emotions? Why we feel loved or unloved, angry or joyful? Or sad and depressed?

To be human is to feel emotional pain. It's natural and unavoidable. The loss of a loved one, a job setback, or divorce, a bad race, injury, or illness can turn the sunniest disposition into a darkened cloud of doom and gloom. The real trouble begins when this pain begins to intensify, and life's normal challenges become seemingly insurmountable obstacles. One psychiatrist, Dr. John Ratey of Harvard, calls these developments "shadow syndromes" of mental disorders, which can sabotage us by contributing to chronic sadness, obsessiveness, anger outbursts, inability to finish tasks, acute anxiety, stress, diminished productivity, and impaired social situations.

When these shadow syndromes blossom into major or large depression, if left untreated, they can destroy all that one holds dear. They can lay waste to remarkable talent and careers. Like Marco Pantani's.

• THE PIRATE'S PAIN •
Anatomy of Severe Emotional Meltdown

The Italian cyclist's sudden death at the age of 34 shocked the bike world in early 2004. The Pirate, as Pantani was known for his swashbuckling style and bald head, was a national hero, beloved by his countrymen, a demigod and climber without equal, who earned multiple stage wins and overall wins at the Tour de France and Giro D'Italia. His unexpected death in a messy hotel room in the seaside town of Rimini, Italy, didn't make sense to the legions of fans who worshipped his bandana-wearing, piratical ebullience.

The circumstances surrounding his death were poked over and scrutinized by cycling journalists worldwide. Just what happened in that room?

According to *Bicycling* magazine's Web site and other press reports, "Hotel staff said he appeared out of it when he checked in. Marco Pantani was a recluse all week, seen only at odd meals. Hotel staff, apprehensive at best, checked on his room after not having seen him all day Saturday. His half-clothed body was found on the floor. While notes and several pill bottles were found nearby, the medications were entirely legal (mostly low-dose antianxiety and antidepressants) and the notes, while described in the Italian daily *La Repubblica* as 'troubled' were not a suicide letter."

The coroner later reported that Pantani had died from a cocaine overdose. He had been depressed. He was close to 40 pounds over his racing weight of 133 pounds. He had not raced for almost a year. He had even checked in to a clinic to treat depression for two weeks.

Because of recurring drug use allegations, Pantani had been ostracized from the sport that had provided him with an identity and mission in life. The first widely publicized signs of trouble occurred at the 1999 Giro d'Italia during a mandatory drug test. His hematocrit levels bled off the charts—evidence of possible blood doping—and he was subsequently suspended from the race despite wearing the leader's jersey. Publicly humiliated, Pantani kept a low profile until the following year's Tour de France, where he dueled like a buccaneer of the bike with Lance Armstrong in the Alps. It was the pirate versus the gunslinger. His courage catapulted him back into the warm, forgiving graces of the press and fans.

This "good" period wouldn't last; further humiliation awaited him when Italian police raided riders' hotels in 2001 and found insulin syringes. Pantani denied drug use, but the allegations stuck, and once again he withdrew from bike racing in disgrace. He plunged back into a deeper trough of depression. The longer he stayed away from cycling, the worse he felt, too embarrassed to return to the sport where he had forged his recklessly lovable identity. If only he could put his life and racing back together, friends and fans thought. But depression doesn't work that way. Antidepressants don't guarantee automatic success. Nor can you show up on Dr. Phil and get a 30-minute lecture about what you must do to turn your life around. Depression leads a solo life, estranged from the peloton. The sufferer often tries to confront life's headwinds, without assistance.

A note found by Pantani's bed said: "No one has been able to understand me. Not even in cycling, not even in my family. I've ended up alone." He had even pushed away his former teammates. A tragic symmetry brackets Pantani's life and death. Riding up the mountains, he preferred riding solo, in front. Confronting life's downhills, he also rode alone.

What does Pantani's struggle with depression mean for everyday cyclists? Haven't we all experienced those periods in our lives when we felt sluggish, listless, moody? Perhaps an illness or training injury has taken the wind out of our sails. A personal setback like getting sacked at work or a failing marriage or relationship that affects your riding. A lackluster race, a century ride that you couldn't finish, or a constant lessening of your training times can chip away at your confidence. Some are

Antidepressants: Hope in a pill

ONE way to keep depression in check is by taking antidepressant drugs like Prozac, whose use is surprisingly becoming more common among athletes, though few choose to reveal this information. Unlike banned drugs like EPO and steroids, which are designed to illegally improve performance, antidepressants fall in a much different category of merely allowing the athlete to reach a functional level of normalcy. Maybe even to get out of bed in the morning to go on a training ride or visit the gym for a spinning class, or not suffer long periods of sulking and moodiness following a below-average performance at the local triathlon.

The task of chemically altering levels of serotonins through prescribed medication has kept the big pharmaceutical companies busy—and profitable. According to the latest statistics, close to 3 percent of all Americans—that's 19 million—suffer from depression, while 28 million Americans are now taking selective serotonin reuptake inhibitors (SSRIs), which is the particular class of drugs to which Prozac belongs. According to Slate.com science writer Brendan Koerner, "These medications work by slowing the brain's absorption of serotonin, a neurotransmitter that helps control mood. Serotonin is attracted to receptors within the brain, and those receptors contain enzymes that break down—or 'reuptake'—the mood-regulating chemical. SSRIs inhibit the action of those enzymes, so a person taking such a drug experiences a resultant rise in their serotonin levels.

"But serotonin is not the only brain chemical that plays a role in mental well-being," Koerner continues. "Neurochemistry researchers believe that a lack of dopamine or norepinephrine also contributes to depression."

The effectiveness of antidepressants varies with individuals, and it can take up to several weeks before noticeable changes are evident. Which medication to choose is often a function of side effects that can range from low sex drive to insomnia. In March 2004, the Food and Drug Administration asked pharmaceutical companies to revise the warning labels of ten drugs to notify users of the possible risk of suicide. Talk about experiencing unpleasant side effects! Over a decade ago, pharmaceutical firms began marketing newer drugs that work to heighten the brain's supply of dopamine or norepinephrine. These drugs act like atypical antidepressants since they target multiple receptors in the brain. "Antidepressants are pharmacologically specific," observes Elliot Valenstein at the University of Michigan, "but not behaviorally specific. The chemistry of products is ever more specific, but God knows what's really happening in the brain."

"Only about 80 percent of depressed individuals are actually responsive to medication, with about 50 percent responsive to their first, or subsequent medication," says John Greden, director of the Mental Health Research at the University of Michigan. "Plus, there's an 80 percent relapse rate within the year once someone goes off the pills." If drugs like Prozac possess a Lourdes-like aura for their therapeutic powers, we can thank the marketing and public relations folks at the pharmaceutical companies for effective consumer branding.

Belgium's 2000 Olympics silver medalist in mountain biking, Filip Meirhaeghe, trained, raced, and lived through depression. The difference here is that he discussed his problem in the media. Such candor for cyclists is rare. In an interview with Joe Lindsey for Bike.com, the Belgian revealed, "when the [Olympic] race was over, my life was over. I didn't know what to do." Stuck in a depressive rut and unable to train, Meirhaeghe turned to doctors, who prescribed antidepressants. His 2001 season was lackluster, but in 2002, and off the meds, he dodged a psychological bullet and became world champion.

haunted by some kind of internal "fear factor" on the eve of a big race or even in the middle of a ride when you feel like quitting.

These negative feelings may create performance anxiety, stress, insomnia, and even low energy. Yet athletes feel awkward discussing their private feelings. It's almost an unwritten code to stay mute on this topic. It's taboo. A tight-lipped stoicism is required, if not admired, in sports. That overworked, overused adage "no pain, no gain" ignores its hidden counterpart: the mental pain some of us carry inside ourselves, which has nothing whatsoever to do with anaerobic thresholds and lactic-acid buildup.

Why are some people better equipped to handle stress and emotional pain? What effect do emotions have on athletic performance? What roles do biology, lifestyle, training, and environment play in affecting our mental outlook? And what exactly triggers despondency or a depressive episode, a precursor, so to speak, of the Big Meltdown? Furthermore, doesn't staying healthy and active through sports prevent the occurrence of negative feelings and depression? Isn't cycling the ideal antidote to anxiety and despondency?

·

The answer to those questions has led to a fascinating two-way street, which this chapter will now explore:

1. Exercise can have a remarkably positive effect on the mind as well as the body, potentially alleviating even major cases of depression, and . . .
2. Too much exercise, and pressure to exercise, can lead to and exacerbate several psychopathologies, including depression.

We'll look at the positive effects of exercise first, and explore its downside afterward, including therapies to treat or prevent depression.

· EXERCISE IS THE ANSWER ·

It's probably no surprise to hear that exercise can do wonders for the mind as well as the body. "The proof has been accumulating since the 1970s," says Dr. Charles Brown, a certified sports psychologist and triathlete in Charlotte, North Carolina. A 1985 University of Kansas study reported that physically fit subjects handled divorce, death of a loved one, and job layoffs and switching with fewer health problems and symptoms of depression than less-fit counterparts. Studies in Norway showed that military recruits, affected by wintertime depression when stationed in the dark and frigid north, experienced no slump in mood when they participated in sports during off-hours.

A 1999 Duke University study found that exercise and the antidepressant Zoloft relieved depression almost equally—with added self-esteem benefits for the exercisers. "We found that 50 minutes of exercise a week was associated with a 50 percent drop in the risk of being depressed," said psychology professor and study author James Blumenthal, quoted by *New York Times* health and fitness writer Gina Kolata in her book, *Ultimate Fitness.* "People who exercised more had a greater reduction in symptoms," the study stated. Yet due to the lack of a control group, Blumenthal conceded that his study does not quite prove that exercise alleviates symptoms of depression; it remains possible that the test subjects (156 depressed people, aged 50 or older) might have gotten better on their own. "What people really want to know is, can you simply write a prescription for them to exercise rather than take Zoloft?" asked Kolata. "The answer is, he still doesn't know."

But others are more sure about the mood-elevating power of exercise. Richard Friedman at the Cornell Medical School prescribes a mix of medications and exercise. "Patients have little to lose," he told Kolata. "It's never made anyone worse. Most interventions, most medicines, have lots of side effects, but I have never seen a case—ever—where a patient complains that they are more anxious, or more dysphoric after they exercised. Nearly everyone who does it feels better, and no one says anything bad about it."

"One of the first things a clinician should do is get depressed patients on an exercise program," says Robert Thayer, PhD, a California State at Long Beach psychology professor and author of *The Origin of Everyday Mood.* He cites several salubrious effects: "Exercise gives you energy,

BIKE FOR LIFE

whereas depression saps your energy. When energy levels are high, negative thoughts, sadness, and low self-esteem—all components of depression—decrease. Exercise increases metabolism, heart rate, breathing, and decreases muscle tension. The result is a handy sense of calm, well-being, and eventually a zoned-out bliss. And exercise provides a greater sense of efficacy—you can't change your boss, but you can control something in your life."

As for type of exercise, an aerobic sport like cycling seems best. A study by Rod K. Dishman, head of exercise research at the University of Georgia, found that the repetitive, steady, lulling nature of aerobic exercises like running, biking, swimming, or cross-country skiing produces a calming effect.

But how much exercise? At what kind of intensity? For how long? Spinning three times a week at the gym, doing several centuries over the summer, or spending 15 to 20 hours a week training as a competitive amateur rider?

The answer is a personal one, varying among individuals, because it all comes down to listening carefully to your mind and your body, of knowing when to ease off if you can't handle the increasing pressure and stress due to competition or overtraining. It means going easy on yourself if you experience insomnia, fatigue, or are affected by a lingering injury or illness.

What we do know for certain is that it doesn't take much exercise to mitigate mild depression. Dr. Thayer cites studies that found that a brisk five- or ten-minute walk at lunchtime can improve a person's outlook on life as long as a full hour. A 1994 University of Wisconsin study found that depressed women who pedaled an exercise bike for 20 minutes stayed upbeat for as long as four hours afterward.

But we do know that if exercise were all good, top athletes who exercise several hours a day would be the most blissed-out, stress-free people on earth. Many are not; they're stressed-out, prone to illnesses, unhealthy. Here's why.

• THE DOWNSIDE OF EXERCISE •

A sidebar in chapter 1 describes the causes (too much work, too little recovery) and effects (weakness, fatigue, elevated heart rate, frequent illness, insomnia) of overtraining, which is rife in the cycling world. Here we will focus more on the emotional toll that overtraining takes.

"Some athletes' toughest opponents are addictions, eating disorders, and depression," says Dr. Antonia L. Baum of the department of psychiatry at George Washington University Medical Center Washington, D.C., whose study examining the effects of too much exercise on moods was published in the January 2003 edition of Current Psychiatry Online.

"Psychiatric illness in an amateur or professional athlete may arise from coincidence, a predisposing pathology that first attracted the athlete to the arena, or a psychopathology caused by the sport itself. Stressors unique to athletes that may cause, trigger, or worsen psychopathology include pressure to win and constant risk of injury."

"Stress creates a functional imbalance in the brain's chemistry that modifies the way we think, feel, and act," says multisport coach Phil Maffetone, author of *In Fitness and in Health*. "Sometimes the brain may have too much of one type of chemical or not enough of another, altering the 35 or more neurotransmitters that make us feel certain ways: high or low, sleepy or awake, happy or sad, agitated or depressed."

Maffetone, who comes at the issue from a holistic point of view, points out that "mental problems" can happen to anyone, not just those who are inherently unstable. "We should distinguish the mental state from the psychological," he says. "Realize that many athletes struggle with mental distress, but are psychologically stable. If the brain gets distorted, from the chemical effects of diet, nutrition or training, a mental injury may result. The problem is not uncommon in the athletic community, which values overtraining at the expense of personal health. Overtraining frequently is preceded by too much anaerobic work. Increased lactic acid—more specifically, lactate—in the body may provoke depression, anxiety, and phobias. This occurs due to an overstimulation of the adrenal glands (and occurs with the release of endorphins) and an overexcitation of the nervous system.

Too often, Maffetone has seen athletes lose their competitive drive not through physical injury, but through anxiety, phobias, and depression—all of it brought on by training stress heightened by internal and/or external pressures, unwillingness to seek help, and poor diet choices. Below, we'll look at each of these three in detail.

▶ **Poor diet.** "Most neurotransmitters are made from amino acids derived from dietary protein and often influenced by the amount of dietary carbohydrates via the hormone insulin," says Maffetone. "Brain imbalances may be caused by a mismatched diet, a lack or excess of certain nutrients."

Fortunately, with few exceptions, many training problems can be prevented and reversed through a better diet. As an example, Maffetone cites the neurotransmitters serotonin and norepinephrine; a shift toward the former may produce depression.

"Serotonin has a calming, sedating, or depressing effect in the brain, so a high-carbohydrate meal, such as pasta or oatmeal, or eating sweets, results in more serotonin production, a benefit for an overactive person," he says. "On the other hand, those who are a bit low to start may get worse, even to the point of depression. Sweets are traditionally thought of as providing energy, but in actuality they are sedating." (Sometimes, sweets may give the feeling of a pickup, but that is very short-lived.)

By contrast, norepinephrine has a stimulating effect on the brain. "A high-protein meal with little or no carbohydrates will provide the brain with increased norepinephrine levels," says Maffetone. "Therefore, the person who needs a pickup or is depressed could often benefit from more of this brain chemical. An imbalance in serotonin and norepinephrine—with a shift toward the former—may produce depression." For more information about controlling emotions with diet, see the sidebar later in this chapter.

▶ **Lack of professional help.** According to Maffetone, another possible remedy that stressed/depressed cyclists might use to combat mental fatigue and distress is outside counseling help. Unfortunately, he says, the idea of psychological counseling is a difficult choice for many athletes. Unlike a physical ailment such as a sore back or knee that can be treated by a sports medicine doctor or massage therapist, it's doubtful that a competitive cyclist will publicly acknowledge that the black dog of depression is nipping at his heels. He or she might be riding in denial—for years! Imagine the stigma attached to being known as "mentally ill" or "depressed" by sponsors, coaches, teammates, or bike club members. Who wants to wear that kind of yellow jersey? If this sounds unfair, it is. And sports remains one of the last remaining bastions in our society where an open dialogue about depression has no home. (Politics is the other.) Conventional wisdom says "get over it" or "it's all in your head." Ironically, that's the point.

▶ **Pressure to win and injuries.** On top of the dietary issues and physical stress of "normal" overtraining, athletes have "unique stressors that may cause, trigger, or worsen psychopathology," says Dr. Baum. This relentless pressure from coaches, fans, sponsors, and your own expectations, can lead to intense stress.

Using animals instead of people, University of Michigan researcher Juan Lopez arrived at some startling conclusions: "If you stress the hell out of a rat, the rat will have high levels of stress hormones. If you look at his serotonin receptors, they're clearly screwed up by stress. The brain of a highly stressed rat looks very much like the brain of a very depressed rat."

Cycling journalist Joe Lindsay, in a Bike.com report on depression, took this line of inquiry to Dr. Monika Fleshner, a kinesiology professor at the University of Colorado: "Research shows that exercise can improve mental disorders, but also that there's a threshold that, when crossed, causes harm," says the doctor. "When rats were given a wheel to run on, they showed a marked decrease in behavioral symptoms of depression. But when forced to run at certain times of the day and for certain periods of time, stress spiked—dire news for pro athletes, who train and race on a sponsor's or coach's schedule." Add heightened expectations, and stress levels blow though the roof.

That brings us to Bobby Julich, the young American who shocked the bike world with a third-place finish in the 1998 Tour de France. The following year, he crashed in a time trial and broke a bunch of bones. Thus began his decline and erosion of confidence, which lasted five years before he began placing high again in races. In an interview with the *New York Times* during the 2004 Tour, he admitted, "I've had terrible results for four or five years. Once that snowball starts rolling downhill, it's kind of hard to stop. You need a team effort to get that snowball going back up the hill. Now I've got the team." Speaking of the crash, he continued, "I didn't feel secure. It was not only the crash itself but everything that happened after that. I never again could get the energy I had in my body out. I was frustrated, my confidence was blown, I was scared, I was afraid. It was a life-changing experience." But when pressed to explain his newfound strength, he answered, "Let's call [those years] a very unfortunate, untimely interruption."

But that's the past. Julich placed 40th at the Tour, a successful result given that he crashed a few times. And six weeks later, he nabbed a bronze in the time trial at the Athens Olympics.

A Triathlete's Battle with Depression

JUST as depression eludes a 100 percent cure (it's not like mending a broken bone), and may require a blend of pills, counseling, support from friends and family, there are active ways to stem its paralyzing effect, of breaking its tenacious hold. Fortunately, as you have seen from the previous paragraphs, exercise helps—a lot. Consider the roller-coaster history of Sandy Gresko, who was profiled in a 2001 *Triathlete* magazine article originally titled "Ironman, not Prozac," by *Bike for Life*'s Roy Wallack. Following that piece, reproduced in its entirety below, we caught up with Sandy for an update in early 2004. Here's her story.

Sandy Gresko, a 38-year-old lawyer-turned-personal-trainer from Western Springs, Illinois, is clinically depressed. Not momentarily bummed-out or just going through a bad spell, but organically, diagnosed-by-psychiatrists, occasionally-wants-to-kill-herself depressed. Depression has made her life hell. It has wrecked relationships, destroyed a lucrative career, gave her recurrent suicidal tendencies as an adult, sent her to a mental institution, and had her on Prozac for years.

But there is a silver lining.

"It [her condition] got me to where I'm happy—a place most people never find," she says. "And I owe a lot of it to triathlon."

Gresko, who came out of nowhere to win her 35–39 age-group in the Hawaii Ironman in 1998 and 1999, and sixth last year, is not the first person to beat depression with exercise— just one of the most dramatic. Psychologists have known for over a decade that depression can be alleviated with exercise, which raises your levels of natural feel-good neurotransmitters and pain-reducers (i.e., dopamine and endorphins), improves your appearance, and boosts your sense of self-worth, achievement, and control over your life. What's unique about Gresko is that she is pharmaceutical-free, a rarity in clinically depressed patients. She makes a very strong case for the life-changing power of exercise.

As a youth, Gresko didn't know she was clinically depressed, although there were signs. "I'd get really low when the pressures of life seemed overwhelming," she said. "All I knew was that working out made me feel better about myself and my body." Always athletic, she competed on the swim team at her Chicago-area high school and at Northwestern University.

Her first major depression occurred when her athletic safety valve went away: 1985, year one of Notre Dame law school. Although she was an honors student set on a legal career— "I was Type AAA—I wanted to make big money and buy a vacation home for my parents in Hawaii," she says—law school was culture shock.

"The overwhelming studying, the lack of exercise—depression exploded on me. The only way I handled it was to start running," she says. The pattern continued the next few years— deep depression relieved by sports. From 1987 to '89, she turned to triathlon, which she did so well in that she fantasized about turning pro. That lasted until she began working at a high-powered law firm in Newport Beach, California.

All work. No triathlon. Real-world pressures. A broken relationship. In 1990, Gresko became suicidal.

She turned herself in to a hospital. A doctor told her what she instinctively knew: Some chemicals in her brain were slightly amiss. She was clinically, permanently depressed, a lifelong condition. She began taking the antidepressant Prozac.

The next seven years were a rollercoaster. To keep her anxiety in check, Gresko only worked part-time, and saw a psychiatrist once a week for 3½ years. She ran (but didn't do triathlons) to keep in shape, stopped taking Prozac out of fear of its side effects, got engaged, broke up, and moved back to her parent's home in Chicago. By July '97, when her psychiatrist moved and another boyfriend split, she spiraled into depression and was hospitalized.

Enter triathlon, again. Knowing how she'd loved the sport, Gresko's father bought Sandy a new Trek road bike four days before the Chicago Danskin triathlon. She took tenth in her age group.

Ecstatic, Gresko dove back into the tri life. Unfortunately, when the season finale in Muncie ended in October, a new crisis began. "I felt empty, depressed, my focus gone," she said. "I'd steadily improved, but now wanted to die."

She almost did, deliberately overdosing on antidepressants. A last-second 911 call landed her in a state facility for the indigent. "It was like a scene out of *One Flew over the Cuckoo's Nest,* she says, "Crazy people, many just out of prison, screaming and threatening. I lied through my teeth to convince the doctors that I was sane."

Released three weeks later and determined never to return, Gresko committed to two goals to make herself happy: Give up the law for good to become a personal trainer, and try to qualify for the 1998 Hawaii Ironman.

In April of 1998, Gresko became a certified personal trainer. And in October, after winning all five triathlons she entered that summer, she finished the Ironman in 10:39:08, good for first in her age group and 27th woman overall.

And 1999 was even better, in a way. "I learned I could overcome obstacles without slipping into depression," she says. A stress fracture in her hip meant she couldn't run from May to September—but she biked, swam, and discovered water running. The result? Gresko won in 10:13:24, barely missed the age-group record, finished second amateur overall and 27th overall.

"I feel like a guardian angel is watching over me," says Gresko. "There were so many opportunities for me not to be here (i.e., die). I will never be able to be completely depression-free, but I don't think I will ever be back in a hospital again.

"After all, that would screw up my training!"

Follow-up in 2004

If Hollywood ever bought the rights to Sandy's life story, the screenplay would end right here—on a high note. But life isn't always a movie of the week.

While triathlon remained an important aspect in Gresko's life—she continued to excel in the sport, winning All-American honors for several consecutive years—depression ambushed her in 2001. She needed to be hospitalized again. She sat out the entire next racing season. Why the recurrence? Even Sandy is at a loss to fully explain, "Sports has definitely helped me," says Sandy, who got married that year, "but then I got really competitive. If I didn't meet my own high standards, it just added more pressure. I'm an all or nothing person. After winning races, I began to become afraid of losing. I grew fearful. I started to get scared. I was always looking back in a race, instead of ahead."

Blessed with unshakable resilience and fierce willpower, she somehow returned to Ironman training and finished the Hawaii Ironman (2003) in the top half of the field. Then the psychological bottom dropped out for her—yet again. "I kinda felt that the depression was creeping back during my training, so I did all I could to make it to Hawaii. After the race, I mentally crashed. I did nothing for five months." Sandy went back on antidepressants, and only after her self-imposed layoff from all physical activity, she began working out in a boot camp program five hours a week at the local gym. "That's all the exercise I need to be doing," a far cry from the 20-plus hours of weekly training she endured as a triathlete, regularly racking up 200 miles a week on her bike. Seeking to adopt a more delicate lifestyle, she signed up for Spanish classes and joined a book club. "I'm just trying to be normal, to be in the middle. I just want to be happy, because I know I have this predisposition to depression. It's something I was born with. It's something I live with, but working out has definitely helped me feel better about myself. Maybe someday I will start doing triathlons again, but I'm not there yet."

• CONCLUSION •
Your Goal Is to Lower Your Stress

"Illness of the mind is real illness," states Andrew Solomon, who himself suffers from depression and has been hospitalized. "It can have severe effects on the body." One can be experiencing symptoms of depressive tendencies—irregular sleep patterns, changes in appetite, erratic energy levels—without even realizing the underlying root causes. This means one thing: decreased performance—and can affect all types of riding, from racing and touring to those who simply want to do their first century.

Ultimately, the answer comes down to individual preferences—of listening carefully to your mind and your body, of knowing when to back off if you can't handle the increasing pressure and stress due to competition or overtraining. It means going easy on yourself if you experience insomnia, become fatigued, or are plagued by a lingering injury or illness.

Even star riders like Bobby Julich must learn to view problems as temporary setbacks, which take time to resolve. If untimely, unexpected interruptions can plague riders of all abilities and ages, what are the best ways to handle them? The answer: it's an individual choice. On the positive side, a layoff can actually rejuvenate and strengthen you. The body comes back stronger after the taper. Or you may choose to take up walking or swimming to maintain your cardiovascular fitness.

Bottom line: you want to lower the stress in your life, not keep piling it up. Three words are all it takes to keep counterproductive thoughts at bay—*keep biking fun.* "What we all agree upon is the whole

BIKE FOR LIFE

notion of a goal—a diversion from a self-defeating pattern," says Dr. Brown. Match the challenge to your skill level. Don't set such lofty, unrealistic goals that failure is an option. Back off when you need to. An extended layoff can actually rejuvenate and strengthen you. The body comes back stronger after an extended taper given sufficient conditioning. Or you may choose to take up walking or swimming to maintain your cardiovascular fitness if an injury is keeping you from riding.

If you do take a cycling hiatus, however, keep in mind that biking can be addictive like any drug—those damn pleasure-seeking receptors in the brain!—you might even experience minor withdrawal symptoms, like a change in sleeping patterns, by taking an extended bike break. But don't despair. It's not as if you'll need to check into the Betty Ford Clinic or obey the strictures of a 12-step program. You have a much healthier addiction. And it will make time back on the bike all the more enjoyable.

Alternate Therapies to Curb Depression

"**DEPRESSION** is a disease of thought processes and emotions, and if something changes your thought processes and emotions in the correct direction, that qualifies as a recovery," writes Andrew Solomon in *The Noonday Demon*. "Frankly, I think that the best treatment for depression is belief."

By belief, he means hope—because isn't sunny hope a far greater friend than black-hued despair? Judging from the number of available alternative treatments, belief is certainly equated with optimism in curbing emotional pain. Here then are a few popular alternative treatments, but keep in mind this tip from Dr. Richard Friedman: "Exercise is the first step for all my patients. It boosts everyone."

Good Nutrition

You are what you eat. You can help outfox depression by simply altering your diet to modify your brain chemistry in the most appropriate way. Decreasing the amount of sugar and other carbohydrates can help, since both raise the absorption of tryptophan in the brain, which in turn boosts serotonin levels. "If the diet can affect the mental state, then clearly certain nutritional supplements can do the same," says Philip Maffetone. "Taking too many serotonin precursor nutrients, especially when combined with a high carbohydrate diet, may contribute to depression." Carbo-intolerance does not mean stay away from all carbs, but choose those foods that won't cause erratic blood sugar spikes. Caffeine, juice, and sweets (beware of high levels of fructose in energy bars!) may provide those speedy bursts of alertness and energy but should be avoided, since they end up provoking anxiety responses by taxing the adrenals. Depressed people can also have low levels of zinc, vitamin B_6, and chromium. Fish oil, which is rich in B vitamins, helps raise the level of omega-3 fatty acids that are positive mood enhancers.

Eye Movement Therapy (EMDR)

EMDR (Eye Movement Desensitization and Reprocessing) is designed to dislodge trauma-based experiences to lift you out of a particularized depressive fog. Here's how it works, according to Andrew Solomon, who went through a 22-session course and was surprised to learn how rapidly he uncovered long-buried secrets in his brain, including powerful images from his childhood. "The therapist moves his hand at various rates across a field from your right-side peripheral vision to your left-side peripheral vision, so stimulating one eye and then the other. In a variant on the technique, you wear headphones that alternate sounds to stimulate one ear and the other." Basically, what the patient is doing is stimulating a rapid-fire exchange between the left brain (thinking, analytical, verbal, past/future, planning) and the right brain (feeling, intuitive, present, images, in the moment). Combined with psychoanalytical treatment, EDMR, according to Solomon, is a wonderful tool: "I always come out of my EMDR therapist's office reeling (in a good way); and the things I learned have stayed with me and enriched my conscious mind."

Hypnosis

Like EMDR, hypnosis is used to unlock memories from the past, memories that can be emotionally crippling. By reliving those experiences, the patient just might be able to break through to the other side—past the blockage—and reach a resolution. Hypnosis is most effective, according to Michael Yapko, who is the author of several books on depression, if there is a particularly troubling episode in the patient's life, and the goal is to come to a different understanding of that memory. Hypnosis also uses positive imagery to paint a brighter future by discarding negative thought patterns.

St. John's Wort

This shrub is a godsend to northern Europeans who exalt over its ability to lessen anxiety and depression. Ancient Romans even used it for ailments like bladder problems. It is sold as extracts, powder, supplements, or tinctures. How the plant works is still a mystery. Some researchers have zeroed in on one of St. John's Wort's biologically potent substances, hypericum, which is thought to inhibit the reuptake of several neurotransmitters. Because the plant has been endorsed by natural-medicine bigwigs like Andrew Weil, St. John's Wort, though unregulated by the FDA, has a nonthreatening talismanic charm among natural health adherents who believe in the healing power of plants over lab-produced medicines. Despite being a popular remedy, St. John's Wort shouldn't get a 100 percent clean bill of health; it can lead to harmful side effects if used in conjunction with oral contraceptives, beta blockers, and certain cholesterol-lowering drugs.

• EPILOGUE •

Did I ever fully recover from my post–La Ruta mental meltdown? In retrospect, it's clear why I flatted. I overestimated my level of conditioning and foolishly underestimated just how tough the race really is. It's easy to wing a one-day event like a century with minimal training and sufficient prior experience, though your body won't like you the next few days. But you can't fake a three-day mountain bike race. It's too much to ask your body. And an overtaxed body is ill-suited to ward off emotions that rob you of self-esteem. I now saw myself as a quitter for the first time in my life.

It took me five months following La Ruta to get back on my mountain bike for short 90-minute rides. I mixed it up with a lot of hilly trail hiking, but I did not push the personal exhaustion boundaries like before. Other factors played a role in my low mileage. I was still feeling low myself. My father got sick and was diagnosed with Alzheimer's, and for several years, observing his slow demise as the cruel disease wiped away his memory contributed to my own permanent state of sadness. My father had been such a strong supporter of all my wild athletic exploits, such as encouraging me to continue biking across America and not quit after a freak accident in Wisconsin, or of giving me a long-distance phone pep talk on the eve of my first Ironman when I confessed that I didn't think I could finish the swim in the required time (I made the cutoff by almost 30 minutes). During this period that my father disappeared under the fog of dementia, I felt like I too was disappearing; I was stuck in a perpetual state of mourning, waiting for his second death. He died in January 2004 just as Bike for Life was getting under way. His death in a way freed the shackles of the depression that once bound me. I plan on doing extensive bike touring again—up and down the California coast, through the deserts. I will be riding for myself, of course, but thinking always of the inspiration my father provided me. He turbocharged my endorphins. —BK

What's an Endorphin, Anyway?

WE hear and use that term quite a bit to describe that post-workout euphoric rush of happy, pleasant feelings. Many label this experience the "runner's high" (sorry, cyclists). Such feelings are caused by endorphins. Yet endorphins' role in affecting brain chemistry is still not wholly understood despite years of scientific research. Endorphins transmit signals to the brain and help alleviate pain or make you feel pleasure. Eating chocolate does this by releasing endorphins. So do sex and drugs. But how do you measure endorphins? Can they be quantified?

In her book, *Ultimate Fitness, New York Times* health and fitness writer Gina Kolata spoke with several neurologists and researchers looking for clues to endorphins' relationship with exercise and well-being. Surprisingly, she was unable to locate a consensus in her attempt to pry folklore from hard science. There is a kind of holy grail aspect to identifying endorphins.

Research first studied opiate receptors in the brain, since they thought that certain drugs were mirroring a "naturally occurring brain chemical." Solomon Snyder, a neurobiologist at

Johns Hopkins University School of Medicine, and his colleagues were at the forefront of this field in the late 1970s. "All of a sudden, opiate receptors became a popular area," Snyder says. "The chemicals were so new that they that had not even been named." So a committee was formed, and voila—the endorphin was born. While some researchers examined endorphin levels in the blood, noting their rise or fall during exercise, Snyder believed that this was an insignificant line of inquiry. "Endorphins in the blood are irrelevant," he told Kolata.

Huda Akil, an endorphin researcher ar the University of Michigan, agreed with this assessment, telling Kolata, "What people do is they conflate the change in endorphins in the blood with what might be happening in the brain." No one has been able to find direct evidence that endorphins make it from the blood to the brain, because when a person exercises, " a large precursor protein called propiomelancortin is released from the pituitary gland, entering the bloodstream. It travels to the adrenal cortex, the outer layer of the adrenal gland, which cuts it into pieces, one of which is the stress hormone ACTH. Another piece is further cut up into two more fragments, one of which is known as the beta endorphin." But according to Akil, "No one knows for sure what beta endorphin does when it is released into the blood."

One way to measure if these endorphins do make it to the brain is by getting a spinal tap— a painful procedure that would need to take place while the subject is exercising. Bottom line, for Akil, is that the endorphin runner's high is pure speculation, "a total fantasy in the pop culture. . . . While exercise may elicit euphoria in some people some of the time, I think it's really simplistic to make one hormone the heart of it all. I would think it is a cocktail of goodies and that it is probably a delicate mix."

Marla Streb

A PhD IN THE DOWNHILL SCIENCES

It's difficult to imagine a greater bundle of contradictions than champion downhiller Marla Streb, who prefers to take the least direct line—unlike descending—through life. Growing up in Baltimore, Maryland, she trained as a classical pianist, supported herself through college as a cocktail waitress, did her post-graduate work as a research chemist studying oysters and mussels, then discovered the joys of mountain biking in her late 20s after doing the bike relay leg in a local triathlon. She moved out west to La Jolla, California, in her VW microbus named "Indifference," picked up a job in a medical lab testing HIV strains in monkeys, and filled her free time exploring San Diego's sprawling network of canyons, gullies, and hills on her mountain bike.

She soon graduated to racing cross-country and accelerated up the amateur ranks. She looked forward to a potentially lucrative career as a pro rider, until reality in the form of a VO$_2$ Max lab test suggested that genetics can't be fooled. Her coach recommended that because she could never be the fastest cross-country woman biker—her lung capacity for precious oxygen molecules was not high enough—she should rethink her role in the sport. You can't argue with data; Marla knew that from years working in the labs. So she took up downhill racing. And she became increasingly more proficient at taming gravity despite a litany of injuries. In fact, she became celebrated for her starring role in an off-beat television commercial for VO$_2$ Max energy

bar in which she barrels into a tree on a downhill run. "That commercial paid for my house," Marla told Bill Katovsky in her Bike for Life interview in March 2004, before she won the national championship at age 37. Her autobiography, The Life Story of a Downhill Gravity Goddess, opens with this passage: "I used to be a normal woman with a promising career as a research scientist, but a mountain biking bug bit me, and I changed."

I'VE ALWAYS HAD an awkward approach to everything I do, especially forming sentences. For some reason, I abhor predictability. I've broken up with boyfriends because of it. Conforming makes me uncomfortable and weak. That's why I was initially so reluctant to wear sponsors' logos all over my body and look like a "team member." I felt like a sell-out. And in that respect I'm now the Gravity Goddess of Sell-out. But if it can further what I love to do and help with this great act of nonconformity, then I have to concede.

Unlike many women, I am reluctant to get married or commit to a relationship. I often refuse to drive in a car. I'll go to great lengths to get somewhere—hitchhiking, difficult train schedules, dangerous bike routes, etc.—just for the principle. I'll put my life in jeopardy to get there "my way."

Babies frighten me. I sought out the most broke life-partner, Mark, I could find. Guys with money turn me off. Mark doesn't have a bank account or a dime to his name—perfect! I don't smoke pot. Although I own three houses and a 50-foot sailboat, I still sleep in my VW bus or the cold floor of my garage. I prefer to sleep outside alone than stay in a comfortable house with friends.

Of course biking is beneficial to relationships, because it's a stress reliever. I'll go out for a long, painful one after a difficult day, and I come home relaxed. It is a problem though if a couple tries to ride together and they have different riding philosophies. My boyfriend and I will fight bitterly, so we don't go on "rides" together anymore. Just happy, slow commuting after I've already trained that day.

My pride or insecurity is my motivation. I go out on a massive cross-country ride with no food or water and get dreadfully lost and bonk terribly, eventually finding my way back home in the dark. Then I feel much better. If I am ever feeling apathetic, which can happen after eleven years of racing, I don't try to force an aggressive feeling. I just enjoy the moment of being able/paid to ride my bike in the woods on a weekday at a beautiful mountain resort. Then something always kicks in when that start beep goes off and the throttle always opens. Usually a more relaxed downhiller is a faster one. But some people perform better if they think of their competition as the enemy. They think of something that pisses them off. It always worked for [wildman downhiller] Shaun Palmer.

Breaking Ground—and Bones

I HAVE HAD my share of injuries. I've broken my right collarbone five or six times. I broke this mostly during training, a couple times getting hit by cars (one lady gave me her car, a Dhiatsu, for my compensation). This was during my steep learning curve. I finally had a piece of it removed, so now it's collapsible. A collapsible shoulder can be a huge benefit, so I try to fall on that side when I tuck and roll. It literally folds inward on impact. But even if your collarbones are intact, I recommend tucking and bringing your arms into your body and rolling to the side. You want to get as small as possible.

I broke my ankle during the World Cup qualifiers in South Africa. Two hours later I had my mechanic duct-tape my foot to the pedal and I went on to place third in the race.

I broke my arm during practice for a Mammoth Mountain NORBA. This injury was responsible for a 70 percent salary cut the next year.

I've broken several fingers—in training mostly, but no big deal. I usually just race right through these—as with all the other injuries I suppose—and tape my fingers together.

I had a torn thumb ligament, but this happened in high school. The lack of a ligament caused my hand to slip off the bars occasionally. So I voluntarily had my thumb joint fused together so it "hooks" on to the handlebar.

I haven't found any pain more intense than the pain of a scratched cornea. I did this at an IMAX movie shoot, where I poked my eye putting on a street motorcycle racing jacket (from the Velcro of the arm). I crumbled over and couldn't walk for seven hours, my eye spasming while I lost control of all my other bodily functions.

In a qualifier, I crashed and my leg hyperextended behind my head, tearing my hamstring. I continued down the course and crashed and tore it almost completely. This was my second most painful injury ever.

At an X Games winter competition, I impacted an icy jump with my hip at about 50 mph. The bruise lasted for two years, and now I have a small, gelatinous melon-shaped protrusion on my butt. Looks like a nasty saddlebag.

I broke my leg with torn PCL [posterior cruciate ligament] from riding motocross. This was my most expensive injury. I've

BIKE FOR LIFE

had it operated on three times now, and the cadaver graft with complicated bolt system's really holding up!

And I have a shattered ego, which happens frequently in racing and training.

As I get older, the only noticeable change has been a slowdown with recovery from several hard training days strung together. I still have to maintain a higher fitness level than my competition (from what I've read), and this seems to cancel out the slower recovery. Often at the end of the day, my 21-year-old teammate is more beat that I am! Perhaps because I tend to be very mellow, my high-strung younger counterparts get worn out equally.

For the last few years, I've tried to incorporate protein in every meal, even snacks. Seems to starve the craves. I used to eat zero animal flesh, but I got too skinny and kept breaking bones. Now I'm much healthier with vitamins and daily salads. Although I still have a problem with sweets, coffee, and multiple Red Bull vodkas. But that makes me happy and that's what life is about!

In the off-season, my weekly training is: two to three dirt-bike sessions, one BMX/downhill workout, two cross-country rides, lots of road (usually commuting, of which I am a big advocate), gym two to three times, running on the sand dunes two to three times. In season, it's one big cross-country ride, one easy run, four days downhill or mountain cross-training/racing.

The most important thing that mountain biking taught me is that if I can climb a mountain, I can do anything. Mountain biking taught me that I am strong, tough, and brave. That I am never too old. That I like to get dirty and play like a child. It's taught me that guys like women who can beat them at something. That there's a lot more beauty in the world than what you can see from the sidewalk or the driver's-side window.

12

ROLLING RELATIONSHIPS

*Rules for reconciling significant cycling
and significant others*

THE MOMENT THAT *people hear that my wife and I bicycled 600 miles from Monte Carlo to Rome on our honeymoon in 1994, the accusations fly.* "You forced *her into it,*" they charge, contrasting my lifelong cycling obsession with her revulsion of anything more taxing than turning an ignition key. So it's fun to see their jaws drop when Elsa smiles, points to herself, and proudly says, "Wait a minute—it was *my idea.*"

Explanation? Elsa hates riding a bike. But she loved riding a tandem.

In fact, it was her idea that I buy our $3,600 Santana Sovereign. Originally, it was a test bike I'd brought home to review for Bicycle Guide magazine. One ride, however, and she was hooked on tandeming's famed win-win: a fitness fix for me, toned legs for her, and "quality time" for the relationship. Although Santana cut me a deal (hey, I was the editor), it's still the most I've ever spent on a bike. But it paid off. I got the girl.

Today, the Santana is covered with cobwebs, but I tandem more than ever. My bike is a $650 Raleigh Companion. My partner is my son Joey, whose legs perfectly fit on the frame's kid-friendly lowered rear seat. We ride the Raleigh almost every day—to and from his school, up the Back Bay bike path to Newport Beach, on steep local dirt trails, even once on the 38-mile L.A. Fun Ride from Downtown to Hollywood, where he was one of maybe a half-dozen kids among 2,000 riders. It's a great workout for me, and a captive audience for Joe; he talks and asks questions endlessly.

"Why do you love bicycling so much?" he asked me on a ride in August 2004, when he was nine.

"It's brought me many good things," I said, "adventure, health, a career, and . . . you."

"Me? What do you mean?" he asked.

Joey was born exactly nine months to the day his mother and I tandemed into Rome. That led to a discussion of world geography, eggs and sperm, and gestation periods. Soon, he homed in *on the delivery system. "How did the sperm get to the egg . . . did a doctor inject it . . . did you have S-E-X?" he spelled it out, not exactly sure what it entailed. "Uh . . . s-sex, yeah, we did it," I stammered. Detailed questions followed; soon, my future "birds-and-the-bees" lecture was done, way ahead of schedule.*

We looped the Back Bay, stopped to pet a black Lab (Joey loves all dogs), discussed global warming (he is a rabid environmentalist), and headed home at 18 mph (he always asks our speed). A typical day on a tandem, the ultimate relationship vehicle. —RMW

Front side of a T-shirt seen at a Southern California double-century ride: "My wife said if I do one more ultra-endurance cycling event she'll leave me."

Back side of T-shirt: "God, I'll miss her."

•

John Axtell's first wife used to get so mad when he'd go off on all-day or all-weekend rides with his friends that she'd go out to the garage the night before and let the air out of his car tires. That way, he'd be so late meeting his friends that he'd have to ride alone—or, she hoped, not at all. "So I started parking on the street and putting the sprinklers on all night," said Axtell, a 44-year-old wildlife biologist from Minden, Nevada. He began his marriage riding 2,000 miles a year, and ended it 14 months later logging 4,000.

"The problem was that she had no friends in the area, no hobbies, and felt lonely," he said. "I used to joke with friends that my divorce really helped my riding."

•

Cycling can bond you, and cycling can separate you. Axtell's experience will hit home for many. After all, the all-day weekend events, the early-morning rides, the chain lube on the carpet, the travel, the expense, the doctor visits, the all-consuming, round-the-clock focus on the sport, can make the noncycling spouse (often the wife) feel ignored, abandoned, jealous, and angry. We aren't talking about professionals here; their job requires them to work out all day. But for Masters racers, double-century Death Riders, and mountain bike expeditioners—often Type-A personalities working just as intently on their careers—the cycling lifestyle can include little time for TV, a novel, a movie, or a spouse.

But the issue isn't just cyclist/non-cyclist. There can be similar problems even when both spouses ride, due to conflicting cadences. Take Robert and Sandra Hendricksen of Mar Vista, California, both 38, both athletic. Both enjoy mountain biking. But not with each other.

"I hated riding with him," says Sandra. "We'd start off doing the climb to dirt Mulholland at the top of the Santa Monica Mountains, then I wouldn't see him for 45 minutes. Then, when I get to the top, he's impatiently circling at the trail juncture, and says, 'C'mon, let's go, what took you?' Finally, after a couple of months of this, I just exploded, 'I never want to ride with you again!' I think he was relieved—he felt the same way. Cycling together was driving us apart. But cycling apart, we never spend any time together."

No one knows how many relationships are negatively affected by cycling. No studies have been done. But riders talk about it enough for someone to sell T-shirts about it—and for it to be codified as a recognized condition: *the "Cycling Widow Syndrome."*

Although also known as the Cycling *Widower* syndrome if the affected party is the man, CWS is clearly weighted toward women, given that roughly 90 percent of the participation in cycling events is male. (For ease of reading, this chapter will refer to the aggrieved party as female.)

"It's a very real issue for serious cyclists and others involved in endurance activities," says sports psychologist Kate F. Hays, professor at the University of Toronto and coauthor of *You're On! Consulting for Peak Performance.* "How do we go about balancing individual interests with your needs as a couple?

"If you don't try to reach common ground, rigorous cycling training can become an irritant and source of immense frustration to the noncyclists," says Hays. "If you want the relationship to survive, you must take steps to prevent your lives from becoming unconnected parallel lines."

One of those steps may be a tandem. Another may be setting up proper expectations. Another may be "bribing" your forlorn significant other with things he/she desires: jewelry, a new hardwood floor, a trip to Mazatlan, dinner at the Sizzler (if she loves cheap, all-you-can-eat shrimp, that is). Those and many more "Anti–Cycling Widow/Widower" tips are outlined in the lists and true-to-life sidebars included in this chapter. But be beware that those tips might simply be temporary stop-gap measures if taken in isolation.

According to Hays's *You're On!* coauthor Charlie Brown, a Charlotte, North Carolina,

sports psychologist and one of the world's foremost authorities on family therapy as it relates to endurance sports, random Band-Aids may do little to address the deep, long-term fissures that a die-hard athletic lifestyle can impose on a relationship. "But they can work," he says, "if they are used as *part of a systems approach that forces you to pay attention to balance."*

Systems approach. Balance. Swallowing these unfamiliar concepts in one sentence is difficult. But once you understand them, you may gain the ability to true a wobbly cycling-affected relationship and make a good one even smoother.

First, some background: while most marriage and family therapists hail from the "conflict resolution" school of psychology (that is, they identify a problem in a relationship and try to fix it), Brown's background is "systems"—a deeper, more macro view. "It's like being a relationship anthropologist," he says. "You dig down through the layers to see how the culture of the marriage turned those problems into a big deal."

Read that last sentence again slowly. You see, as it turns out, resolving conflicts—such as a wife being mad at her husband for going on six-hour rides every Saturday—is *not* the key to a happy relationship. Conflicts themselves are okay, a part of life. No two people agree on everything. The key to relationship bliss, however, is *not making a big deal out of them.*

"Some of the most compelling research on relationships shows that 69 percent of conflicts in successful relationships are not resolved," says Brown, citing the landmark book *Masters of Marriage vs. Disasters of Marriage,* by frequent "Oprah" guest John Gottman, PhD. "Instead, the couple simply learns how to regulate [lower] the tension of these conflicts."

BIKE FOR LIFE

• AIM FOR A 5-TO-1 RATIO •

Gottman found that successful couples have three things in common:

1. They know a lot about each other—their opinions, their needs, their perspective.
2. They maintain respect/admiration for each other.
3. They maintain a *high ratio* of "emotional deposits" (thoughtful acts) to "emotional withdrawals" (self-centered acts). In fact, the highest predictor of a failed relationship, says Gottman, is a low ratio.

Example: An early-morning, six-hour Saturday ride might be considered an emotional withdrawal to your noncycling spouse. But its negativity can be canceled out somewhat by positive emotional deposits, such as kissing your sleeping wife on the forehead as you leave (she'll notice), bringing in the newspaper and setting it on the table for her, then bringing home her favorite blueberry muffin from Starbucks after the ride, or just telling her you were thinking about something she said as you were riding. Surprisingly, it doesn't matter how small or big (one muffin or a whole box) or expensive or cheap (a new Lexus or a new sheepskin seat cover) the emotional deposits are; if there is a large ratio of them to the emotional withdrawals, the latter are better tolerated, says Gottman.

So, the big questionis, *What is the winning ratio of "good" emotional deposits to "bad" emotional withdrawals?*

Brown found that most men, when asked, think the proper ratio for a good relationship would be at least 2 to 1. Women tend to think the best ratio is 3 to 1.

The correct answer? Gottman found that the magic number is *at least 5 to 1.*

Here's how the math works in practice: "Depending upon the ratio, your significant other may look at the same thing in different ways," says Brown. "Say you walk in from a mountain bike ride tracking dirt on the floor. If you have a good [5 to 1] ratio, your wife will say to herself, 'Poor baby, he was so tired that he forgot to take his shoes off. I'll clean it and bring him a beer.' But if you have a bad ratio, she'll probably blurt, 'Frickin' slob!'"

While there are no known studies of cycling-affected couples, Brown studied the next-closest thing—triathletes. His conclusions, based on a study of 292 responses he received to a questionnaire passed out at three 1995 triathlons and published as "Trials and Tribulations of Triathlons for Twosomes," were startling: 68 percent of the triathletes and 73 percent of triathlete spouses said that *triathlon training had a positive impact on their relationships.* In fact, triathlete family happiness scored higher than the general population, even though the average triathlete in Brown's survey worked out twelve hours a week.

How can this be, when tales of broken triathlon relationships are legion? (See Case Study #8 in this chapter.)

"It may be that we only hear the horror stories," he said. "Yes, there are a core of 'tri-heads' who don't have much balance in their lives. But they aren't the majority."

Brown's study found that triathlon gave the nonathletic partner many opportunities for supportive, affiliated roles—i.e., family nutritionist, race photographer, training-schedule watchdog—that helped make him/her feel like an important part of the enterprise. Clearly, there are many potential emotional deposits at play here: the bonding of a shared experience, respect and admiration for the triathlete, and compensation from the appreciative triathlete. If, for instance, the distance to the race venue is far, triathletes might turn the trip into a family vacation, adding to the emotional payoff.

Is the "Cycling Widow Syndrome" similarly overblown? Even if it only affects a minority, cyclists could clearly improve their relationships by making their family part of their "team." *Bike for Life* saw vivid examples of this at the World Solo 24 Hours of Adrenalin Championship in Whistler, British Columbia, in September 2004. We found that nearly every competitor relied on a deep commitment from family, extending from training to staffing, feeding, and wrenching for 24 hours at the race site. The support was especially striking from nonriding husbands to competitor wives (see Case Studies #5 and #6), wherein the men exhibited a rabid enthusiasm that brought to mind die-hard dads supporting their softball- and soccer-playing daughters.

There's only one problem: 24-hour solos, despite a rapid growth in popularity, are so difficult that no more than a few hundred people a year do them. The Race Across America, arguably another family affair, is annually attempted by a couple of dozen people, max. That contrasts with the tens of thousands of enthusiast cyclists who participate in centuries, double-centuries, benefit rides, and Masters racing—activities that generally require no help from spouses, have no common transition/pit area for interaction or even eye contact, and simply do not involve 24-hour-racing-style bonding, support, appreciation, and emotional deposits. In fact, just the opposite, some might argue. You train for most cycling events alone or with a network of friends outside the family. You drive to these events alone or with friends, and there is very little that family members can share—other than bitterness over being excluded, forgotten, and abandoned. Therefore, unless you're able to figure out a way to turn a century ride into a family event, your relationship might benefit from developing a strategy to counteract cycling's emotional withdrawals. Here's how to raise your ratio.

A RATIO-RAISING PLAN

Cycling is a demanding lover, a black hole of passion with an awesome gravitational pull. It can make you feel great about yourself while it sucks away most of your attention and affection from your family without your realizing it. Saul Miller, PhD, a Vancouver sports psychologist and author of *Sports Psychology for Cyclists,* likes to tell a joke that can quickly help put a cycling-affected relationship into perspective:

A farmer has a prize cow that is not giving milk. The farmer calls an animal doctor, who finds nothing wrong and suggests that he bring in a cow psychologist. The farmer calls a cow shrink, who comes in and talks to the cow privately. After ten minutes, the psychologist emerges from the barn and explains the problem to the farmer: "The cow tells me that you keep pulling her teats but you never tell her that you love her."

Miller chuckles at the punch line. "You think that just coming back in a good mood from a ride means it's good for her, right?" he says. "Wrong. There's got to be more."

Gottman calls it emotional deposits. "You," says Miller, "can simply call it *payback*."

Designing a payback scheme that raises your emotional deposit/withdrawal ratio and saves your cycling and your relationship starts with honesty—with yourself and your partner.

First, if your relationship is worth saving or improving, let your partner know it. "Aretha got it right," says Miller. "R-E-S-P-E-C-T. Show it. Be upfront: 'The first thing is that I love you and want to be in a relationship with you. But keep in mind that as a racer/endurance rider, I need to ride. Are you willing to support me? What can we do?'" This approach immediately works from a PR and practical perspective. Recognizing the problem in itself is an emotional deposit. And since women often consider themselves "relationship experts," says Dr. Hays, putting the ball in their court "engages their expertise in the issue in a positive way."

Keep in mind, however, that superficial "respect" means nothing unless you try to understand the noncyclist's perspective. Look at yourself closely; cycling probably dominates your life a lot more than you think.

"Training triangulates the relationship," says Stu Howard, a psychiatrist and Ironman Triathlon finisher from Cranbrook, British Columbia. "Your passion is seen by the noncyclist as an addiction, like addiction to alcoholism. In fact, it is. Be honest with yourself and call it that."

Like a 12-step program for treating alcoholics, Howard advises that you admit your training program isn't just the time on the road—it's the time talking about it, support activities, looking in the window of bike shops, worrying endlessly about not having the lightest titanium seat post.

"After all, you have to be somewhat obsessive-compulsive to do well in cycling—even competing against yourself," says Howard. "You need to clean your bike, master heart monitor computer downloads, research power meters. On top of that, many cyclists are Type-A people who push themselves, further draining the energy you have to devote to the relationship. It's very hard for serious cyclists or triathletes to do junk training—even though we read that we should take it easy."

If you add up the sheer hours you spend on the sport, on and off the bike, you may begin to understand why your spouse feels her needs aren't being met. "She has limited hours in a day to relate to you," says Howard. "So whereas you gain self-esteem, fitness, and social bonding from cycling, your spouse views it as, 'I'm losing something.'"

She can't get all that missing time back. But a good start to compensating her is by expressing a willingness to compromise. "All relationships on some level are about compromise," says Dr. Hays. "Merely expressing a willingness to compromise is reassurance to the aggrieved party that the relationship is functioning."

Of course, there's a point at which the compromising, the emotional deposits, and the greatest ratios in the world are for naught. "If your significant other isn't sharing some of your passion with you, doesn't understand it, it's more than a minor problem," says Mickie Shapiro, a marriage and family counselor, psychology instructor at UC Irvine, and longtime runner, cyclist, and triathlete. "You aren't sharing a lifestyle."

Shapiro knows of what she speaks. Not long after she got seriously into 10k's, marathons, and cycling back in her early 40s, around 1980, she walked away from a supportive husband and a rock-solid, 21-year marriage that produced four brilliant children. Athletics not only gave her a sense of independence and control that she never had before, she said, but rerouted her from her family's focus on intellectual, academic, and cultural pursuits to a fully athletic lifestyle.

"My husband starting jogging, but it wasn't enough," she says, "I didn't want to go to concerts and plays and read so much anymore—because I wanted to work out." The thought of going to Paris to spend three days in the Louvre held no attraction for her anymore. Flying over to do the Paris marathon, then ducking into the Louvre one afternoon at most—that was where she was coming from.

Shapiro felt no guilt over plunging into a sports lifestyle, and you shouldn't either. Passions that lead to relationship problems are not specific to cycling or endurance sports, and they don't indicate that you are uncaring or unintelligent. In fact, history's smartest bicyclist, Albert Einstein, saw his marriage strained as his stature and obligations increased after 1905, when he wrote four articles that altered physics, including the Theory of Relativity. "I am starved for love," his wife, Mileva, wrote to a friend in 1909. Einstein had sent Mileva a list of conditions that she would need to meet to remain married to him, such as, "You shall make sure . . . that I receive my three meals regularly in my room" and "You are neither to expect intimacy nor reproach me in any way." Albert may have predicted the existence of space-time continuum, but obviously didn't foresee the development of Gottman's 5 to 1 ratio.

Remember John Axtell, whose first marriage—and car tires—went flat? For his next relationship, he went out of his way to find a cyclist. But as his mileage mounted, this girlfriend felt abandoned, too, and she left after two years. Today, Axtell's mileage is up to 8,000 a year, including a 100-miler every Friday and numerous double-centuries. But he gets no grief from his second wife.

"I learned from my previous relationships that I had to make more of an attempt to explain my lifestyle and lay out my schedule," he says. "So she went into this knowing what to expect." Mrs. Axtell II isn't a cyclist, but has a lot of friends and is working on her PhD, so she can find plenty to do on those few weekends a year (14 of them in 2004) when John's out of town. "It's the perfect relationship," he says.

Perfect for him, anyway. Tactics may vary, but a framework of proper expectations, common ground, mutual respect, and a 5 to 1 emotional deposit/withdrawal ratio is a good start for anyone trying to reconcile a cycling lifestyle with the needs of a significant other. Next, check out the dozens of tips, strategies, and case studies outlined in the rest of this chapter. Finding the right mix for your relationship may not come easy, but the payoff can be great.

Ultimately, athletic accomplishments taste that much sweeter when you have someone to share them with. "After all," said former pro triathlete Brad Kearns, whose own marriage barely survived his rocky career, "what if you win your age group and no one's there clapping for you?"

• BRIDGING THE GAP •
Scenarios, Strategies, Tips, and Case Studies

There's no right or wrong in a cycling-stressed relationship—just an inevitability that if both parties are not similarly involved in cycling or related sports, vastly different needs will arise. It is hard for the noncyclist to understand the cyclist's feelings of triumph or pain. It is hard for the cyclist to understand the nonrider's feelings of abandonment. It is impossible to see each other's perspective without an open dialogue. Therefore, this section begins with communication strategies, follows with tried-and-true tips culled from sports psychologists and athletes, and puts it all together in four realistic rider/nonrider scenarios and case studies from riders themselves, giving you a wealth of ideas that you can use to bridge the gap in your own relationship.

COMMUNICATION STRATEGIES

"Communication" sounds cliché, but if you talk the talk, good things happen. In his study "The Trials and Tribulations of Triathloning Twosomes," Dr. Charlie Brown found that a calm one-to-one about the impact of training, without defensiveness, accusations, or time pressures, did wonders for cycling-stressed couples. Merely agreeing that it is stressful helped couples get along better. "Remember," he warns, "training stress causes relationship stress." Here's what a dialogue should accomplish.

Step 1: ***Get your partner on the same page.*** Express the passion, joy, feeling of accomplishment and goals you get from cycling. Over time, make a laundry list: I've lost 38 pounds. I'm proud of my body. I eat healthier. I go to work with more vigor—I see more clients, make more money. This is my window of opportunity to be competitive. I was a nerd in high school and this makes me feel cool. I always wanted to wear tight shorts in public.

Step 2: ***Find out what bothers her about your involvement in cycling.*** She may not mind that you ride all day every Saturday. She may be bothered by the fact that you fall asleep immediately when you come home and she can't tell you about her day. Your problem might be solved by a strong cup of coffee. True, you might get an earful of what you don't want to hear: "You spend more time on that bike than you do with me. You are addicted. I am not a priority for you. I feel abandoned, unneeded. I'm overwhelmed by the kids when you aren't here on weekends. The lawn doesn't get mowed. We don't go out anymore. We don't talk. We don't have enough sex. You don't want to be with me any more. I am supporting you in your goals, but getting nothing in return." But at least she'll feel better getting it off her chest, and a dialogue can begin.

Step 3: ***Set common goals and proper expectations.*** Setting common goals shifts focus to the positive, agreeable aspects of your relationship, rather than the negative. Proper expectations allow the two parties to devise a plan that can reduce the emphasis on cycling's negatives and highlight its positives. (See next section for details.)

• A HODGEPODGE OF • RELATIONSHIP TIPS AND SOLUTIONS FOR CYCLING-AFFECTED COUPLES

Best intentions notwithstanding, you could well fall short of Gottman's 5 to 1 ratio of emotional deposits to emotional withdrawals simply because you don't know the options available. Below, we've outlined two dozen cycling-relationship stressbusters, divided into cyclist's and spouse's responsibilities, that are designed to help you raise your ratio.

THE CYCLIST'S RESPONSIBILITIES

1. **Carve out an important role for the noncyclist:** Ask her to join the steering committee of your bike club, or take a massage class so she can work on your battered legs. This will provide common ground, plug her into a similar social network, and make her feel important to your training and performance.

2. **Try to train or exercise with the noncyclist**: In his triathlon study, Dr. Brown found exercising together to be the most effective coping strategy. If cycling is out, consider crosstraining activities. If cycling separate bikes is out, consider inline skating, running, and even mixing sports. If she rides slow, use her as a pacer as you run.

3. **Try a tandem, but make it fun:** Bill McReady, the founder of Santana tandems, has made a lucrative career out of convincing people that tandems are the best way for a couple of different cycling abilities to secure their relationship—and has hundreds of success stories to prove it. But the noncyclist can lose enthusiasm and drop out if you move too fast and expect too much. Focus on making tandem rides fun, not serious hardcore riding, until the weaker half pushes the pace.

4. **Show appreciation:** If you don't provide some attention to your spouse, she'd have to be a doormat not to get mad. Merely conveying appreciation, such as a simple thank-you ("Geez—I couldn't have gotten my PR without your help"), is a good start. as well as bringing a race T-shirt home for your wife and the neighbors who watched the kids for you. Also, simply ask, "What can I do for you today, sweetheart?" when you get home. It's a statement of appreciation.

5. **Quid pro quo (aka bribery or payback):** Involving your partner in the sport (see #1 above) doesn't always work. Many men love to get away from their woman, love the solitude, love the camaraderie with the guys, the chance to challenge and exhausting themselves. Similarly, many women have no interest in sports. So, if you go do a century ride, be smart: take her out to dinner afterward. If it's a double-century or overnight event, take her to Santa Barbara for a weekend soon thereafter.

6. **Off-season payback:** "I tell pro and top amateur athletes, 'Let your significant other know that you need to be supported,'" says Dr. Ross Goldstein, a San Francisco sports psychologist. "But in the off-season, it's payback time." Basically, you're her slave from October through February.

7. **Beware radical changes in riding quantity:** Don't be surprised when sudden spikes in your mileage create strains. Ramp up the payback before she notices.

8. **Limit hard events:** Monumental events like the eight-day TransAlp Challenge require a tunnel-visioned

BIKE FOR LIFE

focus to do well, but can be unfair to other family members year after year. So compromise; do the event every other year. For smaller events, like double-centuries, limit the compulsion by doing, say, seven races a year instead of ten. Then take the family camping three weekends.

9. **Get home chores done:** If you know in periods of heavy training that the lawn doesn't get mowed, the leaves don't get raked, and the wife gets embarrassed by it, think ahead. "It's not the commitment to fitness that causes family problems," says Dr. Brown, "but whether or not things get taken care of at home." So hire your nephew or the neighborhood kids to do it—you need the help and they need the money.

10. **Ride to family events:** If she wants you to go to her niece's birthday party, don't blow it off because you have a ride that day. Just get up an hour earlier and bike to Chelsea's house.

11. **Train in non-family hours:** Ride early in the mornings, or before the spouse gets home from work. If it's too cold or dark, see next entry . . .

12. **Use a bike trainer**: Yeah, it can be boring. But with a heart rate monitor, a favorite TV program, and no coasting, time flies and you pack double the workout in half the time. Triangle trainers are dirt cheap (some performance models start at $100). Get distracted easily? Pay the big bucks and stay motivated with a CompuTrainer or similar device that measures and graphically displays pulse, watts, cadence, distance, speed, and more.

13. **Make your event a vacation:** You can do cycling events anywhere in the world, so make it someplace she likes. Build a vacation around the Cycle to the Sun hill climb of Mt. Haleakala on Maui, and she'll eagerly help you train.

14. **Reserve special time for the relationship:** Make Wednesday night "Date Night," and stick to it. It'll assure that you get together and function as a couple, regardless of your training schedule.

15. **Stay socially active–individually:** Create stories to share by spending time apart. Make sure you both are developing your own sense of identity.

16. **In the end, do the right thing:** Be fair and move on if you're incompatible. But don't give up relationships—or cycling. Your cycling/relationship problem may be a manifestation of bigger problems. If the relationship is bad, it doesn't matter if it's cycling or playing bridge. In that sense, maybe cycling provides a valuable service by helping put bad relationships out of their misery.

17. **Be straight with the next one:** If you do, the outlook for a new squeeze is probably brighter, since this person will know you only as a cyclist. It may seem ideal to marry a triathlete or someone very athletic, so you can share the passion, the motivation. But beware. Don't dive into a relationship with someone just because he/she is a cyclist. Hard-core cycling may tend to attract addictive personalities.

THE PARTNER'S RESPONSIBILITIES

1. **No name-calling:** Don't pathologize your spouse with labels like "addict," "freak," and "hyper." No one likes to be condemned for an activity they love.

2. **Get with it, gal (or guy):** Fitness and competition is a good thing for body and soul. If you're not physically active, you hurt yourself and the relationship.

3. **Be positive:** Come up with constructive suggestions for ways that your cycling-spouse can get in a workout without wrecking your day.

4. **Share a common goal:** You have a choice: be supportive or antagonistic of his passions. Help your spouse to set and get goals—it'll make you closer. You don't have to ride a bike alongside while your spouse runs around the block, or hand him a special energy drink at the turnaround on race day. But if you stop at Trader Joe's, why not pick up a dozen $.89 Clif Bars in that Carrot Cake flavor he likes?

5. **Develop some hobbies:** You need a feeling of accomplishment, too. What better way to fill eight hours on bike-ride Saturday than learning Chinese, taking a guitar class, joining a book club, volunteering to help teach the homeless interviewing skills, even stamp collecting—or all of the above?

6. **Look on the bright side:** There are several advantages to having a cycling spouse: he's out of the house, can wear shorts at a company picnic without embarrassment, has his time accounted for (just check the training log), is probably a good Type-A provider, has good diet and health habits, and can teach you a nice stretching routine. According to many *Bike for Life* interviewees (see case studies, below), there may be sexual-performance benefits conferred by the high fitness levels.

• STRATEGY •
Four Common
Cycling-Relationship Scenarios

Wonder how to put the above tips together? Here's a strategy from Dr. Kate Hays for resolving the following stressful cycling-relationship scenarios.

SCENARIO 1: Man rides, woman doesn't

1. **Try to engage her in some aspect of your training:** Have her meet you halfway for lunch, and use a tandem for some training.

2. **Get her involved in the sport:** Take her to events. Even take her to the Tour de France (see Case Study #1, below).

3. **Get her riding somehow:** A tandem works—if you start slow and make it fun. Push it too fast, and you risk her hating cycling forever and never trying it again. Take her to a bike shop to buy clothing.

SCENARIO 2: He loves riding, she hates it

1. **Set up a quid pro quo:** Promise to watch the kids on Tuesday and Thursday to balance her watching them all weekend.

2. **Beware developing parallel lives:** Carve out time together, such as dinner on Wednesday nights. Talk it out and plan, as you would a business. Joint problem-solving is important, because it makes the couple feel like a couple.

3. **Bribery:** She allows you the double without causing trouble, so you reward her with tickets to "Les Miserables" and agree to go antiquing with her next Saturday.

SCENARIO 3: Both ride, but one is stronger

1. ***Faster partner uses slower partner for "recovery day" rides:*** Avoid situations where frustration will arise. If you hate waiting for her at the top of hill climbs, stay on the flat beach bike path. Or use the "Rich White double-back method" (see his interview at the end of this chapter): When you arrive at the top of the climb, don't wait—turn around, double back past her, and climb again. That way, you get to ride more. And she thinks you went back to check on her.

2. ***Buy a tandem. Use it for hard rides:*** The stud gets a great workout; the spud gets a thrill ride.

3. ***Train together, but the strong one adds artificial difficulty:*** Pedals with one leg, pushes the weak one up the hills, rides/climbs in too big a gear, pulls a brick-filled baby trailer.

4. ***Split the day:*** Strong one hammers with the club in the morning, then comes back and pedals easily with the weak one in the afternoon.

SCENARIO 4: Woman rides, man doesn't

Men don't tend to want to subordinate themselves unless the woman is a superstar, according to Dr. Hays (see Case Study #6). "That way he can take on an important role—like being her coach. But if she is just in it as an average person, he might not be as amenable." So her best strategy?

1. ***Get the man riding:*** He is likely to have sports somewhere in his past, and may enjoy it. A possible downside, however: the cycling may awaken a macho competitive streak, and they may not enjoy the time together pushing the pace.

• CASE STUDIES •

Every cycling-affected relationship has its own unique spin. The following eight case studies offer valuable real-life lessons about bridging the gap between your significant other and your significant riding.

CASE STUDY #1: The education of a widow-maker

How a cycling psychologist banished the "Cycling Widow Syndrome"

One weekend in late August 2004, Ross E. Goldstein, PhD, made a decision that he says would have surprised him a decade earlier. Not only did the 57-year-old San Francisco psychologist and Masters racer decide not to ride one day, but he decided to do so *without resentment.*

"Both my kids were in soccer tournaments," said Goldstein, who logs 175 to 250 miles per week. "So I simply did what was best for the family, without complaint. But when I was younger and obsessive-compulsive like many riders extremely involved in the sport, I would have sulked. Back then, racing seemed almost incompatible with my relationship. Living from race to race, it's hard to see that anyone or anything else is important. I couldn't tolerate taking a day off."

The result? In 1993, when Goldstein was featured in a superb *Bicycle Guide* article about problematic cycling relationships by Barbara Hanscome, his wife was a classic "cycling widow," clearly resentful of playing second fiddle to his bike racing. The relationship was on thin ice. "It was a problem," says Goldstein.

But with age came wisdom—and a smoother relationship with the missus. "Over the years, I've learned that it is my responsibility to do cycling in a way that it does not negatively impact the family. In other words, I pull my own weight—even though I actually ride more now. I share the driving to soccer games. I'm there rooting on my kids. I spend more time with my wife. If I have to give up a morning ride with my friends, so be it.

"Besides, I've learned that if you give concessions, you get back more in the long run."

A Harvard PhD and author of *Fortysomething: Claiming the Power and the Passion of Your Midlife Years*, Goldstein has spent the bulk of his career analyzing generational trends and consumer behavior. Applying his expertise to cycling, he offers the following tips to those who hope to keep their relationships as healthy as their riding.

1. ***Don't be rigid:*** "Know when to back off. You make yourself crazy and your loved ones angry if you don't make time to be with them at important times," says Goldstein. "I used to train every Saturday and Sunday morning, but my wife felt that I was giving the best hours of the day to cycling. There are times when trying to do both is like pushing a rock up a hill. I solved the weekend problem by getting up early and riding three days during the week."

2. ***Adjust according to your life stage:*** "Look at your life as a series of episodes," says Goldstein. "And fit in as much cycling as is appropriate for the times. When my kids were very young, I actually had to be around more (to watch them). Now that they're teenagers, I actually ride more."

3. ***Think quality, not quantity, in your training:*** Goldstein's shorter weekday rides often more than make up for his longer weekend rides, because he makes them count. "You can get a lot done in 90 minutes if you're focused," he says. "Keep in mind that training programs are guidelines. They don't necessarily have to be followed to the letter to work."

4. ***Don't abuse others' time:*** Give your significant other a reasonable estimate of how long you'll be riding. "If you tell your partner you'll be gone for two hours when you know you'll be gone for four, you insult them," says Goldstein. "They feel as if they've been stood up."

5. ***Negotiate and communicate:*** It doesn't matter if your thing is cycling, golf, or coin collecting, says Goldstein. "Together, negotiate the boundaries. Tell her what you'd like to do and see how it fits with her plans. Don't be stubborn and insist on getting your way all the time. Since I learned to do that, my cycling is no longer an issue."

6. ***It's all about balance:*** "You don't have balance between your cycling and your family all the time," says Goldstein. "But if you recognize it, you can easily get back in balance before your significant other realizes it."

BIKE FOR LIFE

WIDOWS: Read This . . .

Goldstein says the onus for curing a cycling-impacted relationship is not only the man's. Cycling widows, remember this advice:

- ◢ *Don't diss his passion:* Your partner's commitment to cycling may ebb and flow over the years, but for now it is important to his life. He certainly won't give it up and will resent it if you demand this. If you make him choose between you and cycling, you're likely to lose.
- ◢ *Don't nag:* It'll make him happier to ride away from you.
- ◢ *Figure out what bugs you:* Are you upset because you don't spend enough time together, and feel left out and undervalued? Or do you simply want to discuss other things besides cycling? "Most people don't resent their partner's involvement in the sport," says Goldstein. "It's the feeling that they don't matter that bothers them."
- ◢ *Be honest:* Can you cut it? A relationship with a serious cyclist may be too frustrating for you. You might be happier with someone else.

CASE STUDY #2: Bribery, Le Tour, and killer sex

"My cycling was an issue with my first wife," said Mike Miller, a 53-year-old electronics engineer from San Diego. "I biked on-and-off my entire life, but got serious in 1989, when I started hitting 5,000–6,000 miles a year and going on two- to three-week cycling camping trips with a friend of mine. My wife really didn't like those, but they are the cheapest, most fun vacations you can have. In 1992 we went 3,200 miles in 28 days, averaging 114 miles a day, and spent less than $1,000, including the airfare home from Virginia Beach to San Diego. I figured the trips were good for her, too, because I subscribed to the theory that absence makes the heart grow fonder. You're full of joy and energy to see her after a couple of weeks. Still, it was balancing act. The complaining and whining wouldn't stop. She was starting to battle breast cancer, while I was doing double-centuries. I got a lot of flack for doing a 150-mile prep ride on the Saturday before the double.

"My solution to the problem? *Bribe her.* I'd take her out to dinner, flowers, clean up around the house—all the things I wouldn't normally do."

Miller's wife passed away in 2002 after 28 years of marriage. With his second wife, whom he married in the summer of 2004, he reports fewer problems, even though he upped his mileage to 8,000 per year. "That's because I explained my lifestyle to her up front," he says. "She's not into cycling or athletic. But I've done a couple of things to work on her.

"We bought a tandem right after we got married. She loves it. Then I took her to the Tour de France and didn't bring my bike. We'd see the race for 30 seconds going by then watch it that night for an hour on TV. She really got into the excitement. I guess I brainwashed her.

"Still, my wife gets jealous if I spend too much of the weekend cycling. But overall, I think my cycling helps the marriage, since when we're together things are great, and sex is out of this world. My wife jokes about my prowess. And her friends are jealous of my condition. I get a lot of compliments on my looks. I'm 53, have seven grandkids, but look 43. I have only 6 percent body fat.

People are amazed. I lift weights. I don't look like the other cyclists.

"I do tough doubles in 13 hours. I did the 24 Hours of Adrenalin event in Idyllwild with my sister. My most difficult challenge: finding time to ride. I'd cycle a lot more if I wasn't happily married."

CASE STUDY #3: Tandem family affair: Building bonds with the kids

"Relationship" isn't just male-female; it's also parent-child. This story, which ran in the March 1993 issue of Bicycle Guide, *received more positive letters than any other I've ever written. It even affected me. As soon as my son was old enough, I bought a tandem.—RMW*

"Hey, Butt-head," says ten-year-old Kirsten Von Tungeln to her dad, Jim.

Instead of reprimanding his daughter, however, Jim just laughs and replies, "What, brat?" In this case, butt-head is simply a term of endearment between two riding buddies, and it makes perfect sense from Kirsten's view of the world: sitting behind her father for hundreds of hours a year on the stoker seat of their tandem bicycle.

In 1992, Kirsten, a red-haired fourth grader from Irvine, California, became the youngest tandemer to have ever completed the L.A. Wheelmen Grand Tour double-century (in 17 hours and three flats) *and* to have soloed the popular Solvang Century (nine hours)—at age nine. That paved the way for her toothy, blonde-haired sister, Allison, seven. She did her first century at age five on a tandem with their mom, Cindy, and went on to many solos.

Traveling without the girls along was not a consideration for the bike-crazy Von Tungelns, whose garage once housed twelve bikes, including Trek and Nishiki front-suspension mountain bikes, Fuso, Bertoni and Specialized Epic Comp road bikes, and a Mongoose Iboc mountain bike with fenders, slicks, and touring bags, which Jim uses to commute 23 miles to work on every day.

"Hey, in the long run, doing this was cheaper than a babysitter," jokes Jim, pointing to the two Santana tandems with the wooden blocks taped to the rear pedals. "But in truth, I just don't believe in babysitting at all. You need to spend quality time with your kids."

Jim speaks with authority. A 38-year-old teacher of juvenile delinquents, he owns a doctorate in theology and family counseling. "There is no quality time like traveling together," he explains. "No interruptions. No phone calls. No TV. No superficial two-minute conversations after work quickly asking them 'how'd it go at school today?' and getting a clipped 'okay' as a response. It's all about being together, having an open ear, letting them lead. The conversations are on a deeper level.

"It enables you to be a friend to your child, because it's just you and the kids having full, uninterrupted talks for hours."

One long conversation that Jim remembers fondly lasted for one and a half hours during the fall Solvang Century. The girls were so impressed with the beautiful green hills and rolling pastoral countryside between Solvang and Santa Maria that they repeatedly asked, "Why don't we buy a home and move up here?"

"That gave me a chance to explain a little about economics," recalls Jim. "I told them, 'there are no jobs up here—that's why no one lives up here.'" Kirsten and Allison asked questions on the subject of their parents' occupations—Cindy is a nurse—for the next 30 miles.

Riding teaches them a lot more, too. Jim ticks off self-confidence, knowledge of time and distance, understanding of grades—as in steepness, not report cards—and even food and diet.

"When we say the ride is 30 miles long, they immediately know that's about one and a half hours," says Jim. "When we say nine percent grade, they groan. And when we go shopping, they automatically read the nutritional labels and figure out how much fat and carbohydrates are in it."

Not surprisingly, the girls' favorite food and drink are PowerBars and Cytomax. They are exceptionally fit, says Jim, and quite knowledgeable about regional terrain and sights.

Allison's favorite place is the Back Bay of Newport Beach, an ecologically protected area the family rides through on one of their 50-mile Saturday loops. "We always stop and see the ducks," she says. "They are so beautiful."

Kirsten's favorite moment of her life came when she and her dad went for a long ride on a densely foggy day, then struggled up an 8 percent grade in nearby Dana Point harbor. "When we got to the top, we all of a sudden popped through the fog into bright, bright sunlight and pure, blue sky," she remembers. Father and daughter just stood together speechless for ten minutes looking at the stunning carpet of fog over the Pacific Ocean.

The funniest moment for the Von Tungelns came on a 350-mile biking vacation they took last Easter vacation to Borrego Springs, in the desert east of San Diego. "Little did we know that we had to climb up Montezuma's Grade—12 miles at an 8 percent slope," says Cindy. "It took Allison and I four hours. During that time, someone called the sheriff's department and told them that some crazy lady was climbing up the hill with a baby."

Speaking of crazy, Kirsten's friends at school don't know what to make of her hobby. "They think I'm weird," she says. "Half the time, they don't believe me." Sometimes, Jim says that Kirsten, an "A" student and acknowledged teacher's pet, gets a little depressed by her classmates' taunts and talks about giving up bicycling to concentrate on her flag football, roller-skating, Junior Brownies, and peer tutoring, where she helps teach the special-ed kids. But even though her parents don't push her, Kirsten keeps on stoking. "Sometimes when I ride I feel so good I could just ride 5,000 miles," she says. Her goal for 1993 is to do another solo century: the mountainous Ride Around the Bear from the desert floor to Big Bear and back. (She wanted to do it on a new bike, Klein's diminutive "Kirsten" model, and was disappointed when told that Klein changed the name of the bike to the sexually neutral "Panache" to attract small male riders. Luckily, Gary Klein says he has a few Kirsten stickers left over.)

The family's next goal together will come this summer [1993]: to San Francisco and back on the tandems—three weeks and 1,000 miles. The girls shake their heads and say in grade-school parlance, "I don't *think* so."

But they'll surely be there on Highway 1, singing their old standard, "99 Bottles of Beer on the Wall" and telling the corny elementary school jokes that have been passed down through the generations. "Why did Santa Claus have only seven reindeer?" asks Kirsten. "Because Comet stayed home to clean the sink." "What did the fox say to the owl?" challenges Allison. "Howl you doin'?"

And then it's Jim's turn to chime in—and teach his kids a little about the real world at the same time. "What animals can open an IRA?" After a brief discussion of tax-deferred retirement plans, Jim finally gives the answer: "A deer, because it has a buck. And a skunk, because it has a scent."

Epilogue

Eleven years later, we followed up with the Von Tungelns.

"When you have kids, most people drop out of cycling," said Cindy Von Tungeln in October 2004. "People feel awkard taking their kids to events, as we did. But they shouldn't. My kids got a number of benefits: they have no fear of talking to adults, who treated them as peers on those rides. They became star basketball players in junior high, high school, and college due to their strong legs and lungs. They learned to never give up when it gets tough, like in the last 50 miles of a double-century or the last five minutes of the fourth quarter. And we have some great memories of riding down the coast from Seattle to San Diego over three summers."

The Von Tungeln girls, as their parents expected, "did their own thing" and dropped out of cycling when junior high activities took precedence, but not before the family racked up an amazing 93 double-centuries between them.

Cindy finished the California Triple Crown series (at least three double-centuries in a year) six consecutive years (1992 to 1997), oldest daughter, Kirsten, finished it five times (1993 to 1997), and younger daughter, Allison, won the coveted T-shirt three times (1995 to 1997). Jim, a two-time president of the Orange County Wheelmen, was the first person

inducted into the Triple Crown Hall of Fame, rode a career total of 50 double-centuries, completed the series every year from 1990 to 1998, including all 11 of the 1997 events, completed Paris-Brest-Paris (750 miles with 31,000 feet of climbing) twice, and is one of two people to have completed the L.A. Wheelmen Highland Quad Century of the Grand Tour (400 miles in 24 hours) four times.

Unfortunately, all the riding affected Jim's health and his relationship. Injuring and reinjuring the nerves in his hip when he refused to rest, he underwent five operations and had to give up cycling in 1999. "The pain was 24-7," said Cindy. With Jim unable to bike, and his source of achievement gone, the marriage became stressed. The Von Tungelns' divorce became final in 2003.

Tandem Gear

The Von Tungelns used two adult tandems with wooden blocks on the pedals to accommodate their kid's legs, but the market now offers a few dedicated kid-friendly tandems with lowered stoker seats. (Incidentally, these telescope up to accommodate an adult, too, so they can be used by a couple.) Models include:

1. Raleigh Companion ($680; uses 26-inch mountain bike wheels)
2. Bike Friday Family Tandem ($1,000; uses 20-inch wheels and folds up for easy transport)
3. Co-Motion Periscope ($3,600; mountain bike wheels; fits into an airline-legal suitcase due to four take-apart couplings)

A less expensive way to get the tandem experience is by using one-wheel attach-a-bikes, made by Adams, Burley, and Trek, that connect to the adult bike. The least expensive option (which I used with my son from age four to seven) is an ingenious telescoping tow-bar called the Trail Gator ($89; www.trail-gator.com), which attaches the headtube of the kid's regular bike to the adult's seat tube in ten seconds. It lifts the front wheel of the kids' bike three inches off the ground, giving the "captain" (front rider) complete steering control while allowing the "stoker" to contribute real pedal power.

CASE STUDY #4: Get a sugar momma

Dan Cain, a 46-year-old bicycle retailer and consultant from Borrego Springs, California, has advice for any man who dreams of riding as much as he wants—even to the point of giving up work to ride: "Fall in love with an independent woman who makes a lot of money," he says. "That's usually an older woman."

Living a cycling fanatic's fantasy life in this mountain community south of Palm Springs, Cain is essentially a kept man happily supported by a woman with a full-time career. "Jody's the breadwinner," says Cain. "She lets me ride 20 to 30 hours a week, race every other weekend. She's my Sugar Momma."

She's also his second wife. The first one, a state parks worker who Cain was married to from 1990 to 1994, "wasn't as permissive of my time," he says. She bailed when he refused to buy a house. The couple had been living cheaply in a state park property.

"I was already working full-time at my bike shop, which I founded in 1985 hoping to combine business and pleasure," he said. "Trouble is, there wasn't enough pleasure. I only had time for one all-day

ride and a half-day ride a week. I didn't want to work more." No more revenue, no house, no more marriage. Cain didn't look back.

Fortunately, he later found a woman who could take care of her own material needs. "Jody, very attractive, five years older than me, no kids, a runner, a well-to-do investment-relations writer, came into my shop one day and I ended up taking her on a tandem ride," says Cain. More rides led to marriage and to a big, beautiful house she bought in Borrego Springs in 2002. With her permission, Cain closed the shop he'd run full-time for 14 years, moved it into his garage as a part-time operation, and dramatically ratcheted up his cycling. During the week, when Jody lives 150 miles away in an apartment in Los Angeles and commutes to work, Cain rides up to 30 hours per week. He races every other week, including three team and one solo 24-hour race in 2004. He finished top Masters and fourth overall at the 24 Hours of Temecula. At all other times, he's with Jody—fit, attentive, eagerly providing her with what he calls "endless sexual pleasure."

Ironically, Cain and Jody don't ride the tandem anymore. "She took one too many falls, and she's such an independent-thinking woman that she actually doesn't like being on the back of a tandem too much," he says. He rides alone for the most part, except when ex-Yeti pro Russel Worley comes out to visit.

Does Cain mind that he might be called a "trophy husband?" "Hey, I get my freedom to ride and she gets her city ya-yas out and a fit man happy to see her," he says. "We both get what we want out of our situation. Isn't that the definition of a good relationship?"

CASE STUDY #5: The lady and the guinea pig

"We need to start exercising."

Tammy Darke said "we" because she was too nice a girl to say "you." The registered dietician from Mission Viejo, California, then 27, was a triathlete and marathoner, with boxes full of medals. Her husband, Mark, was fat, plain-and-simple. What else could you call 210 pounds on a 5-foot-9 frame? "I was resentful," said the audio-video shop owner, then 32. "But I immediately started thinking, 'Now, which of the sports that she does is the coolest?'"

It was mountain biking. But that would have to wait six months. You see, it took that long for the man that Tammy now refers to as "my guinea pig" to slowly work himself into shape. The step-by-step plan they laid out together called for walking, then jogging, then running, but no biking until Mark hit a threshold—185 pounds. On that joyous day in early spring 1997, he, Tammy, and mutual friend Tony picked up a new Raleigh M600 hard-tail at Sports Chalet and headed to Aliso Woods Park in Laguna Beach. Then wife and friend patted Mark on the back, left him at the bottom, and rode off up the steep hillsides of the Cholla Trail for two hours.

"After three months, I climbed Cholla," said Mark. "After a year, I finally rode with my wife. That was a cool day. For the first time, I could actually say, 'I'm a mountain biker.'"

After three years, the mountain biker was riding a dual-suspension Rocky Mountain Element and out-riding his wife. At his urging, they entered a team in the 2000 24 Hours of Adrenalin relay race at Idyllwild, California. Their team, "The Chick and 4 Nuts," enjoyed the round-the-clock scene so much that they did four more races, once winning the co-ed division. Then Tammy broke up the team.

"I'm not getting enough laps," she told her husband in 2003. "I wanna do a solo."

Today, the former fat man is the pit crew of the woman who nurtured him to fitness. Tammy took second at the 2003 Idyllwild solo. She qualified for the 2004 world's in Whistler, British Columbia, where *Bike for Life* met her. She took 12th place.

The Darkes weren't satisfied. "We're in this together," said Mark, "and we're going to train harder next time." This time, of course, "we" really means both of them.

CASE STUDY #6: Twenty-four hours of love

In 1993, after a year of marriage, Barbara and Bill Kreisle were stressed out. As a social worker, she'd bring home depressing stories from her job. As an oncologist treating terminal cancer patients, he'd carry home the weight of the world. "I knew we had to do something fun, something fit, to bring happiness into our lives," said Barbara. "We had no money. But we did have two old bikes in the garage. The guy at the bike shop said, 'Try mountain biking. Lotta good trails here in Phoenix.'"

That changed everything.

Barbara, never athletic, immediately discovered that she was a good rider. So good that the guy at the shop said, "Why don't you race?" By 1995, she was on the podium. By 2000, she turned pro. And after a few years, Bill, who had enjoyed riding with her, began to say, "Hey, there's more to life than mountain biking."

That's when it hit Barbara: "Our mountain biking was all about me-me-me—so I became more supportive of his needs," she said. "It seemed unfair that I had a very happy lifestyle while he's holding people's hands in death, that he needed to get out and pursue his own hobbies. So I take the boys [their two sons], and urge Bill to go do his fly-fishing, his skiing, his backpacking."

When the family moved to Boise, Idaho, Barbara discovered round-the-clock racing. While on a vacation, she and Bill flew to England's biggest 24-hour race, the Red Bull Rampage . She competed in the 2003 World Solo 24 Hours of Adrenalin Championships at Whistler in 2003, taking 18th place. She and Bill went back again to B.C. in 2004, where *Bike for Life* ran in to her husband manning the pits.

"We ride together once a week, and I keep up with her," said Bill. "I know her friends. I'm in the network. But I'm really happiest in this role—as her manager."

"Bottom line? I'm happy if my wife's happy. And she's happiest on a bike."

CASE STUDY #7: The 60s: turn on, tune in, roll on

As Capitol Hill politicians endlessly debate the future of Social Security, some of us like to take matters of active retirement into our own private hands. Like retired health-care public relations and marketing manager Ginny Champion, 61, and her husband Jim Bonner, 63, a former mechanical engineer, who bike-toured coast-to-coast in 2003. Starting out in Portland, Oregon, the Flemington, New Jersey, couple carried all their own gear, averaged 50 miles per day, and pedaled 5,000 hard-earned miles. Now the hard part—ten questions with *Bike for Life*.

1. **Why do it?**

    Ginny Champion: This was Jim's dream, which he accomplished solo twenty years ago and always wanted me to do. My 60th birthday was the deciding factor. I wanted the challenge. Another factor was the encouragement of people in our bike club, including a 76-year-old woman who made the trip when she was 60.

2. **How'd he sell it?**

    GC: I have always enjoyed cycling, but was not sure I could or would want to cycle long distances for days at a time. It took several years of cycling with Jim, a high-performance bicycle, a 650-mile trip from Montreal to New Jersey, and a few weeklong trips before I felt comfortable on the bike and confident of my abilities. Jim's patience and encouragement have been key. Once we both retired we had the time to cycle frequently; cycling for health and for fun became our new "job." It has been a great way to be together, travel, and enjoy our leisure time.

3. **The preparation?**

    Jim Bonner: Ride, ride, ride. We did not train with packs, however. We have been riding more than 5,000 miles a year since we retired a few years ago.

4. **The best part?**

    GC: The friendliness and kindness of people, many of whom invited us to stay with them or share a meal. Secondly, the grandeur of our country, from the mountains to the plains. A stretch along the TransAmerica bike trail through Idaho and into Montana was a scenic highlight.

5. **The worst part?**

    GC: Jim had no bad days. What a partner! However, I was discouraged by the hot, humid, hilly Ozarks of Missouri.

6. **How about your health?**

    JB: We had few rest days but we traveled only 50 miles a day, so we had time each day off our bikes to rest and relax. We focused on eating well (though each of us lost over 15 pounds) and keeping hydrated. In general, we felt good throughout our trip. In a previous cross-country trip, I had some problems with sore feet, saddle sores, and numb hands. I attribute my comfort on this trip to Shimano sandals, a Brooks leather saddle, and a better fitting bike. Knowing how to pace ourselves also made a difference.

7. *Describe your gear.*

JB: We took matched Trek 520s to reduce the number of spare parts we had to carry. We also used the best heavy-duty wheels available. These wheels consisted of Phil Wood hubs, Mavic T520 rims, and Continental Top Touring 2000 tires (700 × 37). We each carried an extra tire and a few tubes, but we only had one flat. I think if we switched the tires from front to back, we could get another 5,000 miles out of them. We used mountain bike gearing with triple chain-rings and Arkel panniers (and a pair of old Cannondale panniers).

8. *Any effect on the relationship?*

GC: Cycling together has brought us closer, more patient, and caring of one another. We are fortunate, I think, that we have found an activity that we both enjoy and can do together. Regarding our trip across the U.S., I know Jim understood that the trip would be a challenge for me and that I would have some tough times, since he had made the trip himself 20 years ago. He was consistently patient, encouraging, and I think he was proud of me.

9. *Any fights on the trip?*

GC: We never had a major disagreement. We had worked out a lot of issues before we left, for example, how far we would go each day, that we expected to have "bad" days, or how we would spend the time when we were not riding. We were both excited to be making the trip and understood that what we would gain would be greater than any inconvenience or problem. We looked forward to an adventure.

10. *How about some advice?*

GC: Ride together; take a several-day trip together; be open to one another, to people you meet, and things that happen along the way.

JB: Keep in mind that a long trip should not be a race. If it becomes one, then not enough time was allotted and anxiety may lead to short tempers. Always remember that you are doing the trip together. You are doing it as a team of two. Either you both succeed or you both fail. If one person has a problem, then the team has a problem.

CASE STUDY #8: Triathlon relationships: And you thought cycling was tough

When Denise Berger of Mission Viejo, California, then 39, arrived home from the 1992 world duathlon championships in Frankfurt, Germany, with the 35–39 age group bronze medal around her neck, her husband of two years, Tim, excitedly congratulated her. That seemed strange, since he'd grown increasingly antagonistic toward her devotion to racing and training. But it soon made sense.

"Now that you've won a medal, this is it—no more training, right?" he asked, hopefully.

"Absolutely not!" Berger responded, flabbergasted. "This is who I am. I've been athletic my whole life—and into this sport way before I met you. Give it up? I want more medals!"

Tim took off his wedding ring and threw it at her, then stormed out the door. Five years together gone forever. Another multisport relationship kaput.

If dedicated cyclists think they've got a hard time balancing their sport and their relationships, how about training for *three* sports? No one actually knows if the triathlete divorce rate is any greater than that of the general population, but speculation is rife. "It seems like it's astronomical," says Triathlon USA deputy director Tim Yount, who talks to American triathletes and duathletes at dozens of races all over the world. "When I go to events, I inevitably hear, 'Oh, her? That didn't work out.'"

The worst imbalances of all may involve those trying to qualify for the Hawaii Ironman, composed of a 2.4-mile swim, 112-mile bike, and 26.2 mile run. "Like cycling, triathlon triangulates a relationship, but Ironman is worse," says Canadian psychiatrist Stu Howard, a two-time Hawaii finisher. "Ironman can be like an addiction, like alcoholism."

Like an addiction, Ironman training can go on for years. "Once you go to Hawaii, you gotta go back," says Ray Campeau, 43, a New Jersey apartment owner who made it to Kona by lottery in 1998. "I chose Ironman training over my marriage," he said. His wife had left him a year earlier after he rebuffed her ultimatum to cut back on his heavy training,

"It's like a drug—it takes over your life," Campeau says. "You can throttle back on

triathlon if you do the shorter distances, but if you get the Hawaii bug, you're screwed."

Bruce Buchanan, a dentist-turned-personal-trainer from Fernandina Beach, Florida, clearly explained the role triathlon played in his life when he married his second wife. She was proud and supportive of him when he swept the 50–55 age group in 1991, 1992, and 1993. Then, after five years together, they got divorced. The problem was typical: "I didn't make her feel like a priority," says Buchanan. "You get tunnel vision and self-centered training for Ironman. I wouldn't let anything interfere with it—except my dental work. Not her."

Proving that old dogs can learn new tricks, however, Buchanan made amends with his third wife, Lee. "I realized from the previous marriages that you must always put your spouse first," he says. "That's critical for saving the relationship." He now gives up training time for Lee, her projects, and cultural events. He will skip a swim practice to go to a movie with her, or a run to go to dinner. He found that his small sacrifice not only makes her feel important, but does not impact his performance. He won his age group again in 1999, 2001, and 2002, the latter in a new 60–65 age-group record.

"In your first year of Ironman, you can get away with being obsessed," says Buchanan. "But after that, you can't expect her to be the only one making sacrifices. Besides, triathletes probably need the time off anyway, since we all train more than we need to."

There's an ah-ha moment: the smart triathlete or cyclist doesn't look at time with his spouse as a skipped training session. He just views it as recovery time.

Rich White

THE REVEREND

Manufacturers may think they gain new converts by advertising in magazines aimed at cologne abusers from Manhattan. In truth, people get into mountain biking the way they get into anything: word of mouth. And when it comes to riding, Rich White just won't shut up.

—Rob Story, Bike magazine, 1997

We all know a Rich White—the guy who makes the calls, maps the route, introduces new people to the sport, makes the ride happen, keeps the tradition alive. But for those people in Southern California and in the bike industry lucky enough to have met him, there is only one Rich "The Reverend" White—our own personal cycling celebrity, a superb athlete with a Bruce Lee body, the outsized personality of a comedian/late-night talk show host, and the blunt, commonsense wisdom of your neighborhood's most grizzled old granddad.

Rich, variously a bike shop manager/salesman/mechanic, manufacturer marketing manager, and occasional freelance writer, owns no property and few possessions—except bikes. He lives and breathes mountain biking—all cycling, actually. His passionate pontificating about all things—music and history and culture and books, but especially cycling—earns him sizeable real estate in any conversation and press from any magazine editor within earshot. I've written stories about Rich and because of Rich. When I want to ride somewhere local or international, he's the guy I want along. Rob Story, one of the finest sports/adventure writers of this era, called Rich "the head cheerleader for mountain biking's 40-million member team." He titled the column about Rich excerpted above "The Reverend," and the name stuck.

A customer walks into the shop. "I'm looking for something with a RockShox and costs no more than $800," he says.

"OK," Rich says, "but what do you wanna do with it?"

"Umm . . ." he ponders.

"Well," says Rich, "next weekend I'm hitting this buff single-track that drops 3,500 vertical feet through four different climate zones. Last time, I couldn't believe how cool that view was, when we were on top of the mountain looking down on the clouds as the sunset turned them red. Does that sound like something you'd do? 'Cuz you're welcome to join us if you want."

In no time the shopper's wheeling a $1,500 bike out the door. Whether he rides with Rich depends only on his motivation. But the offer's genuine. Rich White, like Barry White, always wants to spread the love.

—Rob Story

As you'll see in this Bike for Life interview conducted on December 15, 2004, Rich was on the wrong path in life until the day he found cycling, and it changed him. That was a good day for all of us. —RMW

ME? BEING INTERVIEWED along with the likes of Gary Fisher, John Howard, Mike Sinyard, Ned, Missy—such an esteemed list of heroes and dignitaries? Unbelievable. First, my picture on a magazine cover [Bicycle Guide, 1993], next a story about me [*Bike,* 1997], then a few bylines, then crossing the Alps by mountain bike, and now this. In the Library of Congress forever. Pretty good for a guy who hasn't accomplished anything, really, except wake up every morning and shout to the world, "I love riding my bike!"

I was born in 1959, but my life actually began in 1984, on the day I won a bike in a poker game. I wouldn't have believed it at the time if someone had told me that that bike—a Raleigh Traveler, a 21-inch steel road bike, way too tall for me—would change my life. Get me out of an unhealthy lifestyle into a healthy one. But it did.

At that time, I was all about entertainment. Sex and drugs and rock 'n roll. I was into going to Hollywood and seeing bands and being around nightclubs. After I got out of high school, if I'd had a business card it might have said "part-time gambler, nightclub host, nightclub security, concert security." I was a regular in Vegas at the Dunes poker table and I had a regular game at my house three times a week. You could sit in with 50 bucks. Also, we were into fighting—because that's what we did at our nightclub, as security guards. Scrawny guy like me, I wasn't the bouncer, I was more of a host-diplomat. That means I had the mouth; I was the guy who talked guys out of fighting. I patrolled the line outside to make sure the pretty girls got inside. I don't have a black belt, nothing. What I had was a bunch of big guys kick my ass all the time and teach me how to keep them from doing that.

I worked the L.A. Olympics for two weeks in 1984 as a trained observer. I was paid to walk around just observing people, because they thought there was going to be terrorist activity. I was actually working out at the area where they had the cycling events, and I got into watching it. It was a couple days later when I won the bike in a poker game. A guy owed me money and didn't have it, so I just took the bike and rode it until he paid me, and he never did.

Immediately, I found that I just liked the feeling of riding, traveling from A to B, human-powered. I'd forgotten that I rode as a kid—a lot, actually. I used to ride my bike 17 miles to school without my parents knowing it. I lived in Carson, but I went to this Christian school in Harbor City, down by San Pedro. I'd sneak my bike out of the shed, skip the bus and ride my bike. But I didn't consider myself a cyclist. I just didn't want to take the bus; I wanted the freedom. I never thought about it as something to compete with or ride for pleasure. But now that I had a bike again, that big-mileage gene kicked in. I was living in Downey and I'd ride that beat-up old Traveler down the riverbed to the beach and back—40 miles or so. One day, about a month after the poker game, I ran into a friend who I didn't know rode. He was all surprised, and said, "Man, I got to get you a better bike." And he got me a Raleigh USA bike, just like the ones they rode in the Olympics.

I just totally fell in love with it. I instantly knew that that was me. I was addicted. Because I worked at night in a nightclub, I had free time to ride all day.

Before the bike, I hung out by the pool all day and hit on all the strippers getting tanned. I actually married a stripper—in '83, I think. Beautiful Chinese girl with big fake hooters. I met her before I got into cycling. Lilly. After she married me, it was Lilly White, which always got a laugh. But she stuck with me, even when I went to jail five years later. . . .

Why did I go to jail? Because I got involved in the most popular industry of

BIKE FOR LIFE

the '80s—selling drugs. I worked in a nightclub, where you can make money being a bartender—or a . . . *facilitator*. Money's coming in, money's going out, all the time. Rock 'n roll, gambling, and drugs.

It wasn't prison. It was just jail. Only did five months, but I say a year. I got a job in the jail school. I helped everybody write letters home to their family and friends. I used my diplomatic skills to get along with everyone—all the various races and factions. Once it was over, all I knew was that I never wanted to do anything again that got in the way of cycling.

Jail had a significant impact on me. It was an exit gate from one life and an entry gate to another. I did what I had to do. I paid for it, and I moved on. I knew that I didn't want to do that anymore. I didn't think I necessarily had to do cycling to keep me away from my old life, I just liked it enough to where I didn't want that old life. That's the whole thing about the "Reverend" deal. It's pretty easy to preach cycling when it saved me from the purely low-goals life. I could have done other things for a living I guess, but I didn't have anything that I liked more than that. I had options, I just didn't know what they were. Everyone has options; that doesn't mean you want to take 'em. If people are out there having problems, and they don't go out and find what's them, they're just flailing, right? I just got lucky and found what was supposed to be me already.

As soon as I won the bike in that poker game in 1984, I knew where I was going. I knew I was going to get into the industry. But I figured I didn't know anything, and the best way to learn was to go to school, and that school was retail. So about eight months before I went to jail, I worked part-time at Bike Outpost in Fountain Valley—

for Bill McReady, owner of Santana Tandems. For me, it was college. I was getting paid dirt, but I was going to school. I had a full plan: I was going to start a bike shop and get out of the security business. I was going to call it Rock Hard Cyclery.

Two days after I got out of jail, I went in to get a tube for my mountain bike, and the manager was a friend of mine, Dave Crosby, who I worked for at Bike Outpost. He hired me on the spot. I didn't ask for a job. He said, "We would love to have someone like you working here. If you don't have a job, I want to hire you right now to sell bikes." He never knew I went to jail. He thought I went away to take care of my sick mom or something. Soon, they fired him, and I was the manager.

The Mountain Dogs and the Reverend

I GOT INTO mountain biking in 1986, two years after I won my bike, two years before I worked in a bike shop. I was always an off-road, dirty kind of guy and thought it'd sure be cool to go off into the mountains. My friend Lance and I went to the bike shop and bought mountain bikes together. It was around the start of the year, I think. It's hard to remember, exactly—that was the decade of decadence. I had long hair like everyone else. Very long, practically down to my ass. Picture Sampson with a bad haircut. Anyhow, Lance just got some Christmas cash. I always had money because I was dealing drugs. We went down with $1,200 and bought the bikes, and rode in Whittier Hills. I bought a map, made peanut butter and jelly sandwiches, and rode as far as we could until the sandwiches and water ran out.

Three miles into that first ride, I was obsessed. It felt like my legs were about to cramp up, I was about to pass out. My lungs were fried. Sweat was pouring into my eyes and they were burning. My hands were sweating on the grips. I felt like I was about to fall over and die on the spot. And I figured I needed to go a little bit further.

I absolutely loved it. I was ahead of everyone else, and I thought that was cool. Lance was dying worse than me; he weighed about 80 pounds more. Actually, though, I just liked the fact that when I looked up to the top of something, if I kept going, I'd get there. When I got there, I thought, *Now, I just want to go to the next-highest thing.*

I loved riding road bikes just as much. But now I couldn't stop riding either one. Every time I was on one, I felt like this is where I'm supposed to be.

Everyone I knew bought a mountain bike as soon as I bought one. My whole social circle instantly converted to mountain biking—a bunch of hippy freaks.

We wanted to get matching shirts so that if we got drunk in a bar we could identify each other. We looked at all the other clubs and they all sounded kind of arrogant, elite, and noninclusive, that we just wanted a name that described our lifestyle—we were just a bunch of dogs that liked running around a mountain, whether it was on a road bike or a mountain bike. So we were the Mountain Dogs.

Roadies invited the Mountain Dogs on club rides, but all they really wanted were people to beat. People to make them feel that they were special. Some people think a bike makes them important, but it really doesn't. It made me start thinking mountain biking is different [than road biking]. People who are willing to go out and get dirty and stuff don't look at each other for the jersey they're wearing or how clean their bike is or how bitchin' it

is. They go out and suffer and thrash and get dirty together.

And then there's the ride, the scenery, the experience. Lot of road riders don't talk about the ride. They never ride alone, just to do it. They talk about the clothes, the bike they're riding; they never talk about the simple beauties that they saw along the way. They never stop to take a picture. We did.

I'd like to think the Mountain Dogs and I knew most of the trails in the San Gabriel Mountains. That's because I took a map, I laid it on the ground, I started from the left, and I rode every damn trail that was listed.

By 1990, things were great and getting better. I'm working at the Mulrooney shop in Cerritos. I started racing. Then one day this Asian gentleman walked in and said in a thick accent, "Hey, I want to talk to Moun-Tain Dog." He was all Chinesed-out, and I say that without any bigotry, being married at the time to Lilly. But he's the prototypical Taiwanese businessman, with the blue suit and tie, black shiny shoes, and white shirt—the antithesis of mountain biking. I was like, "Okay, I'll be right with you." He was from a parts maker called Zoom and needed marketing help to crack the U.S. market. He had gone to a couple of bike shops, and they were all roadies. To them, the Mountain Dogs were the only real mountain bike club around, and I was *the* mountain biker—the only one with a mouth as big as mine, anyway. Truth is, no one had gone to as many places as I had locally. Everyone else did the same old rides, and I went off the map. No question, I'm loud. I don't need a bell. The bears need a bell to warn me of them.

So I began consulting for Zoom and eventually left the bike shop. I went on the road with Zoom for five years. Did their national marketing. Went to most of the NORBA races, went to most of their distributors.

Through a stroke of luck, I was on the cover of *Bicycle Guide* in February 1993. The editor started riding with the Mountain Dogs and he asked us to review 19 of the new $700 front-suspension mountain bikes, at that time a breakthrough price point for the technology. The exposure was awesome. Dream come true. It was one of those weird things where, once you're in a magazine, people think you're important, so then they give you things to do, and give you products, and then because you have all those great new things, other magazines think you're somebody, and then they start putting you in their magazine. It kind of perpetuated things for me, no doubt.

In 1997, I was ordained by the bishop of *Bike* magazine—editor Rob Story, one of my heroes and friends. He called me the Reverend—and the name stuck. He wrote a story about my behavior on the trail that captured me to a T.

I'd ride a lot with big groups, and everyone has a different pace. It's just as difficult to ride faster than someone can than slower than someone can. So everyone has to get into their own groove. But when you're in the back, you feel a little anxiety that you need to keep up, that everyone's waiting for you at the top.

My style was to alleviate that, so everybody would feel comfortable on rides. Instead of getting to the top first and sitting there and waiting for everyone and cooling down, I didn't let myself down. I came here to ride—so I'd roll back down to the last guy, make sure he was all right, give him some encouragement, and in the process get myself more training time. It

wasn't just because I was thinking about everyone else. It also gave me more ride. I got to climb it again, work out a little bit more, do more of exactly what I came to do. A lot of guys rode up to the top and then they didn't want to ride down and have to do it again. It's like, well, you came to ride—or you came to sit? It makes everyone feel better. The slower guys feel better. The faster guys ride more, and nobody's waiting on anyone. It just makes sense. It's a simple thing. It's a win-win. Nobody loses. There's nothing worse than being left somewhere and not knowing where everyone is. And then when you ride hard and get somewhere and cool down, you gotta warm up again. I don't blame guys for being bummed out for waiting. I just wonder why they wait.

Today, people who meet me ask me what the whole Reverend thing is all about. It's easy. It's not about preaching about your afterlife; I think your body here on Earth is a temple, and you should take care of it. And my way of taking care of it is through cycling as much as I can.

Fitness Advice from a Lean Machine

HONESTLY, IT'S KIND of weird to have someone say to me, "I want your body.'" Well, you know what? That means you have to climb into my mommy's womb and come out exactly like I did. I'm the only person who has my body; we're all individuals. Don't judge yourself by the mirror. You don't have to be perfect. You just have to be fit enough to do the things that you want to do. That's the most important thing.

On a daily basis, you have to get up in the morning and kickstart your body. Your metabolism. Soon as I wake up, I do half an hour of light aerobics, rowing machine, or a tai chi kickbox workout before breakfast.

Food-wise, remember that the hole up on your head is bigger than the hole in your ass. You can't shove tons in, have a little bit come out, and not expect to have the rest stick on your fat gut.

All these bullshit diets with this trend and that trend, it really always comes around to eat a balanced diet. Eat a lot of fruits and vegetables. Cook fresh food. Avoid anything that says "all you can eat." Just because it says that doesn't mean you have to. Soup is a really good thing. You take a lot of really good things and boil them all together. Eat things you like to eat that you know aren't bad for you.

Then put a lock on the TV for one hour after you eat. Until then, you have to move. Do anything—just don't lay down. I was into that thinking before cycling; it's just that cycling made it easy because it's fun. That's the difference. I don't go to gyms to work out all the time. Find something you like to do, whether it's cycling or hiking or bowling, do it a lot. Work up a sweat. Make yourself suffer. One of the things about adventure racing, which I'm now getting into, is that if you can be comfortable being uncomfortable, you'll be a good adventure racer. Well, to work out in any sport, you have to teach yourself to be a little uncomfortable—just for a little while. Just long enough to burn more calories than you consume.

That's easy to do if you find something you like doing, like cycling. That's fitness in simple terms: find something you love to do—and do it a lot.

Don't Be Afraid to Be Afraid
IN FACT, I think a lot of the attraction of mountain biking is the joy of overcoming uncomfortable situations—the hard work, the fear of the unknown, the fear of getting hurt. Put them all together and you have incredible potential for adventure.

A bicycle's way more fun to adventure on than to race. I've raced; racing is just going in circles. Mountain biking at its best is exploration, the great unknown, pushing the boundaries. Once I did a 13-hour death hike–bike death march in Jacumba in the Southern California desert along an abandoned railway with no lights through tunnels so dark during the day that you couldn't see your seat, cactus bigger than your entire bicycle, more flats than a year of NASCAR racing. Of course, I didn't do these alone. The TransAlp Challenge— eight days, 400 miles with 60,000 feet of climbing—is one thing, but doing it with one of your best friends brings a whole new kind of sentimental value to it. The TransRockies was pretty incredible.

If there is racing that combines the adventure and the camaraderie, it's 24-hour events. Take the first 24 Hours of Moab, 1995. I've never ridden in a snowstorm in the middle of the night before. Four o'clock in the morning, stoned out of my mind, coffee'd up like Juan Valdez.

But the beauty of mountain biking is that you don't need to travel the world to make epic memories. My philosophy is sort of borrowed from my favorite book, *The Way of the Peaceful Warrior*, by Dan Millman. It woke me to the simple way of thinking that I think is important on bike rides—that there are no ordinary moments.

You don't need an exotic place to find a great ride. If you're out there with a friend on any ride, it can be a great ride if you just pay attention to that day, that moment. A lot of people, especially those who come where we come from—the Orange County, city-urban areas—are in such a hurry to do other things that a bike ride to them just

BIKE FOR LIFE

fits into their schedule. They rush it; they have a time frame; they hurry up and ride and go home. They have no time to notice the ride, because they can't stop and really see what's going on—it's just a workout. They did it, they're done. They didn't feel it, enjoy it.

A lot of people I know do loops, these little carved loops. They never go off the loop. They never go somewhere and just ride somewhere—even if it's wrong. They don't ride the dead end roads, down past where they know where they're going. They don't go if they don't know if there is going to be water or food or a Power Bar or a flat repair station waiting for them.

They are afraid to be afraid.

You ride with guys who only want to take one tube, one patch because they are afraid of carrying something. "I filled up my backback, when I'm done I'm coming back." A lot of people have important things to do. They do the ride between important things. The important thing for me to do is to do the ride. I do everything else between rides.

I always liked hiking and tennis and running. But I always wanted to do them and then come home. But when I got into cycling, I didn't necessarily want to come home. That's where I wanted to be the whole time. I just had to come home. Come home to get supplies and go out and do it again.

Tai Chi and Singletrack

OF COURSE, SOMETIMES you need a little extra help to go out again. I started doing tai chi after my first huge crash in 1987. I knew that I had a problem; my crash put a lot of fear in me, and I knew that I wasn't as focused as I was, because I kept thinking about the crash and thinking about the pain. So I went and took a tai chi class so I could redirect my focus and learn a couple basic breathing and stretching and focus exercises. No matter how smart you are, no matter how good you are at what you do, sometimes if you just go take some kind of class or good instruction from someone, it helps you have a direct and complete focus, a really regimented focus on a particular goal. Tai chi gives you principles that teach you about focus and mental preparation, how to move your body very slowly and to feel your every movement.

I was familiar with tai chi from my old life. While working at the club, I was having a lot of problems defending— stopping drunk, nasty people from hitting me. My biggest problem was that I was having problems not looking at what I wanted to avoid. Looking right at them, and not getting beyond that. I was focusing on every little obstacle and not the big overall problem.

Tai chi helped because I practiced focusing. Every minute of tai chi you're focusing on your breath, your movement, your position, your next breath, next movement. A particular exercise called the archer, where you focus on shooting an imaginary arrow at an imaginary target. If you really practice enough, you can almost hear the arrow hitting the target.

How it translates to the bike: it trains you to look where you do want to go and not where you don't. Helps you relax and give a few little things to focus on. Like anything, if you don't practice skills, they don't come to you easily in panic situations or when you're tired and fatigued. Muscle memory is trained to do something—so things happen without you're having to think about them. Like instead of me being scared about the trail being gnarly, I focused on exactly where I needed to ride, and get across the gnarly shit no sweat.

One of my Mountain Dog friends, Jim "Popeye" Thompson, an old grumpy bike dude, helped me in this regard. He taught me not to fear anyone. He told me every day to ride as hard as you can. If the trail beats you, it beats you, but at least you didn't give up because you're scared.

Middle Age: What's next?

I've enjoyed the Reverend thing, the notoriety. But let's put it in perspective. I'm no visionary or do-gooder. No matter how good you get at riding it, you're still just riding a child's toy. You're doing a real cool thing, it's real exciting, it's real fun, but you're really not doing anything for the planet, except riding a bicycle around, like kids do every day, in every neighborhood. I do it because it's really fun, it's really good for me. Not for anybody else. It's kind of selfish. Cyclists are the most selfish people around, except for triathletes. It's all about me, riding my bike, as fast as I can.

Over the years, I got invited to do a lot of fun things. I got a lot of publicity that other people didn't get. I had a lot of free time to take people on rides, and of course I'd like to think I've spread some joy to others. The coolest thing in the world is when I see people riding bikes and they're going to crazy places, and I remember taking them on their first rides. That's way better than trophies and medals.

After the Zoom thing was over, I went back to the bike shop. Sold a lot of bicycles.

It was fun.

But soon it gnawed at me. I didn't want to live at the beach anymore. I gotta live in the mountains. It didn't make sense to be a mountain biker and to have to drive to the mountains to ride my mountain bike, when I could live at the mountains and ride my bike out my door. In 2000, I got a job at Hardcloud.com, a sports Web site, now defunct. They hired me to be one of the writers. I could now live anywhere I wanted. A buck a word. Supposedly 2,500 words a month, plus reviews and expenses. All of a sudden I was making a lot of money—for me and my barebones lifestyle. It was stupid money. Internet money. Of course it didn't last.

But it got me to move to Big Bear. And now I live at 7,000 feet, two hours from the concrete chaos of L.A., in mountain bike heaven.

I'm 45. Where do I see myself in the future? In my dreams I want to do La Ruta, road-bike down the Pacific Coast, tour across the States, around the world.

How long can I keep it going? Well, remember in 1993 when we rode down the Trans-Canada Highway in Jasper and Banff and saw those specks off in the distance? Remember that? And going into Pocahontas where the big totem poles were? And we kept riding, and we caught those little specks on the highway, and they turned out to be old bastards on a bike tour, 70-, 80-year-old men? We were amazed. "Wow, they're still riding at that age!" we said. Right? Well, what the hell? Why not us?

BIKE FOR LIFE

13

HOW TO SURVIVE

*Staying safe amid mountain lions, bike-jackers,
lightning storms, careless drivers, poison oak,
rabid dogs, and other unexpected dangers*

CALL IT CONTINGENCY planning, emergency procedures, or just Plan B. Because even if you do everything we advocate in *Bike for Life*—ride a perfect bike with a perfect fit with perfect form and a perfect training plan that ramps up your fitness without injury—fate can intervene. Your hard-won health can suddenly be wrecked for the weekend or forever if you're cut off by a car, attacked by a dog or a mountain lion, bike-jacked, or riddled with saddle sores or poison oak. Your progress suddenly may slow when you're slammed by headwinds, caught in a thunderstorm, or get a flat when carrying no repair kit. After all, you can't deprogram bad luck, but you can and should be prepared when it happens. This chapter tells how to survive some of cycling's unexpected roadblocks.

· 1 ·
HOW TO SURVIVE . . .
A Mountain Lion Attack

On January 8, 2004, Anne Hjelle of Mission Viejo, California, 30, literally survived the jaws of death. On a mountain bike ride in Whiting Ranch Wilderness Park, just a few miles from her Orange County home, the personal trainer and ex-Marine was attacked by a 122-pound mountain lion that had killed and disemboweled another mountain biker, 35-year-old Mark Reynolds, hours earlier. As Hjelle descended twisty, cacti-studded Cactus Ridge Trail at 15 miles per hour, the animal, also known as a cougar, leapt on her right shoulder and bit hard into the back of her neck.

As Hjelle screamed and punched him, the animal worked his way around to the front of her neck, and clamped down. Cougars, typically 7 to 10 feet long and 65 to 150 pounds, have 300 pounds per square inch of crushing power in their jaws— about six times as much as a wolf. With the right-hand side of her face torn off, and her carotid artery and trachea missed by millimeters, Hjelle blacked out. It took a team to save her: her courageous riding partner, Debi Nicholls, 48, who hugged her friend's leg and was dragged 20 feet with her down the hill, and three male rock-throwing mountain bikers, who pelted the lion from the trail. Soon, the cat released his prey and loped a short distance away. Sitting under a bush next to Mark's body, the killer watched as paramedics quickly arrived to carry Hjelle to the hospital, then was killed himself later that day by rangers. Despite the attack, Hjelle had no internal injuries. A few weeks after undergoing six hours of facial reconstructive surgery, she was back hiking. She's disfigured and will require many more surgeries, but feels lucky to be alive.

The incident shook up mountain bikers around the country, including *Bike for Life*'s coauthor Roy Wallack, who regularly bikes at Whiting Ranch. Wildlife experts speculate that attacks on people in the wilderness are likely to increase as humans' homes and recreational activities continue to impinge on animals' habitats. "It's completely unnatural behavior—their normal prey is deer and sheep, then raccoons, and even other mountain lions," says John Ganaway, a former head ranger at Whiting and current boss at nearby Caspers Regional Park, where in 2003 a cougar almost pounced on a five-year-old boy until the mother threw a shoe at him. "One animal behaviorist believes that seeing us on a

daily basis makes them lose their fear of us—and look at us as a food item."

Ganaway arrived on the scene at Whiting with other rangers hours after the attack on Hjelle and surveyed the scene the next morning. "There was blood everywhere," he said. "It was a fight for her life. And it's a good thing she fought; that's one of the first rules of surviving an attack. As we tell our visitors, mountain lions are used to animals running—not fighting back. And they don't have good endurance, so you can tire them out. The mother at Caspers saved her kid because she read the literature that we pass out."

According to the California Department of Fish and Game, 15 verified mountain lion attacks on humans have occurred in California since 1890; ten of those since 1992. Six of the attacks resulted in fatalities—two from rabies, which is common in the animals, especially during summer months. The last death before Reynolds's was in 1994. Here's what the CDFG suggests you do to survive the trails in a cougar habitat.

1. **Don't ride alone.** Cougars are less likely to attack groups. Ride with a partner, and stay close togther. If attacked, you can help one another.
2. **Don't run if confronted by a lion.** They instinctively chase—and are so fast that they'll catch you in seconds.
3. **Stand tall.** Cougars try to bite the head or neck, so try to remain on your feet, don't bend over or turn away. Make yourself look bigger. Raise your arms, move them slowly, and speak in a firm, loud voice. If you're wearing a jacket, open it. Maintain eye contact with the animal.
4. **Raise hell.** Yell, scream, act aggressive. Whatever you do, don't be quiet.

Noise unnerves the animal and is an audible call for help.

5. **If attacked, jab the animal's eyes.** Use something sharp—sticks, rocks, a bike pump, or your bare hands.

6. **Keep fighting.** Kick and punch until you can't anymore. Mountain lions have poor endurance. He might think that this isn't worth it and decide to go back to deer and other weaklings that flee.

7. **Don't ride or jog after dusk.** Sundown in the mountains is near feeding time for cougars.

8. **If you do ride after dusk, affix two lights to the back of your helmet.** "They look like eyes to the lions," says Dan Cain of Borrego Springs, California, who rides up to 30 miles per week in the desert mountains south of Palm Springs and has run across the big cats on several occasions. Charged by a lion in 1998 on the Pacific Crest Trail, he stood his ground, screamed "like a rock star," aimed his lights into the lion's face, and sighed with relief as the cat backed off.

9. **Most of all, don't take the mountain lion threat lightly.** Beautiful, tawny-colored animals with black-tipped ears and tails, mountain lions have been hunted for bounty for decades, given "protected" status since 1990, and now number 4,000 to 6,000 in California. Half the state is prime cougar country, especially where deer are plentiful. As suburbia marches toward the foothills and mountains, as in Orange County, expect more encounters. "A week before the attacks at Whiting," says Ganaway, "a Fish and Game warden told me, 'It's not a matter of *if* we have another attack, but *when*.'"

Even so, Ganaway notes that "you're still far safer riding in the mountains than swimming in the ocean," according to statistics.

· 2 ·
HOW TO SURVIVE . . .
A Fall

Mountain bike legend Ned Overend was one of the rare riders to go a whole career—an exceptionally long one, at that—without suffering a broken bone. That wasn't by accident (no pun intended). His method, below, applies to both mountain and road riding.

▶ **Balancing act:** Practicing track stands and general balancing will help you avoid slow-speed falls. "It'll give you that extra second to clip-out," says Ned. And avoid toppling over on your hip.

▶ **Slip out fast:** Set up your pedals to get out of them easily in a crash. Clean 'em out, keep 'em oiled, and you can pull your foot out quickly and avoid a knee injury.

▶ **Soft landing:** Minimize impact when you hit the ground. Fight the urge to stick an arm out; that'll risk a broken collarbone. Instead, keep your body in and try to let the handlebar and pedal hit the ground first. Before you hit, tuck your arm in and roll, letting your whole body absorb the blow.

· 3 ·
HOW TO SURVIVE . . .
A Flat Tire Without a Patch Kit

It's happened to everyone—a flat tire when you're alone, without a spare tube or

BIKE FOR LIFE

patch kit, and too far out to walk home before nightfall. How do you survive? "I usually wait until other bikers come along and bum a tube off them," says Jim Langley, a former bike mechanic, longtime *Bicycling* magazine technical editor, and now an industry consultant. But if you're in outer Mongolia and yurt drivers only come along every three days, Langley advises the following.

> ▶ **Stuff it with grass:** This age-old survival trick is so well-known it's cliché, but it works. Simply jam your tire with grass, paper, rags—anything that'll solidify it—and keep rolling.

> ▶ **A slow leak? Pump it up:** Even if it lasts 60 seconds, that gets you a long way on a bike. Ride until it's flat and repeat. Great upper-body workout.

> ▶ **Ride it:** Flat be damned. If it's on the rear tire, keep pedaling. "No kidding. This usually works as long as you watch out for things that might damage the rim," says Langley. "I've ridden up to five miles on flat road and mountain bike tires with no damage to the wheels. Be careful in corners though—it can get pretty squirrelly." Note: Riding a front tire flat is near-impossible; swap it with the good rear inner tube.

Here's Langley's fixes for other common mechanical maladies.

1. **Broken chain.** You can't jury-rig a chain, or carry a spare. So Langley won't leave home without a chain tool and a special repair chain link, such as from HKC and Sachs. Some snap the link in place with your hands.

2. **Taco'd wheel.** A wheel so bent that it takes on a potato chip or taco shape needs to be replaced, but you can temporarily straighten it enough to get home. Here's how: remove the wheel, find the largest wobble on the rim, then raise the wheel with two hands over your head and swing it down so you smack the bump on the ground. "Wham! Check the wheel," says Langley. "Closer to straight? If not, whack harder. Move on to the next wobble and whack it until the wheel is straight enough to ride."

3. **Bent derailleur hanger.** If you crash on the right side of the bike and bend the derailleur, your shifting is gone. To get it back, try this neat Langley trick, which works only if the bend is on the hanger itself, the little finger on the frame where the derailleur bolts on: take off the rear wheel, remove the quick-release skewer, and unscrew the derailleur so that it's off the frame. Now, you can thread the end of the axle into place where the derailleur used to be. If you can, use the wheel to gently coerce that bent piece of metal straight. Then reinstall the derailleur.

4. **Broken shift cable.** You're stuck in one gear if the shift cable breaks, so at least make it one you can ride comfortably in until you get home. That involves tightening the cable, which you can do by pulling it to the nearest water bottle mount screw and tightening it down. If the remaining cable is too short for that, Langley advises tightening the limit screw on the derailleur to force it to stay in an easy gear.

·4·
HOW TO SURVIVE...
A Bike-Jacking

On June 23, 2004, five-time national mountain bike champion Tinker Juarez was putting in big road miles in preparation for the TransAlp Challenge, a 400-mile off-road race across the Alps that was two weeks away. Heading back to his home in Downey, a Los Angeles suburb, the 42-year-old briefly pulled off the L.A. River bike path at Atlantic Boulevard to change his cassette tape. "Just as I was about to hop back on my bike, someone tapped me on the back," said Tinker. "I turned around and saw a gang member guy with a gun camouflaged next to his T-shirt—pointed right at me."

"Give me your bike," the man said coolly.

Wordlessly, Tinker handed him the bike. The gunman rode off on the brand-new Cannondale 613, a unique carbon-aluminum mix so light—15 pounds—that it was banned from the Tour de France the previous summer. The $5,000 bike moved fast, Juarez guesses, probably selling for a hundred dollars within the hour.

"I wasn't going to question the guy," he said. "There was nothing I could say to him. I knew to say nothing, just living here all my life. I have cousins like that. I live around it, I see it. There's too much senseless killing every day, for a shoe or a watch—or a bike."

"I don't have to live here. I could live in Colorado with mountains and animals, or I can live here [in L.A. County] with my family and millions of other people, a few of them bad, like this guy."

Juarez knows he'd screwed up: "Maybe I need to get an MP3 player, so I don't have to stop to change tapes anymore. I definitely got a little too complacent, stopping in a bad area." That's putting it mildly; he was bike-jacked in North Long Beach, a low-income area next to Compton, where his brightly colored bike jersey and tinted sports glasses made him conspicuous. "Normally, when I see people on a bike path who look like gang members, I turn off onto the streets, go around them, and get back on the bike path further down."

Of course, you can't avoid what you can't see. In a case that made the papers in 1993, Oliver Thompson, then the 51-year-old police chief of nearby Inglewood, was deliberately rear-ended on his custom-made Davidson road bike while riding home from work. Three men jumped from the car and demanded his backpack at gunpoint, and he quickly complied. As his assailants ran back to the car, he pulled a .45-caliber service revolver out of his fannypack and fired, wounding one and causing him to drop the pack. "Good thing they hadn't demanded my bike," says the lifelong cycling aficionado. "Somebody would have died."

The last statement was made in jest. Chief Thompson advised that bike-jacking victims keep it in perspective. "Walk through the what-ifs," he said. "Even if you do the right thing—plan your route around bad areas and avoid riding at night—bike-jacking can happen to anyone at any time. Give them what they want, and hopefully your life will be spared."

The day he was bike-jacked, Tinker Juarez stayed cool and survived. Three weeks later, he won the Masters Division at the TransAlp.

BIKE FOR LIFE

· 5 ·
HOW TO SURVIVE . . .
Poison Oak, Ivy, and Sumac

East of the Rockies, it's ivy. Down South, it's sumac. Out West, oak. Mountain bike enough, and you'll eventually be exposed to urushiol, the poisonous sap that can make you regret a day of epic single-track. For some, the immune response to urushiol-contaminated skin cells is a tiny itchy spot on the arm that lasts two days. For others, it means three weeks of oozing, burning, seeping, pus-drenched welts spreading all over your body that cause loved ones to recoil in revulsion and make you scratch like you've never scratched before. But that's not the worst of it. About 15 percent of the 120 million Americans who are allergic to poison oak, ivy, and sumac are so highly sensitive that they break out in a rash and begin to swell in four to twelve hours, not the normal 24 to 48. Their eyes may swell shut and blisters may erupt on their skin. Considered one of the few true emergencies in dermatology, it requires you to get to a hospital as soon as possible for a shot of corticosteroids to bring the swelling down.

For most people, the sores usually go away on their own in two weeks. But that fortnight of hell has led to a cottage industry of poison oak remedies, rumors, and urban myths. First step: immediately after the ride, wash the affected area and all the clothing you wore with soap and cold water; the easily spread oil can persist in crystalline form on clothing or other contacted items (including pets) for several weeks. Then, to shorten the agony, try out some of the following over-the-counter and home-brewed cures culled from www.gorp.com, www.poisonivy.aesir.com, and www.otan.us:

▸ **Rhuli:** This popular medicine, found in Anti-Itch Gel by Band-Aid, leaves a dry, menthol-tinged film over the affected area. Some say washing beforehand with soap or dishwashing liquid will speed the effect. Besides rhuli gel, try Caladryl, calamine lotion, or Benadryl; the alcohol in each cools and dries the area. Possible downside: some say that the gel can leave chemical burns that are visible as scars a decade later.

▸ **Tecnu:** Firefighters and wildlife rangers prefer to wash off with this popular urushiol-dissolving skin cleanser right after exposure. A good idea: keep a small bottle stashed with your tire repair kit.

▸ **Ocean salt water:** Some believe that poison ivy sores will disappear a day or so after you swim in the ocean and apply a salt-water-soaked cloth to the affected areas for 20 minutes twice a day.

▸ **Hot water:** Increasing the shower temperature to near-scalding, a popular remedy, was so painful that one rider wrote on his blog, "I thought I was nuts." But the first dousing dried up his blisters overnight, allowing isolated holdouts to be mopped up with Rhuli. Possible downside: hot showers stop itching for a while (because the nerve cells have been deadened, say detractors), but may cause the itching to spread, possibly due to the opening of pores and increased blood flow in the area.

▸ **Vicks VapoRub, Clorox, a warm epsom salt bath followed by**

calamine lotion, peroxide, and dish-washing liquid: Champions of all the above say they stifle itching immediately and can dry out sores in two or three days. Apply Vick's twice a day; it slightly burns at first, as does Clorox. Laying a peroxide-soaked washcloth on the infected area for 15 to 20 minutes will make the oozing poison oak bubbles turn white, at which time you can scrape off the dead skin. Rubbing Joy dishwashing liquid onto the skin and letting it dry overnight supposedly kills the itch and also works for mosquito bites.

If none of those do the trick, try urban legends: hairspray; burdock root tea; and hemorrhoid ointment. Scrub the wound with a hard bath brush lathered with rubbing alcohol and soap, followed by a coat of Calohist. Desperate? Boil the root of a polk sallet plant into a smelly paste form, and rub it on the sores until they burn or sting; works overnight, some swear. Tired of rubbing goop on your skin? Make a lead fishing-sinker necklace by pounding a sinker flat with a mallet, punch a hole in it, thread a string through, and wear it around your neck. "I live in the country, am very allergic to poison ivy, and have been using this thirty plus years. It really works!" said one old-timer.

Best advice of all: leaves of three, let them be.

· 6 ·
HOW TO SURVIVE . . .
Headwinds

The solution is one word—an *aerobar*. Club riders deride this add-on handlebar extension, which lowers and narrows you into a pointy aerodynamic shape, as "for triathletes only." Pro riders only use it in time trials, not the peloton, because it compromises handling in a pace line. Yet when it comes to surviving headwinds, the speed- and spirit-sapping bane of all cyclists, the aerobar works for racers, average Joes on the bike path, and fully loaded bike tourers pushing cross-country with 60 pounds of gear.

I was one of the latter in June of 1989, when my triathlete friend Larry Lawson and I pedaled the length of the Mississippi River from beginning to end for three weeks and 1,987 miles, fighting constant headwinds all the way. I was the experienced tourer of the two, having pedaled all around the world in the 1980s, while Larry was on his first trip. But it instantly became obvious that he knew more about handling the headwinds that relentlessly blow north from the Gulf of Mexico than I did. Within minutes of departing Lake Itasca, Minnesota, from which the Mississippi emanates as an innocent 10-foot-wide stream, Larry was out of sight. I struggled to stay in double figures as the gusts whistled in my ears, slowing me to 7 mph on the flat prairie. Larry greeted me 20 miles down the road, having read the first chapter of Mark Twain's *Life on the Mississippi*, then bolted off, establishing a pattern that held all the way to LaCrosse, Wisconsin.

The difference? Larry had an aerobar; I didn't.

Over a couple of cold ones at the Old Style brewery in La Crosse, we decided to switch bikes: my steel Univega touring bike with two panniers—bloated with touring books and camera equipment, a tent, and a sleeping bag, total weight 64 pounds—for Larry's aluminum Klein Quantum with Scott triathlon bars and a round Tupperware cake container suspended under the seat that held one change of bike clothes, a wallet, and a sleep sheet. Total weight: 21.72 pounds. (He'd weighed it before we left.)

His aerodynamic dream machine made a huge difference. Down in the aerobar tuck, I effortlessly sliced through those headwinds at 14, 15, 16 mph easy—it almost felt like cheating. I could see Larry struggling with my barge, banging into the wall of wind. But I didn't see him for long. Soon, he was ahead again and out of sight.

But the experiment was an unqualified success. When I caught him four hours later on the west side of the Mississippi at a drive-in liquor store in Pikes Peak, Iowa, Larry was so exhausted he hadn't read a page of Twain. I'd arrived fresh, just minutes back. The point? Aerodynamics counts.

From that point we rode in a pace line, the Quantum first, like the bow of a ship, its arrow-point profile cutting wind resistance by a third, all the while creating a draft for the rear rider to rest in. Aerobar inventor Boone Lennon, who modeled the form after the tuck of a downhill skier, later told me that an aerobar could save a pro rider three seconds a mile in a time trial, but I'm convinced that it's worth far more for bike tourists battling headwinds. The second we flew home from New Orleans, just two weeks before Greg LeMond won the 1989 Tour de France by eight seconds on one, I bought an aerobar and haven't ridden without it since. —RMW

·7·
HOW TO SURVIVE . . .
Urban Riding

The good news is that cycling on the roads is safer than it used to be. Deaths are down by a third since 1975—probably due to increased use of helmets and tougher drunk driving laws, speculates Patrick McCormick, communications director of the League of American Bicyclists. Now the bad news: cyclists still die at a rate far beyond their numbers. In 2002, according to the Highway Traffic Safety Administration, road accidents caused 42,643 deaths in the U.S., of which 662 were bicyclists, down from 728 in 2001 and 859 since 1990. That means roughly 2 percent of the people who die on the road were riding a bike, grossly out of proportion to their numbers and total mileage.

But you don't have to be a statistic, say cycling safety experts like John Forrester, author of *Effective Cycling*, considered the bible of bike safety. His advice, in a nutshell: *Act like a car.*

It's simple. If you act like a bike, riding in the gutter, trying to stay out of the way, you're invisible. If you act like a car, you make yourself obvious and give drivers signals they understand. Here are Forrester's rules for living to ride another day.

1. *Ride in a straight line.* Many cyclists can't, either through poor bike fit or poor skills. Make yourself predictable for drivers.

s. *Look over your shoulder.* Safe merging and turning isn't possible in a car or on a bike without this basic traffic skill. Practice it. And keep your neck muscles stretched.

3. *Leave the curb area and ride closer to the middle of the lane.* This is a key to survival. First, the curb area is dangerous—debris, car doors opening, and being cut off by right-turning drivers who now think they have room to pass you. Second, moving left to the

right-middle of the lane makes you visible to cars and won't tempt them to squeeze by. They can easily drift into the left lane to pass you safely.

4. ***Don't ride on the wrong side of the road.*** This is the greatest cause of car-bike accidents. Drivers don't expect you, especially at intersections and driveways.

5. ***Avoid sidewalks.*** They're dangerous and slow. Besides conflicts with pedestrians, every driveway becomes a new intersection.

6. ***If you lack skills, get off the street.*** Uncoordinated? Out of shape? Unskilled? If you don't have what it takes to ride in traffic, don't risk it. Safe cycling takes more concentration, alertness, and judgment than driving. If you lack these qualities, stay on the bike path.

7. ***Wear a helmet.*** You're a fool if you don't. Most bicycle fatalities are due to head injuries. And helmets look cool and provide more visibility.

Yet while Forrester's widely accepted rules seem beyond reproach, they may be flawed, according to Robert Hurst, author of *The Art of Urban Cycling*. "Riding 'like a car' will keep you safe from 99 percent of drivers, but do you want to take a chance on the 1 percent who don't pay attention?" says the Denver bike-messenger-turned-writer. "His rules make you complacent, but you need to be paranoid. Be ready for disaster. In the era of the cell phone, where distracted drivers are weaving all over the place, you can't assume anyone sees you." He agrees with Forrester on one rule, but adds a caveat: "Wear a helmet—and ride like you don't."

How to Survive the Insurance Companies After an Accident

IF you don't meet your maker in traffic, but are one of the estimated 45,000 cyclists per year who are injured in a bike-car accident, the hassle is just beginning. At least 30 percent of bike-car injury cases go to litigation, compared to only 10–15 percent in traffic cases involving only automobiles, according to West Los Angeles attorney Bill Harris, who handles several hundred bike cases a year. In other words, insurance companies don't make it easy for injured cyclists to collect for their injuries. In fact, the police and the courts are also, to some degree, stacked against cyclists, Harris adds. "Their thinking is, 'you bikers are doing something as dangerous and as crazy as riding in traffic with a bicycle. You'd better be prepared to stop fast–or be careful!'"

Although cycling safety guru John Forrester believes that up to half of all accidents may be the fault of the cyclist, the fact is that innocent injured cyclists often don't get a fair shake. To protect yourselves after an accident, *Bike for Life* has compiled the following tips from Harris. They'll give you a basic guideline of what to do–and what not to do–when dealing with the driver, the police, the hospital, and the insurance companies.

1. **Insist on a police report:** Evidence will vanish and stories will change over time as witnesses move, memories fade. Make sure your claim is investigated. The first and best

evaluation is a police report. Even ask the cop at the scene if you can look at the report to make sure everything you know gets put on it. You have the right to request a copy.

2. **Get cops (and paramedics) to the scene by stressing that you're hurt:** Cops often won't come out unless there's injury. Make sure cops come out and look at physical evidence, such as: (1) Point of impact, and (2) where and how far the bike was thrown. This will make them material witnesses to the accident.

3. **Collect witnesses immediately:** Get the names and numbers of everyone who saw the accident. Many people come to help—then leave. You'll probably never see them again. In our system, you have to prove fault, and if you have no witnesses, it is more difficult to reconstruct the accident.

4. **If it wasn't your fault, if possible don't move anything:** Let the driver move the car. Don't move your bike. Let the policeman get a look at the most accurate view of what happened.

5. **Get all the facts to show who's at fault:** A typical insurance adjuster gets only a few—three or four—bike cases a year. Like the cops, they often automatically assume that the cyclist is wrong, so they won't believe you unless your facts are ironclad. They'll jump on bike cases because they think they can play with liability. This is why a higher percentage of bike-car claims go to litigation than car-car claims: over 30 percent compared to 10–15 percent.

6. **Contact is not required to make a claim:** If you have enough evidence and witnesses, you may be able to make a claim of damages based on a near-miss. This is a proof problem, a much tougher case, but winnable if you have independent, unbiased witnesses.

7. **Don't exaggerate or admit too much to the cops:** If you brag that you were going 25 mph, it may make it look like you were going too fast for the circumstances. The speed of the rider will be scrutinized very closely when pursuing a claim. Also, be careful about what you say. If you didn't see the car, it could hurt your case. They'll assume "if you would have seen it, you could have avoided it."

8. **Don't be a tough guy—list all your injuries, take an ambulance, and get quick follow-up care:** List even your slightest injuries on the police report. Transportation by ambulance to hospital is safer for you and documents your injuries better than going in yourself. Don't hesitate to seek follow-up care. Insurance people don't believe your claim—they only believe medical records. Tough guys don't get points in this business. Seek as much medical care as you need—and can afford.

9. **Immediately photograph your visible injuries:** They often heal quickly.

10. **Use small claims court:** If you are wiling to accept $2,500 or less, generally too small an amount for an attorney to handle, try to collect it yourself. If you're persistent, that is.

11. **Use an attorney for big cases:** Don't ever handle a big case yourself. You don't know how to value it. An attorney normally takes a standard one-third for attorney's fees, but is worth it. Don't delay. Keep several deadlines in mind: one year for bodily injury and three years for property damage. Don't wait that long, however; with time, witnesses disappear or forget, and credibility wanes in the eyes of judges. If you sleep on your rights or forget to file, the court will not help you.

BIKE FOR LIFE

12. **Collect full replacement value for your bike:** Don't allow the insurance company to prorate your bike. There is no market for a used, broken bike.

13. **Don't rush the bodily injury claim:** Settle property claims immediately, but wait until you are completely healed to settle bodily injury claims. Permanent scarring—especially facial—is worthy of a large settlement.

14. **Count on your own auto insurance (if you have it) to cover you:** It's a little-known fact, but almost all cyclists are covered by their own auto insurance policy. Look under the section titled "medical pay coverage"; it may be $10,000–$20,000. If you paid your premiums, you absolutely have the legal right to get your own benefits. If the guy who hit you isn't covered, you are covered under "uninsured motorist." But don't expect much cooperation on this; remember that your own insurance is still an adversary. You may have to demand arbitration.

15. **Don't be nice to the driver of the car who hit you:** Don't make any gratuitous remarks or any statements of admission to the driver; just trade names and addresses. Get registration, driver's license, insurance company. Don't be nice, just businesslike. In car-bike accidents, nice guys often get screwed.

· 8 ·
HOW TO SURVIVE . . .
A Lightning Storm

It was July 5, 1982, U.S. Highway 14, Bighorn Mountains, Wyoming. To avoid the heat, we'd waited until dusk to begin a 6,000-foot climb, the longest of our Pacific-to-Atlantic tour, to the top of 8,950-foot Granite Pass. Everything went perfectly at first. The sky was a cloudless blanket of black velvet, embroidered with tiny, glistening pearls. It was like a dream, looking out 25, 50, maybe 100 miles and seeing no cars and no city lights—only stars. Off in the distance, tiny silent lightning bolts flashed every 10 seconds. It was a storm, but so far away that I got out my camera, set the shutter open, and shot time-exposures. What a concept: photographing a storm as if it were a tourist sight, watching it like a movie.

Before we knew it, however, we were movie actors. The storm turned, raced closer and closer, and pinned us against the mountainside. Howling winds knocked us sideways. Plum-sized raindrops pounded us. Lightning splattered on the ground 100 feet away, making my skin tingle and hair stand on end. My god—we were human lightning rods, ready to fry! We threw our steel bikes down, sprinted downhill a ways and squatted down like forlorn gargoyles. For an hour we gazed at the electric light show around us with amazement and horror, wondering if this was the end.

All these years, I've wondered, *Did we do the right thing, or was it just luck that we survived?*

The U.S. National Oceanic and Atmospheric Administration publishes a preparedness guide for severe weather that the League of American Bicyclists has adapted for cyclists. Here's their advice for handling a thunderstorm.

1. ***Thunder = trouble***: If you can hear thunder (it sounds like a loud crack

close-up and a low rumble farther away), get shelter; you are close enough to the storm to be struck by lightning. To estimate your distance from the storm, remember that light (186,000 miles per second) travels faster than sound (around 750 mph); every five seconds between seeing the flash and hearing the thunderclap equals a mile. If the time grows shorter, take cover in or under a nearby building or underpass.

2. *Shorter is better:* Don't be the high point on flat terrain. Lightning always takes the quickest path to the ground and usually strikes tall isolated objects such as trees or tall buildings; the Empire State building is hit about eight times a year. If in the woods, take shelter under the shorter trees.

3. *No trees*: If exposed, find a low spot away from trees, fences, and poles. (But get to higher ground if flash flooding is possible, like near a creek bed.)

4. *Get down*: If you're on a hill with exposure to the sky, head downhill and seek an overhanging bluff or a valley or ravine to lower your exposure.

5. *Off the bike*: If you feel your skin tingle or your hair stand on end, dismount fast, get away from your bike. Metal attracts lightning and rubber-soled shoes and rubber tires provide NO protection from it.

6. *Squat down*: In the middle of a storm, crouch low to the ground on the balls of your feet. Place your hands on your knees with your head between them. Make yourself the smallest target possible, and minimize your contact with the ground.

Up on Granite Pass that night long ago, it seems a rare occurrence came to pass in my life: the right decision. After the lightning moved on, we walked the bikes uphill in the drenching rain—cold, soaked, and scared. Three miles up, we came to the Shell Falls Interpretive Site, a nature display with an attached restroom. Inside it, high and dry in sleeping bags, were two other bike tourists we'd last seen at the bottom of the mountain eight hours earlier. They didn't like riding at night and left early. And they didn't seem to appreciate being awakened or to hear us endlessly recount our tale of survival in the eye of the storm. —*RMW*

· 9 ·
HOW TO SURVIVE . . .
Saddle Sores

As Ethan Gelber, director of the peace-through-cycling organization BikeAbout, put it on Gorp.com, "being saddle sore and having saddle sores are two different things." The former is a complaint from anyone who hasn't ridden in a while that diminishes as you ride more, while the letter is the "bitter result of steps not taken that let a minor problem get worse."

Saddle sores, cyclists' most common complaint, can wreck a ride. These dreaded pimples, boils, and raw skin are caused by saddle friction incubated in the hot, moist, bacteria-laden environment inside your bike shorts. Saddle sores have stopped RAAM riders, first-timers, bike tourers, and bike racers. According to www.road bikerider.com, the excellent Web site run by former *Bicycling* magazine editors Ed Pavelka and Fred Matheny, famed men of steel like Eddy Merckx and Sean Kelly had to abandon races when saddle sore pain became too great, and old-time riders would put slabs of raw steak in their shorts to cushion the tender area. Modern methods are more convenient, but by the time you use them, it may be too late; your ride's over. Here's what to do to stop saddle sores before and after they begin.

1. *Correct your saddle position:* Too high and your hips rock as you pedal, creating excess rubbing against the nose of the saddle; same with saddle too far forward.

2. *Numb it/shrink it/corn-pad it:* Dull the pain with Ibuprofen, knock it down to size with Preparation H (Hey, it shrinks swollen tissue, right? Apply it before putting on your shorts), and cushion it with corn pads, the donut-shaped adhesive pads found in the foot-care section of drug stores.

3. *Stand up:* Standing while pedaling relieves the pressure on your crotch, restores circulation, and lets you shift things around. Roadbikerider.com recommends standing 15–20 seconds every few minutes. Use natural opportunities such as short hills, rough pavement, or accelerating from stop signs. Stand and stretch when you're at the back of a pace line or group.

4. *Keep shifting position on the saddle:* Sit mostly toward the rear where your sit bones get maximum support and take pressure off your crotch. But also move farther back on seated climbs, and more to the middle when bending low to make good time. Each shift relieves pressure points.

5. *Change saddle and shorts:* Your saddle sore may be isolated in one small area, and changing your saddle and/or shorts can reduce pressure on it. Chronic sores may mean you have too wide a saddle—possible if you are a man using a women's saddle.

6. *Lube it up:* If you've noticed irritation on previous rides, reduce friction by dabbing petroleum jelly, Chamois BUTT'r, or Bag Balm on your crotch and the chamois (the material in the crotch of the shorts) to reduce friction.

7. *A fresh saddle:* To reduce the transfer of dirt and bacteria, buy a new saddle when yours wears out. And bring your own saddle or a saddle cover if you're planning on renting a bike out-of-town.

8. *Keep clean:* Always wear clean shorts for each ride. If you seem susceptible to saddle sores, you may find it helpful to wash your crotch with antibacterial soap and warm water before lubing up. Dry your skin well first.

9. *Chuck your undies:* Not only can underwear irritate skin like fine sandpaper and trap moisture against the body, but its seams can dig into your crotch. Good bike shorts have seamless padding where it is most needed, reduce sweat where you should be dry, and cut down on chafing. Yes, they are skin-tight and make the self-conscious feel even more so. But they work. If you really don't want to show it off, use the baggy, mountain bike style shorts with the chamois-lined padding hidden inside. Look for shorts with a one-piece liner or one that's sewn with flat seams.

10. *At day's end, strip and clean up quick*: Don't give bacteria time to invade saddle sores. Get out of your shorts, wash out with TLC and a gentle soap, and sleep naked to allow everything to dry.

11. **Stop riding and medicate:** If it's too painful, you're doing damage. Get off the bike. Go swimming. Wear loose clothes. Take some time off the bike to help it heal. It's far better to lose three days now than a week or more after infection sets in. If you continue to ride on an open sore, it may eventually form a cyst that requires surgery. Some recommend treating it with an acne gel containing 10 percent benzoyl peroxide or Emgel, a topical prescription product. Whatever you do, don't scrub and clean sores with alcohol, which will only dry out the skin and irritate it further.

12. **If sores are chronic, go recumbent:** The laid-back 'bents take the stress off strategic spots a traditional bike might bother. And they're faster, too.

· 10 ·
HOW TO SURVIVE . . .
Numb Hands

A loss of sensitivity in your paws, caused by reduced circulation, usually stems from the following: too-stretched-out position, too-forward body lean, and unchanging hand position. In theory, some simple fixes apply.

▶ **Raise the handlebar gradually.** Too-low bars (and/or stem) put too much weight on your hands. An ideal, balanced fit distributes roughly 30 percent of your body weight across your seat, bars, and pedals.

▶ **Lower the seat post and/or level the seat.** A too-high and/or tilted saddle throws your upper body weight forward and puts lot more pressure on your hands' contact areas.

▶ **Slide the seat forward or shorten stem.** Given a correct-sized bike frame, numb hands indicate you're too stretched out from the rear of your saddle to the handlebars. Note: Beware moving the seat too far forward. The changed positions vis-à-vis the cranks could cause back/knee probs.

▶ **Switch hand positions often.** Especially limit time in the top-of-the-bar position. Carpal tunnel syndrome, a crimping of the ulnar nerve, may result from the hyperextended wrist position of the top bar. Shift from top of bar to hoods to drops. The hoods put hands in the wrist-safe "handshake" position.

▶ **Kill the "death grip".** Squeezing the bar too tightly can cut circulation. So relax, gently rest hands on the bar. As long as one thumb is always under the bars, your hands can't slip and you can steer and control the bike, even when riding fast, with only a very gentle touch.

▶ **Use mountain bike bar-ends.** Although out of style, they position hands for better climbing and a wrist-safe "handshake" grip.

▶ **Shake-out hands.** Centrifugal force pushes blood out to the fingertips and capillaries.

▶ **The right gloves.** Use models with more padding, full fingers for cold weather. Avoid too-tight gloves that restrict blood flow.

· 11 ·
HOW TO SURVIVE . . .
Dog Attacks

I had 30 more miles of Wisconsin farmland to ride before reaching the Mississippi

River and Dubuque, Iowa, when it saw me. A maniacally barking mutt, loping beside some kids riding motorcycles along a fence, suddenly changed directions and headed for my right ankle. No problem—I'd outrace it, I thought. But as I pressed hard on the pedals, the sudden torque dislodged the out-of-true rear wheel (it was missing a spoke), yanked it out of the rear dropout, and tangled it in the derailleur. The frame became a limp, metallic pretzel; I collapsed on the ground in a bloody mess. So much for Dubuque, so much for the bike, so much for my 1978 cross-country trip. Its work done, the dog stopped barking. The kids on their bikes came by and eventually brought over their mother, who drove me to Dubuque. My father wired me $300, which I used at the only bike store in town to buy a frame from a brand-new company based in a Wisconsin barn called Trek.

They say that Iowa is all corn. How about pig farms and dogs? As I biked across the Hawkeye State, canines seemed everywhere, and once bit, twice wary. Having already demonstrated the folly of **(1) Standing Up and Outsprinting Them** (the logical first option for most riders given that most dogs are merely defending their territory and lose interest when you're off the property), I tried to reason with them. In other words, I'd **(2) Scream!** They'd hesitate, surprised, aware of what can happen when a human is angry with them; escalating if need be, **(3) I'd Raise My Hand** threateningly as if it contained a heavy object, because dogs understand the meaning of a throwing gesture. If I had had time to prepare, I'd play **(4) Drench the Dog**. Seeing your water bottle in hand, even before squirting it, may make Fido stay away. When none of that worked, especially with big dogs, I would deploy **(5) The Bike Barrier**—dismounting quickly and holding my bike between me and its chompers, swinging it or a bike pump like a weapon and yelling out for help.

Tired of being understanding, I eventually decided to go on the offensive and buy a **(6) Boat Airhorn** and **(7) Halt Pepper Spray**—the latter the weapon of choice for U.S. postal carriers. Unfortunately, it only works if you hit the target in the eyes—a difficult enough feat when standing still, much less riding. I taped the Halt to one side of my handlebars. On the other side, I affixed the small high-decibel airhorn. I was ready for battle. But I never used the Halt. And the airhorn was more often used to ward off dive-bombing red-winged blackbirds nesting in roadside ditches. As I headed farther west, and farms gave way to the cattle ranches of Nebraska and then the dry wastes of Wyoming, I gratefully encountered fewer and fewer dogs. I didn't mind this at all. I never liked dogs, though years later a Golden Retriever named Rockee had entered and stayed in my life for 14 wonderful years. The day before this rambunctious, loving animal died in my arms at the vet from a ruptured spleen, I had towed him up Mt. Tam in Marin in a Burley children's trailer behind my Klein mountain bike. I was his beast of burden. —BK

·12·
HOW TO SURVIVE...
A Bear Attack

First mountain lions. Then dogs. Now grizzly bears? On August 29, 2004, a quick-thinking mountain biker in Wyoming's

Shoshone National Forest fought off a grizzly that repeatedly charged him until a companion drove the animal off with pepper spray. Kirk Speckhals, 46, escaped being mauled, though he sported these trailside mementos: four dirt marks from the bear's claws on his forearm, a punctured bicycle tire, and a bent rim.

The encounter took place during a ride around Pinnacle Buttes, near the Yellowstone ecosystem, where the grizzly population has increased from 200 to 500 over the past 30 years. Riding with pepper-spray-carrying Tom Foley, Speckhals, a ski patroller, had been ringing his bicycle bell at regular intervals to warn possible bears of his approach. For some reason, he had stopped ringing his bell when he saw a grizzly off in the distance, about the length of a football field, in full charge, coming right at him. "He charged six or seven times," Speckhals later told an Associated Press reporter, but each time it was deterred at the last moment by the bicycle. "Finally, he grabbed my bike out of my hands. He started stomping on it." With the bear distracted, Speckhals started creeping away, but Yogi immediately left the bike and put its front paws on Speckhals. "This time he just took me out—drug me to the ground," he said. "I knew I was in trouble. I rotated and got on my chest." Foley, arriving to find the bear sitting atop his friend, grabbed his pepper spray, aimed for its eyes, and yelled as loud as he could. The grizzly ran off.

Fear factor, indeed. Grizzlies have been known to attack campers and hikers in Montana's Glacier National Park. It is not a pleasant way to die; hence their Latin name, *ursus horribilis*. If you happen to go mountain biking in areas known to support grizzlies—Alaska and British Columbia sport significant bear populations, including brown and black bears—here's some practical advice to heed, according to *Safe Travel in Bear Country*, by Gary Brown (Lyons Press).

- Since wash basins often smell and food odors permeate your tent, sleeping bag, and panniers, wash or clean all of them before you begin your trip—especially if you've cooked in or near it.
- Body odors (food, medicines, lotions, repellents, etc.) may attract bears, as well as human sexual activity. So keep as personally clean as possible; wash up after cooking, eating, sex, and before retiring.
- Other items that attract bears: fragrant and sweet-smelling items like perfumes, deodorants, cosmetics, lotions, shampoos, soaps, suntan lotions, and toothpaste; some first-aid items and medicines (such as Campho-Phenique); also lip salves and balms, insect repellents, pot scrubbers, vinyl, foam rubber, and motor oil.

The Alaska Bureau of Land Management field office offers these pointers.

1. **Look and listen:** Bears are active both day and night and may appear anywhere.
2. **Don't surprise them:** A startled bear may attack.
3. **Make noises:** Let bears know you are in the area—sing, yell, or clap your hands loudly. Bells may be ineffective. Be especially careful in thick brush or near noisy streams.

4. **If you encounter a bear, don't try to run or bike away:** They've been clocked at speeds up to 35 mph, and running may elicit a chase response. If the bear does not see you, backtrack or detour quickly and quietly. Give him plenty of room. Back away slowly if he sees you, speak in a low, calm voice while waving your arms over your head.

5. **If a grizzly makes physical contact, play dead:** Lie flat on your stomach and lace your fingers behind your neck.

6. **If a black bear attacks, fight back:** In Alaska, you can protect yourself with firearms if you have a permit. In the lower 48 states, you need to make do with pepper spray.

Most bears tend to avoid people. Seventy percent of the killings by grizzly bears are by mothers defending their cubs, says wildlife biologist and black bear expert Lynn Rogers. "But nobody's ever been killed by a mother black bear defending her cubs. Black bears are not territorial toward people and are usually afraid of being attacked themselves," Rogers says. "Their most common aggressive displays are merely rituals that they perform when they are nervous. Most likely bears will run away or seek safety in a tree. A bear will break off its attack once it feels the threat has been eliminated. Remain motionless for as long as possible. If you move, and the bear sees or hears you, it may return and renew its attack. In rare instances, particularly with black bears, an attacking bear may perceive a person as food. If the bear continues biting you long after you assume a defensive posture, it likely is a predatory attack." She too urges fighting back.

·13·
HOW TO SURVIVE...
Road Rage and Lousy Drivers

Over the years, I have been swerved at by young hot-rodders in California, honked at by malicious cretins in Montana, the object of thrown beer cans and firecrackers by Michigan motorists, knocked off my bike by a drowsy elderly man outside Ann Arbor, and nearly run over by a feckless 15-year-old driver in Nebraska who was learning to drive with his mother as his passenger.

One of the most bizarre incidents occurred near my home in Mill Valley, California. I was riding about a foot to the left of the white shoulder line to avoid roadside trash when a late-model Cutlass swerved at me. The driver then stopped in the middle of the road, got out of his car and blocked my path. Naturally I was forced to halt.

Fiendishly puffing on a cigarette, he began yelling at me, standing just inches from my face: "All you foreigners coming to my state are ruining it. You're not a native, I am!" I didn't say a word during his insane tirade. Nor could I follow his logic, except to speculate that he might have equated cycling with foreign imports such as Brie and Perrier.

As he spewed angry nonsense, I silently weighed the pros and cons of defending my roadside rights and possibly getting into a fistfight on a glorious Saturday morning in the middle of the road on busy East Blithedale Avenue. When he was done with his roadside rant, he got back in his car and drove off, his broken muffler making throaty, bronchial noises.

Why is everyone in such a hurry? I might scold motorists if they are driving too close to me, or if they cut me off. But with road rage being all the rage these days, I've learned to look before leaping into an altercation. A bike is no match for a 7,000-pound SUV. Or even a driver carrying a gun. A study by the American Automobile Association (AAA) in 1997, found that 37 percent of road rage drivers used firearms against another driver, and 35 percent used their car as a weapon

The rules of the road? The League of American Bicyclists offers an Emily Post–like guide to sensible riding when faced with road rage: "Remove yourself; make every attempt to get out of their way; yield lane position by turning or slowing down and getting behind them; be prepared to execute emergency maneuvers; do not return any gestures or shouts; do not make eye contact; do not push for proper lane position to avoid challenging the driver."

So swallow your pride. You can't change the behavior and driving habits of distracted or ill-mannered drivers. All you can do is keep your own eyes on the road, both hands on the handlebars, and your ego tightly fastened underneath your bike helmet. And report the miscreant's license plate and description to state and local police as fast as you can. —*BK*

14

THE JOURNEY

Centuries. Touring. Hill-climb challenges.
Twenty-four-hour relays. Cross-state rides.
With its immense variety, cycling offers
motivation for everyone.

W HEN I WAS *in my early 30s, I used to think that there were two types of bicyclists in this world: the people who like the Donut Shop Ride, and the people who don't. I was one of the latter. I used to think the former were narrow-minded fools, mainly because they seemed unaware that any type of cycling—or anything at all, for that matter—existed beyond their 30-mile neighborhood loop, whereas cycling for me was all about escaping the neighborhood and seeing the world.*

I didn't know Donut Shop riders existed until late 1992. One day earlier that year, I had ridden my bike into my new job as editor of Bicycle Guide magazine, a rather ordinary action for the editor of a bike magazine to take, I thought. When I came back from lunch, I saw several members of the ad and editorial staffs, all hard-core racers, gathered around my bike, a Trek 1200 road bike with fenders, huge, triathlon-style Scott aerobars with bar-end shifters, a frame pouch for food, three water bottles, and a special bracket holding lights and a bell. They all wore puzzled expressions and were shaking their heads. "Yeah, rode that thing in Paris-Brest-Paris last year," I said as casually as I could as I went by. "Hardest thing I ever did."

No one said a word. Which was weird, since P-B-P is probably the hardest ultra-distance race in the world, aside from the Race Across America, 750 miles in three and one-half nearly sleepless days, from Paris to the Atlantic coast and back. For 5,000-plus endurance riders who show up in Paris every four years, a P-B-P finish is like graduating from Harvard.

Weeks later, my boss called me in to his office and told me that several people in the organization had asked him to fire me. Seems they didn't like the idea of a sissy who used fenders being the voice of the magazine. It was at that moment that I realized that none of these hard-core road racers in the office had heard of P-B-P. As I quickly set about explaining to everyone exactly what

Paris-Brest-Paris meant and why fenders and lights were required for it, then added that I had ridden my bike 25,000 miles around the world, including through the Soviet Union, and was described as "America's most traveled bike tourist" on my just-published book, the ice thawed and several invited me to join them on a ride in the South Bay on Saturday morning. That's when I found out many cyclists' concept of what the sport is all about is limited to the Donut Ride.

Starting in Redondo Beach, they hug the cliffs and zig-zag up and down the steep climbs of Palos Verde Peninsula for 37 wheel-sucking miles on their aerobar-less road bikes, back then mostly of Italian make. I love the route but hate pace-line riding; it's nerve-wracking and you can't look up for a second to take in the view, much less stop for a photo. Everyone was so serious—and going so fast. We ended up, just about two hours after the 7 AM start, at a Starbucks, where everybody sat back and sucked down a frappacino and a muffin and talked about component groups. Different groups of twelve and twenty cyclists came in at a time; I saw maybe 100 altogether during my 30 minutes. Most had been doing this ride ever since a donut shop stood on this corner. In fact, for most, the Donut Ride is all they did in cycling. I talked to a dozen people, all hard-core racers or wannabes. Not one had ever been on a bike tour, owned a pannier, or ridden a century, much less heard of P-B-P. No one had ever ridden in the nearby Santa Monica Mountains, full of hundreds of miles of twisty, challenging two-lane roads. That's crazy, I thought. They don't know what they're missing. The bike is a machine of infinite travel possibilities. The cycling world is a huge smorgasbord of events—cross-state rides, double-centuries, hill-climb challenges, cross-country touring, and, nowadays, epic mountain bike adventures. How can they get motivated to do this same-ole-same-ole week after week, year after year?

Well, it's a dozen years later and I get together nearly every Saturday morning with three forty-something guys and do a casual two-hour mountain bike ride. Nothing epic, just a couple of predictable local loops in Silverado Canyon or at Whiting Ranch in Orange County. Anyhow, Matta, the contractor; Kennedy, the magic-trick inventor; and Grant, the machinery salesman, aren't the most hard-core riders I've ever met and don't have any interest in dawn-to-dusk death rides, but we've shared bad crashes, broken chains and blown tires. They motivate me to get up at 6 AM, instead of sleeping in. On the way home, we almost always stop at a Greek deli for 45 minutes of shooting the breeze about cycling and politics and technology and the Lakers.

I still draw a lot of my motivation to ride from planning and training for big epic adventures in far-off places. The bike is, first and foremost, a vehicle of exploration for me. But after all these years, I've come to see the value of the Donut Ride, too.—RMW

For excitement, motivation, challenge, competition, and sheer variety, cycling can keep you engaged indefinitely. This book's coauthors have spent much of their adult lives sampling the riding variety this sport has to offer, and in this chapter will leave you with a wide-ranging list of great cycling events that can provide years of challenges. Before those, however, we've included two personal favorites from our files that we think illustrate two important, underutilized themes—exploration and team competitions—that can help provide cyclists with huge motivation to *Bike for Life*.

How I Learned to Stop Worrying About Mileage Markers and Love the Scenery

13 road-tested lessons from a solo trip across the U.S.

By Bill Katovsky–Published originally in *Adventure Cyclist* in Fall 2003

A SUPERBREED OF marathon cyclist now tears across America in eight, nine days. That's almost as fast as traveling by Greyhound, and probably about as comfortable. These sleep-deprived speed demons live on Ensure for liquid fuel and the kindness of their support staff who trail behind in cramped motorhomes that reek of Tiger Balm and WD-40. In the Race Across America (RAAM), there is absolutely zero time for photo-snapping at historical national monuments. What's required by competitors can be whittled down to these simple truths: Keep your legs spinning in an even cadence, with your body and head in a tucked aero position, while your front tire kisses that lonesome highway from here to eternity.

The transcontinental urge to cross the U.S. has been our manifest destiny. "Go west, young man." And we as a nation did. But it's a different kind of Land Rush for cyclists. Traveling west is the wrong, slower direction on account of prevailing headwinds. Nonetheless that was the compass direction I selected back in the summer of 1978, when I left Ann Arbor, Michigan, where I was attending college. I was relatively new to cycling, with only two century rides to my credit (Cleveland to Toledo, and back again).

By peering back into the rearview mirror of a quarter century, the memory of biking that summer through Michigan, Wisconsin, Iowa, Nebraska, Wyoming, Montana, Idaho, and Oregon still remains an indelible one, as well-worn, contoured, and creased with fond remembrances as the Ideale leather bike saddle (with copper rivets the size of pennies) that made the voyage with me.

In retrospect, my bike trip was as much physical as it was mental. That first day on the bike had to be one of the loneliest days in my life. After a quick good-bye to my girlfriend who was standing in front of our boarding house in Ann Arbor, Michigan, I pointed my wobbly-with-extra-weight Falcon westward, yet later ended up only biking 45 miles that day. It was not because I was tired. Instead, I needed to mentally regroup. I was uncertain about this quest, a walkabout on two wheels. Call it fear of the unknown. So I checked into a cheap $12 a day motel in Jackson because I wanted to hear human voices, even if they came from a television. I ended up watching a Dialing for Dollars matinee movie. There was no phone in the room so I didn't call my girlfriend, who was never chatty to begin with. She never quite understood what I was trying to prove by pedaling across the United States. Did I?

So many emotions were madly swirling through my head that first day. It was a day punctuated with rather bleak roadside realities: A car full of teenagers lobbed a firecracker at me. Several other motorists tried to run me off the road. This was Michigan, the motor state. Bikes are anathema. I was still too close to Detroit. One other fact intrigued me: the number of dead, squashed animals littering the side of the road. So much highway roadkill—squirrels, opossum, birds. I tried not to extrapolate any deeper existential meaning from all this flattened fauna.

Seven weeks and 2,800 bike-miles later, I arrived in the small coastal town of Lincoln City, Oregon, where I took the much-anticipated baptismal plunge into the cold Pacific surf. Triumphant with pride and accomplishment, I screamed to the sky, the waves, the empty beach that I had done it—I had biked across America! It was such a sweet personal victory and triumph that still tastes delicious—a quarter century later.

Here then is a list of thirteen lessons I learned that summer—hard-fought lessons that I followed for years afterward on bike trips through Califonia, the American Southwest, the Rockies and elsewhere. And these lessons can be especially relevant to anyone planning a self-supported multi-day bike trip.

1. ***No matter how many miles you travel in a day, you will always want to bike more.*** Does it really make a difference whether you clock 60 miles instead of 75 miles? Oftentimes, you will want to mix in a little sightseeing, which cuts into time in the saddle. Distances are only important if they represent where you can find a campground or motel before dusk. The authentic test of truth occurred for me one afternoon in north-central Nebraska. It was raining hard. A plumber's van stopped, and the driver waved me over. "How about I give you a lift," he said. "How far you traveling?" I asked. "All the way across the state into eastern Colorado. About 270 miles, I reckon." I silently considered his offer for several seconds, but before I had time to change my mind, I hurriedly said, "No thanks. I'm fine with cycling." He wished me well and drove off. I biked another 15 soggy miles that day to a one-saloon town, pitched my tent under some trees, while the storm persisted. The Devil had tried to tempt me, and I had told him to get lost.

2. ***Ninety-nine percent of the people you will meet along the way won't have a clue as to what you're doing.*** In a restaurant parking lot in Riverton, Wyoming, which was less than 100 miles from the Continental Divide, I encountered several couples on their Honda Goldwing motorcycles. One husband and wife were dressed in identical leisure suits, both Pillsbury Dough Boy plump. I asked them, "How far have you come?" They didn't even answer my question. They just stared at me and my pannier-loaded bicycle, shaking their heads in disgust or bafflement.

3. ***If strangers do have a clue as to what you're doing, the three questions that you will most likely be asked are: (1) where you from? (2) where you headed? and (3) how many flats you have?*** This friendly interrogation generally doesn't venture beyond these three questions, but if there happens to be a fourth, it will usually be less of a question than a statement: "You still have a long way to go."

4. ***A hill beats a headwind any time.*** Because I was traveling east to west, I spent virtually every day battling persistent headwinds, especially in late afternoons. One time, along the eastern plains of Nebraska, gale-force winds forced me to pedal in my lowest gear even while going downhill. I was lucky to average five miles per hour that blowing day. On the other hand, a hill or mountain grade has an endpoint, a summit where all that effort expended on ascending is rewarded with the descent. But an unforgiving headwind takes no prisoners, gives no quarter; it's relentless, a brute force that mocks those who dare to defy it. You must charge into it, like a bull with its horns lowered.

5. ***Don't be hung-up or fixated on equipment, since what fuels your trip is your head and heart.*** Yes, so much of cycling long distances is mental. It's not really a matter of whether you're riding a $4,000 titanium steed. Or whether you have state-of-the-art componentry. I rode a 10-speed Falcon before switching to a Trek. For clothing, I wore cotton Adidas gym shorts, an old tattered blue dress shirt, and a pair of Robert Haillet tennis shoes. During the day, I dined on Snickers bars and endless cans of Mountain Dews. This was an era before Lycra, hard-shell helmets, aerobars, clipless pedals, triple chain-rings, and energy bars. Yet, by summer's end, I was in great shape, with chiseled quads and calves. I used to boast, "I feel like I can walk up walls!" At the same time, if the right bike and equipment will make your trip more enjoyable, then by all means, embrace these necessary expenditures.

6. ***Take rest days.*** The occasional extended pit stop will keep your trip fresh and invigorating, because there will be some days when the mere thought of getting on your bike in the morning will make you want to book a flight home. The bike becomes your enemy instead of your ally. One of my trip highlights was the two days I spent off my bike in Grand Teton National Park, where I went hiking in the canyons, swimming in Colter Bay Lake, and lounging in the campground.

7. ***Share notes with other cyclists heading from the other direction.*** While days, and sometimes weeks, would pass when I wouldn't see another cyclist, I always welcomed the opportunity to talk shop whenever I did encounter one. You might discover new information about road conditions or the best diner with real homemade cooking. Also, don't try to be outpsyched when these strangers start to boast about how many miles they average per day. Remember: You are doing this trip for yourself. (Unless you're riding a tandem.) At one campground in western Montana, I encountered a tour group from Bikecentennial. There were about a dozen riders. We swapped stories, compared

notes. (I was following the Bikecentennial route for much of the second half of my trip, relying on those handy guides which I kept tucked inside my Kirkland rear panniers.) These riders envied my individual freedom from tangled-up, messy group dynamics. "I wish I was biking alone," several of these cyclists let me know in soft conspiratorial tones. I appreciated their vote of confidence for my style of traveling, but I didn't have the heart to tell them about all those lonely, miserable hours of privately watching those highway mileage markers incrementally record my progress, my sole companion the constant steady rush of the wind always whistling in my ears.

8. ***Know how to fix a flat.*** For two days in north-central Nebraska, I rode with a guy named Kevin whom I met in a campground. He was nineteen, and was cycling from La Salle, Wisconsin, to Bozeman, Montana, to attend his brother's wedding. He told me that he had never fixed a flat before, though he came prepared, since he had brought along a thick bike repair manual. "If I get a flat, I will just read how to fix it." The book must have weighed several pounds. One shouldn't count on luck, however. One day, in western Iowa, I had three flats within two hours. Frustrated and seething with unfocused rage, I was ready to quit my bike trip right then and there—50 miles from the Missouri River—and with half a continent still waiting for me. (At the next bike shop in Sioux City, I found my lifesaver in a pair of thorn-proof inner tubes.)

9. ***You can't be fussy about where you end up sleeping.*** Though I carried an eight-pound Eureka tent, there were many times when I was too tired to want to set up the tent; I just wanted to lie down and go to sleep after a solid day of riding. A tent is useful when it rains or in mosquito-infested areas. Otherwise, keep the tent at home. It's not worth the extra weight. My tent sort of came in handy during a storm-tossed night in northeastern Nebraska. The thunderstorm seemed to hover right over the campground, sending down bolts of lightning and ear-splitting booms of thunder. The wind whipped around the tent, yanking out the stakes, so I was forced to lie down in a spread-eagle position to keep the tent from blowing over. Several inches of water covered the bottom after it had seeped up from the grass. That soupy, sleepless night was the worst night of my trip. I had been so unnerved by the tempest that I only went 20 miles the next day, checking into an $10 a night motel room. I experienced another uncomfortable night in Natrona, population 5, just east of Casper, Wyoming, where the only bare patch of bare ground was a patch of gravel next to two gas pumps at the service station/cafe—which also functioned as the "town center." (At the cafe, a beefy foreman from Burlington Railroad offered me a job to shovel cinder along railway beds. "It pays $10 an hour, but you need to watch out for rattlesnakes. You just kill'em with your shovel.") Generally speaking, I found that some of the best places for camping in small towns were found in the commons area located within the town square. The grass was usually thick and soft, and

nobody would bother you. I avoided campgrounds because of the ubiquitous RVs and their noisy electric generators. One cyclist I met said he preferred sleeping in cemeteries. "No one disturbs you there," he said.

10. ***Keep a journal.*** It takes only a few minutes each night to record your observations and experiences. I still like to thumb through my sweat-ruined, grease-smeared, spiral-ringed notebooks that I kept as company. During my trip, it became a nocturnal ritual, that after I had eaten dessert, I would take out the tiny notebook, in which I would record my mileage that I calculated by taking a piece of string and measuring it along an AAA road map. (Even in the modern era of cyclometers, this is still my preferred mode of measuring mileage. Old habits die hard.)

11. ***Learn to deal with pain and discomfort***. It took about two weeks of riding for my legs to get in shape. My quads were terribly sore and fatigued those intitial riding days. I hadn't really trained for the journey—maybe two hundred miles of riding the previous six weeks. However, small physical ailments soon began to accumulate along with the mileage. I experienced numbness in both hands. It became difficult to turn doorknobs or use the phone. Even though I kept changing my hand positions on the handlebars, the numbness from nerve damage increased. I finally alleviated some of the numbness by cutting off a section of my sleeping pad and wrapping the handlebars with the foam pad. Yes, I also got saddle sores—which are a bummer. Also, if you have a lingering ailment before your trip, take care of it prior to your start. I had painful ingrown toenails on both big toes. As long as I was cycling, I didn't feel the pain. But once I hopped off the bike, I could barely walk. Finally, in Idaho just east of Boise, when the toe pain became too severe, I checked into a medical clinic on a small Indian reservation, and the young doctor there performed quick podiatric surgery.

12. ***Expect the unexpected, but savor the thrills.*** When I reached my first Continental Divide, high up on Togwotee Pass in Wyoming, with the snow-capped Tetons off in the distance, I camped that night by a stream and lulled myself to sleep by the soothing sound of the moving water and the satisfaction of a job well done. Though I had another 1,000 miles to go before I arrived at the coast, I had reached a major milestone. It would be erroneous for me not to mention all the times that I had wanted to quit way back in Iowa when I was adrift in a sea of green cornfields. Or how disgusted I felt one morning riding through a locust-infested swath of an unpaved 20-mile stretch in northwestern Nebraska, when swarms of these hopping demons covered my legs and arms almost the entire distance. The four subsequent times that I would later cross the Divide as I angled northwest, I would get off my bike and toast my good fortune with a swig from my water bottle.

13. ***Be vigilant.*** You are sharing the road with cars, SUVs, semis, RVs, joyriding teens, sleep-deprived folks driving home after work. RVs can be especially

BIKE FOR LIFE

lethal, because the vacationer behind the wheel doesn't always remember how far that oversize rearview mirror on the passenger side extends. You need to stay focused and alert while you ride. Even on my very last day of riding, with only 20 miles remaining before I arrived at the Pacific Ocean, a dark cloud of superstition hovered over me. I kept telling myself, "Be extra careful. You don't want to have an accident, especially now." Still, how could I have prepared for the near mishap when a toaster fell off the back of a pickup truck piled with household junk? The appliance bounced once on the asphalt and missed my front wheel by about a foot. I almost was toast, so to speak, but fortunately the cycling gods were smiling on me, as I continued westward on the final day of my 2,800 mile cross-country trip.

Go Team Go

The primal need of 24-hour mountain bike racing

By Roy M. Wallack–Published originally in *Dirt Rag,* May 2002

"DID YOU CHARGE your lights? Are you sure you charged your lights?" Rich screamed.

"Yes, yes, yes," I assured him. "Don't worry. Brand-new. Used once. Recharged for hours back home. Done deal."

And so began the most memorable lap of 24-hour racing in my life. Which might seem kind of strange, given that it was a lap I didn't ride.

While I retreated back to the campfire, reached in the cooler for another beer, and dangled another hot dog over the flaming logs, Rich rode off into the night. With my lights. Under my name.

You see, I was supposed to be riding in the 1996 24-Hours of Moab, not him. But the day before the event, as the members of Team Mountain Dogs, our bike club, casually pre-rode the 10-mile loop, I bit the dust. Hard.

Distracted by a "hey!" yelled by a photographer off to the left, I buried my front wheel in a rut and face-planted. I have no memory of falling or of the impact. When I awoke, my friends said I'd been unconscious for three minutes. After another two minutes, I began to remember my own name. By the time I was able to recall the name of my then-two-year-old son, Joey, a four-wheel-drive ambulance had arrived to take me to a Moab hospital.

That night, the sight of my face actually compelled a child at the local McDonald's to clutch his daddy's leg in fear. On race day, with six stitches in my lip, a throbbing sensation in my cheekbone, and an oozing crust congealing over the right side of my mug from mouth to eye to ear like a gory Phantom of the Opera mask, it seemed best to let Rich take my place.

Not that anyone seemed to mind. Mountain Dog founder Rich "The Reverend" White, known for his passionate pontificating about all things mountain biking, is a superb rider, way faster than me. Although he hadn't planned to race—he was chronically short of cash and didn't want to pay the $100 share of the entry fee and expenses—he had a confirmed seat on the 12-hour road trip from L.A. because we all wanted to channel his energy. In fact, I was here in Utah because of Rich. Four years earlier, after we'd met when I tried to sell my first book to the bike shop he managed, he'd taught me how to mountain bike, introduced me to the beauty of the mountains. I was almost honored to will my lights to him.

Still, I was bummed—this would have been my first 24-hour race. Now, it was a lost weekend.

THE REVELATION

In the hours before the race, I pondered the gruesome shell hardening over my face and watched with envy as the Mountain Dogs scurried about, worrying over this and that. I had no purpose; I was worthless. But as I moped around the 1,000-strong tent city, something strange happened.

A camaraderie. A getting-away-for-an-adventure-with-my-friends vibe. A "where-ya-from-dude-and-what-the-hell-happened-to-your-face?" neighborliness. It was infectious. And suddenly, riding or not, this event was giving me something I needed, something I craved, something I didn't experience much in everyday life: the feeling of being part of a team on a great quest.

I'm no psychologist, and I know that lots of women do these events, too, but it seems that 24-hour races tap into a primal compulsion that men can understand best: the need to get together, take on a challenge, get sweaty, get bloody, and, most of all, get tales to tell. Tales for next week's ride. Tales for the next family barbecue. Tales for 50 years from now, when we're using wheelchairs instead of bikes, pacemakers instead of HRMs, and diapers instead of Lycra shorts.

If I'd known then that I'd do a half-dozen 24-hour events after this, including a solo, I wouldn't have been surprised. If you had told anyone at Moab that by 2005 there would be dozens of 24-hour races across North America, 20,000 participants, NORBA-sanctioned team and solo championships, and a Solo world title race with hundreds of age-group participants, they might have said "of course." After all, we'd been practically crying for something like this for years.

Yes, I was out of the race as a rider. But a team needs more than that. There would be chains to lube, dozing riders to wake, beers to chill, hot dogs to roast, and stories to record for posterity. And who better to do that than me, a former wedding videographer?

THE GUARDIAN ANGEL

It's midnight, about the time I figured Rich ought to be finishing his lap, and the start-finish zone is electric. Too early to sleep, too dark to ride without fear, hundreds of spectators and competitors clog the finishing chute in a frenzy of sound and sweat. In the middle of it all is yours truly, a regular Geraldo Rivera, asking the hard questions on videotape. "What's it like to share the same bike shorts for 24 hours?" I grill two clothes-swapping members of Team Largeass.

Soon it's 12:10, 12:15, and I pan over to Craig, our Mountain Dog teammate awaiting the baton. Where's Rich? He shoulda been here by now! Did he crash? Is he hurt?

Finally, at 12:20, Rich comes flying into the pits, drenched in sweat and quivering with excitement. He hands the baton to Craig. And he tells me something that makes me cringe: "It was the lights."

My lights—the ones I assured him were potent enough to beckon a supertanker to harbor. They burned out around 11:30, halfway through the most treacherous part of the 10-mile loop. I remember his words as if they were my own: "Suddenly, I find myself blind, invisible, freezing, and terrified in the wet, moonless night. One false step in my slippery clipless shoes could put me into the path of mountain bikers flying downhill at 30 mph—or plunge me 50 feet into jagged rocks below. So I inch along in baby steps. At this rate, it'll be hours before I get back."

I feel like hell. I let a teammate down. I start to apologize. Then Rich stops me.

"Roy, don't worry about it," he says. "Because of those lights, this turned into one of the greatest rides of my life."

Huh?

"After about 20 minutes in the middle of nowhere," he explains, "a featureless biker screeches to a halt, his handlebar-mounted lights blazing like the eyes of a snarling animal. 'Get on my wheel, now!' he barks.

"And for the next 30 minutes I hang on for dear life, tethered to the halogen beams of a human seeing-eye dog who screams at me to stay with him, to speed up, to turn right or left or standup, to ride with more exhilaration and terror and pure speed than I've ever ridden in my life.

"Who he was, I don't know. But he was an animal. A guardian-angel animal!"

The second he says that, I notice a muscular, dark-haired biker from L.A. who I've interviewed several times before. It's Johnny G., renowned fitness guru and inventor of Spinning, the ultra-popular health-club stationary cycling program. He'd brought a team to Moab—Team Spinning, of course. He'd just finished a lap in 1 hour, 5 minutes—which was quite fast, especially at night. I remark how impressed I am with his time.

"I might have gone even faster," he notes in his distinctive South African accent, "if I didn't have to stop to tow a guy in."

I'll never forget seeing Rich grab Johnny's hand and shake it, especially since the moment is immortalized on videotape. "Thank you, thank you, thank you," he babbles to his rescuer. He becomes almost reverential when he looks at the posted standings, which show Team Spinning in the top five.

"Wow, you're a contender," Rich says, "And you stopped to help me. Unbelievable."

Johnny G., always the motivator, shrugged off the thanks. "Above everything, these 24-hour events are all about teamwork," he says, his tone modulated like an Indian wise man. "Even if it's not your team."

Wow. Teamwork—*even if it's not your team*. I bask in his words, so true, so poignant, so perfectly capturing the beauty of this remarkable 24-hour bonding experience. Then I put the camcorder down. Johnny's eyes instantly narrow, then dilate.

"My god, Roy," he says, "What in the hell happened to your face?"

• AN EVENT SAMPLER •

Cycling is a big umbrella that covers a wide variety of riding challenges, from hill-climb events, to cross-state tours, to mass one-day city rides that draw thousands, to multi-day mountain bike stage races, 750-mile nonstop endurathons, to epic centuries and overnighters. Experiment, sample a few from each category, push your boundaries; it's one way that cycling can keep you excited for a lifetime. Here are a few good ones to get you started.

ROAD BIKE HILL-CLIMB EVENTS

Fancy aero handlebars, disk wheels, and wind-cheating bike frames won't help you on a hill climb, where fitness, stick-to-it-tiveness, some technique, and raw pride matter most. Nothing beats the epic satisfaction of conquering a mountain, especially when it's steeped in cycling lore and gives you a finisher's medal as proof, as do the following hill-climb events. For more info on these and other events, check www.altrec.com/published/cycle/other/hillclimbs/

1. **Mt. Haleakala, Maui, Hawaii**

    One of the steepest, longest climbs on Earth—37 miles, 10,000 feet—rises from the sea-level town of Paia into Haleakala National Park, passing through several distinct climactic zones before reaching the top of the crater.

    When: August

    Contact: www.cycletothesun.com; 808-572-4400 or 808-244-5502

2. **Mt. Evans, Colorado**

    This 28-mile climb in the Rockies starts at 7,540 feet and tops out at 14,250 feet. It's been canceled twice in 38 years due to snow; be prepared for goats, sheep, awesome scenery, and bitter cold. Pro Tom Danielson set the record of 1:45:30 in 2004.

    When: Late July

    Contacts: www.americancycling.org; www.bicyclerace.com; 303-322-3420

3. **Snowbird, Utah**

This 10-miler climbs 3,500 feet up spectacular Little Cottonwood Canyon.

When: August

Contacts: www.bicycleutah.com; 801-933-2113

4. **Mt. Tamalpais, Marin County, California**

This classic 12.5-miler rises 2,200 feet from Stinson Beach and ends with a stunning 360-degree panorama of the Pacific Ocean, the Golden Gate Bridge, and San Francisco. The record is 37 minutes, 26 minutes, set in 2003.

When: September

Contacts: www.californiaroadclub .org/races04/mt_tam_hill_climb.html

5. **Mt. Greylock, Massachusetts**

This 9.8-miler rises 2,793 feet as it tops out at 3,491 feet, the highest point in the state.

When: September or October

Contacts: www.ne-bra.org

6. **Mt. Graham, Arizona**

This 20-mile, 5,600-feet-of-elevation climb starts in dry brush and winds up through pine forest in 12 hairpin turns to the peak's aspen-covered 9,600-foot summit.

When: September or October

Contacts: www.azcycling.com; 520-795-7006

7. **Sandia Crest, New Mexico**

Located on the Turquoise Trail, a forested national scenic byway between Albuquerque and Santa Fe, the climb to the 10,678-foot summit of Sandia Crest leaves you at the Sandia Peak Tramway, the longest jig-back tram in the world.

When: June

Contacts: www.nmbikensport.com; 505-235-8720; or www.turquoisetrail .org/sandiacrest; 505-242-9052

8. **Mt. Charleston, Nevada**

This 17-mile, 5,700-foot climb begins on the parched desert floor 30 miles north of Las Vegas and ends in cool (sometimes freezing) pine-tree-studded, snowcapped mountains. Pack a fleece vest.

When: September

Contacts: 702-228-9560

9. **Mt. Washington, New Hampshire**

This ultra-steep 7.6-miler averages an otherworldly 12 percent grade while gaining 4,727 feet, with the last 50 meters maxing out at a tendon-tearing 22 degrees. Beware of harsh weather, high winds, and occasional sub-zero windchill near the top of the northeast's highest, steepest mountain road.

When: August or September

Contacts: www.tinmtn.org/hill climb/index.cfm

10. **Mt. Diablo, California**

You won't be lonely on this 10.8-mile, 2,751-foot climb, which gives great views of San Francisco Bay from the summit. It regularly draws over 1,000 participants.

When: October

Contacts: www.mrsnv.com/evt/ home.jsp

11. **Western Montana**

A tradition for nearly 30 years, this 4-mile, 840-foot romp to the 4,000-foot finish has a division for everyone: tandems, unicycles, recumbents, and even high-wheelers.

When: October

Contacts: www.missoulabike.org /Rides/HillClimb

12. **Mt. Equinox, Vermont**

The 5.2-mile, 2,800-foot-high route up this Carthusian monastery toll road offers a spectacular view of four states.

When: May

Contacts: www.tinmtn.org/hill climb/index.cfm

13. **Bogus Basin**

Starting in dry brush near Boise, the nation's oldest hill-climb contest travels 17 miles and 3,500 feet high to a ski resort, named after the two prospectors who sold worthless land to fortune seekers here in the 1860s.

When: September

Contacts: www.GeorgesCycles.com

14. **Mt. Lemmon, Arizona**

Soars above Tucson. Spectacular views come one after another on this 27-mile climb east of Tucson, which peaks out at 8,400 feet. The longest climb in the state rises through seven climate zones

When: August

Contacts: www.azcycling.com or www.hlhap.com/azroadclimbs.html

MOUNTAIN BIKE MULTIDAY STAGE RACES

Enjoying immense popularity today are Tour de France–like stage races for amateur mountain bikers. Averaging around 50 grueling miles per day off-road, riders typically spend the night in gymnasiums or tents (or hotels in the case of La Ruta), then head out at 8 AM to do it again.

1. **La Ruta de los Conquistadores**

What: 3-day, 250-miles

Where: Costa Rica

When: Mid-November

Contact: www.mountainbikecosta rica.com or www.adventurerace.com

From the Pacific Ocean to the Caribbean Sea, this grandaddy of mountain-bike stage racing snakes through rain forest, over 11,000-foot volcanoes, banana and coffee plantations, and tiny farm hamlets, alternately drenching you in heat, humidity, or rain and cold during high-elevation segments. Founded in 1992 by famed adventurer Roman Urbina as a cycling reenactment of trail-blazing sixteenth-century Spanish conquistadors.

2. **TransAlp Challenge**

What: Eight days, 400 miles, 61,000 feet of climbing.

Where: Germany to Austria to Italy

When: July

Contact: www.transalp.upsolutmv .com; www.bikeforums.net

This epic race rolls from the southern German pre-Alps to Italy's Lake Garda through the most jagged, beautiful, and daunting parts of the eastern Alps, the Dolomites. Note: It's you and a *partner* against nature. Every checkpoint must be crossed in tandem. Cross a minute apart, you get a two-hour penalty.

3. **TransRockies Challenge**

What: 7 days, 350 miles

Where: Alberta, Canada

When: August

Contact: www.transrockies.com, 403-299-0355 or 877-622-7343

Begun in 2002, this primitive bike, hike, and camp endurathon has a fearsome reputation even among La Ruta and TransAlp vets. Beware: there are hours and hours of hiking, and the Canadian Rockies are wet and cold in the summer.

4. Cape Epic

What: 8 days, 900 km, 20,000 feet of climbing

Where: South Africa

When: April

Contact: www.cape-epic.com/ or www.siyabona.com/event_cape_epic .html

This two-man team race leads over 800 mountain bikers through the Western Cape past wide-open African plains, majestic mountains, deep ravines, arid semi-deserts, indigenous forests, and flourishing vineyards, including a Big Five Game Reserve housing elephants, giraffe, gemsbok, springbok, or even lions.

24-HOUR MOUNTAIN BIKING & OTHER EPICS

Nothing beats the camaraderie and bonding of 24-hour mountain-bike relay racing, which now draws tens of thousands of participants throughout North America. There may be 50 or more races on the continent, with a third of those staged by two big operators.

1. 24 Hours of Adrenalin

Contact: www.twenty4sports.com; www.24hoursofadrenalin.com

The biggest 24-hour event organizer, it stages a dozen races in the U.S. and Canada, and founded a popular solo world championship in 1999.

2. Granny Gear

Contact: www.grannygear.com

The pioneer of the 24-hour race, it stages four races in the U.S.

3. Ride 424

Contact: www.ride424.com

Lists hundreds of 24- and 12-hour races and other one-day events.

Non- 24-hour Epics

3. Leadville Trail 100

When: August

Contact: www.leadvilletrail100 .com

This thin-air 100-mile mountain bike ride based in Leadville, Colorado, ranges in elevation from 9,200 to 12,600 feet. Race vets warn you to race with dark sunglasses during the day, because the thin-air sunshine will burn your retinas and leave you with night blindness.

4. Alaska Iditasport Ultramarathon

When: February

Contact: www.iditasport.com

From Knik Lake to Finger Lake, Alaska, this gruelathon of cold and pain pits skiers, mountain bikers, and runners against 130 miles of the famed Iditarod Trail, site of the Iditarod Dog Sled Race. "Cowards won't show and the weak will die!" once said racer Laddie Shaw.

ENDURANCE ROAD BIKE EVENTS

1. Furnace Creek 508

What: 508-mile bike race

Where: Valencia to Death Valley to 29 Palms, California

When: October 11–13, 2003

Contact: The508.com or adventurecorps.com

A legendary 25-year-old Race Across America qualifier that has grown into an annual destination event drawing competitors and media attention from around the world. Solo and team riders cross a huge swath of Southern California, including Death Valley.

2. **Paris-Brest-Paris**
   What: 1,200 km in 90 hours or less
   When: Every four years since 1891; the next race is 2007
   Participation: 5,000 riders
   Contact: www.rusa.org (Randonneurs USA); www.audax-club-parisien.com
2. **Boston-Montreal-Boston**
   What: 1,200 km (750 miles), under 90 hours
   When: Mid-August
   Participation: Limited to 150 riders
   Contact: bmb1200k@att.net

MULTIDAY CROSS-STATE RIDES

In 1973, when *Des Moines Register* feature writer/copy editor John Karras suggested that he ride his bicycle across Iowa in six days in July and write columns about what he saw, a tradition was born. The public was invited, and about 300 riders showed up for the start of the ride in Sioux City on July 26. By actual count, 114 riders made the entire distance, with 500 riding the last day into Des Moines.

Since then, more than 40 other cross-state rides have been established throughout the years. They have a lot of catching up to do. By the end of the 31st The Register's Annual Great Bicycle Ride Across Iowa® (RAGBRAI) in 2004, more than 223,650 people had ridden at least some part of the 14,650 total miles covered over the years. In three decades, RAGBRAI has passed through 742 Iowa towns (78 percent of the states' incorporated towns), spent the night in 117 different overnight towns and with completion of the 25th ride in 1997, has been in all of Iowa's 99 counties.

Below is contact information on RAGBRAI and some of the other popular state rides. Most are quite inexpensive, even considering that riders camp out or sleep in high school gyms on most rides. If your state isn't listed, try to find it at www.adventurecycling.org or nbtda.com, which has information and links to over 60 rides, including some in Mexico and Canada.

Alabama: BAMA Bike Across Magnificent Alabama
7 days, 350 miles
When: Early June
www.bikebama.com; 256-658-5189

Colorado: Ride the Rockies
6 or 7 days, 350–400 miles
When: Late June
Participation: 2,000, lottery basis
www.ridetherockies.com; rtr@denverpost.com; 303-820-1338
Also in late June is BTC, Bicycle Tour of Colorado
www.bicycletourcolorado.com/

Florida: Bike Florida
7 days, 350–400 miles
When: Late March, April
Participation: 1,000 riders maximum
info@bikeflorida.org; 352-376-6044

Georgia: BRAG—Bike Ride Across Georgia
8 days, 400 miles
When: Mid-June
Participation: 2,000 riders maximum
www.brag.org; 770-921-6166

Idaho: Spuds Cycling Around Idaho
7 days, 429 miles
When: August
Participation : 150 maximum
biking@cyclevents.com; www.spuds.cyclevents.com.

Illinois: Bicycllinois
7 days, 498 miles, Cairo to Chicago
When: Early July
www.bicycllinois.com/; 773-868-1495

Indiana: Cover Indiana Bicycle Tour
7 days, 350 miles
www.habitatindiana.org; 765-449-8900
Also: Touring Ride in Rural Indiana (TRIRI)
www.triri.org; 812-332-6028

Iowa: RAGBRAI
6 days, 450 miles
When: Late July
www.ragbrai.org; 515-284-8285

Kansas: BAK—Bike Across Kansas
8 days, 500 miles
When: Early June
Participation: 800 riders maximum
www.bak.org; 316-284-6811

Louisiana: Cycle Louisiana
450 miles
When: May
ppitzer@crt.state.la.us.; 225-342-8173

Maine: Trek Across Maine
3 days, 180 miles
When: Mid-June
Rider limit: 1,800
American Lung Association, www.maine lung.org.

Maryland: Cycle Across Maryland
7 days, 300 miles
When: Late July
Rider limit: 1,500
info@cyclexmd.org or www.cyclexmd.org
410-653-8288; 888-CAM-RIDE

Massachusetts: Mass Bike Tour
7 days, 375 miles
When: Mid-July 18–24
Rider limit: 200
www.massbike.org

Missouri: CAM—Cycle Across Missouri
7 days
When: Mid-June
davereiter1@earthlink.net; 314-406-2359

Montana: Cycle Montana
7 days, 280 miles
When: Mid-July
Participation: 170 riders maximum
www.adventurecycling.org/tours/index.cfm;
800-755-2453

Nebraska: BRAN—Bicycle Ride Across Nebraska
7 days, 519 miles
When: Early June
Participation: 600 riders maximum
www.bran-inc.org; 402-397-9785

North Carolina: Cycle North Carolina
8 days
When: Start of October
Participation: 1,200 riders maximum
www.ncsports.org or www.cyclenorth carolina.org; 919-361-1133

North Dakota: Cycling Around Sakakawea Country
8 days, 452 miles
When: Late July–August
Rider limit: 350
www.state.nd.us/ndparks

Ohio: GOBA—Great Ohio Bicycle Adventure
8 days, 350 miles
When: Mid-June
Participation: 3,000 riders maximum
www.goba.com, 614-273-0811, or www.outdoor-pursuits.org

Oklahoma: Oklahoma Freewheel
8 days, 400 miles
When: Mid-June
Rider limit: 2,000
Tulsa World, www.okfreewheel.com

Oregon: Cycle Oregon
When: September
www.cycleoregon.com; OREGON 800-CYCLEOR

South Carolina: Cycle South Carolina
7 days, 340 miles
When: Early June
MR10speed@aol.com; www.members.aol.com/cyclesc.

Pennsylvania: Pedal Pennsylvania's Great Northern Crossing
7 days, 600 miles
When: Mid–late July
Rider limit: 300
www.pedal-pa.com

Tennessee: BRAT—Bicycle Ride Across Tennessee
7 days, 420 miles
When: Mid-September, early October
Rider limit: 500
www.state.tn.us/environment/parks/BRAT; 888-TN-Parks

Utah: Cycle Utah
7 days, 250 miles
When: Early September
Participation: 130 riders maximum
www.adventurecycling.org; 800-755-2453

Virginia: Bike Virginia 2005—the Valley Byways Tour
5 days, 300 miles
When: Mid–late June
Participation: 2,000 cyclists
www.bikevirginia.org; 757-229-0507

Washington: Cascade Peaks
7 days, 450 miles
When: Early July
Rider limit: 150
Adventure Cycling; www.adv-cycling.org

Wisconsin: GRABAAWR XVII—Great Annual Bicycle Adventure Along the Wisconsin River
7 days, 490 miles
www.bikewisconsin.com

Wyoming: Tour de Wyoming
6 days, 370 miles
When: Mid-July
Participation: 300 riders maximum
www.cyclewyoming.org; 307-742-5840

MASS-PARTICIPATION ROAD RIDES

"Humans have a fascination with transportation and they have a primitive urge to congregate," wrote Jackson Lynch, a profound cycling writer of the 1990s. "Put the two together and you've got either a stock car race or a fun ride." This book is definitely not about stock car racing, and you definitely won't be lonely on these well-populated rides.

1. **Le Tour de L'ile de Montreal**
    What: 45-mile bike ride around the island of Montreal
    Where: Montreal, Quebec
    When: Early June
    Participation: 35,000 to 40,000 riders
    www.velo.qc.ca/tour

2. **The Great Five Boro Bike Tour**
    What: 45 miles
    Where: New York City: Battery Park, to the Bronx, Queens, Brooklyn, then crosses the Verrazano-Narrows Bridge to Staten Island
    When: May
    Participation: 30,000 riders
    www.bikenewyork.org; 212-932-2453

3. **Seattle to Portland Bicycle Classic**
    What: 200-mile one- or two-day ride
    Where: From Seattle to Portland
    When: July
    Participation: 8,000 riders
    www.cascade.org/EandR/stp

4. **The Hotter 'N Hell Hundred**
    What: 100 miles
    Where: Wichita Falls, Texas
    When: Late August (always nine days before Labor Day)
    Participation: 8,000–10,000 riders
    www.hh100.org

5. **AYH Great San Francisco Bike Adventure**
    What: 15 miles—a family ride
    Where: San Francisco
    When: June
    Participation: 12,000 riders
    Rhody Productions; 415-668-2243

6. **Rosarito Ensenada 50-mile Fun Ride**
    Where: Rosarito Beach, Baja California
    When: Late September
    Participation: 9,000 riders
    www.RosaritoEnsenada.com; 858-483-8777

7. **Apple Cider Century**
    What: 25, 50, 75 or 100-mile bicycle tour of the orchards, forests, and wine
    Where: Three Oaks, Michigan
    When: Late September
    Participation: 5,000 to 7,000 riders
    www.country.applecidercentury.com

8. **TOSRV–Tour of the Scioto River Valley**
    What: 210-mile out and back from Columbus to Portsmouth
    Where: Columbus, Ohio
    When: Early May
    Participation: 3,000–4,000 riders
    www.tosrv.org

9. **The Moonlight Ramble**
    Where: St. Louis, Missouri
    When: August. It begins at 2 AM
    Participation: 10–15,000 riders
    www.moonlightramble.com

GLOSSARY

Aerobar: Add-on handlebar device that puts the riders in a lower, narrower, wind-cheating shape that adds significant speed.

Anaerobic threshold: The point at which a physical effort becomes so taxing that your body's respiratory system can no longer take in enough oxygen to maintain its speed.

Bonked: When your muscles literally run out of fuel and you must slow down or stop.

Bottom bracket: The juncture of the frame's down tube and chain stays, which holds the rotating pedal mechanism.

Brevets: A series of time-limited qualifiers for Paris-Brest-Paris.

Bunny hop: When a mountain bike rider lifts both wheels off the ground at the same time; useful for clearing trail obstacles.

Century: One hundred miles.

Cleat: The metal fastener added to the bottom of a bike shoe that snaps into a companion pedal; this "clipless" shoe-pedal system helps a rider derive more power from all ranges of the pedal stroke.

Crank arm: The lever that the pedal attaches to.

Creep: The gradual, and dangerous, stretching of the spinal-column ligaments, caused by sitting or stretching in a rounded-back position.

Critical Mass: Organized rides by cycling advocates that take over city streets during busy drive times to illustrate need for greater funding of bike paths and facilities.

Cruiser: Low-tech, one-speed balloon-tire bike typically used to ride slowly on bike paths or in neighborhoods.

Cyclocross: A winter cycling racing sport that is run on a grass and dirt course. Uses a road-bike bike with knobby tires.

Derailleurs: The devices, found outside the hub of the rear wheel and at the cranks, that switch or derail the chain from gear to gear.

Double-century: Two hundred miles.

Drops: The section of a road bike handlebar that loops down in a semicircle, putting the rider in a lower position for sprinting or descending hills.

Fast-twitch fibers: The short, bulky muscle fibers responsible for rapid contractions.

Flat-bar bike: Any bike that uses a straight, mountain-bike-style handlebar.

Flywheel: A heavy, solid, high-momentum wheel used on stationary bikes.

Forkstand: Device that holds a bike in place for repair or stationary workouts by locking the empty fork of the front wheel in place.

Free radicals: Wayward electrons, thought to be released by exercise and some diet, that shoot through the body and can cause unspecified damage over time.

Freewheel: The ability of the rear wheel of a geared bike to coast when the rider is not pedaling.

Granny-gear: The easiest gearing on a bike, typically a combination of the smallest chain-ring on the crank and the largest cog on the rear hub, that is most often used during steep hill climbs.

Headset: The metal rings and bearings that hold the stem and the fork in place in the headtube.

Headtube: The short vertical-frame tube at the front of the bike that houses the stem holding the handlebar and the support sleeve of the fork.

Heart rate: Pulse, usually measured in beats per minute (bpm).

Hoods: On a road bike, the rubber coating that surrounds the brake-gear shifter unit. A common hand position that allows for control of steering, braking, and shifting.

Hub: The axis around which a wheel rotates.

Hybrid: A bike, typically used by casual or fitness riders, that combines the large, fast-rolling "700C" wheels of a road bike with the flat handlebar and more upright seating position of a mountain bike.

Hyponatremia: Water intoxication; drinking too much water without replacing lost electrolytes.

Interbike: The annual cycling industry trade show, typically held in September in Las Vegas.

Leg speed: The pedaling cadence, typically measured in revolutions per minute. Most riders' leg speed is 80 to 90 rpms.

Masters: Older riders, typically 40 and up. Some events consider the Masters category as anyone over 30.

Mountain bikes: Bike for riding on steep dirt trails that has "fat" (up to 2-inch wide), knobby tires, flat handlebars, and a wide range of gearing.

Neutral spine: Erect, natural, effortless posture characterized by a concave lower-back position, which puts very little stress on muscles and bones.

NORBA: National Off-Road Bicycle Association.

Off-road: The opposite of on-road; typically a euphemism for dirt trails.

Pace line: Cyclists riding together in a tightly-packed line to go faster than one rider could alone due to the effect of drafting, in which the front rider breaks through the wind and succeeding riders pass easily through his wake.

Pannier: A pack or basket hung over the rear wheel of a bike.

Paris-Brest-Paris: Quadrennial 1,200 kilometer (750-mile) timed ride from Paris, France, to the Atlantic Ocean town of Brest and back.

Pedal axle: The horizontal post around which a pedal spins.

Peloton: French name for "bunch," as in a bunch of riders riding en masse, as in the Tour de France.

PR: Personal record, usually referring to a person's all-time best, fastest, longest ride, run, or other athletic benchmark.

RAAM: Race Across America.

Quick-release: Handled device at the wheel hub that, when twisted by hand, instantly loosens the wheel for removal and repair without the use of a wrench or other tools.

RAD: Rotational alignment device, typically used in a bike fitting.

Recumbent: An unconventional bike, once shunned but now growing in popularity, that has out-front pedals and a chair-like back support to put the rider in a highly comfortable, back-friendly, feet-forward, lounge-chair like position. The position is also highly aerodynamic, and recumbents own many bicycle speed records.

Road bike: A bike with tall, narrow tires and drop handlebars designed for fast, low-friction riding on paved surfaces. Once known as a "ten-speed," it now may come with as many as 30 gears.

Road racer: A competitor who rides a road bike. Colloquially called a "roadie."

Saddle: Bike seat.

Sag wagon: A support vehicle that offers food and repair services to riders, typically on a long ride or event such as a century ride.

Slick tires: Low-friction tires, without knobs, used for road riding.

Spin class: Group indoor cycling sessions, typically found at health clubs, with an instructor and music—like an aerobics class with stationary bikes.

Suspension forks: Shock-absorbing devices with springs and rubber bumpers that hold a mountain-bike front wheel in place.

Tandem: A bicycle built for two people with two seats, two handlebars, and two sets of pedals.

Time trial: A solo, timed ride. Typically expressed in distance, i.e., a 25-mile time trial, or TT.

Top tube: The tube on a bike frame that connects the headtube with the top of the seat tube.

Triathlon: An athletic contest that is a long-distance race consisting of three phases: swimming, bicycling, and running.

Ultra events: Usually, a cycling event longer than 200 miles (a double-century).

Velodrome: A track designed for cycling.

VO$_2$ Max: Aerobic Capacity. The maximum amount of oxygen your lungs can take in, typically measured in milliliters per kilogram. Pro riders are 80+.

X-Bike: A novel stationary bike for spin classes that has a freewheel and laterally rocking handlebars.

BIBLIOGRAPHY

Adamson, Ian. *Runner's World Guide to Adventure Racing* (Rodale, 2004).

Anderson, Bob, and Jean Anderson. *Stretching: 20th Anniversary* (Shelter Publication, 2000).

Baker, Arnie. *Psychling Psychology* (Argo Publishing E-book, 2003).

Brown, Dr. Charlie, and Kate F. Hays, *You're On! Consulting for Peak Performance* (American Psychology Assn., 2003).

Cooper, Kenneth L. *Dr. Kenneth L. Cooper's Antioxidant Revolution* (Thomas Nelson, 1994).

Friel, Joe. *The Cyclist's Training Bible* (VeloPress, 2003).

Hurst, Robert. *The Art of Urban Cycling* (Falcon Press, 2004).

Ilg, Steve. *Total Body Transformation* (Hyperion, 2004).

Kolata, Gina Bari. *Ultimate Fitness:The Quest for Truth about Health and Exercise* (Farrar Straus Giroux, 2003).

Maffetone, Philip. *Training for Endurance* (David Barmore, 1996).

———. *Eating for Endurance* (David Barmore, 1999).

Miller, Saul, and Peggy Maass Hill. *Sports Psychology for Cyclists* (VeloPress, 1999).

Pruitt, Andrew L., with Fred Matheny. *Andy Pruitt's Medical Guide for Cyclists* (RBR Publishing, 2002).

Johnson, Richard, and Patrick R. Mummy. *Symmetry: Relieve Pain, Optimize Physical Motion* (Quantam Media, 1999).

Ryan, Monique. *Sports Nutrition for Endurance Athletes* (VeloPress, 2002).

Solomon, Andrew. *The Noonday Demon: An Atlas of Depression* (Scribner, 2001).

Streb, Marla. *The Life Story of a Downhill Gravity Goddess* (Plume, 2003).

Yessis, Michael. *Kinesiology of Exercise* (Masters Press, 1992).

NOTES

• CHAPTER 4 •

1. "Your muscles contain three different power systems, but only one source of fuel can be used for muscle contraction, adenosine triphosphate (ATP). ATP is a high-energy chemical compound found in all muscle cells. When ATP is broken down, the energy released is used for muscle contraction. Because your muscles contain only a small amount of ATP; it must be steadily recharged. The rate at which ATP is recharged in your body must meet the demands of the exercise. Because your body stores ATP in only small amounts, you require plenty of stored energy to recharge ATP and the energy flowing. Body stores of carbohydrates, protein, and fat release varying amounts of ATP when they are burned for fuel." Monique Ryan, *Sports Nutrition for Endurance Athletes* (Boulder: VeloPress, 2002).

2. Chris Carmichael. "The Tour Marches On Its Stomach." www.lancearmstrong.com /lance/online2.nsf/htmltdf03/ccrest1

3. Edward F. Coyle, Department of Kinesiology and Health Education, University of Texas, Austin.

• CHAPTER 5 •

1. Shephard RJ, Berridge M, Montelpare W, Daniel JV, Flowers JF, "Exercise compliance of elderly volunteers." *Sports Med Phys Fitness.* 1987 Dec; 27(4): 410–8.

2. Hagberg JM, Allen WK, Seals DR, Hurley BF, Ehsani AA, Holloszy JO. " A hemodynamic comparison of young and older endurance athletes during exercise." *J Appl Physiol.* 1985 Jun; 58(6): 2041–6. PMID: 4008419 [PubMed - indexed for MEDLINE]

3. Ibid.

4. Orlander J, and Aniansson A. "Effect of physical training on skeletal muscle metabolism and ultrastructure in 70- to 75-year-old men." *Acta Physiol Scand.* 1980 Jun; 109(2): 149–54.

5. Rodeheffer RJ, Gerstenblith G, Becker LC, Fleg JL, Weisfeldt ML, Lakatta EG. " Exercise cardiac output is maintained with

advancing age in healthy human subjects: cardiac dilatation and increased stroke volume compensate for a diminished heart rate. 1984 Feb; 69(2): 203–13.

6. Stratton JR, Levy WC, Cerqueira MD, Schwartz RS, Abrass IB. "Cardiovascular responses to exercise. Effects of aging and exercise training in healthy men." 1994 Apr; 89(4): 1648–55. PMID: 8149532 [PubMed - indexed for MEDLINE]

7. Moller P, Brandt R. "The effect of physical training in elderly subjects with special reference to energy-rich phosphagens and myoglobin in leg skeletal muscle." *Clin Physiol.* 1982 Aug; 2(4): 307–14.

8. Coggan AR, Abduljalil AM, Swanson SC, Earle MS, Farris JW, Mendenhall LA, Robitaille PM. "Muscle metabolism during exercise in young and older untrained and endurance-trained men." *J Appl Physiol.* 1993 Nov; 75(5): 2125–33.

9. Frontera WR, Meredith CN, O'Reilly KP, Knuttgen HG, Evans WJ. "Strength conditioning in older men: skeletal muscle hypertrophy and improved function." *J Appl Physiol.* 1988 Mar; 64(3): 1038–44.

10. Ames et al., 1995 review.

11. *Women's Sports and Fitness* July/Aug 98 p. 115.

• CHAPTER 8 •

1. Dehaven, KE, WA Dolan, and PJ Mayer, "Chondro-malacia patellae in athletes—clinical presentation and conservative management," *Am J Sports Med* 7(1) 1979): 5–11.

2. Owen Anderson. 2004. "Cyclists' knee injuries—patellofemoral syndrome," *Sports Injury Bulletin.* www.sportsinjurybulletin .com/archive/1044-cyclists-knee-injuries .htm [December 9, 2004].

3. "Abnormal patterns of knee medio-lateral deviation (MLD) are associated with patellofemoral pain (PFP) in cyclists." *Med Sci Sport Exercise* 28(5) (1996): 554. Also, ER Burke, ed., "Injury prevention for cyclists: a biomechanical approach." *Science of Cycling* (Champaign, Ill: Human Kinetics Pubs Inc., 1986), 145–84.

4. Robert E. Margine, *Physical Therapy of the Knee* (New York: Churchill-Livingstone, 1988), 127–9.

5. Ibid.

• CHAPTER 9 •

1. Oregon Health Sciences University.

2. *Men's Health,* November, 2003.

3. *Men's Health,* August 2003.

4. *American Journal of Clinical Nutrition,* 2002; 75(4): 773–79; and the Framingham Osteoporosis Study *J Bone Miner Res,* 2000; 15: 2504–12.

5. *Lancet,* 1990; 335: 1013–6; *Ann Intern Med,* 1998; 128: 801–9.

6. *Men's Health,* September 2003.

7. www.ncbi.nlm.nih.gov.

8. National Osteoporosis Foundation.

9. *Men's Journal,* June 2004.

10. *Los Angeles Times,* May 3, 2004, p. F3.

11. *NEMJ,* 2004.

12. Source: www.nemj.org and the Associated Press, May 12, 2004.

13. Gonadotropin-releasing hormone (GnRH), which controls the follicle-stimulating hormone, which stimulates the synthesis and secretion of estrogens.

14. A 2004 study published in the *New England Journal of Medicine* found that Fosamax strengthens bones for at least a decade, dispelling fears that it might eventually boomerang and start making hips and spines brittle and prone to breaking.

ACKNOWLEDGMENTS

MANY HELPING HANDS and patient, wise counsel were critical in pushing this book along from original conception to what you are now reading. Our literary agent, Andrea Pedolsky, surely inspired by memories of an old, still-functioning English three-speed with a wicker basket, helped shape and refine our book proposal. Our editor, Matthew Lore, a New York City bike commuter, shared our passion and enthusiasm for the sport. Our assistant editor, Peter Jacoby, handled all our changes and missed deadlines with unflappable grace. Also, special thanks to the dozens of coaches, university researchers, event directors, and cycling journalists who shared their knowledge and tolerated all our questions during countless hours of telephone and in-person interviews: Chris Kostman, world-class athlete, event organizer, trainer, thinker, friend; Robert Forster, peerless physical therapist/endurance cyclist; Steve Ilg, the world's fastest, fittest yogi; multifaceted world-champion adventure racer Ian Adamson; renowned stretching guru and cycling maniac Bob Anderson; personal trainer and Iron-man Christopher Drozd, who pumped us up; Canadian Stuart Dorland and Costa Rican conquistador Roman Urbina, whose 24 Hours of Adrenalin and La Ruta races, respectively, have brought joy and purpose to thousands of cyclists, including us; conditioning coach Rob Bolton, for driving down from Santa Barbara for the valuable tutorial on functional finess; Dr. Jeanne Nichols, whose landmark study helped us bone up on osteoporosis; Bill Stickland, for the sage advice on the original *Bicycling* magazine bone-loss story; Dr. Christopher King, for an eye-opening morning in the University of Southern California's human performance lab; fit-meister Paul Levine; Andy Pruitt, the go-to guy of cycling ergonomics; bike journalist Joe Lindsey, for telling it like it was;

Dr. Charlie Brown, the world's leading cycling psychologist; Philip Maffetone, for important holistic ideas about fitness and health; postural therapist Patrick Mummy, for watching our backs; *Competitor* magazine's ubiquitous publisher/editor Bob Babbitt, whose keen article assignments over the years led to heaps of information scattered through this book; and to many others.

Friends for Life.

INDEX

Bold page ranges indicate substantial discussion of the subject;
bold page numbers indicate a glossary definition.

BIKE FOR LIFE

BIKE FOR LIFE

off-road, **330**

off-season, 18–22, 127, 262, 271. *See also* crosstraining; weight training

O'Grady, Patrick, 241–43

Old School coaching, 47

OPC (one-pointed concentration), 18

orthotics, 167–69

Orwoll, Eric, 220, 223

osteoporosis, **211–24**
　Giove's experience of, 225–30
　Jacques's experience, 221–22
　mechanics of, 219–20, 222–24
　overview, 211–14
　plan for avoiding, 215–18

Overend, Ned "The Lung," 125–31, 295

overtraining
　cycling position and, 184
　emotional side effects, 250–52
　overview, 7–8, 27, 42, 255

overuse injuries. *See also* overtraining
　aging and, 128
　avoiding, 13, 178–80, 181
　chondromalacia, 180, 185–93
　tendonitis, 181–85

paceline riding, 39–40, 209–10, 238, 300, 312

paceline technique, 39–40

The Paleo Diet (Cordain), 76

Pantini, Marco "El Pirata," 246–47

parathyroid hormone (PTH), 218

Paris-Brest-Paris, xix, 1–2, 159, 311–12, 325, **330**

patella, 186–93, 202–3

patellar tendonitis, 181–85

Pavelka, Ed, 304–6

peak and taper, 7, 9, 126–27

Peale, Norman Vincent, 233–34

pectorals, weight training for, 14

pedal axle, 163, **331**

pedals, maintaining, 36, 295

penis, biking and the, 135–38, 143, 144–46

Penseyres, Pete "Half-Million Mile," 213

perineum, 135–38, 142, 143

Periodization, 4–9

Perls, Thomas, xvii

Physiology in Bicycling (U.S. Cycling Federation, et. al), 188

plan. *See* training plan

Plan B. *See* emergency procedures

plank with leg raise, modified, 13–14

Plotnick, Gary D., 110

poison oak, ivy, and sumac, 298–99

Poland, 170–72

police, post-accident interaction with, 301–2

Pollan, Michael, 78

Pollock, Michael, 106

positive thinking, 232–34

posterior tilt, **330**

posture. *See also* back pain
　aerobar and, 166
　aging and, 104–5, 121–22
　awareness of, 42
　bike fit and, 160–61, 178–79
　exercises for improving, 15–16, 18, 116–17, 193–96, 200–202
　neutral spine position, 160–61
　Symmetry approach to, 193–96, 204–5

power and strength, 111

Powers, Chris, 191–92

power words and thoughts, 234

prehab, **177–205**
　back pain (*See* back pain)
　knee pain (*See* knee pain)
　overview, 177–79

"Pressure during cycling" (*BJU International*), 134

protein, 83–84, 86, 89–90, 215–16, 262

PR (personal record), **331**

Pruitt, Andy, 8, 178, 185

Psychling Psychology (Baker), 237

psychological counseling, 251–52

psychosis. *See* depression

push-ups and pull-ups, 12, 15

quads
　anatomy of, 186
　climbing and, 38, 57
　exercises for, 10, 11, 13, 16, 120, 189, 196
　imbalance from cycling, 10, 204–5
　saddle tilt and, 162, 191
　tendonitis and, 181, 183
　quick-release, 296, **331**

RAAM (Race Across America), 45–46, 48, 53, 67–69, 313, **331**

racing. *See specific races and types of racing*

Radiological Society of North America, 133

RAD (radial alignment device), 168, **331**

raloxifene, 218

"Rapid Bone Loss in High-Performance Male Athletes" (*Sports Medicine Digest*), 213–14

raw foods, 80, 99–101

reaction time, xvi, 10

reciprocal inhibition, 14

recovery
　aging and, 31, 242, 262
　base training and, 6–7
　body's job during, 5
　Eddie B. on, 173, 174–75
　hammer and, 123
　immune system and, 87, 108–10
　of muscles, 86
　as "ride with slower spouse" day, 274
　touring and, 315

recumbents, 143, 169, 202, 306, **331**

relationships and cycling, **263–84**. *See also* sex and cycling
　case studies, 274–84
　Cycling Widow(er) Syndrome, 265, 267, 274–76
　overview, 263–64
　scenarios, 273–74
　strategies and tips, 269–74
　systems approach to balance, 265–70

relaxation, 21–22, 37, 118–21, 194, 236–37. *See also* neutral spine position

repairing bikes on the road, 296

Resh, Tom, 37, 38–39

resistance training, 124

rest and recovery. *See* recovery

rhuli gel, 298

Ride Around the Bear, 278

road bikes and biking, **331**
　climbing technique, 37–39
　endurance events, 324–25
　hill climb events, 321–23
　mass participation rides, 328
　mountain biker's view of, 290
　multi-day cross state rides, 325–27
　Sinyard's role in developing, 152, 155

road racer, **331**

road rage, 309–10

Rodham, John, 71, 76

Rogers, Lynn, 308–9

rollers, 63

Rosarito-Ensenada Ride, 53–54

rotator cuff exercises, 116

Roubaix, 155, 198

running
　fighting depression with, 253–55
　knees and, 117, 179–80

BIKE FOR LIFE